RESUME PRO: THE PROFESSIONAL'S GUIDE

RESUME PRO: THE PROFESSIONAL'S GUIDE

by Yana Parker

TEN SPEED PRESS

Ten Speed Press
P.O. Box 7123
Berkeley. California 94707

Cover design by Fifth Street Design

Library of Congress Cataloging-in-Publication Data

Parker, Yana
   Resume pro : the professional's guide
   / Yana Parker
       p. cm.
   ISBN 0-89815-466-9
   1. Resumes (Employment)   2. Self employed.
   I. Title.
HF5383.P355   1993
650.14'068—dc20   91-33281
                        CIP

First printing 1993

Printed on recycled paper

Printed in the United States of America

1 2 3 4 5 — 97 96 95 94 93

Acknowledgments

Many people helped make this book possible, and I would like to acknowledge them for their contributions:

- Susan Ireland, who helped create this book at every step of the way over a two-year period and who is now the editor of the *Resume Pro Newsletter*

- Jackie Wan, Ten Speed copy editor-from-heaven, who saved my buns as well as this book

- Valerie Lau, Rhonda Findling, Eve Abbott, Lynn Desker, Patricia Delich, and Cynthia Mackey, who helped organize and proofread the text

- The resume writers, the other professionals in the career field (and even a few job hunters) whose experience, knowledge, and resume-writing examples appear in this edition

- Marilyn Hill and Ellen Sasaki, who did the drawings

- Ten Speed Press, who once again trusted that we could create another winner

THANK YOU.

Contents

NOTE: *A detailed table of contents appears at the beginning of each chapter.*

Introduction

A Career in Resume Writing: How I Got Here from There

When I started my own resume business, back in 1979, I went to the public library and downtown bookstores and looked, in vain, for a book like THIS one. I wanted some advice and inspiration on how to make a living doing something I could feel good about.

I had figured out, by then, that I didn't like working nine to five doing other people's "flunkie" work, and I knew I was good at writing—and specifically, good at writing *resumes*. But I had NO experience at running a small business and I had NO idea how my work compared with others.

I didn't even know for sure what business I was in! I loved chatting with people about their work scene, what they were good at, how they might escape demeaning jobs and get a chance to do something meaningful with their lives. But I wasn't a career counselor—I had neither the specific training nor the patience for it. I needed to achieve more immediate results, and to do something I could complete in one sitting, given my very short attention span.

But I wasn't just a writer or a word processor, either. I wasn't content to work with what was put before me, and always had to *meddle* with it, always had opinions about it, always had creative ideas about it.

Never really fitting into any career categories myself, I slogged along on the fringes of the business world for years, struggling to find a niche that could feel right for me. I was tugged back and forth by various forces: "I MUST pay the rent," "I MUST find a way to enjoy my workday," "I MUST make some sense out of my life."

And finally the path did, very slowly begin to emerge: I would be called a Resume Writer, but I would get to define that role in my own unique way, and apply to it any and all of the special talents that I had to offer. It did not matter that I had no credentials because the public was judging THIS job solely by its results: IF you could put out a good product, you were IN.

During the next ten years I worked hard to master this craft, succeeding beyond my expectations, and lo and behold, here I am publishing a *third* book in a field I discovered by accident!

How This Book Is Organized

This book is about the entrepreneur's path, beginning with how one person developed a satisfying career centered on resume writing. It then expands to embrace the experience and wisdom of many others around the country—virtually all ardent fans of *The Damn Good Resume Guide*—whose daily work overlaps mine in this one respect: we ALL, at one point or another, help job hunters develop a resume.

The book has two main sections:

- The first part, Chapters 1 through 8, is all about the WRITING aspect of doing resume work professionally.
- The second part, Chapters 9 through 13, is all about the BUSINESS side of operating a one-person resume-writing service.

Because I experienced such an uphill battle to find my own way, I find it immensely gratifying to help others take a step in the right direction along THEIR career path.

Out on a Limb

In assembling this book, I have gone out on a limb, presenting material that I thought would be—first and foremost—useful and engaging.

This policy posed inevitable risks:

a) Some of the material will seem inappropriate for some readers.

b) There will probably be some inaccuracies.

c) Some material will probably need immediate updating.

Perfection, then, was not a high priority. I decided I would rather risk criticism and bring you material that I found truly HELPFUL, timely, and interesting. Sometimes this came out looking corny or even unprofessional but I took the position, "Why bother, if it can't be at least a LITTLE bit fun?"

The flavor I've been striving for is much like that of the *Damn Good Resume Writer Newsletter*, which was published for over a year as a first step in assembling this book. Like the newsletter, this book is an eclectic mix of real-world advice, breezy articles and letters, and hard-core professional reports. The tone sometimes seems irreverent and playful, but it is always done with respect and affection for individuals, and with appreciation for how important our daily work really is to each of us.

I think you'll like this book and find it extremely helpful. Your indulgence is requested when it comes to the imperfections that you will certainly find here. (Please DO report them, however, so we can fix them!)

I wrote this book to show you how to create superior resumes, but I had another goal in mind beyond that. I want this book to get you excited and inspired about how YOU could use YOUR talents in this field. I want you to see that there IS a place for your VISION here, that this isn't a cut-and-dried business! You can make a difference. Your job can actually influence the world of work and contribute to the quality of a lot of other people's lives. That's something to get excited about!

Finally, I want to say that this book is not a finished product. *Resume Pro: The Professional's Guide* is meant to be the *beginning* of an ongoing

dialogue and sharing among resume writers across the land. A quarterly newsletter of the same name (this new one will be called the *Resume Pro Newsletter*) will keep that dialogue going between editions, and I am EAGERLY awaiting your contribution to it.

So now I invite you to come "out on the limb" with me.

Sincerely,
Yana Parker
January 1993

DISCLAIMER:
No Recommendations Here

Inclusion of a resume writer's work in this book does NOT constitute a recommendation of that particular writer. There is a fairly broad range of skill and experience shown here—from novice to expert.

If readers are using this book to help find a local resume writer, they can, however, gain a sense of the relative quality of that writer's work by comparing it with other examples.

Please feel free to contact directly any of the resume-writing beginners and professionals whose letters or articles or resume work appears in this book. You'll find a list of names, addresses, and phone numbers on page 399. Inevitably a few of them will have different addresses and phone numbers by the time you read this. You can call or write me for their current listing.

A RESUME WRITER'S PRAYER

by William Seavey
Sierra Madre, California

God grant me the serenity to stay cool under the pressures of "Can I have it by noon today?" and "What can you do for $5?"

God grant me the patience to repeatedly explain that "resume" is not pronounced "re-zoom" and doesn't mean "life story."

God grant me the power to turn men over fifty into young lions, divorced women into childless singles, and job hoppers into corporate careerists.

God grant me the presence of mind to find one more synonym for the words "dependable," "hard working," and "establishes good rapport."

God grant me the courage to calmly remind my clients that the "$8 and up" services provided by other resume businesses usually turns out to cost "and up."

God grant me the intelligence to understand the chicken scratches a client euphemistically calls "notes" or "outline."

God grant me the empathy to console one more frustrated job seeker who has already been everywhere but my resume service.

And God grant me the wisdom to type one last resume, put a sign on the door, "Gone Fishin'," and get back to work on my real love, the Great American Novel.

1

Gaining Perspective: What IS Good Resume Writing?

1
Gaining Perspective:
What IS Good Resume Writing

Let's Begin with Definitions

Before launching into the specifics of how to write excellent resumes, let's **step back a moment and try to gain some perspective** on this issue.

Let's say **you and I believe we have a certain group of skills**—perhaps writing, organizing, analyzing, interviewing. And let's also say that we've looked around in areas that interest us, and we've got the idea that **writing resumes for job hunters MIGHT be an appealing way to apply these skills.**

What, then, can we DO about that idea? Is there a school for resume writers? Are there any credentials required? Any standards to adhere to? Is there a measure of good and bad for resumes? Indeed, **is there a generally accepted DEFINITION of a resume?**

And how do we know if we'd really be any GOOD at this? On what basis do we decide what to charge for our services? What are our services worth?

All of these questions plagued me in the beginning. I had leaped in and started my business without the luxury of knowing just what I was doing! Over the months and years, I browsed through dozens of resume books, career guides, and even a few entrepreneurial manuals—most of which were dismally disappointing—and I listened to "experts" at tons of workshops, seeking some guidelines.

To my amazement, I learned that **there was NOT a clear-cut universal definition of what a resume IS!** Everybody *acted* as though there was agreement about this. Yet the actual examples I saw ranged everywhere from severely formal academic documents ("curriculum vitae") to outrageously avant-garde gimmicks of self-marketing! In between were vast quantities of B-O-R-I-N-G job histories, which I suspected were destined for one-way trips to the waste basket. Where could my skills and interests fit in, in this crazy-quilt picture?

Quickly I realized that the "curriculum vitae" end of the resume spectrum did NOT appeal to me in the least! No place for my creativity here. I squirmed my way out of those jobs at all costs. At the other extreme, I felt suspicious of clever, gimmicky hype, especially when it was interwoven with gross exaggerations—although at least this seemed a bit more interesting.

That left the middle-of-the-road alternative, represented, *so far*, by the vast sea of resumes presenting their long-winded, tedious job descriptions. **I rebelled.** I just knew, somehow, that these miserable pieces of paper were serving nobody very well. The sender was done a great injustice, and the receiver was left frustrated (if not fast asleep!).

Then inspiration hit me: As long as there is so much confusion and disagreement here, with even the so-called experts contradicting each other, **why couldn't I simply take a stand for what seemed to me to make the most sense?**

From then on, my resume work got stronger every day. I looked directly at the obvious questions:

- What IS a resume?
- What COULD a resume be?
- What information do employers need?
- What help do job hunters need?
- How can I help these two parties communicate with each other?
- Who am I working for?

I discovered that there definitely WAS room for some fresh and innovative thinking about the definition and role of resumes.

I finally settled on my own definition of a resume—a definition that **made sense** to me and that helped me focus my skills more effectively:

A resume is a personal marketing piece designed to open the door for an in-person job interview.

You'll find this definition repeated throughout this book.

I found that if the finished product helped the job hunter get an interview, and if it looked enough like a resume to satisfy the employer, it was a "good" resume—*a damn good resume!*—regardless of its content or style.

Eventually, though, I came to demand more of my work than just helping job hunters get their feet in the door. **I wanted them to be sure they were knocking on the right door, as well!** But more about that later.

I hope that this chapter and the ones to follow will inspire you to **create your own definitions**—of what a resume IS and could be, and of what a good resume writer is. And I hope you will constantly update your definitions and your standards as you learn more, broaden your perspective, and sharpen your skills.

I want to set the standards high and challenge you to live up to our newsletter slogan, "Exploring and Promoting Excellence in Resume Writing."

No More Boring Resumes!

(There Is Magic to Be Done Here)

What I want to do here is get the new resume writer off to a good start (and stimulate the old-timers who may have fallen into a rut). It is so easy to get hooked into the standard old routine of (yawn) giving the client a form to fill out, taking this data, making it look pretty, and MAYBE inserting some flowery stuff to make it sound impressive.

B-O-R-I-N-G. This is what everybody does. Let's break that mold and start from a new perspective.

First of all, let's NOT give the job hunter any forms to fill out. All that accomplishes is to set us both up for creating a classically dull resume. Sure, let them bring you a work history—a list of jobs they held, with dates and cities and names of companies. Definitely. That will save time. But don't ask them to write out a description of their old jobs, and DON'T ask them to list all their accomplishments. Fergodsake, if they could do a good job of that, why would they be hiring you?! They could simply hire a word processor to assemble and process their words.

If that's all you're doing for them, and that's all you ever intend to do for them, then this book is not for you. And you should be charging word processing rates, not professional resume writing rates. These comments are not intended to put down word processing. It's wonderful to be able to make somebody else's writing look gorgeous, and that's how many of us got started. But you want to go beyond this. Think of yourself as a writer, in-

terviewer, problem solver, and counselor, as well as a good word processor. Only when you put all those skills together can you call yourself a professional resume writer—or resume creator, as one of our colleagues prefers.

Early in my career I made a discovery that helped me break the mold forever. It is part of my routine to interview new clients in depth before we get down to the actual resume writing. I noticed that when we started talking about their hobbies or what they loved or hated about their jobs, things came out about them that I was sure the employers would love to know about. But these were things nobody seemed to be putting on resumes—things about personal and professional values, about commitment, about passion and pride in work.

I began to wonder why we couldn't put this truly important and interesting stuff ON the resume and leave OFF the dull, dry, predictable stuff. But there was the question of tradition: How could we say these interesting things? Could we get away with it? Would the job hunter be taken seriously? Would this really serve their needs? The answer is, "Absolutely."

So let's zero in now on exactly what characterizes a winning resume.

FIVE CHARACTERISTICS OF A GOOD RESUME

1. A good resume is a **marketing tool**—not a personnel document. Its primary purpose is to help land a job interview.

2. A good resume is **about the job hunter**—not about the job hunter's work history.

3. A good resume **focuses on the future**—not on the past.

4. A good resume **focuses on achievements** or accomplishments—not on job descriptions.

5. A good resume **documents and prioritizes skills the job hunter enjoys using**—not abilities they used in the past just because they had to.

In short, an effective resume is about the *worker,* not the *work.* It helps the employer identify a superior candidate because it distinguishes between mediocrity and excellence. And it helps the job hunter because it sets them apart from all the other eligible candidates.

TWELVE CHARACTERISTICS OF A GOOD RESUME WRITER

If you are to help your clients create this ideal document, you need to develop certain basic skills and certain qualities. As you read the list below, you may feel it's a tall order. Well it is, but then, it's a tall job, too.

In my opinion, a good resume writer is:

1. A skilled writer;

2. A skilled interviewer—effective listener; able to size up a situation;

3. A good strategist—decisive yet flexible; able to propose an approach, get agreement, adjust the course as needed, remain in control of the situation, sense when to be authoritative and when to follow the client's lead;

4. Clear about limitations—what they can or can't do, and what they will or won't do;

5. A person with a lust for learning—curious, willing to try something new;

6. A creative problem-solver and intuitive counselor, able to make an unexpected leap on faith;

7. Empathetic and yet able to stay detached; able to put a tearful client at ease while keeping the process moving;

8. A practical business person, with a realistic awareness of the world of work;

9. Personally experienced with the job-hunt struggle (preferably in the recent past) and has held a variety of jobs at different levels of responsibility;

10. Able to produce under time pressure and meet deadlines;

11. Skilled in word processing and page layout.

12. Able to understand—and then convey to clients—the seeming paradox that vision and practicality are inseparable when it comes to careers.

These qualities and their skillful and appropriate use to "repackage" the job hunter, account for the difference between superior resume writing and the work done in fast-food-type resume "factories." Superior work takes time and thought, as well as careful collaboration between the job-hunter and the resume writer.

Throughout all this, you need to conduct your work with the conscious intent of supporting a client's self-esteem in relation to the job search. If your client already enjoys a healthy level of self-confidence, then your job is simply to help document their value in the workplace. But if their confidence is lagging—and it may simply be a by-product of the stress of job hunting—then your skill as resume writer can transform the resume-writing process into a powerful vehicle for self-appreciation as well as a tool for focusing. (The client may need to see this documentation of their value in black-and-white even more than the employer needs to see it!)

As resume writers, we are in a unique position to make a difference. Virtually every job hunter believes they have to have a resume, so our services are not considered frivolous, but in fact, are a basic necessity. And many more people will come to us for help than will go to a professional career counselor. Yet many of those job hunters do need some help with getting focused, making choices, and developing the skills of an effective job search. Since we are right there on the front lines, we *could* make a difference.

There is a tremendous opportunity here for the exercise of creativity—in the actual art of writing, in the solving of classic problems, and in the very difficult challenge of transforming a traditional document into a meaningful career-search tool that makes a difference in somebody's life. It involves approaching each one afresh, with no canned techniques, but actually listening attentively to each new client to discover the special qualities that may never have been conveyed before but *will* be conveyed this time, thanks to our skill and commitment.

So there! It is said! There is magic to be done here! The magic is like opening the door for a beautiful caged bird and luring it out to fly free. But in this case the caged creature is the job hunter's precious talents, their "light that was hidden." Everybody has these special gifts that haven't yet been fully brought forth, haven't been articulated, haven't been appreciated. And it is wonderful to be able to help people draw this stuff out, see it, and get it down in writing to share with the world—just wonderful!

Your clients will love their resume to the extent that you're able to draw out of them what it is that they're most proud of and get that to show up on the resume, so their unique talents are documented. When you succeed in that, your clients will say *"Thank you, Thank you!"* and they'll send all their friends to you for more of that same "magic." And you will have the satisfaction of having a career that matters.

More on What Makes a Superior Resume Writer: Ethics

In addition to all the skills, abilities, and awareness that go into superior resume writing, we need to concern ourselves with the overall issue of professional ETHICS. Since resume writers are not licensed or credentialed, and there are no tests to pass nor minimum educational requirements to be in this business, it is up to us to set some standards.

Don Asher, San Francisco resume writer and author of *The Overnight Resume*, noting that "there is a wide variation in conscientiousness and quality of product available to the consumer," penned this proposed code of ethics.

THE RESUME WRITER'S CODE OF ETHICS
by Donald Asher

1. Every client will receive original work. Given that certain phrases and sentence constructions are common in this industry, we will not copy prior work or portions of old resumes. (I call this the "No Boilerplating" rule.)

2. Resumes shall be truthful. No lies or misrepresentations of fact shall be allowed in a resume produced in this office, and we will decline projects from clients who insist on lying on their resumes. (The "No Lying" rule.)

3. We will not oversell the client's qualifications or skills. Employers rely on resumes to assess the qualifications and skills of job candidates. Although it is our duty to maximize our clients' presentations, we will not undermine the credibility of our profession by compromising the utility of resumes. (The "No Overselling" rule.)

4. Clients will be charged a fair, equitable, and standardized rate for services performed by us. There may be a wide variance in rates for the diverse services we provide, but similar clients with similar projects will be charged comparable rates. (The "No Highballing" or "No Overcharging" rule.)

"The Resume Writer's Code of Ethics," Don adds, "is designed to promote professionalism, discourage scoundrels from practicing in this industry, and preserve the resume writing business as a viable profession for the long term."

Don closes with admonitions I heartily stand behind:

- "Make a personal commitment to lifelong learning in your field."
- "Read every major and most minor books available on the subject of resumes and job-search tactics."
- "Follow up on your learning activities to test the efficacy of your theories."
- "Understand your field in its macro-economic context."

The Job Search

"The job search is a search for daily meaning as well as daily bread, for recognition as well as cash, astonishment rather than torpor.

"In short, for a sort of Life rather than a sort of Monday-to-Friday dying. Perhaps immortality, too, is a part of the quest."

—Studs Terkel

AND MORE ON SUPERIOR RESUME WRITING:
Tuning In to the Employers' Needs and Interests

Superior resume writers have their eyes and ears wide open, tuning in to all the players in the job search game—and *especially* tuned in to the employers' needs and interests. They know that **resumes work only when they meet the needs of BOTH of the major players:** the job hunter and the employer. And they know they will have to make an ongoing effort to **educate themselves about what employers need and want.**

"The easiest part of the resume writer's task is using personal computers and laser printers to produce attractive job histories and cover letters. The *hardest* part is gauging what will trigger real interest from employers."

So says Davis Bushnell in a special report to *The Boston Sunday Globe* (December 30, 1990) on the role of resume firms in aiding laid-off workers to land jobs. (Thanks to resume writer Joe Roper of Hingham, Massachusetts, for pointing out the article.)

Employer Survey as Learning Tool

What do YOU know about what triggers employers' interest? This is a critical issue, so I would urge you to find out. Perhaps once a year or so, you could conduct your own local mini-survey. *This is not necessarily a big deal to do!* Just dial up any five employers you can think of, who you know personally OR whose opinion would be of interest to you. State that you are a professional resume writer, and you want to be sure you are writing resumes that WORK for both your clients and the employers they apply to. And therefore you'd like to know **what triggers their real interest** enough to call a person in for an interview.

Remind them that you don't want to know "in general" what they think most OTHER employers think—you just want to know what triggers THEIR interest, in particular. Then LISTEN really carefully, draw them out as much as possible, and write down the response as accurately as you can. Resume writers are good listeners and interviewers, so this is "right up your alley." The results should be invaluable. **(Of course you're invited to share your findings in the *Resume Pro Newsletter*.)**

If you need a little more "priming" before you do your local survey, I have some suggestions: Here is Yana's List of (only two) Questions for an Employer Survey:

Question #1. "**Overall, what is it that sparks your interest on a resume**? Turns you on, makes you interested, makes you sit up and take notice?"

For example, Yana's answer: "If I were looking at a resume sent to ME . . .

"FIRST: Something uniquely creative, or bold and self-confident, some sign of a creative mind reaching out to engage me, saying something unexpected and provocative—definitely doing or saying something that's NOT traditional and expected and predictable.

"SECOND: Some indication of their awareness of ME, some clue that they paid attention to the person they are addressing and actually had something to say to ME, specifically —like appreciating and enjoying my work, or having a good idea to share about it."

Question #2. **What's your strategy for screening resumes?** How do you quickly sort through them and locate the good ones?"

For example, Yana's answer:

"FIRST: I'd look for some obvious dumb things to see if I can toss the resume out—like sloppiness, misspellings, inappropriateness, bad writing, extremely conservative and boring form and content. Those go straight in the trash.

"SECOND: I'd look to see what they say they want—what their objective is, and then (assuming their objective sounds something like my job opening) I'd check to see if their background makes them look well qualified for it. If they don't name an objective, then I'd look to see if their direction is somehow made clear to me."

Following is an example of a resume writer "doing her homework" to stay on top of an issue that's important to resume writers. This kind of commitment to learning will keep her on the cutting edge in her business.

WHAT DO EMPLOYERS REALLY THINK?

by Vicki Law-Miller

I sent a questionnaire to a few employers in my area, along with a letter asking them to help me evaluate my service. *(Letter shown on page 13.)* Here are some of the responses, for the most part unedited.

1. When in the process of hiring, how do you decide if a resume is good or not?

- Not handwritten, organized and easy to read, with headings for each category. I want to see all pertinent personal information, especially age and sex, even though not required.

- Well organized; if so, then usually the person is methodical and ready to do what's asked.

- Eye-catching, good quality paper, a good format that lets all information be found easily and readily.

- I look for past experience and facts about ability and previous job duties.

- I usually form a first impression when I open the resume package. Sometimes there is a very neatly done resume behind a hand-scratched cover letter. I am impressed if the applicant has taken time to find out something about my business. Many times, it is evident that the applicant knows nothing about the business and makes many wrong assumptions. Finally, I always look for gaps in work history. If there is a gap, it is always nice if the applicant has explained why the gap is there.

- Short, not wordy, light beige paper. No copies, must be originals. No great big, long paragraphs.

2. What makes you decide that an applicant looks like someone you want to interview?

- I look for relevant experience; the rest get tossed aside. I like to see 'Education" listed first.

- Work experience, longevity in jobs.

- Experience—does it fit the position? Is it described accurately?

- If the applicant's education and job experience closely match the job opening, I will interview the person regardless of how I feel about the resume.

3. What do you consider most important on a resume?

- The objective.

- Content, followed closely by overall look.

- How long they stayed at previous jobs, *why* they left.
- Brief; highlight of key areas of abilities; honesty. Let the reader know what YOU would want to know if the roles were reversed.
- The past experience does not have to be in the same business as ours, but I like to see jobs and activities listed that require common sense and a willingness to work and learn.
- Employment references.
- Relevant experience. Remember to "blow your own horn."

4. What turns you off on a resume?
- Personal and irrelevant information.
- Homemade look, errors, hard-to-read.
- Overselling, too much unimportant info not pertinent to the job.
- Too much detailed explanation.
- Frequent job changes.
- No references, gaps in employment, handwritten, no personal information.

5. What would you like to see different on resumes that would help employers identify a good candidate?
- List three references with phone numbers.
- Goals—five-year, short-term, etc.
- Personal information.
- Business interests and goals.
- A "Release of Information" from the applicant so that prior employers would be willing to give true and accurate information about the applicant.

Vicki has grouped together a number of employers' answers under each of the questions she posed.

She closes with this observation: "I am surprised and a little nervous about the mention of personal references and information, since I have read that personal information is usually considered irrelevant and should not be included." Also, she points out that these responses are from small-town employers in Montrose, Colorado. Thank you, Vicki, for a terrific effort. I hope that lots of other readers will follow your lead and do their own local survey.

SAMPLE SURVEY LETTER SENT TO EMPLOYERS:

(Readers: Is this a good idea for YOU to try? —yp)

Dear _____:

For the past few months I have been assisting local individuals who are looking for employment by counseling them on resume writing.

A handful of my clients have been gracious enough to give me their permission to use their resumes for the purposes of this survey, in which I am asking personnel managers and business people to critique these resumes. This is an effort to not only serve my clients better, but also to get a feel for what you, as a manager, would like to see on a resume when you are in the process of hiring.

I would greatly appreciate your taking a few moments out of your busy schedule to answer the enclosed questionnaire and return it in the self-addressed, stamped envelope.

If it would be more convenient for you to conduct this survey over the phone or in person, please feel free to call me at the above number. If I am not available, please leave a message on my answering machine as to when it would be most convenient for me to call you back.

To show my appreciation for your help in this matter I would like to offer you 20 percent off of any of the services my company has to offer. I have enclosed some information for your convenience.

Thanking you in advance.

Sincerely,

Vicki Law-Miller, Owner
Scribbles to Script

**Vicki Law-Miller
Scribbles to Script
Montrose, CO**

2
Getting Started with Your Client

A Top-Secret Tip!

My own favorite resume formats—the ones I use MOST of the time—would be:

1. *Combination* Functional/Achievement

2. *Combination* Chronological/Achievement

However, for the sake of brevity, in this book I have referred to these formats as simply functional or chronological WITHOUT tacking on the word "achievement." But then I will urge you, plead with you, may even harass you, to LACE ALL YOUR RESUMES GENEROUSLY WITH ACHIEVEMENTS rather than with tedious job duties or bland and irrelevant activities. In reality I think ALL resumes should be achievement-oriented regardless of their format.

The Basics

We resume writers need to be able to show job hunters how to look at their work experience— perhaps even their whole lives—very differently if they are to create powerful, effective resumes that will make a difference in their job search. They need YOUR HELP to gain this fresh new perspective. In fact, YOUR approach to resume writing could trigger a transformation in your client's whole approach to the job search—and incidentally make you a hero and bring you many referrals from happy clients.

For example, if your clients have thought of their paid work as being unrelated to what really excites them, you could help them look at the work they've already done to see WHERE they have managed to incorporate their personality and their values into the job. Then you could help them switch their focus to THAT aspect of their work experience, rather than on the job content or responsibilities.

The result of this approach is that job hunters begin to see the joy and satisfaction (be it great or small) that they've managed to derive from work situations, and they begin to understand that they might be able to actually INCREASE that job satisfaction dramatically—and still get paid for it!

I believe it is our business to actively support that new self-appreciation and expansion process—if we are to be superior resume writers.

So here's a trick for you to master: Learn to guide your client in examining each past work experience not for its task content, but for its job satisfaction content, and its favorite-skills-developed content, and its pride-in-accomplishment content! *This is one of the most important lessons I've learned, and I want to pass it on to you. It is a central theme of this book, and of all my work.*

You may be amazed at what can happen in a single working session with a client once you master this skill of zeroing in on truly satisfying accomplishments. At the same time, you will be teaching the job hunter to do this in the future without your help.

FIVE CONCEPTS

You will recall that in the Introduction a few pages back, I listed five characteristics of a good resume. Because I think these points are so important, I'd like to repeat them here in a slightly different way—from a resume *writer's* point of view:

FIVE BASIC CONCEPTS FOR SUPERIOR RESUME WRITING

1. A good resume is a **marketing tool**—not a personnel document. Its primary purpose is to help land a job interview.

2. A good resume is **about the job hunter**—not about the job hunter's work history.

3. A good resume **focuses on the future**—not on the past.

4. A good resume **focuses on achievements** or accomplishments—not on job descriptions.

5. A good resume documents and prioritizes **skills the job hunter enjoys using**—not abilities they used in the past just because they had to.

Now let's look at the features of **ineffective** resumes:

1. An ineffective resume is largely an **historical document** presenting past work history, whether or not it relates to future goals. It's a "career obituary."

2. An ineffective resume is **about jobs and job descriptions,** rather than about the unique talents and accomplishments of the person who held them.

3. An ineffective resume **ignores the issue of job satisfaction.**

In short, an ineffective resume is usually about WORK, not about THE WORKER. This kind of document fails to help the employer identify a superior candidate because it does not distinguish between mediocrity and excellence. Nor is it of much value to the job hunter, because it doesn't set the candidate apart from all the other eligible applicants.

Setting the Stage

During our initial phone conversation, I will often give a client some "homework" to do before the resume-writing session—ten minutes of brainstorming to come up with the longest possible list of job titles that sound appealing and appropriate for right now. This technique is effective if, during that initial phone call, the job hunter cannot quickly answer the question, "Just what is it you want to do next?"

My theory is this: At some level they KNOW what they want to do, but I have to create a shortcut to bypass their blocks to accessing this knowledge. The ten-minute limit helps get them PAST the place where they usually get stuck because they don't have TIME to get stuck. I also tell them that they CAN'T do it wrong—that whatever comes up is the right answer for THIS assignment.

Then I jot down a reminder to myself about the homework assignment on my client records. (See the "New Client Intake Form" at the end of this chapter, page 39.)

When the client appears at my office to begin the resume, I start off by explaining my strategy:

1. "First we'll be building a clear picture in YOUR mind of what your next job looks like— what you want to have in the job and what roles you want to play.

2. "THEN we'll work to design a resume that transmits that image to the reader's mind." (My writing teacher called this "image detail.")

Key to Excellence: Full Client Involvement

One of the keys to writing effective resumes is to work directly WITH the client, rather than sending them home while you produce their resume alone. Working with a client takes a lot of practice, but the benefits are significant:

1. The resume will be more authentic, more "theirs," because of their input.

2. You learn to really listen carefully to the client, and to ask the right questions—which makes you a better resume writer.

3. THEY learn a great deal from the process about how to assess their own skills.

When I work on a resume, the client is at my side the whole time. They leave the first-and-only session with their completed resume in hand— and they REALLY appreciate that! I have become skilled and very efficient at this, and therefore I can charge about the same hourly rate that career counselors charge.

EXAMPLE:
Working with a Student

Elizabeth Rohrmann, a Mills College student, was seeking an internship. She came to my office and we spent a little over three hours creating her one-page resume. I took plenty of time to develop an appropriate process with her, and to explain it carefully as we went along.

The steps we took included, in this order:

- Listing the positions that were of interest to her.
- Identifying (and setting aside) the positions for which she would need to complete more studies (she plans to go to graduate school in about a year).
- Determining what she wants to learn in the internship she is applying for, and therefore what tasks she would like to be working on in the internship.
- Specifying the roles she expects to fill in the internship—and thus, the skill areas we need to address in a functional resume.

Then I explained to her that we would be creating a resume that focused on what she could bring to the agency where she interns, in the way of experience related to her goals.

I outlined our strategy as follows:

- Identifying personal attributes, interests, and attitudes of hers that would be of interest to an employer, and summarizing them for the "highlights."
- Identifying and documenting her experience that relates to the areas she plans to work in.
- Determining how to incorporate other information she wants to include on the resume, such as study abroad and knowledge of Spanish.

Elizabeth expected the internship to require some word processing and filing, but wasn't eager to do it, so we included her computer knowledge, but played it down in only one sentence at the bottom, as well as placing "administrative support" as the last paragraph in the resume.

We presented the skills to emphasize what she wanted in the new position: lots of marketing, human relations and program involvement, and minimal clerical work.

Elizabeth's functional-style resume appears on the next page.

ELIZABETH L. ROHRMANN

Permanent address:
514 Crockett
Seattle WA 98109
(206) 284-0303

College address:
P.O. Box 9299
Oakland CA 94613
(510) 729-8767

OBJECTIVE

Internship in the administration of a nonprofit or social service agency.

HIGHLIGHTS

- Committed to work that promotes a more egalitarian society.
- Believe that individuals can make a difference.
- Demonstrated ability to work efficiently and complete projects.
- Able to communicate with Spanish-speaking clients.

RELEVANT SKILLS & EXPERIENCE

Human Relations / Public Relations / Marketing
- Worked in a **cooperative marketing effort** with other students, alumni officers, and admissions officers, on the Mills College Student Recruitment Task Force.
- Gained an **objective understanding of different groups of people** and a greater respect for human diversity through my experience living and studying in Barcelona, Spain (spring 1990).
- Created a **positive learning environment**, as gymnastics instructor for children age 3-12, and as trainer of other gymnastic instructors.

Program Development (needs assessment - follow-up - quality control)
- **Co-developed a recruitment training program** for current students.
- **Followed-up on the needs and goals** of Mills students, and reported this information to program planners.
- **Coordinated "Career Exploration Day,"** a mentorship program providing career education-by-experience for high school students.

Administrative Support / Program Funding
- Currently studying "Corporate Finance."
- Experience with IBM, WordPerfect, and Macintosh word processing.

WORK HISTORY

1990-present	*Chairperson*	Student Recruitment Task Force, Mills College
1988-present	*Customer Service Rep*	Mills College Bookstore, Oakland CA
1987-present	*Full-time student*	Mills College, Oakland CA
1990 Spring	*Full-time student*	Institute for Social & International Studies, Barcelona, Spain
1987-90 Summer	*Clerk Specialist*	Security Pacific Bank, Seattle WA
1988-90 Winter	*Clerk Specialist*	Security Pacific Bank, Seattle WA
1985-87 part-time	*Gymnastics Instructor*	Seattle Gymnastics Academy, Seattle WA

EDUCATION

B.A. candidate, May 1991 - MILLS COLLEGE, Oakland CA
Major: Political, Legal, and Economic Analysis   Minor: Art History

- Resume writer: Yana Parker -

The Job Objective as Starting Point

The JOB OBJECTIVE is the first thing that should appear on a resume—after the name, address and phone number, of course. In my opinion, it is not optional, it is ESSENTIAL.

A good, clear job objective looks something like this:

- "JOB OBJECTIVE: Position as a full-charge bookkeeper"

Or better yet:

- "JOB OBJECTIVE: Position as full-charge bookkeeper with Macy's"

It tells, as succinctly as possible, both the FUNCTION a job hunter wants to fill and the LEVEL OF RESPONSIBILITY they want to assume.

If it's easy to identify a clear job objective, great—you and your client are lucky. If it's tough to get clarity about it—well, you have lots of company. Hasn't this happened to you? At the start of a session, you ask your client, "What kind of job are you looking for?"

"It's just not simple!" she complains, "I don't even know what they CALL this thing I want to do!" In that case, your client may need to do some information interviewing (see page 23) to clarify the terminology of the objective. For now, the two of you could come up with a GUESS at what the job title might be, and put THAT on a draft resume to be used specifically for information interviewing.

The confused job seeker above would probably be relieved to hear that she doesn't have to have the "right answer," right now, about her ultimate job objective. Even if her tentative job objective is not the "perfect" answer, it makes the resume more focused and therefore MORE POWERFUL and EFFECTIVE.

Reassure your clients that they can come back and you will reprint their resume with their explicit job objective AFTER they've done some investigation.

Here's another typical situation: You ask your client, "Okay, what kind of job are you going to be aiming for with this resume?" And he says, "Oh, I don't want to get *specific* about that; I just want to keep all my options open, so let's not bother with an objective at all."

Here's what I tell my clients who insist on "keeping all their options open" and not stating a job objective:

"The reality is that 'keeping all your options open' is not a smart approach, even though it may SEEM logical. The fact is that you are only going to seriously apply for ONE job at a time, and the sooner you decide on which one, the more effective your job search will be and the quicker it will be over. (And who wants to drag out a job search?!!)"

If my client is STILL set on avoiding the use of a job objective, I tell him "You can have MORE THAN ONE resume, if you need to, rather than trying to make one resume cover two or more very different types of work. For example, if you are still undecided about which of two quite different career directions to go in, OR you're looking for two part-time jobs in different fields, then we can do a good, focused resume for EACH of the two areas."

"However," I continue, "if you don't even TRY to state a clear objective, you effectively put the burden on the employer to figure it out for you, and believe me, EMPLOYERS WON'T DO IT. They don't have the time, don't have the motivation, and they don't have the responsibility to figure out what to do with an indecisive job hunter."

Homework (Job-list Brainstorming) to Help Clarify the Objective

In working with a client, my initial task, then, is to get the job hunter clear about a specific job objective so the picture can begin to emerge. At first that picture may look like a rough outline, a quick sketch, a framework.

To move the job hunter toward more clarity about her job objective, I may need to get her to tell me the ROLES she wants to play in the new job. And this is where the "homework" comes in, which was mentioned at the beginning of this chapter on page 19. The homework is simply a long list of specific job titles that are currently interesting and appealing to the job hunter. From this list of specific job titles, we can deduce the various ROLES she is currently attracted to.

As she reads off this "homework" list to me, I jot it down on my computer screen. Then we prioritize the list and group the job titles into clusters of similar types.

Often I take those JOB TITLES and transform them into functional SKILL AREAS. Then after grouping, prioritizing, and condensing, we end up with a few essential skills and a starting point for a functional resume. Look at the "working notes" and resumes for Ned Powell and Kathy Jacobsen on pages 69 through 76 for good examples of this technique.

Information Interviewing to Help Clarify the Job Objective

Very briefly, "information interviewing" is a kind of reverse interviewing where the job hunter finds someone (or better yet, several people) already working in his desired field, who would be willing to let him visit them briefly on their job. He arrives at their office with a carefully prepared list of questions that they could answer in, say, fifteen to twenty minutes—questions that would help familiarize him with this line of work.

The job hunter takes notes like crazy, observes the work environment as best he can, and makes every effort to leave with the names of a few MORE people he could similarly interview. (By the way, *don't use the word "interview"* when you request an appointment for this informative meeting!)

Here are examples of two clients whose job objectives were unclear, and who needed to do some information interviewing.

CASE #1

Lani Simpson, whose resume appears on page 88, liked her job but wanted to work in a more stimulating environment where her input was valued and acknowledged. She also wanted to get back into the textile field. But she wasn't yet clear enough about a specific job objective.

We did a resume that outlined and illustrated **the roles she enjoys playing**, and presented her preferred working modes as assets to management. The final paragraph refers to her knowledge of textiles.

Lani's resume was designed for information interviewing (i.e., exploring possibilities) *and creates an outline of a desirable job* by limiting the experience presented to just those things she enjoyed doing, and wants to re-create in her new job. As long as she is consistent in **omitting** the things she doesn't want to do in the future, and **including** most of the functions and activities she really enjoys, then this resume will fit almost any position that appeals to her, with minimal changes.

Thus, Lani has a strong, focused resume that is customized for the textile world, yet it can be easily modified for other desired environments merely by replacing the paragraph on "background in textiles."

CASE #2

Louella was told that the resumes she had written just weren't snazzy enough, so she brought them in for a critique. She saw that one reason the resumes lacked appeal was that she hadn't allowed herself to imagine getting paid for doing things she could really get excited about. So her resumes lacked passion. They're "okay," but they're not really dynamic because they recount activities that actually bored her. She did a good job in these positions, but her heart wasn't in it, and her lack of enthusiasm showed up in every version of her resume.

I recommended that she discard these resumes altogether and spend some time identifying what she really wants to do next. She should start all over AFTER she does some creative visualization (see below). Then she can design a career-exploration resume (same as "information interview resume") based on her vision of the new career she wants.

I suggested that Louella use the visualization technique of writing a letter to a dear friend as though she had already been at her ideal new job for almost a year. I had her DESCRIBE *in great detail just what her new job is like.*

Also, I asked her to send me a copy of the letter, and come in again to create a resume for *that* job. Then she can do some **information interviewing,** taking this ideal-job resume along with her to try to develop something close to what she really wants to do. I urged her to tap into the "juice," the passion, the excitement, as a source of guidance.

Louella agreed that this is really what she needs to do now, and she will send me the results of her exploration later.

Six Steps to a Strong Chronological Resume

Here are the steps for doing a strong chronological resume:

1. State the job objective as simply and clearly as possible.

2. Determine what the basic functions of the new job are.

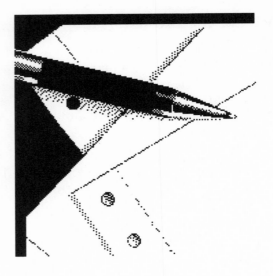

3. Identify the job hunter's primary past jobs, omitting very short-term positions UNLESS they involved important experience that should be mentioned.

4. Determine which of the old jobs provided the experience that's most like what the job hunter will do in the new job, or in some way uses similar skills.

5. Now, **DON'T write a job description for the jobs listed**. Instead, allocate most of the work-history space for detailing achievements. For each of the most RELEVANT jobs, write a few one-liners that present the job hunter's accomplishments—what they brought to the job that was valuable and unique, and how they got results that benefited the organization.

Be specific. Focus particularly on tasks that are similar to those they'd be doing in the new job. (This creates an image in the employer's mind of the applicant already doing the tasks of the new job!)

6. For each of the nonrelevant jobs, write just one one-liner that *captures the essence* of the job hunter's responsibility and contribution, without going into detail about the various job duties.

Now you have covered the bases for those employers who are more comfortable with chronological resumes, yet you haven't bored and distracted them with tedious job duty descriptions that are of no interest to them, and do not support your client's case.

Margaret Dwaite's resume on the following page is done in a chronological format.

MARGARET DWAITE
1224 Seymour Avenue
Elmira, CA
(123) 456-7890

Objective: Recruitment position with Department of Forestry

SUMMARY OF QUALIFICATIONS
★ Extensive **successful experience in recruiting**, with many ethnic groups.
★ 12 year background in **law enforcement, specializing in investigation**.
★ Proven record of **creativity and resourcefulness** in investigative techniques.
★ Dedicated, hard-working, and responsible professional; awarded Certificate of Appreciation for **exceptional performance** by Inspector General's office, USDA.
★ Quick-thinking, intelligent, able to make on-the-spot decisions, and work equally well as a **team-member or independently**.

RELEVANT EXPERIENCE & ACCOMPLISHMENTS

1985-present   Employment Specialist   CITY OF ELMIRA, CA
- **Assessed applicants** for potential employment, matching them to employers' criteria for interpersonal skills, technical expertise, and learning potential.
- Achieved an **excellent record for successful matches** in assisting employers to **meet affirmative action goals**.
- Conducted **community outreach**, developing a broad knowledge of area resources:
  - **Spoke** to community organizations to introduce the "Hire Elmira" program.
  - **Recruited** individuals at local job fairs.

1983-84   Project Administrator   PORT OF ELMIRA, CA
- **Developed and oversaw a highly effective training program**, providing a unique opportunity for disadvantaged youth to develop marketable skills and abilities.

1979-83   Investigator   U.S. DEPT. OF AGRICULTURE
- Conducted hundreds of **successful undercover fraud investigations** for USDA food stamp program.
- **Testified effectively in court**, winning judgements against abusers.
- **Recruited, hired and trained over 70 investigative aides**, of **diverse ethnic backgrounds**, to assist in undercover investigations.
- **Collaborated** with other agencies, providing **technical advice and investigative support.**

1975-78   Full time student
- Worked as part-time Investigative Aide for the Department of Agriculture.

1969-74   Supervising Eligibility Technician - Group Specialist - Counselor
ELMIRA COUNTY SOCIAL SERVICE DEPT.
- **Screened** and interviewed applicants on **complex eligibility criteria** for a range of social service programs.

1973-present   Administrative Officer/Instructor   U.S. COAST GUARD RESERVE
- **Supervise** all administrative functions - payroll, records maintenance, etc.
- **Oversee training** programs and directly trained over 800 reservists.

1964-68   Deputy Sheriff   ELMIRA COUNTY
- **Interviewed and classified** inmates to determine appropriate job assignments.
- **Prepared comprehensive reports** on investigations and crimes.

EDUCATION & TRAINING
112 college units in •Social Science •Business • Criminal Justice
Management and Leadership Training, U.S. Coast Guard
Peace Officers' Standard & Training Certificate (POST)

- Resume writer: Yana Parker -

25

Reminder: Be Sure to Give Enough Information

When there is a **specific minimum experience** called for in a job announcement, the resume must make it entirely clear that the job hunter HAS that minimum. One job hunter whose resume WASN'T clear enough wrote us about this experience:

"Initially the personnel office did not forward my application to the hiring department because my resume didn't stipulate whether or not I worked part-time or full-time, and they couldn't add up accumulated job experience to see if I had the minimum qualifications. They told me to stipulate the hours worked on the job. I added this info to the resume, made an appointment with the personnel department, and convinced them that I DID in fact meet more than the minimum requirements for the job. THEN I got an interview."

Value of the Client's Old Resume

When a client brings along a copy of their old resume—particularly if it's one they've worked on RECENTLY—don't just "fix it" (or ignore it). Be sure to *find out how the client feels about it*. Ask them, for example, "What is there about this resume that you LIKE—or that you DON'T like?"

I stumbled on this guideline by accident when I asked this question, and was amazed at how fruitful the client's response was. In that particular case, the client felt GOOD about the resume she had written, and just wanted confirmation that it WAS good—and perhaps an idea or two for refinement.

That was VERY useful to know because I realized, "Gosh, this looks pretty GOOD—I don't know what this person needs ME for!"

The Fastest Way to Improve Any Resume: Add More Accomplishments

Let's say, you are midway through a resume session and you just aren't happy with the way it's going. The resume doesn't have enough life, or pizzazz. The FASTEST way to get back on track and improve the resume is to draw from your client more accomplishments they haven't yet mentioned.

For each job listed in their work history, ask the client:

1. How did you perform that job in a unique way?

2. What did you accomplish there that nobody expected or asked of you, that distinguished you as a creative, resourceful, or dedicated person?

3. What did you do on that job that you feel most PROUD of?

4. What did you do there that set you apart from others who held that same position?

5. Now that you're gone, what will your co-workers and supervisors remember about you? What will they miss?

If your client is having a hard time articulating accomplishments, suggest one of the Memory-Jogging Scenarios below, or make up some of your own.

Memory-Jogging Scenarios

- GOOD-OLD-WHAT'S-HER-NAME SCENARIO: Imagine you have left your job, and the person who replaces you is not HALF as skilled or ambitious as you. Your ex-boss and ex-colleagues are remembering the good old days when YOU were there. What would they be missing? How was it better when YOU were there?

- MENTOR/PROTÉGÉ SCENARIO: Imagine there is a new recruit on your team—a bright, delightful person you like a lot. You're moving up, but FIRST you need to train this person to replace you. What are the "tricks of the trade" you teach him?

Remember, you are his special mentor; you're trying to pass on to him the very *essence* of what you do that produces outstanding results. This probably reflects your basic philosophy of life and work, your attitude towards service, and your sense of commitment.

More Ways to Pack Some POWER into a Resume

1. ANSWER THE *SO WHAT?* QUESTION

San Francisco resume writer, Susan Ireland, came up with the following example of putting into practice the principle of answering the "So What?" question in the resume reader's mind. This involves telling not just WHAT you did, but also its SIGNIFICANCE or beneficial outcome (preferably all in the same line).

In this case, the client was applying for a position in catering:

- Implemented kitchen procedures which met serving deadlines and maintained cost effectiveness.

- Organized the kitchen to achieve maximum efficiency.

- Prepared and served specialty seafood and desserts, raising a substantial amount for the local school.

- Traveled internationally, obtaining first-hand learning experience of ethnic cooking.

- Studied and experimented with diet menus to successfully integrate nutrition and weight loss.

Susan Ireland
Dynamite!! Resumes
Kensington, CA

2. USE PLENTY OF ACTION VERBS.

See Hinda's List of Action Verbs on page 32.

3. PRESENT YOUR BEST ACHIEVEMENTS IN A FORMAT THAT WORKS FOR YOU

The following two resumes—Bernard Stopfer and Linda Viloria—illustrate two important points:

a) A listing of explicit, relevant accomplishments makes for a powerful resume.

b) A good resume does not have to conform to any specific format as long as it WORKS!

- The Stopfer format differs from the more common varieties in that the accomplishments and the work history outline are presented on page one, and then (to cover ALL the bases) the specific tasks and responsibilities are presented on page two.
  Bernard (who runs Resumes Plus in Phoenix) breaks with tradition and organizes those responsibilities into functional groups that span all the different job titles listed in his work history. This is a unique format that could work well for some clients.

- The Viloria format deviates in yet another way. It is neither strictly functional nor strictly chronological, yet both elements are woven in. This format is uniquely designed to emphasize the various managerial roles Linda has played and the ways they support her objective.

BERNARD M. STOPFER

240 Lexington Drive
River Edge, New Jersey 07661
201 488-9298

OBJECTIVE

MANUFACTURING/GENERAL MANAGEMENT
Plant Operations... Warehousing/Distribution... Production Planning

QUALIFICATIONS

Over 23 years of management experience showing progressive advancement and foresight in planning for company growth. The ability to identify potential difficulties, take preventive measures, and solve existing problems. The expertise needed to implement the most cost effective procedures.

EMPLOYMENT ASSOCIATIONS

SALLY GEE/GREAT TIMES - Ridgefield, New Jersey   1965 to 1989
A clothing and accessory manufacturer and importer with sales in excess of $20 million.

GENERAL MANAGER   1981 to 1989

As General Manager, continued in the capacity of previous positions as follows: **CREDIT AND COLLECTIONS MANAGER** since 1985, **DIRECTOR OF DATA PROCESSING** since 1972, and **DATA PROCESSING MANAGER** from 1965 to 1972.

SPECIFIC ACCOMPLISHMENTS

- Reduced bad debt to 1 1/2% by strict financial controls. The industry standard is between 4 and 7%.

- Spearheaded shipping, general and administrative expenses reduction programs that resulted in cost containment in spite of increased business volume.

- Redesigned and implemented changes in warehouse lay-out to allow for separate financial distribution center. The corporation realized an additional $120,000 in gross profit with no extra operational costs.

- Established a corporate outlet store enabling disposal of all types of excess inventory, and allowing for pricing higher than closeout levels.

- Designed and implemented budget analysis systems, enabling management to project and anticipate significant variance deviations.

- Reduced office staffing needs by 25% by incorporating extensive cross-training and the design of user-friendly software.

- Implemented a highly sophisticated internal plant, warehouse and computer facility security system, reducing and maintaining shrinkages and thefts to a negligible minimum.

AREAS OF RESPONSIBILITY

OPERATIONS MANAGEMENT - Handled responsibility for operations of all departments including warehouse, distribution, production, inventory, purchasing, data processing, and general accounting. Established and implemented policies and procedures in all areas. Motivated employees, which resulted in maximized productivity. Instituted the use of such procedures as microfiching of invoices and bar coding for inventory control. The results were increased office productivity and greater sales. Directed customer service representatives as well as personally handling the larger accounts.

PLANNING - Designed and coordinated budget analysis systems and production requirements schedules including raw materials, work in progress and finished product inventory. Directed corporate-wide systems controls and programmers and planned all phases of systems and design, testing and user training.

FINANCIAL - Established policies and designed highly effective software for on-line cash application, collection on past due accounts and research of payment disputes. Established Credit and Accounts Receivable Department, and brought the department into a factoring position. Assigned credit lines, approved orders and collections. Resolved collection problems resulting in improved cash flow. Worked directly with Vice President of Sales and Controller to establish budgetary and marketing procedures.

SUPERVISION - Displayed open communication approach to all levels, resulting in excellent rapport with employees; union and non-union, as well as Senior Management. Supervised the day-to-day activities of 8 Department Managers, 11 Supervisors and 220 Plant Employees, and reported directly to the President of the company.

EDUCATION

NEW YORK UNIVERSITY SCHOOL OF COMMERCE
BACHELOR of SCIENCE DEGREE - Business Administration

IBM ENDICOTT, NEW YORK TRAINING CENTER
Intensive Operations and Systems

REFERENCES *will be provided upon request*

LINDA C. VILORIA

1224 Seymour Ave - Oakland CA 94610
home **(510) 123-4567** • work **(510) 234-5678**

**Objective: Position in a retail management program,
with emphasis on Buying and Merchandising.**

SUMMARY OF QUALIFICATIONS

★ Over 5 years successful experience in retail store management,
including 3 years as owner/entrepreneur.

★ Expertise in a wide range of management functions, including:
...Buying ...Customer Service ...Accounting ...Inventory Control
...Employee Management ...Store Design/Location

★ Thrive on the challenge of balancing a number of priorities at once.

★ Demonstrated creativity in choosing exciting merchandise and
creating an appealing store atmosphere.

RELEVANT EXPERIENCE & ACCOMPLISHMENTS

– As Owner/Manager, Scribbles-Too –

Business Management
• Designed a business plan, negotiated leases, obtained permits and licenses,
sought and found funding, monitored contracted services.
• Developed budget projections; set up bookkeeping system; handled accounts payable.

Store Design
• **Designed a new retail store**, in collaboration with an architect/interior designer,
working from a raw shell in a new building. **Created a trendy, upbeat environment**, selecting the wall colors, fixtures, lighting, floor and counter designs.

Buying
• **Bought both seasonal and nonseasonal items** including jewelry, novelty clothing,
quality writing instruments, gift items, party goods, alternative greeting cards.
• **Located unusual and trendy merchandise** at gift shows.
• **Developed a unique mix of merchandise** to capitalize on the ethnic diversity of the
Bay Area's customer base.
• **Constantly researched the latest trends** in clothing and accessories, through
popular and trade publications.

Customer Service
• **Established a strong base of repeat customers** through "bending over backwards"
to find what customers wanted; providing unique, appealing merchandise; and
and maintaining warm and honest relationships.
• **Created a reputation as an "in store"** to go to in downtown Oakland.

– As Manager, Scribbles –

Employee Supervision
• **Interviewed, hired, trained, and supervised** staffs of 4-5 employees.
• **Set up work schedules** to coordinate coverage by part-time employees.

Inventory Control
• **Tracked new incoming inventory, restocked, monitored inventory.**

– continued on page two –

– As Office Manager and Supervisor –

- 14 years experience as an administrator responsible for operations, budgets, controls, personnel, and staff development:
  - For Hibernia Bank: **Delegated** work tasks.   **Evaluated** employees. **Interviewed and recommended** new hires.
  - For UC Berkeley: **Supervised a staff** of 3-4, including purchasing & budgeting.

EMPLOYMENT HISTORY

1989	**Admin.Asst./Bookkeeper**	YWCA of OAKLAND
1986-89	**Owner/Manager**	SCRIBBLES-TOO, Oakland
		alternative greeting card/gift shop
1983-85	**Store Manager**	SCRIBBLES, San Francisco
1981-83	**Trust Administrator**	LLOYDS BANK CALIF, San Francisco
1977-81	**Supv., Credit Operations**	HIBERNIA NAT'L BANK, New Orleans
1970-77	**Office Mgr./Admin. Asst.**	UNIV. of CALIFORNIA, BERKELEY

Plus additional experience in retailing.

EDUCATION & TRAINING

B.A., Philosophy - California State University, Fullerton

Additional coursework in business:

•Advertising •Small Business Management •Computers and Data Processing •Accounting
•Real Estate •Real Estate Financing •Investing •Financial Statements

---

A Unique "Combo" Format

Linda Viloria's resume is an example of how you can COMBINE functional and chronological formats. We didn't describe ALL of her jobs, just the most recent and relevant ones. We broke down each of those positions into functional skills that would best support her new job objective, with some compromises, such as "store design" to highlight her unique background.

HINDA'S LIST OF ACTION VERBS

Career counselor Hinda Bodinger expanded on the list of action verbs found in *Damn Good Resume Guide* and came up with this economy-size list of words to help you compose a resume. She advises, "Don't restrict yourself to one or two headings; read through all of the categories and check off those that are relevant to describe your work experience. The underlined words are especially good for pointing out accomplishments."

Management/ Leadership Skills

administered
analyzed
appointed
approved
assigned
attained
authorized
chaired
considered
consolidated
contracted
controlled
converted
coordinated
decided
delegated
developed
directed
eliminated
emphasized
enforced
enhanced
established
executed
generated
handled
headed
hired
hosted
improved
incorporated
increased
initiated
inspected
instituted
led
managed
merged
motivated
organized
originated
overhauled
oversaw
planned
presided
prioritized
produced
recommended
reorganized

Management (continued)

replaced
restored
reviewed
scheduled
secured
selected
streamlined
strengthened
supervised
terminated

Communication/ People Skills

addressed
advertised
arbitrated
arranged
articulated
authored
clarified
collaborated
communicated
composed
condensed
conferred
consulted
contacted
conveyed
convinced
corresponded
debated
defined
described
developed
directed
discussed
drafted
edited
elicited
enlisted
explained
expressed
formulated
furnished
incorporated
influenced
interacted
interpreted

Communication (continued)

interviewed
involved
joined
judged
lectured
listened
marketed
mediated
moderated
negotiated
observed
outlined
participated
persuaded
presented
promoted
proposed
publicized
reconciled
recruited
referred
reinforced
reported
resolved
responded
solicited
specified
spoke
suggested
summarized
synthesized
translated
wrote

Research Skills

analyzed
clarified
collected
compared
conducted
critiqued
detected
determined
diagnosed
evaluated
examined
experimented

Research Skills (continued)

explored
extracted
formulated
gathered
identified
inspected
interpreted
interviewed
invented
investigated
located
measured
organized
researched
reviewed
searched
solved
summarized
surveyed
systematized
tested

Technical Skills

adapted
applied
assembled
built
calculated
computed
conserved
constructed
converted
debugged
designed
determined
developed
engineered
fabricated
fortified
installed
maintained
operated
overhauled
printed
programmed
rectified
regulated

Technical Skills
(continued)

remodeled
repaired
replaced
restored
solved
specialized
standardized
studied
upgraded
utilized

Teaching
Skills

adapted
advised
clarified
coached
communicated
conducted
coordinated
critiqued
developed
enabled
encouraged
evaluated
explained
facilitated
focused
guided
individualized
informed
instilled
instructed
motivated
persuaded
set goals
simulated
stimulated
taught
tested
trained
transmitted
tutored

Financial/
Data Skills

administered
adjusted
allocated
analyzed
appraised
assessed
audited
balanced

Financial/Data Skills
(continued)

budgeted
calculated
computed
conserved
corrected
determined
developed
estimated
forecasted
managed
marketed
measured
planned
prepared
programmed
projected
reconciled
reduced
researched
retrieved

Creative
Skills

acted
adapted
began
combined
composed
conceptualized
condensed
created
customized
designed
developed
directed
displayed
drew
entertained
established
fashioned
formulated
founded
illustrated
initiated
instituted
integrated
introduced
invented
modeled
modified
originated
performed
photographed
planned
revised

Creative Skills
(continued)

revitalized
shaped
solved

Helping
Skills

adapted
advocated
aided
answered
arranged
assessed
assisted
cared for
clarified
coached
collaborated
contributed
cooperated
counseled
demonstrated
diagnosed
educated
encouraged
ensured
expedited
facilitated
familiarized
furthered
guided
helped
insured
intervened
motivated
prevented
provided
referred
rehabilitated
represented
resolved
simplified
supplied
supported
volunteered

Organization/
Detail Skills

approved
arranged
catalogued
categorized
charted
classified
coded

Organization Skills
(continued)

collected
compiled
corrected
corresponded
distributed
executed
filed
generated
implemented
incorporated
inspected
logged
maintained
monitored
obtained
operated
ordered
organized
prepared
processed
provided
purchased
recorded
registered
reserved
responded
reviewed
routed
scheduled
screened
set up
submitted
supplied
standardized
systematized
updated
validated
verified

More Verbs for
Accomplishments

achieved
completed
expanded
exceeded
improved
pioneered
reduced (losses)
resolved (issues)
restored
spearheaded
succeeded
surpassed
transformed
won

CLIENT RELATIONS & BUSINESS

The First and Last Things to Do with Your Client

INITIAL CONTACT WITH A CLIENT

1. Establish your RELATIONSHIP:
   - HOW do they know about you?
   - WHAT do they know about you? (Fill them in if necessary.)
   - What do they think they NEED, and why are they asking for your help?

   Respond with your assessment of whether (and how) you can help.

2. Establish the CONTEXT of their resume, and then plan the work appropriately.
   - Information interviewing needed first?
   - Urgent job application pending?
   - Just completed college or training program and know what to do next, OR they don't have a clue?

3. Establish the MONEY relationship. Tell them your rates and then listen to their response:
   - Is money an issue?
   - Are they shocked at your rates, or does it sound reasonable to them?

4. Establish the level of CHALLENGE to you, and immediately jot down a potential strategy to address it, along with everything else you know about them up to this point.

RECORD KEEPING AFTER THE SESSION

I find it VERY useful to allow five minutes immediately after the session to jot down my observations about the session, and to document the finances.

Here's what I like to cover in those notes:

- **About the client and the resume work . . .**

  1. Physical impressions of the client to help me remember them;

  2. What was unique about our session—a difficult problem we solved, for example;

  3. How I think it went (satisfaction level);

  4. Anything of interest that I might want to follow-up on;

  5. Anything else that would help me in future interactions with the client—for example, that they're very talkative and I may need to ration my time with them.

- **About the finances . . .**

  1. Exactly how long it took and what I charged;

  2. Reminder to be fair to myself and get fully reimbursed for any follow-up services, if I was especially generous about the fee;

  3. Reminder to offer a free minor update if it was a long, expensive, top-dollar session;

  4. Any specific agreements we made—for example, "I told him that the first minor update would be free," or "I gave her a discount in return for delivering my fliers to her neighborhood."

Paperwork Tools and Techniques to Make the Resume Business Go Smoothly

TIMELY, CONSISTENT INTAKE RECORDS

The trick is, *don't count on your memory.* Have a consistent, brief format for getting "intake" data on a potential new client, and transform that info into final form ASAP, meaning *typed,* somewhere. You could use the "New Client Intake Form" found at the end of this chapter, or use this method:

I scribble first-contact notes on a lined pad that is by the phone, then immediately go over to my computer and type the info into a running commentary document I call my "Client Profiles"—a long document containing the "intake" notes of ALL my clients. (I just go to the bottom of the document and add the newest client.)

THEN, I copy and print just THAT current paragraph on this client, cut it (or accordion-fold it) to fit on the lower two-thirds of a 4 by 6 card, and tape the top edge to the 4 by 6 card on which I've already written, in bold black pen, the client's name, address, and phone number.

Then I attach a yellow "Post-It" note with the appointment date in bold letters. Whenever I see a salmon-colored 4 by 6 card, I know that's about a client, and the yellow Post- It tells me it's a NEW client with a future appointment coming up.

TIMELY POST-SESSION RECORD KEEPING

Immediately after a person leaves, I return to the "client profile" in my computer (entered when they first called me) and spend five minutes updating it with this info:

a) my *impressions of how the session went,* what issues we handled (or didn't handle);

b) anything that would help me in my *next* dealings with that client, such as, "A joy to work with, and we're both very pleased with the results" or "Avoid future work, a very draining time-consuming client";

c) *how long it took, how much I charged,* and *agreements* about future work, such as "Agreed that the first minor change is free." This paragraph is then printed and added to the 4 by 6 card.

RESUME ARCHIVES

I keep THREE copies of the client's resume, *printed and filed immediately* after they leave:

a) a scribble copy, folded and clipped onto the back of the 4 by 6 Client Card;

b) a master copy in a notebook, *filed alphabetically* with all the others;

c) a job category copy in another notebook; this notebook is sectioned into different career categories (Finance, Health, Education, Sales, etc.) This notebook is an invaluable quick reference when I'm writing other resumes.

GENERAL DATABASE

I started to develop a database of resume clients in my FileMaker program. I have to say I have stopped doing it, since I made too little use of it.

I DO have an extensive FileMaker database of *other* types of clients, however: readers of my books, subscribers to my newsletter, and workshop participants. This database is incredibly handy, as I don't have to remember a million details—I just go immediately to the computer, open the database, and record the essence of a phone call, or summarize a letter received or sent.

LETTERS

Readers Share Their Concerns About Choice of Format

CHRONOLOGICAL? FUNCTIONAL? WHICH TO CHOOSE?

Dear Yana: More and more of my clients are requesting a chronological format. What do you think?

**Nancy Rosenberg
The Right Resume
Babylon, NY**

Dear Nancy: There's nothing wrong with a chronological resume format, if you use it right. I know it seems as though I have pushed the functional format (and I admit that for years I used it almost exclusively), but there was a reason: When you put together a functional resume, you HAVE to think about the RELEVANCE of the information; so using a functional format HELPS avoid the tendency of job hunters to fall back on a "resume obituary" approach (summarizing past work duties without linking it to the current job objective). The "resume obituary" approach leaves all the work—analyzing and prioritizing the resume data—up to the potential employer.

BUT . . . but . . . but . . . IF your chronological format is used properly, it can have all the virtues of a good functional resume and MORE. The trick is, for each job or work experience, talk only about the accomplishments and activities that are actually RELEVANT to the stated job objective and the skills it calls for. SKIP the "responsibilities included" business entirely, UNLESS it directly relates to the job sought now.

THEN the chronological format will be just as helpful to the employer as a functional format, and have the important added advantage of being more familiar to some employers.

My favorite variation on this strategy: Using a chronological format, insert a **very brief** line or two **in smaller size type** that deals with the "responsibilities included" stuff, such as the overall nature of the business (its size, its products and services). THEN proceed with the RELEVANT accomplishments and activities. —yp

This strategy is graphically illustrated in the **Self-Teaching Resume Template** on page 49 in Chapter 3.

OH, BUT I LOVE MY FUNCTIONAL FORMAT!

Vicki Law-Miller of Colorado called with a new challenge. Her client (we'll call him Jim) is making a transition into teaching after years in the construction field.

He just got his teaching credentials, and took a job-search seminar at the nearby university, where he was specifically advised NOT to use the format frequently shown in the *Resume Catalog*. (The "Veronica London" resume on page 133 was pointed out as "the format NOT to use.")

Vicki, on the other hand, felt that Jim was a perfect candidate for that format, and especially wanted to use the "Highlights" paragraph to show why Jim would be a good teacher despite virtually NO previous direct experience. That's where she would play up his volunteer work as a tutor and as a "big brother" in a dropout prevention program, as well as his required student teaching.

But Jim's academic advisors had recommended "no Highlights." So Vicki wanted some guidelines for handling his resume in another format. I advised her to fully cooperate with her client's direction, assuring her that she COULD work within his preferences and still produce a great resume.

Here is what I suggested she do:

1. Create a section called **"Teaching-Related Experience"** immediately following Jim's name, address, and job objective, containing four paragraphs headed:

- Dropout Prevention Program
- Tutoring
- Student Teaching
- Course Work

In these four paragraphs (the specific areas of experience he identified) she could expand on these experiences and document Jim's interest in and commitment to teaching.

2. Beneath THAT, she could create ANOTHER section called "Other Professional Experience" or "Employment History," for documenting Jim's years of work in the construction field, in traditional chronological format, but without going into as much detail—"just the bare facts."

Vicki began to see that this "problem" could be viewed as a healthy challenge. She will need to ask herself anew, "What are the truly essential ingredients in a superior resume?" And she'll find that "my favorite format" is not on the list!

We resume writers need to guard against the temptation to become rigidly attached to a preferred format or approach. Flexibility is, in fact, one of our most powerful tools—one that's not available to writers using "canned" computer programs and writers employed by fast-food-type resume mills. So don't voluntarily give up this precious tool!

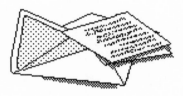

"I HATE FUNCTIONAL RESUMES"

Lynn Desker pointed out an article in the local Business Times entitled "The Making of a Smart and Crisp Resume," and here is a challenging paragraph from it: "One headhunter names as his pet hate the Functional Resume. This is a resume where the information is organized according to the applicant's skills, rather than by jobs and employers. The reader is left with the frustrating task of figuring out what the applicant did for which employer and how much responsibility the applicant had in each job."

Well, let's face it: The head hunter is right; it's a legitimate complaint. BUT—it doesn't have to end there. We aren't stuck with having to choose between CLARITY and the functional format. Why not have BOTH?

Who says, just because your resume is organized by skills, that it has to mystify and frustrate the reader? Come on, we can find a solution to this!

Yana's Apology

Before we go further with this discussion, I want to personally apologize for not recognizing and addressing this problem years ago when the grumbling first began. I just didn't see what now seems obvious: You CAN have a functional resume and STILL tell the reader where and when things happened! And also be clear about the level of responsibility in each job.

I have developed a set of Self-Teaching Resume Templates, and the functional formats in the set (see pages 50–51) show how this can be accomplished. Functional resumes are too useful to abandon just because we didn't get it right the first time!

On Commitment to High Standards

These two letters are included because they illustrate a problem that is unfortunately widespread in the resume business: lack of commitment to high standards. To be blunt about it, **I hope that this book contributes to putting such people out of business**—or at least forcing them to change their attitudes. All it takes to upgrade the profession is a lot more of us doing excellent work, and making sure that potential clients know how to find us.

"B.S., I LOVE YOU"

Dear Yana: I stress short, succinct, active sentences; this helps employers view the resume quickly, without getting too bored.

I try to highlight a job searcher's strength, and fill in jibberish if necessary to help make their career look full (for some, more jibberish than others).

Anonymous One
Somewhere East of Here

(The resume writer signed, but to protect the guilty, we'll just say "Anonymous One"!)

Dear Anonymous One: Filling in with "jibberish" is, sorry to say, a clue that you need to upgrade your counseling and writing skills—not to mention your attitude. If you started with the assumption that EVERYBODY has some fabulous talents and accomplishments, and YOUR business is to discover and document them, then your job would be more fun and your resumes would improve dramatically. —yp

 ### "B.S., I LOVE YOU TWO"

Dear Yana: I have found that when I do not have much to say about a person's background, because they lack experience or whatever, putting a border around the resume is a big plus.

Anonymous Two
Somewhere Farther East of Here

Dear Anonymous Two: I doubt that putting a border around a weak resume is going to impress anybody. Putting a border around a GOOD one might be a nice touch, though.

If your client has been on the planet long enough to be job-hunting, surely the two of you can come up with SOME experience that's more valuable than a border. —yp

New Client Intake Form

DATE   APPOINTMENT

NAME   REFERRED BY

CITY   HOME PHONE

                                        WORK PHONE

JOB OBJECTIVE

WHAT'S THE PROBLEM?

HOMEWORK?

UNDERSTANDING about MONEY and TIME

NOTES

New Client Intake Form

DATE

NAME

CITY
Don't need full address yet, but
it helps to know how far they're
coming, in case they're late.

APPOINTMENT Date/day/time

REFERRED BY
"How did you hear about this resume service?"

HOME PHONE

WORK PHONE

JOB OBJECTIVE
"What is the job you're going for now?" ... or
"What is this resume for? What kind of job?"
"Who's going to get this resume? How will you be using it?"

WHAT'S THE PROBLEM?
"Why do you think you need help? What do you see as the problem?"

HOMEWORK?
If the answer to "What job are you looking for now?" is **anything less than absolutely clear and unhesitating**, give
them this"homework": "Make a list of all the JOB TITLES you can think of that would be acceptable and appropriate for your VERY NEXT JOB . . . and **you must not take more than 10 minutes** to make the list. Then spend 5
minutes (only) making a list of workplaces where you might apply for any of those jobs."

UNDERSTANDING about MONEY and TIME
Rate per hour, estimated hours to complete, estimated fee, cancellation terms.
For example, I might enter: "40/3/120/48", meaning I DEFINITELY DID TELL THEM that I charge $40/hour, it
will take about 3 hours, it will cost approximately $120, and that I NEED at least 48 hours notice if they need to
change the appointment.

NOTES
Warnings, hunches, and strategies go here, such as:
"Talks a-mile-a-minute, goes off on many tangents—BE SURE TO GET HER FOCUSED RIGHT AWAY."
"Concerned about money—be sure to keep an eye on the clock."
"Very vague about the objective—do Homework first—this is going to be tough."
"Scared to death about the job search...needs hand-holding, encouragement."
"Reminder: I asked her to do some information interviewing first if possible. Be sure to follow up."

3

Self-Teaching Resume Templates

3
Self-Teaching Resume Templates

What Are These Templates?

A template is simply a detailed structural outline of a document, providing a starting point and some graphic help in visualizing the finished product.

A *self-teaching* resume template, such as those presented in this chapter, adds another dimension: **explicit instructions**, located right ON the resume template, about the **nature of the material** to be entered in **that particular section or location** on the resume—instructions that link the various parts together to form a focused, coherent, and concise document.

NOTE: There are *software files* on a computer disk that are identical in content to the hard copy (on paper) versions in this chapter. In either form—software or hard copy—we're calling them Self-Teaching Resume Templates.

I designed these templates so that resume writers at all levels of skill could benefit, their primary function being simply to remind writers to:

a) **keep it simple**

b) **keep it focused**, and

c) **keep it relevant**.

Their secondary function is to keep it beautiful!

How I Use These Templates

I promise to go into *excruciating* detail about how I work with a client, using a template as a starting point. For now, here's a quick overview.

Whenever I start working with a client, I first open up a file called Resume Template on my computer screen—usually the Simple Chronological or the Simple Functional version shown on pages 47 and 50. I use this shortcut for several reasons:

- For me, it **simplifies and speeds up the layout of the resume**, because on the template I've already chosen an appropriate resume font, the size and style and alignment of the headings, the location of tabs, and the document margins. All I have to do is start entering the data (typing right over, and replacing, the original directions on the template) and replace the generic headings with real ones.
- The template **serves as a clear OUTLINE** of the new resume, **making it easy for me to**

explain my strategy to the client at the beginning of our session.

- For the client, the template **provides a reassuring sense of direction and structure**. As soon as I type in their name and address at the top, the outline becomes THEIRS; they can see where the resume is going and that we already have a head start.
- For both me and the client, the self-teaching template **serves as a constant reminder to stay on track** and keep the content directly relevant to the job objective.

Using These Templates with YOUR Resume Clients

At the beginning of a resume session you could show your client a copy of two templates—one chronological and one functional—and explain the features and advantages of each. Then start working with the template that you both agree is best suited to the situation. If there is any doubt—and especially **if you are new at resume writing**—select the Simple Functional format. It will get you off on the right foot, because you'll be led, early on, into determining the skills that are relevant to the new job.

Later if you change your mind and want to transform it into a chronological resume, the switch is easy: Just remove the skill headings, and move each one-liner to the work history section, under the appropriate company name.

Incidentally, you may find that this strategy—starting out with the functional format and then switching—results in a more powerful *chronological* resume, because the one-liners have been developed with the relevant *skills* in mind, rather than the job duties of the old position.

Novice resume writers would do well to stick with these two simple formats until they've mastered them, and then begin experimenting with fancier models.

Other Uses for These Templates

Here are a few more situations where the Self-Teaching Templates could be useful, either in hard-copy form, as shown in this book, or in software form in a computer lab (see page 242):

1. In a hands-on resume-writing **workshop** as a graphic step-by-step guideline.

2. In a **classroom** to supplement other teaching tools related to resumes and the job search.

3. In a corporate **outplacement program** or **in-house career center**, as a self-help tool for job hunters and employees.

Features and Advantages of the Different Formats

- **The chronological format is a good choice when:**

  1. You want to call attention to a very stable work history;

  2. You want to call attention to consistent upward mobility and promotions in your chosen career;

  3. You are applying for a job in a very conservative field;

  4. You think your next employer would be more comfortable with a traditional resume.

- **The functional format, which emphasizes applicable skills, is a good choice when:**

  1. The job hunter is making a career change;

  2. The job titles don't do justice to the job hunter's accomplishments and responsibilities;

  3. You want to focus on the skills useful to the future job, rather than on past job content;

  4. The best accomplishments and most impressive work experience are not drawn from the most recent jobs but from farther back in time;

5. The work history is complicated or has long stretches of unsalaried periods. (People are rarely out of work—they are just "out of pay.")

6. The most impressive skills came out of volunteer or otherwise unpaid work.

- **The combination functional/chronological format is good to use when:**

  1. The job seeker has had several very different kinds of jobs, each one illustrating only ONE of several skills to be used in their new career.

  2. The past jobs are familiar to the public so job-description information is not important;

  3. You want to put equal emphasis on the jobs held in the past, and on the skills to be applied to the new job;

  4. You want to make it very obvious where each of the accomplishments occurred.

- **The executive accomplishment format is a good choice when** your client has been laid off from a responsible position and . . .

  1. They haven't worked in their field recently; or

  2. They have been out of work for longer than a few months.

- **The information interview/draft format is useful when a job hunter wants to:**

  1. Explore a desired career field to see if their skills are sufficient for work in that area;

  2. Find a new career field where they could fully express their interests and use their favorite skills.

The **Information Interview Resume** template (page 54) is simply a variation on the functional format specifically for use in career exploration when a client's job objective needs to be clarified. The three primary ways this format differs from an ordinary functional format are:

1. The job objective is clearly TENTATIVE, and relatively general; it may even be a GUESS on the part of the job hunter about a desirable job title that may or may not exist. (They will be doing some research to find out.)

2. The skill areas listed and documented in the resume are those skills the job-hunter WANTS to use in a new career area he is exploring—they do not necessarily represent an existing job.

3. The words "DRAFT RESUME" are an essential component of the resume, so that neither the

job hunter NOR the reader mistakes this for a finalized resume.

Helpful Hints

There is no one right way to do ANYTHING on a resume. Each resume should be uniquely appropriate to that individual and that job objective. Consequently, your resumes won't look *exactly* like these templates. And likewise, our examples illustrating use of the templates don't always look *exactly* like the templates either. That's life!

Here are some alternatives to get you started customizing the templates for your use. PLEASE avoid creating a formula that you repeat over and over for all your clients. Flexibility and innovation are crucial to good resume writing.

ALTERNATIVE WORDING FOR SECTIONS

- For the **Job Objective,** you could also say:
  - Career Objective
  - Objective
  - Career Goal
  - Current Job Objective, followed in smaller type by Long-Term Career Objective, in *rare* cases where this would be helpful.

- Instead of **Highlights** for the overview paragraph at the top of a resume, you could say:
  - Highlights of Qualifications
  - Summary of Qualifications
  - Summary
  - Profile
  - Professional Profile

- The section listing **Relevant Skills and Experience** could be called:
  - Relevant Experience & Accomplishments
  - Skills & Accomplishments
  - Professional Achievements
  - Professional Experience

- For the **Employment History** section, you could say:
  - Work History (especially if you want to include unpaid work)
  - Recent Work History (especially if you want to leave off much earlier jobs)
  - Relevant Work History (especially if you need to omit less-desirable positions)
  - Work History Concurrent With Education (which helps explain a choppy work history during college years)

- Additional Work History for miscellaneous jobs too small to include in the main Work History (or too far back in time) BUT worth mentioning because they're relevant to the objective.

OPTIONAL SECTIONS TO ADD ONLY IF NEEDED *(DON'T GET CARRIED AWAY NOW!)*

- Awards
- Publications
- Community Service
- Credentials
- Relevant Course Work
- Hardware/Software
- Equipment
- Languages

IF YOU HAVE A COMPUTER . . .

Software versions of the templates could speed up the formatting of resumes and show you specifically how each template was created in a word processing program such as Microsoft Word or WordPerfect. *See page 409 for information on ordering the software.*

CUSTOMIZING THESE TEMPLATES

by Susan Ireland

A professional resume writer should not feel constrained by the suggestions and guidelines found in these templates. They provide a foundation for getting started on the right foot, but you should customize them to suit your needs.

Below are some of the ways I might modify the templates for particular situations with my clients.

1. JOB OBJECTIVE

"Focusing on this and that areas" may apply to some job seekers but not to others, where simply the job title will be sufficient. "A position as" could be omitted.

2. SUMMARY OF QUALIFICATIONS

a) The bulleted statements need to be prioritized for each individual resume. The sequence presented here may not be the right sequence for everyone, although "number of years" does seem to be the #1 item in most cases.

b) The "number of years experience" may not be impressive, in which case I would not mention it. Other ways of handling it might be "experience in . . ." or "knowledge of . . . ."

c) "Credentials, training, or education." Include this only if it's a strong point and if the "Summary of Qualifications" isn't followed immediately by the "Education" section.

d) The content of a Summary should be determined by what's appropriate for the field and how the job seeker would naturally express himself. A professional resume writer should be careful not to impose a particular type of statement on a client.

3. RELEVANT EXPERIENCE AND ACCOMPLISHMENTS

a) In some cases the two-line overview of a position is not necessary; the title and company name may tell the whole story.

b) In jobs that are not at all related to the objective, it's okay to say very little or nothing at all about the experience other than the dates, title, and company name.

4. REFERENCES

This is optional on all the formats.

5. EDUCATION

a) Dates are optional. Carefully consider what the date is telling the reader. Does it reveal how old the person is? Or how up-to-date their knowledge in their field may be? In some fields this makes a big difference, and including the dates could work for or against the applicant.

Also, including the date may create an undesirable gap in time between education and work history.

b) The Education section may be moved to the top of the resume if it's highly relevant or if it's the job hunter's strongest qualification—for example, a recent accounting graduate entering the field of accounting.

6. SPECIAL KNOWLEDGE AREA

(See "Snappy Functional" resume format on page 51.)

This category works in some cases but not all. It's optional and should be used only if it enhances the resume.

7. A FINAL NOTE

If you run into problems, consult Chapter 5 for ideas on how to handle difficult parts of the resume.

YOUR NAME
Street Address
City, State, and Zip
(415) xxx-xxxx

Objective: Position as _____

SUMMARY OF QUALIFICATIONS

- Number of years experience in the field or line of work.
- Relevant credentials or training or education.
- An accomplishment* that directly relates to the objective.
- A quality* or characteristic* of yours that supports this goal.
- Another accomplishment*, or another characteristic*.

* reflected in the details below, of course

RELEVANT EXPERIENCE & ACCOMPLISHMENTS

1990-present **Job Title** WORKPLACE, City CA
- Accomplishment/one-liner, from this job, that's relevant to the new job objective.
- Accomplishment/one-liner, from this job, that's relevant to the new job objective.
- Accomplishment/one-liner, from this job, that's relevant to the new job objective.
- Accomplishment/one-liner, from this job, that's relevant to the new job objective.

198x-8x **Job Title** WORKPLACE, City CA
- Accomplishment/one-liner, from this job, that's relevant to the new job objective.
- Accomplishment/one-liner, from this job, that's relevant to the new job objective.

198x-8x **Job Title** WORKPLACE, City CA
- Accomplishment/one-liner, from this job, that's relevant to the new job objective.
- Accomplishment/one-liner, from this job, that's relevant to the new job objective.

198x-8x **Job Title** WORKPLACE, City CA
- Accomplishment/one-liner, from this job, that's relevant to the new job objective.
- Accomplishment/one-liner, from this job, that's relevant to the new job objective.

197x-7x **Job Title** WORKPLACE, City CA
- Accomplishment/one-liner, from this job, that's relevant to the new job objective.
- Accomplishment/one-liner, from this job, that's relevant to the new job objective.

EDUCATION & TRAINING
Degree or classes or whatever
Some credentials, maybe

YOUR NAME
Street Address
City, State, and Zip
(415) xxx-xxxx

Objective: A position as Manager of Whatever, focusing on this and that areas.

SUMMARY OF QUALIFICATIONS

- Number of years experience in work* at all <u>relevant</u> to the objective above.
- Credentials or education or training, relevant to this objective.
- A key accomplishment** that shows you're a "hot candidate" for this job.
- A strength** or characteristic** of yours that's important to you and relevant to this job.
- Something else the employer should know ... a skill**, a trait**, an accomplishment**.

*including unpaid work   ** reflected in the details below, of course*

RELEVANT EXPERIENCE & ACCOMPLISHMENTS

199x-present   *Job Title*
WORKPLACE, City
[A two-line overview of your essential role in this company, mentioning the kind of products or services you offered, and possibly who your customers were.]

- An accomplishment/one-liner from this job, that's relevant to the new job objective above, preferably spelling out your unique actions and the benefits to your employer.

- An accomplishment/one-liner from this job, that's relevant to the new job objective above, preferably spelling out your unique actions and the benefits to your employer.

198x-8x   *Job Title*
WORKPLACE, City
[A two-line overview of your essential role in this company, mentioning the kind of products or services you offered, and possibly who your customers were.]

- An accomplishment/one-liner from this job, that's relevant to the new job objective above, preferably spelling out your unique actions and the benefits to your employer.

- An accomplishment/one-liner from this job, that's relevant to the new job objective above, preferably spelling out your unique actions and the benefits to your employer.

198x-8x   *Job Title*
WORKPLACE, City
[A two-line overview of your essential role in this company, mentioning the kind of products or services you offered, and possibly who your customers were.]

- An accomplishment/one-liner from this job, that's relevant to the new job objective above, preferably spelling out your unique actions and the benefits to your employer.

- An accomplishment/one-liner from this job, that's relevant to the new job objective above, preferably spelling out your unique actions and the benefits to your employer.

EDUCATION & TRAINING
Degree or classes or whatever
Some credentials, maybe

TEMPLATES

YOUR NAME
Your street address
City, State, and Zip
(415) xxx-xxxx

OBJECTIVE

A position as Director of Whatever, focusing on this and that areas.

HIGHLIGHTS

- Number of years experience in work* at all <u>relevant</u> to the objective above.
- Credentials or education or training, relevant to this objective.
- A key accomplishment** that shows you're a "hot candidate" for this job.
- A strength** or characteristic** of yours, that's important to you and relevant to this job.
- Something else the employer should know ... a skill**, a trait**, an accomplishment**.

*including unpaid work   ** reflected in the details below, of course

RELEVANT EXPERIENCE

199x-present   **COMPANY NAME**
Job Title
A two-line overview of your essential role in this company, including the kind of products or services you dealt with.
- An accomplishment from THIS job, illustrating a skill needed in the NEW job.
- Another accomplishment from this job, illustrating a skill needed in the new job.
- Another activity from this job, illustrating a skill needed in the new job.

198x-xx   **COMPANY NAME**
Job Title
A two-line overview of your essential role in this company, including the kind of products or services you dealt with.
- An accomplishment from THIS job, illustrating a skill needed in the NEW job.
- Another accomplishment from this job, illustrating a skill needed in the new job.
- Another activity from this job, illustrating a skill needed in the new job.

198x-xx   **COMPANY NAME**
Job Title
A two-line overview of your essential role in this company, including the kind of products or services you dealt with.
- An accomplishment from THIS job, illustrating a skill needed in the NEW job:
  - A substatement that elaborates on one step in the process of the accomplishment above.
  - A substatement elaborating on another step in the process of the accomplishment above.

197x-xx   **COMPANY NAME**
Job Title
A two-line overview of your essential role in this company, including the kind of products or services you dealt with.
- An accomplishment from THIS job, illustrating a skill needed in the NEW job.
- Another activity from this job, illustrating a skill needed in the new job.

EDUCATION

University of So-and-So, Podunk City
B.A., Basket Weaving, 1989

YOUR NAME
Street Address
City, State, and Zip
(415) xxx-xxxx

TEMPLATES

Job objective: Position as _____

SUMMARY OF QUALIFICATIONS
- Number of years experience in the field or line of work.
- Relevant credentials or training or education.
- An accomplishment* that directly relates to the objective.
- A quality* or characteristic* of yours that supports this goal.
- Another accomplishment* or another characteristic*.

* reflected in the details below, of course

RELEVANT EXPERIENCE & ACCOMPLISHMENTS

ONE RELEVANT SKILL
- An accomplishment* that illustrates or documents this skill.
- Another accomplishment* that illustrates or documents this skill.
- Another accomplishment* that illustrates or documents this skill.

ANOTHER RELEVANT SKILL
- An accomplishment* that illustrates or documents this skill.
- Another accomplishment* that illustrates or documents this skill.
- Another accomplishment* that illustrates or documents this skill.

ANOTHER RELEVANT SKILL
- An accomplishment* that illustrates or documents this skill.
- Another accomplishment* that illustrates or documents this skill.
- Another accomplishment* that illustrates or documents this skill.

* Wherever possible, <u>mention where this happened</u>, linking it to the Employment History to avoid confusion.
NOTE: In all cases, "relevant" means relevant to the above stated job objective.

EMPLOYMENT HISTORY
1990-present	**Job Title**	COMPANY NAME, City
198x-8x	**Job Title**	COMPANY NAME, City
197x-7x	**Job Title**	COMPANY NAME, City
197x-7x	**Job Title**	COMPANY NAME, City
197x-7x	**Job Title**	COMPANY NAME, City

EDUCATION & TRAINING
Degree or classes or whatever
Some credentials, maybe

YOUR NAME
Your street address
City, State, and Zip
(415) xxx-xxxx

OBJECTIVE

A position as Coordinator of Whatever, focusing on this and that areas.

HIGHLIGHTS

- Number of years experience in work* at all <u>relevant</u> to the objective above.
- Credentials or education or training, relevant to this objective.
- A key accomplishment** that shows you're a "hot candidate" for this job.
- A strength** or characteristic** of yours, that's important to you and relevant to this job.
- Something else the employer should know ... a skill**, a trait**, an accomplishment**.

including unpaid work   ** *reflected in the details below, of course*

RELEVANT SKILLS & EXPERIENCE

ONE MAJOR SKILL *(that is directly relevant to the job objective stated above)*
- An accomplishment that illustrates this skill (<u>including where</u> this occurred).
- An accomplishment that illustrates this skill (<u>including where</u> this occurred):
  - A substatement that elaborates on one step in the process of the accomplishment above.
  - A substatement elaborating on another step in the process of the accomplishment above.

ANOTHER MAJOR SKILL *(that is directly relevant to the job objective stated above)*
- An accomplishment that illustrates this skill (<u>including where</u> this occurred):
  - A substatement that elaborates on one step in the process of the accomplishment above.
  - A substatement elaborating on another step in the process of the accomplishment above.
- An accomplishment that illustrates this skill (<u>including where</u> this occurred).
- An accomplishment that illustrates this skill (linking it to the work history below).

ANOTHER MAJOR SKILL *(that is directly relevant to the job objective stated above)*
- An accomplishment that illustrates this skill (<u>including where</u> this occurred).
- An accomplishment that illustrates this skill (<u>linking it to the work history below</u>).

A SPECIAL KNOWLEDGE AREA (essential to the objective named above)
- An accomplishment illustrating/documenting this special knowledge (<u>+ where</u>).
- A list of equipment or processes you're familiar with, consistent w/ expertise in this area.
- A list of courses or trainings you took that shows your expertise in this area.

WORK HISTORY

1990-present	*Job Title*	**COMPANY NAME and city** (+*another line of explanation if needed*)
198x-xx	*Job Title*	**COMPANY NAME and city**
198x-xx	*Job Title*	**COMPANY NAME and city**
197x-xx	*Job Title*	**COMPANY NAME and city**

EDUCATION

University of So-and So, Podunk City
B.A., Basket Weaving, 1989

YOUR NAME
Street Address
City, State, and Zip
(415) xxx-xxxx

Objective: Position as _____

SUMMARY OF QUALIFICATIONS
- Number of years experience in the field or line of work.
- Relevant credentials or training or education.
- An accomplishment* that directly relates to the objective.
- A quality* or characteristic* of yours that supports this goal.
- Another accomplishment* or another characteristic*.
  * reflected in the details below, of course

EXPERIENCE & RELEVANT ACCOMPLISHMENTS

1987-present   **Job Title**   COMPANY NAME, City

One Skill (a primary function of the job above AND directly relevant to the Objective above)
- An accomplishment from this job, that illustrates or documents this skill.
  - A substatement that elaborates on one step in the process of the accomplishment above.
  - A substatement that elaborates on another step in the process of the accomplishment above.
- Another accomplishment from this job, that illustrates or documents this skill.
- Another accomplishment from this job, that illustrates or documents this skill.

Another Skill (another function of the job above, directly relevant to the Objective above)
- An accomplishment from this job, that illustrates or documents this skill.
- An accomplishment from this job, that illustrates or documents this skill.

198x-8x   **Job Title**   COMPANY NAME, City

One Skill (a primary function of the job above AND directly relevant to the Objective above)
- An accomplishment from this job, that illustrates or documents this skill.
  - A substatement that elaborates on one step in the process of the accomplishment above.
  - A substatement that elaborates on another step in the process of the accomplishment above.
  - A substatement that elaborates on another step in the process of the accomplishment above.

Another Skill (another function of the job above, directly relevant to the Objective above)
- An accomplishment from this job, that illustrates or documents this skill.
- An accomplishment from this job, that illustrates or documents this skill.

198x-8x   **Job Title**   COMPANY NAME, City

One Skill (a primary function of the job above AND directly relevant to the Objective above)
- An accomplishment from this job, that illustrates or documents this skill.
  - A substatement that elaborates on one step in the process of the accomplishment above.
  - A substatement that elaborates on another step in the process of the accomplishment above.

Another Skill (another function of the job above, directly relevant to the Objective above)
- An accomplishment from this job, that illustrates or documents this skill.
- An accomplishment from this job, that illustrates or documents this skill.

EDUCATION & TRAINING
Degree or classes or whatever
Some credentials, maybe

YOUR NAME HERE

Street Address   Residence: (xxx) xxx-xxxx
City, State, Zip   Messages: (xxx) xxx-xxxx

OBJECTIVE: _____ (Manufacturing Management, for example)

QUALIFICATIONS: *(items below are idea-generators, not rigid guidelines)*
- Number of years of experience in this field.
- Something about your track record or professional reputation in this field.
- Reference to the specific skills developed that relate to above objective.
- Areas of specialized knowledge or product expertise.
- Work-style attributes that make you a desirable candidate.

ACCOMPLISHMENTS:

An accomplishment that illustrates professional competence, including improvements, innovations, cost-saving measures, etc., with percentages and numbers if appropriate.

An accomplishment that illustrates professional competence, including improvements, innovations, cost-saving measures, etc., with percentages and numbers if appropriate.

An accomplishment that illustrates professional competence, including improvements, innovations, cost-saving measures, etc., with percentages and numbers if appropriate.

An accomplishment that illustrates professional competence, including improvements, innovations, cost-saving measures, etc., with percentages and numbers if appropriate.

An accomplishment that illustrates professional competence, including improvements, innovations, cost-saving measures, etc., with percentages and numbers if appropriate.

An accomplishment that illustrates professional competence, including improvements, innovations, cost-saving measures, etc., with percentages and numbers if appropriate.

An accomplishment that illustrates professional competence, including improvements, innovations, cost-saving measures, etc., with percentages and numbers if appropriate.

An accomplishment that illustrates professional competence, including improvements, innovations, cost-saving measures, etc., with percentages and numbers if appropriate.

An accomplishment that illustrates professional competence, including improvements, innovations, cost-saving measures, etc., with percentages and numbers if appropriate.

EXPERIENCE: Job Title   Company Name, x years
                Job Title   Company Name, x years
                Job Title   Company Name, x years

EDUCATION: Academic degree, if any   University of Whatever

53

DRAFT RESUME
*(Note: the words "Draft Resume" are part of
this format, and could be written in by hand)*

Your Name
Your street address
City, State, Zip
(415) xxx-xxxx

TENTATIVE JOB OBJECTIVE

A position as _____.
*(An approximation or guess, of what you THINK they'd call the job that you
THINK you'd like to do next...after you get some more information about it.)*

HIGHLIGHTS

- Number of years experience in work at all relevant to the tentative objective above.
- Credentials or education or training, relevant to this tentative career choice.
- A key accomplishment that supports this goal.
- Another relevant accomplishment; OR a special strength related to this goal.

RELEVANT SKILLS & EXPERIENCE

ONE MAJOR SKILL AREA *(that you'd LIKE to use in this new job or field you're researching)*

- An accomplishment that illustrates this skill (including where it occurred).
- Another accomplishment that illustrates or documents this skill.

ANOTHER MAJOR SKILL AREA *(that you'd LIKE to use in this new job or field you're researching)*

- An accomplishment that illustrates this skill (including where it occurred).
- Another accomplishment that illustrates or documents this skill.

ANOTHER MAJOR SKILL AREA *(that you'd LIKE to use in this new job or field you're researching)*
- An accomplishment that illustrates this skill (including where it occurred).
- Another accomplishment that illustrates or documents this skill.

A SPECIAL KNOWLEDGE AREA *(essential to the objective named above)*

- An accomplishment that illustrates this special knowledge (+ where it happened).
- List of equipment or processes you're familiar with, related to expertise in this area.
- A list of courses or trainings you took, that shows your expertise in this area.

WORK* HISTORY

199x-present	*Job Title*	**COMPANY NAME** and **city** *(a little explanation if needed)*
198x-xx	*Job Title*	**COMPANY NAME** and **city**
197x-xx	*Job Title*	**COMPANY NAME** and **city**

* Remember, "Work is Work is Work" whether it's paid or unpaid.

EDUCATION

University of So-and So, Podunk City • B.A., Basket Weaving, 1970

54

DALE SIMPSON
P.O. Box 51
Pencil Point, ME 03907
(207) 444-3321

Objective: Position as driver for Britt-Ways Corp.

SUMMARY OF QUALIFICATIONS

- Dependable, hard worker who can be counted on to "get the job done."
- Excellent driving record, with over eight years experience behind the wheel.
- Friendly and well liked; good at customer relations.
- Available to relocate.

EXPERIENCE

1989-91   Driver/Tour Guide   Trolley Tours, Pencil Pt., Me & Larkspur, AZ
- Drove small tour bus through scenic parts of these two resorts, pointing out sights, providing friendly service, and assisting senior citizens.
- Maintained a perfect driving record, always giving first priority to safety.
- Performed light repair work as needed.
- Recognized as #1 employee within this company of 15.

1988   Sales Representative   Recycled Tractor Parts, Townsend, ME
- Sold used tractor and equipment parts by phone and over the counter.
- Handled inventory, shipping, and nationwide teletype service.

1987   Driver   Paris Oil Recycling, Paris, ME
- Managed pickup and delivery of waste oil (until business was sold).

1986   Sales Representative   Old Fashioned Engine & Parts, York, MA
- Opened and maintained new accounts by contacting targeted prospects.
- Traveled approximately 1,000 miles per week, servicing existing accounts and cold calling.

1983-85   Assistant Manager   CarSearch, Southern, ME
- Performed warehouse duties including processing orders, stocking, shipping, receiving, and locating sources for special orders.
- Promoted to Assistant Manager; handled counter sales and customer service.

1978-83   Driver/Dispatcher   Portland-Bangor Oil, Portland, ME
- Drove oil trucks, providing pickup and delivery service for waste oil recycling.
- Supervised product safety while working with thousands of gallons of oil per week.
- Promoted services as "on-the-road representative" for the company.
- Served as dispatcher in the retail fuel oil division, coordinating deliveries and service calls.

EDUCATION
ABA, Business Administration, University of Maine, Portland

- Resume Writer: Susan Ireland -

HAROLD Q. GEARY

1224 Panasonic Way
Boston, Massachusetts 02150
(123) 456-7890

Objective: Program Directorship with Metropolitan Medical Center, involving
•Planning & Program Development •Management •Public Relations •Marketing & Sales

SUMMARY OF QUALIFICATIONS

- Track record of successfully managing complex projects in the health care industry.
- Able to work effectively within a variety of organizational/political structures.
- Extensive experience in developing programs from concept to ongoing operation.
- Solid understanding of marketing and sales strategies in health care.
- Graduate degree plus 15 years experience in health care and senior housing & services.

RELEVANT EXPERIENCE & ACCOMPLISHMENTS

1984-present *Vice President of Operations*
WINDHAM HILLS RETIREMENT HOMES, Boston MA

[Overseeing operations of a retirement center and two skilled nursing facilities serving over 450 residents.]

- Developed uniform standards for corporate operations, including a personnel policy and procedure manual for management staff and a comprehensive set of medical records customized for our facilities to be both user-friendly and in compliance with regulations.
- Led two facilities through their best year in recent history, in terms of both census and bottom line.

1981-84 *Administrator*
TRILLIUM VILLAGE, Millhurst MA

[Administrator, from pre-construction stage to full operation, of this full-service 173-unit retirement center employing nearly 100 staff.]

- Developed pre-construction marketing and sales program which succeeded in getting the project approved and funded.
- Singlehandedly directed startup of facility. Beginning as the sole staff member, built facility systems and staff to full operational level.
- Obtained certificate of need approval for skilled nursing facility.

1979-81 *Director of Membership Services*
MASSACHUSETTS ASSOCIATION OF HOMES FOR THE AGING, Boston MA

[Directed member recruitment/retention program and professional education program for this state-wide association of not-for-profit organizations providing housing, health care, and community services to the elderly.]

- Designed and implemented an improved calendar of continuing education workshops, providing more subjects for a wider range of association membership throughout Massachusetts.
- Introduced a successful marketing program to build membership.

- Continued on page two -

1976-78   *Administrator*
             BURNHAM MANOR, Burnham PA

[Managed day-to-day operations of 44-bed skilled nursing facility.]

- Guided facility through ownership transition from single site family run operation to a multi-facility corporation. Implemented marketing and sales program. Brought the facility up-to-date in terms of regulatory compliance. Directed expansion project.

- Initiated community outreach service which was successful in improving public relations (local meals-on-wheels service).

1974-76   *Program Specialist*
             ADMINISTRATION ON AGING, Washington DC
             (U.S. Department of Health and Human Services)

[Researched and provided information to government agencies and the public on various federal, state, and community programs for the elderly.]

- Authored letters and fact sheets that went out under the signature of various federal officials including the President, Congressmen, and the Secretary of HEW.

EDUCATION & CREDENTIALS

M.A., Gerontology, 1974 - University of Southern California, Los Angeles
B.S., Social Sciences, (Teaching Credential) 1971 - University of Texas, Austin
Nursing Home Administrator's License, California

TEMPLATES

Amy Parker Kurle

19055 Fifth Ave. NE • P.O. Box 676
Poulsbo WA 98370
(206) 779-7544

OBJECTIVE

Sales / Customer Service Manager, AutoBody Experts

HIGHLIGHTS

- 14 years experience in the auto parts and service industry.
- Professional attitude toward customer satisfaction, resulting in an excellent reputation with customers.
- Ability to balance books and handle finances in a responsible manner.
- Purchasing experience and expert knowledge of automotive parts.

RELEVANT EXPERIENCE

1986-90   **H & H DISTRIBUTORS**, San Leandro CA   (import parts wholesaler)
Inside & Outside Sales
Part of a two-person sales team with over a million dollars in sales per year, topping two million the last year.
- Successfully handled busy phones daily, servicing customers while meeting shipping and delivery deadlines.
- Maintained acceptable profit margins without alienating customers, through superior customer service.

1984-85   **OVERLAND PARTS EXPRESS**, Emeryville CA   (import parts wholesaler)
Domestic Purchasing and Inside & Outside Sales
Advanced from order-taker to outside sales person and eventually to domestic purchasing manager.
- Monitored inventory, requested and evaluated price quotes, prepared and placed purchase orders.
- Oversaw receiving procedures and maintained quality control of domestically purchased products.

1978-79   **D & L ENGINES**, Berkeley CA   (VW & Japanese engine rebuilder)
Parts, Service Writing, Bookkeeping, Mechanics
Performed minor mechanical repairs and set-ups for machine work, as well as managing all phases of daily office operations, including:
- Service writing, estimating, and scheduling of work.
- Bookkeeping, banking, and accounts payable.
- Ordering, receiving, and keeping inventory of parts and supplies.

1977   **SMALL CAR WORLD**, Albany CA   (retail import auto parts)
Driver, Counter Sales
Worked with retail customers as counterperson.
Received and stocked parts. Made deliveries.

STEPHEN SILVER
9999 Mountain Road
Claremont CA
(510) 123-4567

Current job objective: Entry position with a computer manufacturer.
Longer-term goal: Position in advertising, sales, and marketing of computer products.

SUMMARY

- Energetic, hard working, willing to learn and accept constructive criticism.
- Strong motivation for advancing in a career.
- Enjoy contributing to a team effort and creating a good working environment.
- Basic understanding of the Macintosh computer.

RELEVANT SKILLS & EXPERIENCE

Maintenance Skills
- As carpenter's helper:
  -painted interior walls -measured and cut lumber -helped with framing
  -operated power tools (saws, drills, sanders).
- Did basic home maintenance:
  -rewired lamps -repaired plumbing and appliance -built shelves.
- Completed classes in:
  -electronics (built a TV scrambler from a circuit board)
  -architectural drafting -basic carpentry.

Office Support Skills
- Assisted in inventory control and priced merchandise, as stock clerk at Jorgensen's Market.
- Cashiered at Jorgensen's, computing and handling large sums of money; answered phones as needed.
- Completed class in Marketing:
  -invented unique products
  -developed simulated marketing strategies.

Computer Familiarity
- Basic understanding of Macintosh programs, MacWrite and MacPaint.

WORK HISTORY

Oct. 1991-present	**Stock Clerk/Cashier**	JORGENSEN'S MARKET, Claremont CA
Summer 1989*	**Valet Parking Asst.**	MENLO COUNTRY CLUB, Claremont CA
(* while in school)	Plus short-term jobs: Carpenter's Helper, Waiter, Busboy, Stockwork.	

EDUCATION

Claremont High School, Claremont CA, 1991

ELIZABETH L. ROHRMANN

Permanent address:
514 Crockett
Seattle WA 98109
(206) 284-0303

College address:
P.O. Box 9299
Oakland CA 94613
(510) 729-8767

OBJECTIVE

Internship in the administration of a nonprofit or social service agency.

HIGHLIGHTS

- Committed to work that promotes a more egalitarian society.
- Believe that individuals can make a difference.
- Demonstrated ability to work efficiently and complete projects.
- Able to communicate with Spanish-speaking clients.

RELEVANT SKILLS & EXPERIENCE

Human Relations / Public Relations / Marketing

- Worked in a **cooperative marketing effort** with other students, alumni officers, and admissions officers, on the Mills College Student Recruitment Task Force.
- Gained an **objective understanding of different groups of people** and a greater respect for human diversity through my experience living and studying in Barcelona, Spain (spring 1990).
- Created a **positive learning environment**, as gymnastics instructor for children age 3-12, and as trainer of other gymnastic instructors.

Program Development (needs assessment - follow-up - quality control)

- **Co-developed a recruitment training program** for current students.
- **Followed-up on the needs and goals** of Mills students, and reported this information to program planners.
- **Coordinated "Career Exploration Day,"** a mentorship program providing career education-by-experience for high school students.

Administrative Support / Program Funding

- Currently studying "Corporate Finance."
- Experience with IBM, WordPerfect, and Macintosh word processing.

WORK HISTORY

1990-present	*Chairperson*	Student Recruitment Task Force, Mills College
1988-present	*Customer Service Rep*	Mills College Bookstore, Oakland CA
1987-present	*Full-time student*	Mills College, Oakland CA
1990 Spring	*Full-time student*	Institute for Social & International Studies, Barcelona, Spain
1987-90 Summer	*Clerk Specialist*	Security Pacific Bank, Seattle WA
1988-90 Winter	*Clerk Specialist*	Security Pacific Bank, Seattle WA
1985-87 part-time	*Gymnastics Instructor*	Seattle Gymnastics Academy, Seattle WA

EDUCATION

B.A. candidate, May 1991 - MILLS COLLEGE, Oakland CA
Major: Political, Legal, and Economic Analysis   Minor: Art History

TEMPLATES

ELISSA PETERSEN
14934 Stanford Ave
Oakland CA 94608
(510) 123-4567 (messages)

**Objective: Social work position, providing individual and/or group
counseling services for children and their families.**

HIGHLIGHTS OF QUALIFICATIONS
- Over 3 years experience working with children and families.
- Enthusiastic and committed to a career in services to children; welcome opportunities for professional growth and development.
- Readily develop rapport with children.
- Able to remain calm and effective in handling crisis situations.
- Excellent communication skills, for both community networking and written documentation.
- Reliable and hard working; able to collaborate in a team effort.

RELEVANT PROFESSIONAL EXPERIENCE

1988-92   **Program Coordinator/Therapist** FAMILY SERVICES, Wilson VA
                                        Child Abuse Treatment Program

Child Therapy
- Conducted **individual and group play therapy** for preschool children:
  - Designed imaginative play forums as treatment for family-related stress.
  - Supported and directed play as themes emerged, to allow successful integration of family experiences.

Parent Education
- **Collaborated with other therapists** in leading **concurrent therapy groups** for children and their parents:
  - Conducted **assessments** of family stressors impacting on parents and children.
  - Developed **treatment plans** addressing the needs of both parent and child.
  - **Designed activities** for **supervised parent/child interactions** to develop improved family relationships.
- Provided **support and psycho-education** for parents at high-risk for abuse or neglect of their children, or other family violence.

Crisis Intervention
- **Intervened** in cases of child abuse and neglect:
  - Conducted an immediate assessment of risks to the child;
  - Collaborated with Social Services, other community therapists, and family members, to ensure the safety of the child.
- **Intervened** in cases of family violence, i.e., spouse abuse and threat of suicide.

- Continued on page two -

RELEVANT PROFESSIONAL EXPERIENCE (continued)

1986-88   **Adoption Worker/Therapist**   CATHOLIC FAMILY & CHILDREN'S SERVICE
Hampton, VA

Family Therapy
- Investigated and **evaluated families** as to their appropriateness for placement of adoptive children.
- Designed **support group meetings** for adoptive parents focussing on issues of **healthy child-parent relationships.**
- Led individual and family therapy sessions.

1984-86   **Clinical Social Work Internships**
- Provided **individual and group counseling for students** at the Student Mental Health Center of Louisiana State University.
- Conducted **individual and group counseling with children** ages 7-12 at the L. Smith Community Mental Health Center, Mandeville, LA

EDUCATION
M.S.W., LOUISIANA STATE UNIVERSITY, Baton Rouge, LA
B.A., Psychology, LOUISIANA STATE UNIVERSITY

CARL A. ZEHNER

7664 Bowen Dr.   Residence: (213) 555-2741
Whittier, Ca. 90602   Messages: (213) 555-4824

OBJECTIVE: Manufacturing Management

QUALIFICATIONS:

- Profit-oriented manufacturing manager with more than 10 years experience.
- Excellent record of resourceful cost reduction and product improvement.
- Strong planner with technical background and demonstrated initiative in analytically defining and solving problems.
- Metal working professional proficient in directing material control, purchasing and production departments.

ACCOMPLISHMENTS:

Designed and installed material management system which reduced inventory $3.8 million dollars (52%) in two years.

Reduced factory burden 34% in three years saving $580,000 annually by critical review of expenditures and analysis of personnel utilization.

Improved labor efficiency in fabrication, welding and machining by 20% in two years, producing annual savings of $142,000.

Specified and negotiated purchase of $500,000 of EDM capital equipment, reducing tooling manufacturing costs 50%.

Initiated and implemented over 50 cost reduction and design improvements, resulting in $75,000 annual savings.

Reorganized Production and Inventory control functions, reducing staff by 67% without impairing department performance.

Sourced three major components offshore, resulting in an average cost reduction of 40% and savings of $55,000.

Reorganized and combined department functions in shipping, receiving and warehousing, reducing manpower while supporting increased sales.

Reduced material costs through more aggressive purchasing management, producing a $120,000 annual savings in two years.

Designed fixtures and specified machining sequence for casting, reducing machining costs between 20% and 50% on over 200 products.

EXPERIENCE: *Director of Manufacturing*   Elgin Engineering Co., 2 yrs.
              Director of Manufacturing   Precision Tool Mfg. Co., 3 yrs.
              Plant Manager   Precision Tool Mfg. Co., 5 yrs.

EDUCATION: Bachelor of Electrical Engineering   University of Pennsylvania

- From Job Hunters: Packaging and Marketing YOU, *with permission from Somar Press -*

TEMPLATES

Tricia Q. Martinez

1193 Bellview Blvd.
Oakland CA 94602
(123) 456-7890

TENTATIVE JOB OBJECTIVE

Public affairs position, with a focus on:
- •Community Relations •Legislative & Policy Issues •Public Presentation

HIGHLIGHTS

- **Insider's knowledge of the health care system,** through 15 years experience as a registered nurse.
- **Thorough understanding of the impact of public policy decision-making** on the lives of individuals.
- 5 years **active political involvement,** with a **lifelong commitment to public service.**
- A **natural leader,** spokesperson, and role model in my field.

RELEVANT SKILLS & EXPERIENCE

Community Relations

- Developed **strong and effective leadership skills,** as hospital-wide supervisor of nurses and support staff, gaining ability to:
  ...think on my feet   ...maintain a broad perspective   ...set priorities
  ...delegate authority   ...resolve problems and remain calm under stress.
- Recognize and understand the **widely diverse cultural practices and belief systems** of thousands of people served in 15 years of nursing.
  Especially effective as **cross-cultural educator and negotiator.**
- **Assessed public policy impact** on the care and services available to medically indigent adults, AIDS patients, and high-risk/low-income populations -- especially pregnant women, children, and drug-addicted mothers.

Legislative & Policy Issues

- As Legislative Intern in the office of Assemblymember Tom Rivers, **served as advocate for constituents,** negotiating with local and state agencies on unresolved health care delivery problems.
- **Monitored legislation** for nurses' legislative interest group; **met with legislators, lobbying** on behalf of registered nurses.
- Currently **chair of Platform Committee,** MGO Democratic Club, charged with developing a plan of action on urgent local issues.

Public Presentation

- **Organized events** for 300-500 people, featuring national political figures.
- **Planned and oversaw a fund-raising dinner** for incumbent City Council member.
- **Spoke before groups** of 100-800, as presenter, trainer, and chairperson.

RELEVANT WORK HISTORY

1989-present	**Fund Raiser**	CITY COUNCIL MEMBER, Jenny Kurle
1978-present	**Registered Nurse**	CITY CENTRAL HOSPITAL, Berkeley
	Nursing Supervisor 1983-'86	CITY CENTRAL HOSPITAL, Berkeley
1988 fall	**Alameda Co. Events Coordinator**	UNITED DEMOCRATIC CAMPAIGN
1985	**Legislative Intern**	ASSEMBLYMEMBER Tom Rivers
1984-86	**Committee Member**	PROFESSIONAL PERFORMANCE COMMITTEE
1984	**Council Member**	NURSES/ BARGAINING COUNCIL
1977-78	**Head Nurse**	HIGHLAND HOSPITAL, Oakland

EDUCATION

B.S., Health Sciences, CAL STATE HAYWARD, 1986
A.A., Nursing, CHABOT COLLEGE, Hayward, 1974

TEMPLATES

4

One Pro's Technique: Working Notes

4
One Pro's Technique: Working Notes

TECHNIQUES

The bulk of this chapter consists of eleven resumes I created, paired with the WORKING NOTES developed in the process of writing each resume. **Working notes contain all the key words, brainstorming notes, ideas, tentative job objectives, etc., that I jotted down on the computer screen as I worked.** This material, I think, will be instructive to some readers of this book.

Here's why I decided to include this free-form material:

1. It explicitly illustrates one person's resume-writing technique, presenting an alternative for you to consider.

2. It contains some ideas about the different kinds of data or information you could draw out of a client, that may help you in developing a powerful resume.

3. It illustrates specifically how some problems were handled. Look for mention of problems in the notes, and then examine the corresponding resumes to see how those problems were resolved.

Working Notes—The First Step in the Resume-Writing Process

When my client arrives at my office to work on a resume, my computer is already turned on and a basic RESUME TEMPLATE appears on the full-page screen, ready for action. (The template is a simplified version of the ones you see in Chapter 3, Self-Teaching Resume Templates.)

I invite the client to sit beside me at the computer screen and I type her name, address, and phone number onto the template. Right then we double-check to make SURE this critical information is correct—a precaution learned from sad experience!

Next, we talk for awhile about her current Job Objective, and when that is clear we insert the objective immediately beneath the client's name, address, and phone number. Sometimes it takes a painfully long time to extract a clear statement from a client about what kind of job she is looking for. But I have learned not to take short cuts here: **Until we have some clarity about her goal, we can't move forward** because we won't know where we're going!

Once we have the name-address-phone-number section typed and the Job Objective clearly written, I usually move to a "blank page" on the

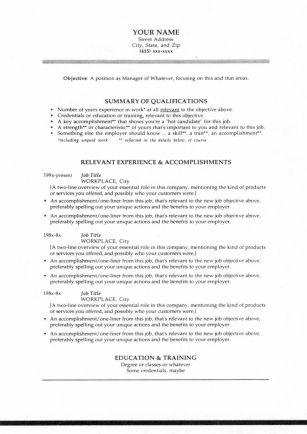

screen—i.e., a place beneath the actual template where we can "scribble" freely.

I will have encouraged my client to bring along a DESCRIPTION OF HER DESIRED JOB, if a description exists—say, a job announcement bulletin, or a classified ad—anything that spells out the duties of the job, as well as the credentials and work experience called for. If no such written description is available, then I ask my client to tell me, in detail, HER UNDERSTANDING of what the job entails and what the requirements are for applying.

All the while we talk, I am jotting down notes on the screen, typing out the entire classified ad if one exists, and recording the KEY WORDS of our conversation that I don't want to forget as we actually develop the resume wording. This technique of extensive note-taking WHILE interviewing is crucial to the way I work. I just can't keep a lot of detail in my head for hours, day in and day out—or I'd go crazy!

The computer, by the way, is a fabulous tool for developing Working Notes like this, because it allows me to work quickly without breaking the flow of thought. On my Macintosh, I can very easily move text around as I go, reorganizing, grouping, and prioritizing things. ALSO, I find that my client gets EXCITED and inspired by the process because she can see the resume begin to take shape before her very eyes. The Mac shows the text in WYSIWYG form (what you see is what you get)—precisely as it will appear when printed out, so I can make some of the text oversize or bold to help us visualize the emerging resume.

Generally the next section to tackle is the "HIGHLIGHTS OF QUALIFICATIONS," and this is probably the SECOND HARDEST part to do, after the Objective. I ask my client—gently!—questions such as:

- "Why do you think you'd be a good candidate for this job?
- What do you have to offer the employer?
- Generally speaking, how much experience do you have and what are your credentials?
- If you don't have credentials or experience, then how do you know (and I believe she DOES KNOW) that you'd be good at this?
- What does the employer need to know about you, to realize you're the right one to hire?
- In other words, what can we say about you, in about fifty words, that would get the employer excited about you as a candidate?"

After my client recuperates from the shock of all these questions, we dig in together and answer all of them. When we consolidate the answers into a tidy, compact paragraph or series of about five powerful statements, we have what I call the Highlights of Qualifications. This paragraph now gets inserted on the resume template directly below the objective. (Ironically, we often come up with *one last Highlight* AFTER we've completed the entire resume, and it may be the most important Highlight of all.)

Next (back in our "scribble space") we will determine what SKILLS we'll need to document on the resume for this particular job. That, in turn, influences whether we stick with my default FUNCTIONAL Resume Template which is already on the computer screen, or we switch to a chronological format. (If the client's aim is to make a big career change—either going to a totally different field, or staying in the same field but changing her job functions significantly—then a FUNCTIONAL resume format will probably work best. For this discussion, let's assume that we're sticking with the functional format.)

Now that we've decided on the skill areas to document, we return to the Template (which by now has her name, Job Objective, and Highlights already on it), and create paragraph headings for each of the several skills identified.

Now I ask, pointing to the first skill, "What have you already done that shows you HAVE this skill?" I encourage her to think of ways she's used this skill with the greatest SUCCESS and gotten good RESULTS, and we record these accomplishments with just enough detail to create a lively image in the resume reader's mind. We continue like that until all the skills related to this job objective are well documented.

Continuing on down the Resume Template, we fill in her Work History and her Education—which often involves lots of questions about what to include and what to leave out. The answer to those questions depends directly on the Job Objective.

When we are finally done, we have on the computer screen a completed resume of one or two pages, followed by our Working Notes—all the informal "hen scratching" from our brainstorming and problem solving and prioritizing. These left-

TECHNIQUES

over Working Notes will include references to goals that are off in the future, plus skills, qualities, or strengths that were not relevant to the job objective appearing on this particular resume. I always give my clients a copy of these Working Notes to take home for future reference, and they appreciate it.

YOU may also benefit from scanning the Working Notes and comparing them with the corresponding resumes.

Only the FIRST set of Working Notes (for Ned Powell) is presented as a DIALOGUE between me and the client, so you can more easily envision my interviewing process. In other words, I have inserted the questions we were discussing, as well as my name and my client's name, just so you could easily follow the progress of the resume session.

So, while reading the OTHER notes and resumes, you'll have to imagine the questions and answers that resulted in those Working Notes, and then examine the resumes to see the results of the work.

In some cases I have included additional comments that I jotted down after the client left. These might include how she (or I) felt about the process, and even perhaps a physical description of the client—all serving as an aid to my memory.

Interview with Ned Powell

Yana Parker: Ned, the first thing we need to establish is your job objective. What job would you like to go after next?

Ned Powell: That's the problem, I'm not really sure. I know that I want to be in the hotel industry and I want a management position, but I'm not sure exactly what I want to do, or at least, what they would call it.

Yana: Then let's start with a little brain-storming about what your ideal job would be. Tell me what some of the possibilities are. What titles sound vaguely like what you might be doing—even if you're not sure there really is such a title?

Ned:
- Assistant Manager
- Creativity Enhancer
- Director of Opportunity Development
- Director of Business Development
- General Manager

- Group Director of Human Resources Development
- Group Director of Public Relations
- Group Director of Program Development
- Group Director of Internal Sales
- Group Guest Services Manager/Coordinator
- Group Operations Manager

Yana: Now, let's talk about what you imagine your ideal job would involve. What would give you the most satisfaction in this position?

Ned: I'd like to make guest services part of the culture, and I'd like to use innovative ways to do that.

Yana: And how will that be different from what you're doing now?

Ned: I want to do it in a bigger scene—some place where there's more opportunity to work in guest services.

Yana: What would you be doing in this ideal job?

Ned: In this ideal job:
- I'm clarifying what the culture of the organization is and needs to be
- I'm creating a strategy for how to get there
- I'm working with key staff people who will get us there—working on development with them, working one-on-one
- I'm implementing innovative organizational development processes
- I'm setting policy
- I'm seeing results in the enthusiasm of the staff
- I'm seeing results in positive guest experiences
- I'm seeing results through better bottom line for properties—get more market share
- My hotel group is developing a reputation for service and staff
- Owners are willing to take some risks . . . new approaches on how to develop business

But that's the ideal situation. In the real world it's not easy. There are a lot of barriers.

Yana: What are some of those barriers, or should we say challenges?

Ned:

1. To be able to communicate my vision to traditional hotel people; and

2. To establish credibility—to develop a relationship with the decision-maker.

Yana: Who will you have contact with in this position?

Ned: I want to have more people to work with—both peers and employees. I'll also have contact with guests.

Yana: Let's look at the list of job titles we made when we started talking. Are there any other possibilities?

Ned:
- Group Troubleshooter
- Networking Specialist
- Operations Manager
- Special Assistant to President
- Special Events Coordinator
- Vice President, Guest Services
- Vice President, Inside Sales

Yana: Looking at these two lists; tell me which one comes the closest to describing your ideal job? Are there certain words in the titles that ring a bell with you, that get you excited?

Ned [*after some thought and discussion*]: The one that hits home for me is "Group Operations Manager."

Yana: Okay, let's take that title and create the Job Objective for the resume, using some of the brainstorming we've just done.

[Ned and I continued to discuss the objective and come up with the following]:

Objective: Position as Group Operations Manager—with a focus on increasing market share and outperforming the competition through exceptional guest service and innovative marketing strategies.

[The following is part of the discussion that went into developing the "Summary of Qualifications" and the "Professional Experience & Accomplishments" statements for Ned's resume. Ned had a hard time saying good things about his previous performance. These are some of the tricks I used to draw him out—in a way that surprised even him!]

Yana: What are the characteristics of one who's a disaster at this business?

Ned: They:
- Are unmindful of what people in the organization need
- Are not motivators
- Don't understand how to build a team
- Don't think creatively
- Don't see the staff as a sales force
- Don't see the marketing plan as an organizational development tool
- Are not willing to take risks
- Don't see challenges as opportunities
- Have limited foresight for growth
- Don't know how to tap into people's inherent energy and enthusiasm
- Cannot bring humor into the workplace, thus failing to enable staff to cope with challenges and relate to stress effectively
- Don't know how to have fun at work
- Don't have a handle on the numbers
- Don't understand how to interpret numbers
- Can't relate to all employees—from staff to executive
- Don't know when to be firm/demanding versus conciliatory and accommodating in situations involving both staff and guests
- Don't know operations thoroughly
- Don't understand how the various departments interrelate.
- Don't understand this concept: "If you're not serving guests, then serve someone who is."
- Don't understand the service concept in broad terms
- Are unable or unwilling to perform front-line tasks (make beds, check people in)
- Don't develop the management staff
- Don't recognize outstanding performance
- Don't have a strong code of ethics, high values

Yana: So what does it take to be good in this business?

Ned: The reverse of what I just said. They:
- Are mindful of what people in the organization need
- Are motivators
- Understand how to build a team
- Think creatively
- See the staff as a sales force
- See the marketing plan as an organizational development tool
- Are willing to take risks
- See challenges as opportunities
- Have great foresight for growth

- Know how to tap into people's inherent energy and enthusiasm
- Have a sense of humor, thus enabling staff to better cope with challenges, and relate to stress effectively
- Know how to have fun at work
- Have a handle on the numbers
- Understand how to interpret numbers
- Relate to all employees—from staff to executive
- Know when to be firm/demanding versus conciliatory and accommodating in situations involving both staff and guests
- Know operations thoroughly—understand how the various departments interrelate with each other
- Understand this concept that: "If you're not serving guests, then serve someone who is."
- Understand the service concept in broad terms
- Are able and willing to perform front-line tasks (make beds, check people in)
- Develop the management staff
- Know the importance of outstanding performance
- Have a strong code of ethics, high values

Yana: Now let's talk about what experience you've had that qualifies you specifically for this objective. If someone were to recommend you for this job, what would they say about you?

Ned: They'd say:
- He has worked internationally—with various cultures
- He has experience with several management models
- He has worked both inside and outside the organization as a consultant
- He has consulted to different industries

Yana: So one of the statements in the Summary of Qualifications could be about your international experience, both in operations and as a consultant. That would be a strong selling point for you, wouldn't it?

Ned: Yes.

[Ned and I talked about this some more and came up with the statement you see in his resume]:

"Eighteen years' professional background in the hotel field, including international experience in both operations and consulting."

[The interviewing and cowriting process continued in this way. We carefully reviewed each line to be sure it was relevant to the objective and that it reflected Ned's real aspirations for his next job.]

Notes Written After the Client Left

NED POWELL—Tall, slim, professional-looking man. He's a "nice guy," career-oriented, and takes pride in his work. He's a little bit shy.

This resume took two sessions. The first one was about four hours long, and we started off "pulling hen's teeth"—it was really hard for him to get into what I was proposing we do. However, he was very cooperative and actually ended up enjoying the process. By the time we got into it, much time had passed and we had to stop because of exhaustion. He agreed to do some work at home and return the next morning to finish.

Fortunately, he really learned fast; he came back with the rest of the material fully written out. I had practically nothing to do then except type it and tweak the layout.

TECHNIQUES

NED L. POWELL
455 Golden Avenue
Raven Run, PA 17966
(509) 222-2221

Objective: Position as Group Operations Manager, with a focus on increasing market share and outperforming the competition through exceptional guest service and innovative management strategies.

HIGHLIGHTS OF QUALIFICATIONS

★ 18-year professional background in the hotel field, including international experience in both operations and consulting.

★ Expertise in team-building and organizational development; thorough understanding of how various departments interrelate.

★ Solid understanding of service as the product of the total organizational process.

★ Reputation for ethical relationships with staff and guests.

★ Successful at involving the entire staff in implementing the marketing plan.

PROFESSIONAL EXPERIENCE & ACCOMPLISHMENTS

OPERATIONS

- Developed and implemented a **sales and marketing driven management strategy,** enabling a new property, the Great Eastern Hotel, to successfully compete in a fiercely competitive environment.
- As **General Manager for two hotels**:
  (Raven Run Suites; and The Villa, a luxury resort in Relay, CO)
  -Initiated greatly **improved operating systems**, resulting in smoother hotel operations, improved staff morale, and better quality customer service.
  -Introduced **state-of-the-art organizational models**, allowing hotel staff to develop a new understanding of their relationship to the guest.
- In 9 years with Queen Mary Hotels, Rooms Division:
  -**Opened a new hotel** in Washington DC, overseeing recruiting and training for the staff of 100, and developed operating procedures for the front office.
  -Earned consistent promotions, ultimately handling three Queen Mary properties.

HUMAN RESOURCE DEVELOPMENT (HRD)

- As Director of HRD for Great Eastern Hotel:
  -**Developed a recruitment plan** to attract and select a staff of 800 people in a full employment economy.
  -**Designed the training facilities** and organization-wide training plan for 800 people, with a focus on sales skills and exceptional guest service.
- **Designed the regional training center** for 1200-room Regent Hotel, Singapore.
- **Co-designed a training model** for Queen Mary Hotels, to be used in their front office departments. **Results**:
  -Improved the staff selection process.   -Reduced staff turnover.
  -Accelerated and strengthened the management development process.

- Continued -

SALES & MARKETING

- **Implemented innovative, workable systems** that enabled all guest contact staff to play an active, supportive role in the sales and marketing process.
- **Reorganized** a hotel front office under the sales and marketing department, greatly **improving interdepartmental communication** and **increasing sales**.
- **Successfully marketed** a resort to local businesses, resulting in approximately $60,000 referral business within a 3-month period.

FINANCE

- **Developed realistic and workable budgets** of up to $700,000, for both departments and entire properties.
- **Created training budgets** for hotels, and for a regional training center, to provide training for hundreds of staff at all levels.
- Performed daily accounting functions: journals, general ledger, bill-paying, budgeting.

HOTEL OPENINGS

- **Opened** a 400-room Queen Mary **flagship hotel**, as Front Office Manager overseeing a staff of 100.
- Served as **HRD Director** for the **pre-opening phase** of an 800-room, five-star international hotel.
- Acted as **Interim General Manager** for an exclusive $80 million resort during pre-opening, at the request of the lender.

CONSULTING

- Conducted **Guest Service Critiques**, enabling hotel management to identify strengths and areas to improve, and to implement strategies for change.
- **Co-developed** and conducted a 5-week **course on effective meeting skills**, successfully adopted for use by several different companies.
- **Trained key managers** in small groups and one-on-one, to improve their individual and team **leadership skills**.
- Conducted a **training needs analysis** for a 1200-room Regent, and followed through with an **organization-wide training plan and training process**.

EMPLOYMENT HISTORY

1991-present	**General Manager**	RAVEN RUN SUITES, time-share hotel
1990-91	**President/Co-owner**	MANAGEMENT ONE CENTER, management consulting firm
1989-90	**Director,** Human Resource Development	GREAT EASTERN HOTEL, Singapore
1986-89	**President**	MANAGEMENT ONE CENTER, U.S. and Singapore
1976-85	**Rooms Div. Manager**	QUEEN MARY HOTELS, Philadelphia & Washington DC

EDUCATION

B.S., Hotel Administration - UNIVERSITY OF RAVEN RUN, 1975

PROFESSIONAL AFFILIATIONS
•Hotel Sales & Marketing Assoc., International   •Raven Run Chamber of Commerce
•Raven Run Convention & Visitors Bureau   •Rotary International   •The Raven Run Club

TECHNIQUES

Kathy Jacobsen's Interview/Working Notes

The following notes were used by Kathy Jacobsen and me to create an information interview resume in 1987, when Kathy was exploring various possibilities for a career. Then in 1991, when Kathy's interests turned in a very different direction, she worked with my associate, Susan Ireland, to write a resume for a therapist position. Notice how the original notes show strengths that apply to her more recent resume.

[Remember, these are ROUGH NOTES left over at the end of a work session on the computer, as explained at the beginning of the chapter.]

POSSIBLE POSITIONS

- Organizational Management
- Management Training
- Personnel Management
- Personnel Advisor/Counselor
- Buying Coordinator
- Merchandising Management
- Fashion Coordinator
- Merchandising Specialist
- Coordinator, Sales Personnel
- Employee Sales Training Program
- Employee Management
- Organizational Training Program (set them up for employees)

WHAT I'M GOOD AT

- can take a drab environment and make it warm and inviting, greatly enhancing the sales and marketability
- thrive on the challenge of applying a wide variety of skills at once
- merchandising
- systems problems
- personnel problems
- organizational development/planning
- training program development
- fashion

Objective: Management trainee position—preferably in the area of fashion or health services, involving training program design, organizational problem solving, personnel counseling, or buying/merchandising.

I CAN PICTURE MYSELF:

- troubleshooting, sitting around a table with management, addressing weaknesses in a company, changing systems that aren't working or systems analysis (visionary leadership)
- influencing people (my best work is in influencing people)
- being a problem solver in terms of personnel/interrelationships

WHY/HOW I'M HOT

- extremely intuitive with people's needs
- extremely organized in my thought processes
- very good at influencing people to open up to change, good at showing them their strengths
- good at helping people understand and explore their strengths and weaknesses
- great coach, can coach and inspire people, will get the best out of them, will push them, very tough, will bring up their performance level
- very clear, go into a problem like a surgeon, get through all the stuff in the way
- a wonderful mirror, people can see where their blocks/resistances are
- can create more positive/desirable environments
- have a great eye for form, line, design
- can spot incongruities in the ways of a smooth-running process
- extremely empathetic
- will give 100 percent of what I've got
- have a great eye for fashion and style
- know what will move commercially

I IMAGINE

- Store is full of people, not enough sales help phone is ringing—people buy like crazy
- I'm like a conductor—I know when the different instruments should come in
- I use my intuitive sense for where the trouble is—to send help there
- I'm juggling many things at same time to produce a harmonious environment
- I'm identifying the rough spots—hearing the not-loud calls for help
- I sense the rough spots, avoid the calamity, catch stuff just before it happens.
- I'm being called upon when everything goes wrong—I have the last say in what happens when responding to emergencies

KATHY M. JACOBSEN
4 New Hamilton Road
Scenic Hills IN
(444) 555-0000

Objective: **Management trainee position,** preferably in the area of fashion or health services, involving training program design, organizational problem solving, personnel counseling, and/or merchandising.

HIGHLIGHTS OF QUALIFICATIONS

- Thrive on challenge and the opportunity to apply a wide range of skills.
- Proven ability to coach employees and elicit their top performance.
- Skill in creating environments that enhance employee productivity.
- Sharp eye for purchasing merchandise that is guaranteed to sell.
- Extremely well organized and analytical in resolving problems.

RELEVANT EXPERIENCE

Systems Analysis/Problem Solving
- Orchestrated the complex interactions between passengers and flight crew, quickly recognizing and resolving problems and emergencies as they arose.
- Successfully directed the flow of salesmen and customers in my clothing stores:
  -Delegated authority to salespeople for making appropriate on-the-spot decisions.
  -Captured and retained customers' interest; broadened awareness of product line.
  -Assured that customers enjoyed themselves and knew their trade was valued.

Personnel Training/Managing
- Supervised 13 flight attendants, coordinating their activities with the needs of 300+ passengers, flight and ground crews, and all support services.
  Delegated work assignments and delivered detailed pre-flight briefings for staff.
- Hired and trained 12 employees, as owner/manager of clothing stores.
  Trained employees to sell, price, merchandise, and efficiently run a store.
- Led groups of tourists through Sebastiani Winery, teaching them the wine-making process.

Buying; Merchandising
- Identified highly profitable fashion trends early on (1976):
  -Introduced natural fiber clothing , particularly 100% cotton goods.
  -Entered exercise wear market (Danskin; Capezio) at onset of its rapid growth.
  -Caught the crest of Hawaiian shirt market.
  -Chose several blue jean labels which subsequently dominated the market (Levi 501's, Chemin de Fer, Pacific Blue/Souvenirs).
  -Transformed used surplus clothing into boutique/adventure fashions (through altering and dyeing) that proved extremely popular with customers.

RELEVANT EMPLOYMENT HISTORY

1985-present	**Owner/Partner**	PONDER'S SURPLUS STORE - Boonville IN
1976-84	**Owner/Partner**	MIDWEST GENERAL STORE - Paregon IN
1976-present	**Buyer**	ASSOCIATED SURPLUS DEALERS TRADE SHOWS - Las Vegas NV
1975	**Tour Guide**	THE WINE CO. - Jaspar IN
1970-73	**Head Steward**	OLYMPIC AIRLINES - Municipal International Airport

EDUCATION & TRAINING

B.S., Education - Lyons College, Lyons IN
Clinical Psychology masters program, Brooks University, Fowler IN
Certificate Program, Organizational Leadership & Management - Lyons College, Lyons IN

KATHY M. JACOBSEN
4 New Hamilton Road
Scenic Hills, IN
(444) 555-0000

(Kathy's more recent resume)

OBJECTIVE: Clinical internship in a mental health facility to further my professional training.

HIGHLIGHTS OF QUALIFICATIONS

• Qualified to facilitate individual therapy with adults and adolescents.
• Experienced at evaluating clients and developing treatment plans.
• Skilled at writing clinical casework reports and maintaining records.
• Background in crisis counseling.
• Personal experience in healing workshops for life-threatening illnesses.

EDUCATION

MA, Clinical Psychology, Brooke University, Fowler, IN (anticipated Sept. '92)
BS, Education - Lyons College, Lyons, IN
Grief Counseling Training Class, New Harmony Suicide Prevention Center

PROFESSIONAL EXPERIENCE

INTERNSHIP

As Intern Therapist at the Community Counseling Center for 18 months:
  • Provided individual counseling to adults, addressing issues of:
   -incest   -grief and loss   -substance abuse   -co-dependency
  • Participated in case presentation seminars.
  • Gained supervised field experience, managing a case load of approximately six clients per week.
  • Served as intake telephone interviewer.

CRISIS WORK

As Grief Counselor at the New Harmony Suicide Prevention Center:
  • Performed community outreach by phone, offering free counseling services to those who had
    recently experienced the death of a loved one.
  • As a co-therapist, provided short-term individual grief counseling with appropriate recommendations
    for continuing professional and/or group support.

As Telephone Counselor at the Paragon County Suicide Prevention Center:
  • Managed a four-hour weekly shift on the telephone crisis line, responding to urgent calls for help.
  • Maintained extensive records to facilitate the immediate tracking of repeat callers and pertinent histories.
  • Extensively researched suicide studies to develop expertise in the field.

As Head Flight Attendant for Olympic Airlines:
  • Effectively managed group crises both in the air and on the ground, assisting passengers to safety
    in a calm and speedy manner.
  • Developed the ability to foresee potential disaster and avert danger without alarming passengers.
  • Gained extensive training in CPR, First Aid, and emergency procedures.

WORK HISTORY

1987-present	Intern Therapist	COMMUNITY COUNSELING CENTER - Terre Haute
1990	Grief Counselor	NEW HARMONY SUICIDE PREVENTION/CENTER - Fowler
1987	Telephone Counselor	PARAGON COUNTY SUICIDE PREVENTION CENTER -
Fowler		
1986	Classroom Assistant	NORWAY SCHOOL for the disabled - Lyon
1985-89	Owner/Partner	PONDER'S SURPLUS STORE - Boonville
1976-84	Owner/Partner	MIDWEST GENERAL STORE - Paragon
1975	Tour Guide	THE WINE CO.- Jaspar
1970-73	Head Flight Attendant	OLYMPIC AIRLINES - Municipal International Airport

TECHNIQUES

Laura Adams's Interview/Working Notes

[Remember, these are ROUGH NOTES left over at the end of a work session on the computer, as explained at the beginning of the chapter.]

JOB POSSIBILITIES

- men's and women's clothing and accessories (Polo/Ralph Lauren)
- home collections—bed, bath, linens, furniture (Polo/Ralph Lauren)
- culinary (Williams-Sonoma)
- fine jewelry, designer jewelry, cosmetics (Tiffany)
- china/silver (Gump's)
- furniture (Macy's)

ORDER OF PREFERENCE

1. Home furnishings and culinary
2. Clothing
3. Jewelry

OBJECTIVES I NEED RESUMES FOR

Objective: Position with Williams-Sonoma in Customer Service or Sales

Objective: Position with Gump's in Customer Service or Sales—China or Silver Department

Objective: Account Associate position with Tiffany

Objective: Position with Polo/Ralph Lauren in Customer Service or Sales

Objective: Position with Macy's in Customer Service or Sales

HOW I CLOSE THE SALE

- show that i'm competent
- observe customers' behavior to assess what their needs and wants may be, as well as their receptivity to suggestions
- respond appropriately to customers' personalities
- elicit more information if necessary
- know when to be more assertive

SUBTLE INTERACTION WITH THE CLIENT

- identify what someone feels when they first walk in the door
- make them feel comfortable (not just a greeting)
- offer help to meet their needs
- assess their needs
- use subtle communications skill

- convey that if they need help, then you are competent to help
- know when to offer help/advice
- know how to open and close a sale
- invite them to learn something about the product

INGREDIENTS OF A GOOD SALESPERSON

- be professional
- develop a rapport with customer

NEEDS ASSESSMENT

- know what the employer's needs are

Notes Written After the Client Left

LAURA ADAMS—Very refined, beautiful, demure woman from Hawaii. Comes across as extremely proper; meticulous in her grooming.

It was an afternoon appointment and I started out very tired, but we survived. We finished in three long hours.

This is a unique resume. We used the entire functional section to outline her strategy and style for effective sales and customer service. It was very different for her, and she seemed to like it.

We printed up a number of copies, each with the same objective but for a different company.

LAURA ADAMS

45 Sunset Hill Drive
Sedona, AZ 86322
(777) 888-8887

Objective: Position in Customer Service or Sales, with Designer Best Company

SUMMARY OF QUALIFICATIONS

★ 13 years successful experience in sales, merchandising and customer service, specializing in clothing, home furnishings, and American & European crafts.
★ Talent for generating enthusiasm and appreciation for fine quality products, establishing a high level of return clients.
★ Ability to represent the company with a poised and professional image.
★ Reputation for reliability, follow-through, and commitment to service.
★ Working knowledge of Japanese and French languages.

PROFESSIONAL SALESMANSHIP • CUSTOMER SERVICE

Developed an **effective sales approach**, applying these basic guidelines:
• Approach the customer with a **welcoming attitude,** conveying an image of friendly competence.
• **Establish a real relationship** and show that I'm personally interested.
• **Continually assess clients' needs**, picking up on subtle signals indicating a receptiveness to more information or suggestions.
• **Watch for appropriate opportunities** to step in and be directive; offer suggestions, inviting interaction with the merchandise, and giving persuasive, convincing product information.
• Determine, and act on, the **optimum time to close the sale**, providing an overall satisfying experience the client will want to repeat in the future.
• Take the time and energy, **"bending over backward"** to assure a proper fit and demonstrate appropriate coordination of articles.
• **Follow-through** by locating merchandise from other stores on request.
• **Provide continued service**, informing clients of appealing new merchandise for "add-on" sales.
• Maintain an ongoing **expert knowledge of the produc**t using all sources available.

EMPLOYMENT HISTORY

1985-92	**Dept. Manager/Sales Associate**	DESIGNER BEST COMPANY, Sedona
1985-87	**Assistant Manager/Asst. Buyer**	LANDLER'S GALLERY, Sedona
1984-85	**Assistant Manager**	QUE RICO! SWIM WEAR, Flagstaff
1981-84	**Sales Associate**	RARE QUALITIES GALLERY, Chino
1979-80	**Sales Associate**	OUT OF THIS WORLD GIFTS, Airport Mesa
1976-79	**Sales Associate**	CANYON GIFT SHOP, Sedona

EDUCATION & TRAINING

UNIVERSITY OF SEDONA, Arizona
1987, Coursework in **Art and Architecture**
1975-77, two years towards Liberal Arts degree

ARIZONA COLLEGE OF ARTS & CRAFTS, SEDONA, AZ
1978, Coursework in **Environmental Design Program**

TECHNIQUES

Michael Evelo's Interview/Working Notes

[Remember, these are ROUGH NOTES left over at the end of a work session on the computer, as explained at the beginning of the chapter.]

POSSIBLE JOB TITLES
- Social Worker
- Driver for Blondie's
- Cashier, Stock Worker at record store
- Bike Messenger

SOCIAL WORKER
- clientele: home service to high-risk families at Home Valley Care

INVOLVES:
- casework
- teamwork
- counseling and teaching parents in their homes: setting limits, role-modeling
- teach parents: setting limits, role-modeling
- help parents to be able to keep their kids

APPEAL OF THE FREE CLINIC WORK:
- like helping people (worked at free clinic)
- referred people to services: gave them information on housing, medical care, crisis services
- 2 month's training
- weekly meetings with other volunteers (encounter-group-like-sessions) to provide group training in effective interactions with clients
- liked the egalitarian & empowerment approach to the clients
- training

TRAITS OF A GOOD SOCIAL WORKER
- to be nonjudgmental, noninterfering, not play God
- identify prejudices
- up-to-date information on referrals
- learn to create an atmosphere that would empower the client (largely by better listening)

WORK EXPERIENCE (uncut)
- Paper route 72-76
- Musician, played clarinet in orchestra 1977-78
- Cook, delivery, kitchen help, recycling, Student Co-op, 1982-85
- Switchboard Operator/Counselor, Free Clinic 9/86-4/87
- Voter Registration, Democratic Coalition Fall 1986
- Leafleting, Cheezy's Pizza, Fall 1986
- Dishwasher, busperson, waiter, Cheezy's Pizza 6/87
- Library Assistant—circulation, checking out books, preparing library cards, shelving books 6/88-9/88
- Golf driving range
- Building Attendant, Intramural Athletic Facility (checked IDs, answered phones, opened/closed building, monitored attendance and cash box) 8/89-10/89
- Loader/Unloader UPS 9/89-11/89

WHAT I LIKE
- writing (cultural anthropology)
- Geography (B.A.)
- reading

TECHNIQUES

MICHAEL EVELO
648 Topeka Avenue
Covina CA 91111
(513) 543-4321

Objective: Entry position in Social Work.

SUMMARY OF QUALIFICATIONS

- **Experience** (5 months) and **Training** (2 months) in **assessing needs** and **referring clients** to community services.
- Committed to helping people realize that they can identify and resolve their own problems.
- Bicultural/Bilingual in Spanish.
- Sensitive to the inherent tension between individual needs and cultural expectations, through academic background in Anthropology.

CLIENT SERVICE EXPERIENCE

As Free Clinic Counselor/Switchboard Operator:

- Received incoming calls from individuals in crisis, homeless, victims of abuse.
- Helped clients identify and articulate their needs.
- Provided information and referral to community services, including:
  ...shelters and meal sources for homeless   ...detox facilities
  ...low-fee medical care   ...psychological counseling
  ...job training programs   ...legal services
- Participated in two-month training period for new volunteer phone counselors:
  ...updated and expanded referral sources through phone interviewing.
  ...met weekly with other volunteers and staff to explore techniques for effectively interacting with clients (being nonjudgmental/noninterfering, not playing God, identifying and eliminating prejudice, creating an atmosphere of empowerment through careful listening and questioning).

WORK HISTORY

1989-Fall	Loader/Unloader	Send it Faster Co., Azusa
1989-Summer	Building Attendant	Athletic Facility, Univ. of California, Covina
1988-Summer	Library Assistant	University of California
9/86-4/87	**Counselor and Switch-board Operator**	**Covina Free Clinic, Covina**
1987-Summer	Dishwasher	Cheezy Pizza Co., Azusa
1986-Fall	Voter Registration	Covina Democratic Coalition
1982-85	Cook, Kitchen Work	Student Co-ops, UC Covina
1977-78	Musician (clarinet)	Azusa Symphony Youth Orchestra

EDUCATION & TRAINING

B.A., Geography, University of California, Covina
Graduate studies in Anthropology, 1987-88 • Danforth Fellowship
Training as Volunteer Counselor with Covina Free Clinic
Driver's License: Z16789, Kentucky

Paula Kennison's Interview/Working Notes

[Remember, these are ROUGH NOTES left over at the end of a work session on the computer, as explained at the beginning of the chapter.]

POSSIBLE JOB POSITIONS
- Assembly
- Production
- Inspection
- Fabrication

HOW I FIT IN
- good at figuring out machines, making them work
- don't want to work with chemicals or have to wear a mask

PRODUCTION SKILLS I POSSESS

a) Assembly
- perform routine production tasks
- on-line assembly
- soldering
- mechanical/semiconductor assembly and fabrication
- work from drawings, blueprints, or instructions
- ability to operate simple hand or power tools
- good eyesight
- able to lift fifty pounds

b) Inspection
- inspect electronics items and process them to be sure they conform to standards

c) Lab Assistant
- work in lab environment
- process, package, test semiconductors
- photographic work
- set up for chemical analysis
- fabrication
- sheet metal, metal finishing, plating, painting, machining, screen printing, riveting

MY VALUABLE QUALITIES
- conscientious
- consistent
- dependable
- not ill
- follow instructions
- meet quality output
- manual dexterity
- come to work on time
- able to figure out how to run machines
- good with customers, help them with their needs, be friendly with them
- get along with my coworkers
- ask questions enough to learn what to do
- honest
- not overdressed, clean
- don't gossip
- fit in with the group
- interest in the organization
- excellent reputation at HP as an employee

OTHER SKILLS
- sew
- answer phone, deal with customers
- selling, collections, ordering, stocking

Notes Written After the Client Left

PAULA KENNISON—Woman of forty-five; pleasant to work with. Looking for blue-collar production position. She had already done an excellent, very simple resume using my book, and it helped her get her present job. Now she wants to get into a somewhat different line of work, using her dexterity with machines at a place like Hewlett-Packard. She didn't feel at all confident about how to express things (even though she had done fine on the earlier resume). She seemed to like what we did, and the resume came out easily on one page. Took about three hours.

PAULA KENNISON
433 Pinehill Drive
Green Gulch CA 91121
(400) 222-9900

Objective: Position with Innovative Computers in assembly, inspection, lab assisting, fabrication, or material handling.

SUMMARY OF QUALIFICATIONS

★ Over 15 years experience in manufacturing assembly, machine operation, and inspection, meeting high standards of quality and productivity.

★ Special talent with machines; easily learn to operate new equipment.

★ Excellent eyesight and dexterity. Physically strong, able to lift 50 lbs.

★ Maintain good working relations with co-workers.

★ Reliable, honest and conscientious; outstanding record of attendance.

RELEVANT EXPERIENCE

1988-present   *Sewing Machine Operator & Customer Service*
SPORTY COLORS, Lansing CA custom boat covers
- Operated sewing machine (both single and double-needle), **producing custom boat covers to specifications** of the pattern-maker.
- Produced other custom products **to customer's specifications** for dimensions, materials, color, with careful attention to **cost-effectiveness** in production.
- **Operated hand tools** such as fastener setters, measuring tools, hot-knife, etc.
- Directly worked with customers, taking incoming calls and orders, billing, and **assisting customers** in selecting products and materials.

1983-88   *Production Coordinator/Supervisor,& Sewing Machine Operator*
WHAT A SEWING CO., Lansing CA, custom boat covers & awnings
- **Hired and trained** sewing machine operators, relaying complex design details.
- Monitored production **quality control.**
- Served as **liaison** between management and employees on working conditions.
- Oversaw **stock control.**
- **Operated sewing machine** to produce custom boat covers, awnings, and other custom products to one-of-a-kind specifications.

1982-83   *Production Coordinator & Sewing Machine Operator*
AWESOME AWNINGS, Barstow CA
- **Trained** machine operators.
- **Fabricated and assembled** awnings.

1977-82   *Co-owner/Operator*
All IN STITCHES Inc., Barstow CA
- Established (with two others) a freelance industrial sewing business.

1973-77   *Co-owner/Operator*
WAY TO GO CO-OP, Barstow CA
- **Original member of manufacturing co-op** (still in operation) producing bike bags, backpacks, rain gear, and yurts.

- References attached -

Ben Taylor's Interview/Working Notes

[Remember, these are ROUGH NOTES left over at the end of a work session on the computer, as explained at the beginning of the chapter.]

JOB TITLES
- Administrative Analyst
- Assistant City Manager
- City Administrator
- Assistant Director
- Business Manager
- Community Development Director
- Development Program Manager
- Director of Operations
- Director of Economic Development
- Economic Development Specialist
- Executive Director
- Manager of Operations
- Management Assistant
- Management Analyst
- Management Intern
- Project Analyst
- Project Manager
- Risk Manager
- Safety Officer

POSSIBLE AREAS OF EMPLOYMENT:
- environmental concerns
- engineering
- consulting
- public administration

APPEAL OF THE ADMINISTRATOR JOB:
- work on different projects
- develop policy
- be an assistant/have a mentor (support top person)

JOB DESCRIPTION MIGHT INCLUDE:
- analysis
- project coordination
- administration

Objective: Administrator/Assistant Manager position involving:
- operations analysis
- project management
- policy development
- administrative liaison

WHAT MY BEST BUDDY WOULD SAY TO THE HIRING PERSON ABOUT ME
- flexible
- can deal with many important deadlines at one time
- prioritize, meet deadlines
- think long-range, cause/effect, what's the relevance of the parts to the whole
- strive to improve everything I touch—optimize systems
- very adaptable, quick learner
- keen business sense, shrewd
- relate very well to professionals, comfortable with doctors and attorneys
- able to cut through the chaff and get to the crux of the matter
- theoretically based person—can focus in on the matter at hand and not get distracted—weed out what matters and deal with it

IF I WERE THE HIRING PERSON, WHAT KIND OF PERSON WOULD I LOOK FOR?
- somebody who listens well to what people have to say
- able to quickly understand what's going on
- use the experience and expertise of other people
- educated in the area—experienced
- somebody who will ask questions, wade in, get out and meet people, be visible, become known quickly
- be a reflection of our business, make a good impression, speak well, deal with professional people in a professional way
- not afraid to deal with unpleasant situations, difficult tasks

HOW I DEMONSTRATED THE ABILITY TO DO THIS IN PREVIOUS JOBS
- conferred with all departments to understand their operations and the conditions in which an accident took place
- gave support to the attorney for anything he needed in the courtroom
- participated in a market survey
- acted as group leader for follow-up meetings

Notes Written After the Client Left

BEN TAYLOR—A young man in his early thirties. Professional looking. Bored with claims work and wanted to use his MBA. He found the process "grueling," but felt very good about it afterwards. This resume took the classic three hours.

BEN TAYLOR
6789 Casa de Luna Terrace
Sebastopol, CA 95472
(707) 900-2345

Objective: **Administrator/Assistant Manager** position involving:
- **Operations Analysis** • **Project Management**
- **Policy Development** • **Administrative Liaison**

SUMMARY OF QUALIFICATIONS
- Ability to prioritize and remain focused on the essence of an issue.
- Strength in formulating policy that addresses organizational goals.
- Experience in handling many projects and deadlines at one time.
- Readily develop rapport with management, staff, and clients.
- Welcome the challenge of resolving conflicts and problems.

RELEVANT EXPERIENCE & ACCOMPLISHMENTS

Operations Analysis • Policy Development
- **Assessed existing operations** in each department of Northern Way, consulting with department managers to identify specific functions, tasks and procedures.
- **Advised NW district superintendent** on potentially hazardous policies and practices that could make NW vulnerable to litigation.

Project Management
- Currently serving as **group leader for a market survey:**
  - Selected the survey sample
  - Briefed participating colleagues on the goals and rationale of the survey
  - Conducted seminars on marketing for management and staff
  - Presented group's findings to a meeting of department heads.
- **Successfully managed** over 100 home restoration projects:
  - Assessed scope of work
  - Scheduled and prioritized tasks
  - Hired and supervised assistants
  - Advised clients on options
  - Estimated labor and materials

Administrative Liaison
- As fire fighter representing the California Division of Forestry, **directed activities** of CCC and convict crews in all phases of fire-fighting, gaining crews' respect and full cooperation under stressful conditions.
- **Supported defense attorneys** in trial preparation and in court:
  - Participated in jury selection
  - **Coordinated complex arrangements** with other departments, to recreate accident events for jury review
  - **Analyzed and summarized status** of trial for supervisor.

EMPLOYMENT HISTORY

1986-present	*Claims Agent*	Northern Way Transportation Co., Sebastopol and Freestone CA
1986 summer	*Field Claims Rep*	Zenier Insurance Group, Freestone CA
1975-86	*Home Restoration*	Self-employed, Guerneville CA
1977-78	*Fire Fighter*	California Division of Forestry, Sespe CA

EDUCATION
M.B.A., California State University, Sonoma, 1981
B.A., Environmental Policy Analysis & Planning, University of California, Freestone, 1979

Hannah Jenkins's Interview/Working Notes

[Remember, these are ROUGH NOTES left over at the end of a work session on the computer, as explained at the beginning of the chapter.]

WHAT I'D LIKE TO DO
Volunteers Coordinator
Spiritual Counselor/Teacher

- help people: build their self-confidence and self-esteem, know themselves better, become free
- love/like themselves,
- be more conscious
- introduce people to helpful books (with synopsis)
- teach self-acceptance (being nonjudgmental)
- infuse the desire to be of service to others

Teacher within business (teaching coworkers and supervisors)

- support employee morale
- help people resolve problems with their coworkers
- help people learn to treat clients and customers in an effective way

Personal Image Counselor

- help people move out of the past
- work with STYLE/Dressing: help people choose ensembles and mode of dressing, point out details they're unconscious of

THINGS I'M GOOD AT

- good as a LIAISON for all kinds of people, at all levels
- helping people, being of service
- assisting in recovery from addictions, offering spiritual help
- helping old people deal with fear of death, fear of the world/people: inspire them, fill them with enthusiasm, confidence, showing them they count. TALK with them, COUNSEL them, ACCOMPANY them, help with business transactions
- networking
- being efficient
- details
- managing things
- investigating, figuring things out
- meeting challenges (solve a problem—get into it, work with it till it's solved)

WHAT I ENJOYED DOING IN OLD JOBS

- work with telephone companies
- computerize all this fee stuff
- deal with millions of dollars
- find the mistakes on the computer printouts (do bookkeeping/accounting stuff, make it balance to the penny, although I was not familiar with this)
- work with lawyers, secretaries, ATT entity staffs
- follow up with accounts payable to see if bills are paid
- check files to see if what lawyers said was right
- research and investigate, work a lot with people
- look at filing systems and see if they could be improved
- make lots of long distance calls and talk with people about problems
- earned the confidence and respect of hotshot sexist bosses
- advise senior management on which staff would best fill a task
- be diplomatic, tactful to maintain law firm's image
- balance caring with getting the job done
- being counted on a lot
- organizing (organized the lawyer's case load, read the documents, created a new filing system by logical key words)
- being on the inside, at the hub, where things are happening
- working with lawyers at national level

WHAT GAVE ME SATISFACTION

- making it perfect, accurate
- computing percentages

WHAT IS THE IDEAL WORK ENVIRONMENT

- where people have a sense of humor

HANNAH JENKINS
1 La Brea, Apt. 605
Forest Hills, CA 94803
(123) 555-1212

Objective: Staff position in a program providing counseling services.

Highlights of Qualifications

★ Experience in counseling individuals and public speaking.
★ Easily inspire trust, warmth and rapport.
★ Nine-year background in volunteer work, involving teaching, supporting and motivating adults.
★ Coordinated staff and activities in a 20-person department.
★ Over 15 years work experience, plus education equivalent to a college degree.

RELEVANT EXPERIENCE

TRAINING/COUNSELING/PROMOTION
As long-term participant (nine years) in a **volunteer** program:
- **Spoke** before large groups (500-1000 people) as main conference speaker.
- **Counseled** individuals of various ethnic and economic backgrounds, guiding and supporting them to successfully apply the principles of addiction recovery.
  Worked with people in jails, hospitals, halfway houses, and recovery homes.
- **Conducted** large and small **workshops** for conference participants.
- **Promoted** increased participation in addiction-recovery programs through direct one-to-one contact and personal encouragement.

ADMINISTRATIVE SUPPORT
- **Managed** and **coordinated** litigation group of approximately 20 staff people, as "right-hand assistant" to senior partner at Silver, Pauley & Mansley. Handed all materials and logistics relating to complex legal issues. **Wrote** daily and weekly reports.
- Served as **interagency liaison** between CA Housing & Development Agency and other city departments: Personnel, Budget, Accounting, Purchasing, Health Services.
- **Coordinated** new office set-up for a research project of the California State Bar Association. **Assessed** job applicants, assisted in **interviewing**, **coordinated** installation of equipment and phones, **supervised** research, **monitored** work flow, maintained bookkeeping and filing systems.

WORK HISTORY

1990-present	**Counselor/Speaker** on addictions, as a volunteer, at jails, hospitals, halfway houses, recovery homes; working with groups and individuals. (concurrent with part-time employment as canvasser and legal secretary)	
1988-89	**Accounting/Billing Coor.**	SILVER, PAULEY & MANSLEY, Forest Hills
1982-88	**Administrative Coor.**	SILVER, PAULEY & MANSLEY
1980-82	**Legal Secretary**	SILVER, PAULEY & MANSLEY
1978-79	**Legal Admin. Associate**	CITY OF FOREST HILLS
1977	**Legal Admin. Assistant**	CALIFORNIA STATE BAR ASSOC., Forest Hills

EDUCATION

•Boston University   •California Institute of Finance
•New School of Social Research, Forest Hills   •Forest Hills City College

Lani Simpson's Interview/Working Notes

[Remember, these are ROUGH NOTES left over at the end of a work session on the computer, as explained at the beginning of the chapter.]

POSSIBLE JOB TITLES
- Customer Service Manager
- Studio Manager
- Administrator
- Vice President of Customer Relations
- President/Manager of M&S Craft Gallery

WHAT INDUSTRIES?

1. Textile
2. Computer/High Tech
3. Publishing
4. Government Bureaucracy
5. Manufacturing

NOTES FOR OBJECTIVES

Administrative/manufacturing support position with a textile manufacturer involving:

- project management
- design
- manufacturing
- customer relations
- troubleshooting

WHAT'S INVOLVED IN THIS JOB

Design Studio Management
- research trends in field
- assign projects to designers
- deal with deadlines
- determine seasonal color schemes
- present results to management

Liaison
- between accounts and creative staff
- between management and creative staff

Troubleshooting (currently with microscopes)
- ability to understand how they work

WHAT I WANT FROM NEXT JOB
- to be involved in a growing/changing business
- work with a company with a more aggressive approach, move to the top
- want to get back into textiles
- learn how the printing process is happening
- want to learn computer uses
- able to do a lot of different things at once
- to be taken seriously
- to have more people around me
- reflect a different attitude of management

WHAT I HAVE TO OFFER
- forward-thinking
- self-starter
- superwoman
- disgustingly reliable
- Aries—being counted on a lot
- if I believe in something, I see it gets done
- good with deadlines

Notes Written After the Client Left

LANI SIMPSON—A very "sharp cookie." She liked her job, but wanted to work in a more stimulating environment where her input is valued and acknowledged. She also wanted to get back into the field of textiles.

We did a resume that outlined and illustrated the roles she enjoys playing and presented her preferred working modes as assets to management.

This resume does not so much document the skills of an existing job as it creates an outline of a desirable job. It limits the experience presented to just those things she enjoyed doing and wants to re-create in her new job. As long as she is consistent in omitting the things she doesn't want to do in the future and including most of the functions and activities she really enjoys, then this resume will fit almost any position she comes upon that appeals to her. Sticking with roles she enjoys will thus minimize the need to change her resume for different job applications while still keeping it very focused.

The only parts of Lani's resume that will need altering if she applies for a similar job in another industry are one line in the Summary and the short paragraph about "background in textiles." In this way she can create what appears to be a very customized resume for the textile world, yet change it very easily for other environments.

LANI SIMPSON

5585 Berkeley Hills Way
Berkeley CA 94706
(510) 555-5732

Objective: Administrative / manufacturing support position with a textile manufacturer, involving •Project Management •Customer Relations •Inter-staff Liaison.

SUMMARY OF QUALIFICATIONS

★ Talent for generating strong support and cooperation of staff, maximizing and integrating their talents to achieve the priorities of management.
★ Ability to "think on my feet" and balance many projects at once.
★ Proven record of success in handling increasing levels of responsibility.
★ Degree in textile design; portfolio of designs available.

- PROJECT MANAGEMENT -

- **Set up a special tracking system** for customer repair units, including design of in-house forms.
- **Developed initial plans for regional newsletter** for field service technicians.
- Collaborated with product manager to **organize a recall-and-return program** for retrofit of customer units, successfully resolving this design problem.
- **Organized all aspects of shipping and receiving** of returned customer goods for repair and restocking, **reducing turnaround time 50%** by careful tracking and attention to detail.
- **Filled in for Department Manager** during vacation periods, attending managers' meetings, arbitrating disputes, authorizing customer credits, screening potential new hires.

- CUSTOMER RELATIONS -

- **Reorganized and streamlined customer service filing system** at Brown-Webber for full staff access.
- **Built a reputation as customer service "Answer Lady"** by developing an expertise in the product line, being available to respond promptly to clients' questions and requests, and taking pride in getting problems handled correctly the first time.

- LIAISON -

- **Served as management/staff liaison** for **conversion to a new software system**:
  - Learned the system - Performed troubleshooting - Trained staff - Recommended improvements.
- **Provided critical management-support** for technical managers:
  - Prioritized incoming communications from customers, factory, and headquarters.
  - Edited important outgoing communications for foreign-speaking technical managers.

- BACKGROUND IN TEXTILES -

- Completed **textiles classwork** as required for A.A.S. degree.
- Independent **fabric design** for use in apparel.

EMPLOYMENT HISTORY

1987-present	BROWN-WEBBER, Optics, San Leandro
	Regional Service Administrator/West 1991-present
	Supervisor/Central Repair Administrator 1988-91
	Group Leader/Central Repair 1988 Apr-Oct
	Data Entry/Customer Service 1987-88
1985 summer	SPORTS CABLE TV, Oakland CA- **Customer Service Rep**
1984-85	FUN FABRICS, Albany CA - **Customer Service Rep**

EDUCATION & TRAINING

B.A., Studio Arts, Montana State University, Bozeman MT - 1980-84
A.A.S., Fashion Institute of Technology, Carmichael CA- 1985-86

Cyprus Smith's Interview/Working Notes

[Remember, these are ROUGH NOTES left over at the end of a work session on the computer, as explained at the beginning of the chapter.]

JOB DESCRIPTIONS AT APPLE COMPUTER

For AREA AIDE

- filing
- sorting and distributing mail
- photocopying
- telephone support

For AREA AIDE C

- distribute mail and paychecks
- answer phones, take messages
- file
- slow typing
- data entry, word processing
- know basic software
- order supplies
- reception
- backup phones
- coordinate distribute paper

WHAT THINGS HAVE I DONE THAT DEMONSTRATE THESE SKILLS

- built models: planes, ships, cars
- rewired a lamp
- built shelves at home
- helped raise a roof for carpenter: got tools, held materials, nailed, measured

RELEVANT COURSES IN SCHOOL

- engineering (part of a class)
- architectural drafting (draw objects)
- history, drafting
- marketing—made up phony products, developed an advertising campaign: logo, TV presentation, benefits, how to hype your product
- drafting
- marketing
- ceramics
- woods

WORK HISTORY (uncut)

- **Stock Work** at Patricia's: produce, pricing, cashier, carry-out, carrying
- **Carpentry,** 1 week: put up Sheetrock, carpenter's helper
- **Deli**, 2 weeks: make sandwiches, clean up
- **Valet Parking**: Country Club, 2 1/2 months: waiter, busboy, help with catering
- **Paperboy**

WHAT I WANT IN NEXT POSITION

- handle money
- work with people
- teamwork—all going for one goal
- support the company, make profits
- get to know people, make friends, make a better working relationship
- Make money—now need around $1000-$1200 per month ($7 per hr)

MACINTOSH SKILLS I HAVE

- MacWrite, Hypercard
- type slowly

TALENTS—WHY PEOPLE WOULD LIKE WORKING WITH ME

- energetic, hardworking
- willing to learn and accept constructive criticism
- strong motivation for advancing in a career
- enjoy contributing to a team effort and creating a good working environment
- learn quickly
- easygoing, get along with everybody (adapt to different personality types on the job)
- nice guy, always helpful
- thorough
- there on time
- concentrate on work
- learn from my mistakes
- great leadership abilities (captain of baseball team)
- energetic young man
- like to make money

GOAL:

- To learn how to sell/market Apple Macintosh

WOULD LIKE

- An apprenticeship program

Notes Written After the Client Left

CYPRUS SMITH—Recently graduated from high school. We used his school and extra-curricular activities as well as paid experience to present his qualifications.

CYPRUS SMITH
233 Sierra Madre Lane
Cotati, CA 94928
(707) 888-0923

Current job objective: Entry position with Apple Computer
Longer-term goal: position in advertising, sales, marketing of Apple products.

SUMMARY

- Energetic, hard working, willing to learn and accept constructive criticism.
- Strong motivation for advancing in a career.
- Enjoy contributing to a team effort and creating a good working environment.
- Basic understanding of the Macintosh computer.

RELEVANT SKILLS & EXPERIENCE

Facilities Maintenance
- As carpenter's helper:
  -painted interior walls -measured and cut lumber -helped with framing
  -operated power tools: saws, drills, sanders.
- Did basic home maintenance:
  -rewired lamps -repaired plumbing and appliance -built shelves.
- Completed classes in:
  -electronics (built a TV scrambler from a circuit board)
  -architectural drafting -basic carpentry.

Office Support Skills
- Assisted in inventory control and priced merchandise as stock clerk at Patricia's.
- Cashiered at Patricia's computing and handling large sums of money.
- Answered phones as needed.
- Completed class in marketing:
  -invented unique products; developed simulated marketing strategies.

Computer Familiarity
- Basic understanding of Macintosh computer: MacWrite, Hypercard.

WORK HISTORY

Dec '91-Jan '92	**Stock Clerk/Cashier**	PATRICIA'S PLACE, Loma Prieta CA
Summer 1989*	**Valet Parking Asst.**	PEPE'S COUNTRY CLUB, Cotati CA
* while in school	Plus short-term jobs as: Carpenter's Helper, Waiter, Busboy, Stockwork.	

EDUCATION

Hamilton High School, Cotati CA, 1991

Ronald Davidson's Interview/Working Notes

[Remember, these are ROUGH NOTES left over at the end of a work session on the computer, as explained at the beginning of the chapter.]

POSSIBLE JOB TITLES

- President
- Executive Vice President
- General Manager
- CEO
- Marketing Manager
- Advertising Manager
- Public Relations Director

FOR POSSIBLE COMPANIES

- real estate company
- insurance company (title, property, mortgage)
- real estate lender
- remodeling company
- brokerage firm
- entrepreneurial venture

JOB INVOLVES

- convincing, persuading
- troubleshooting, innovating, synthesizing
- promoting
- teaching/training
- project development
- dealing with a service: procedures, methods
- risk analysis: investigating, comparing, forecasting, revising, modifying

WHY THEY SHOULD HIRE ME

- connecting the market with the product at two levels: delivery, feedback
- understand how they spend their money
- been around long enough to be realistic about what I can/can't do
- handled a big deal—made money
- get the "big picture" fast, set the priorities
- solve the problems that get results quickest (get the most bang for the buck)
- can handle a hell of a lot of responsibility— handled nearly $1 billion real estate portfolio and successfully handled 20,000 customers
- curiosity: learn ALL about the subject, very quickly gather information—sort it into facts, findings, conclusions, recommendations
- courageous—can take on a tough assignment (can find the help I need)

OVERALL PICTURE OF ME

- Talent for seeing "the big picture," pinpointing an organizational objective and setting goals and priorities to achieve it
- Adept at applying marketing theory to successful business development
- Over twenty-five years' practical, broad-based management experience with a realistic understanding of market constraints and opportunities
- Track record of responsibility for managing complex projects involving thousands of customers with millions of dollars at risk

PROBLEM ANALYSIS

- manage risk/reduce losses
- fact finding, conclusions, recommendations
- work with board of directors

BUSINESS DEVELOPMENT

- convince, persuade, develop, troubleshoot, innovate, synthesize, promote, teach/train

TRAINING

- train managers and salespeople in product knowledge and service

Notes Written After the Client Left

RONALD DAVIDSON—Forty-five to fifty years old, well-groomed, articulate man. He's self-taught in management and has a lot of experience in entrepreneurial and business development. He also has some savvy about management and marketing theory.

This was a difficult session because he was not absolutely focused on one specific job objective. It took much longer than usual to resolve that. We slugged away for five hours, hustling like crazy at the end to get something finalized, after I had all but given up the notion that we could pull it off.

RONALD DAVIDSON
1688 Sky Ranch Blvd.
Eureka Springs, AR 72726
(501) 656-9990

Objective: Position as General Manager/CEO,
providing leadership and direction for **business development** by
increasing market share/profitability, and reducing risk and loss.

HIGHLIGHTS OF QUALIFICATIONS

★ Over 25 years practical, broad-based management experience, with a
realistic understanding of market constraints and opportunities.

★ Track record of responsibility for managing complex projects involving
thousands of customers, with millions of dollars of investment.

★ Conceptual talent for seeing "the big picture," pinpointing an organizational objective, and setting goals and priorities to achieve it.

★ Adept in applying marketing theory to successful business development.

RELEVANT EXPERIENCE & ACCOMPLISHMENTS

BUSINESS DEVELOPMENT
• In 25 years as entrepreneurial CEO, consistently grew organizations in all aspects of sales,
profits, returns, safety, and acceptance, by expanding and strengthening through:
-product development   -system enhancement   -financial controls
-merger   -affiliation   -marketing and sales.

MARKETING MANAGEMENT
• Developed a highly effective customer-oriented **product evaluation process** featuring direct
customer feedback and trade association market research.
• **Created marketing plans,** incorporating 8-10 of the most appropriate media, scheduled by a
PERT method, and budgeted in accordance with expected returns.
• Developed valuable **professional rapport with regulating agencies**, and set standards for
product development, marketplace acceptance, advertising and promotion, sales and product
delivery, customer relations.

OPERATIONS & PERSONNEL
• **Developed operations systems** integrated with production and marketing, greatly improving
profitability.
• **Built a strong team** of front-line managers with excellent esprit de corp, by implementing
regular management meetings, improved training, and incentives.
• Developed a **highly effective management system** for efficiently processing a high volume of
prospective customers through a multi-step sales process.

FINANCE & RISK ASSESSMENT
• **Established initial financial plan and forecast** for several large home-owners' associations,
which are still in effect 7 or more years later.
• Successfully developed SEBASTIAN from under $1 million in gross receipts to over $12 million,
with internally generated funds.

- **Continued on page two -**

TECHNIQUES

RELEVANT EXPERIENCE & ACCOMPLISHMENTS
(continued)

ADMINISTRATION & LITIGATION

- **Created a management information system** that provided, for the first time, the activity of each operational component, making it possible to accurately forecast product development.
- **Adapted** a multiple-department **management system** to successfully administer more than 50 mutual benefit corporations concurrently.
- Developed an **expertise in loss prevention management** through experience coordinating and assessing approximately 100 potential homeowner lawsuits; 75% settled without litigation.

EMPLOYMENT HISTORY

1991-present	**Partner/Chairman**	DEVELOPMENT CO., Eureka Springs & Alston
	(general contracting firm, since 1972, specializing in manufactured modular homes; building, remodeling, and maintenance)	
1990-present	**Principal/Consultant**	SEBASTIAN CORP., Fayetteville
	(real estate/property management consulting firm for the lending, management, and mortgage insurance industry)	
1977-89	**President**	EXECUTIVE MANAGEMENT COMPANY, Inc.
	(real estate management)	Eureka Springs
1976-77	**Vice President**	REAL PROPERTIES, INC., West Fork
	(real estate management)	
1973-76	**Director of Administration**	GILLET HOTEL CORP., Prairie Grove
	(real estate joint venture for condominium and hotel development)	
1970-73	**Program Director**	ARKANSAS SAFETY FOUNDATION, Lewiston

EDUCATION

B.A. Equivalence, Public Administration
US Air Force Institute/University of Maryland

TECHNIQUES

5
Resume Clinic

5
Resume Clinic

CLINIC

This chapter features specific examples of resume problems and their solutions. It is loosely divided into three sections:

In the first part, each page poses one typical resume problem; beneath that, a **solution to the problem is illustrated** just as it would appear on the resume.

In the second part, some additional **"sticky problems"** are addressed in a **question-and-answer dialogue** between the author and several resume writers and job-hunters.

In closing, **one client's problematical resume has been dissected,** and his "before" and "after" resumes both shown for comparison.

Developing Your Bag of Tricks

Resume writers need to have a full bag of tricks at hand—creative solutions ready to apply to the classic resume problems, because PROBLEMS ARE THE NORM when it comes to resumes. Hardly anybody appears in a resume writer's office with a clear job objective and a nice, tidy, uncomplicated work history.

To start developing YOUR OWN bag of tricks— you could call it your **Solutions Notebook**—you might begin this way: Keep a notebook of all the resumes you write, separate from your client records. These copies of your resumes will be about YOU and your developing writing skill, not about your clients.

With each resume you complete:

a) BEFORE your client leaves, ask her to *please* keep you informed on how well the resume is working, particularly the part of it that was difficult and posed a problem to be solved. You *need* this kind of feedback.

b) AFTER the client has left, *immediately* attach a little Post-it note to a copy of the resume and jot down briefly WHAT THE ESSENTIAL PROBLEM WAS and HOW YOU RESOLVED IT. This copy goes in your Solutions Notebook.

c) When the client reports back on the effectiveness of the resume, go back to your Solutions Notebook and update your notes with this information.

Then keep your eyes open and beef up your Notebook with creative ideas you find in OTHER people's work, such as this book, the *Resume Catalog,* and other good books on resume writing by other authors.

The Most Common Resume Problems

In this chapter I'll share many of my own creative solutions to resume problems. Keep in mind that you may have to "tweak" any particular solution so it fits more perfectly with YOUR client's similar problem.

Let's start with the four resume problems that I encounter most often.

PROBLEM #1.

No clear job objective. Either it's missing altogether or it's too general to be useful.

Two strategies that help a client clarify their job objective are job-title brainstorming and information interviewing. These are described on page 23 in Chapter 2. On the same page you'll find my advice to the job hunter who avoids stating an objective and insists, "I want to keep all my options open."

PROBLEM #2.

Lack of experience. This includes:
- lack of ANY experience in the field;
- lack of PAID experience in the desired line of work;
- lack of RECENT experience in the line of work currently sought—for example, when someone is switching back to their old line of work.

There are numerous ways to approach the work experience issue, including the following:

a) **fix it;** immediately get at least some minimal experience in the field, through volunteering (see page 106), or through short-term or temporary employment.

b) **view it differently;** you can look at ALL work, including volunteer work, as experience, whether it involved pay or not, and you can list ALL of this experience under a heading called "*Work* History" rather than "Employment History."

c) **transform it;** using the functional resume format, you can repackage the client's work history to play up the transferability of skills from one field to another.

d) **rearrange it;** turn the work history section upside down, so the earlier (relevant) work appears at the top! There's no LAW saying the most recent work has to appear first on a resume.

PROBLEM #3.

Long-term underemployment, when a highly skilled person has only mediocre job titles in their work history.

Two strategies work best here:

a) **changing the job titles** so they are more accurate and fair. For example, using "Office Manager" as the job title when that is actually more accurate than "Administrative Assistant," even though the employer CALLED it Administrative Assistant. If this makes you uneasy, you could try a compromise such as "Office Manager/Administrative Assistant."

b) **using a functional resume format** or an accomplishment format, either of which will change the focus to skills and results, rather than job titles and job descriptions.

Oftentimes a long-term underemployed job hunter ALSO lacks a clear job objective because they are unaware of their options. In that case I would strongly recommend that they do some research, and take along an "information interview" resume.

PROBLEM #4.

Gaps in the work history. This could range anywhere from one gap to many gaps, and they could be small gaps or giant gaps.

Some special situations are covered in the examples that follow in this chapter, but the following two strategies neatly handle almost all gaps:

a) **Include ALL work** in the "Work History"— paid employment, volunteer work, parenthood, and schooling—as discussed above.

b) **Stick to years** (1987-88) and not months (4/87-10/88). That usually handles any remaining gaps.

Now let's turn to some specific situations and some real-life solutions in the Resume Clinic section that follows.

RESUME CLINIC

A Complicated Work History with Many Problems to Resolve

The job hunter's work history included various complexities:

a) a break in the work history due to maternity leave and education

b) self-employment as the most recent work

c) more than one position with the same employer (on two different occasions)

d) two half-time jobs concurrently

Solution

a) utilization of graphic elements to make the job history as clear as possible, including the use of bold type for only the most relevant job titles

b) inclusion of nonpaid work (motherhood, studenthood) to fill in the gaps for a solid work history

c) use of smaller size type where unobtrusive explanations are needed

WORK HISTORY

1988-present	Independent Consultant	Job development for US placement of overseas nurses
1986-87	**Medical Sales Consultant** and, concurrently	SUPERIOR DATA, San Francisco
	Marketing Liaison	HIGHSTAKES CORP, San Francisco (real estate development)
1985-86	**Health Care Program Coor.**	KAISER HOSPITAL, Oakland
1984-86	Graduate student	University of California, San Francisco
		Compliance Nurse, San Francisco General Hospital
		Coordinator, Refugee Nursing Project
1980-83	Family/maternity leave	
1977-79	**Staff Nurse**	STUDENT HEALTH SERVICE, S.F. State Univ.
1974-76	Full-time student	University of California, San Francisco
		Health Educator, Red Cross
		Staff Nurse, UCSF

Major Career Change, No PAID Experience

In this example, all of Bob's regular full-time work experience appears to be related to engineering. Now he wants to go into media work, where he's done a lot of freelancing and volunteer work.

 Solution

Have TWO work-related sections, calling one "Employment History" and one "Media-Related Work Experience."

- TIP: Whenever you want to include unpaid work in your resume, use the word "Work" in place of "Employment."

Notice that, from the perspective of graphic presentation, we have given Bob's MEDIA-related experience the same weight as his engineering experience. ("The medium IS the message.") The skillful and appropriate use of these techniques to "repackage" the job hunter is one of the prime differences between superior resume writing and the work done in fast-food-type resume "factories." This kind of work takes time and thought, as well as careful collaboration between the job hunter and professional resume writer. There must NOT be distortion of the truth, confusing or evasive chronologies, or "b.s."—that isn't necessary and it won't work.

EMPLOYMENT HISTORY

1988-present	Systems Admin/Engineer	MORGAN FARMS, Seymour, CA
1987-88	Cost Analyst	AMERICAN PRESIDENT LINES, LTD, Oakland, CA
1984-87	Stationary Engineer	JOHN MUIR MEDICAL CENTER, Walnut Creek, CA
1983-84	Marine Field Engineer	GENERAL ELECTRIC CO, Oakland, CA
1980-83	Apprentice Engineer	RED & WHITE FLEET, San Francisco, CA

Additional **MEDIA-RELATED** WORK EXPERIENCE*

1987	**President, Board of Directors**	Diablo View Homeowners Association
1985-86	**Photographer**	DIABLO PRODUCTIONS, Walnut Creek, CA
1984-86	**Public Relations Committee**	Orinda church social organization
1985	**Co-Publisher/Editor**	MODE MAGAZINE, Danville, CA
1984	**Sales Consultant**	HONDA MOTORCYCLES, Walnut Creek, CA

* part time, concurrent with above Employment History

EDUCATION & TRAINING

B.S., California Maritime Academy, Vallejo, 1979-83
Photography and Liberal Arts, Diablo Valley College, 1977-79

A Ragged Work History

One job hunter's sporadic employment history included several short-term jobs and periods of (involuntary!) self-employment. The material on this page (and the next page) was developed for Roving Resume Writers of San Francisco, who work with homeless job hunters. But this problem is fairly common among people with roofs over their heads, too.

 **Solutions**

For jobs that lasted less than six months, mention the YEAR, and perhaps the amount of time, but not the specific dates. *(In this format, if you can make the "2 months" in smaller type, that's great!)*

For example:

1990	**Self-Employed Handyman**, Oakland (4 months)
1989	**Short-Order Cook**, Cheezy Pizza Co., Berkeley (2 months)

The above is honest and gives a better first-impression than:

2/90-6/90	Self-Employed
5/89-7/89	Short-Order Cook, Cheezy Pizza Co.

ROUND OFF employment periods that were more than half a year.

For example:	1986	Teachers' Aide, Podunk School Dist., Marietta, GA
Rather than:	4/86-10/86	Teachers' Aide, Podunk School Dist., Marietta, GA

Periods of Unemployment

Most of us have been unemployed at one time or another. There are several ways to handle these periods on a resume.

(As mentioned earlier, the material on this page was initially developed for Roving Resume Writers of San Francisco, who work with homeless job hunters.)

 Solutions

If you are CURRENTLY unemployed, find an immediate short-term opportunity to get some unpaid volunteer work experience, preferably in your desired line of work. PUT THAT ON YOUR RESUME NOW, even if you don't start until next week. (This will look much better on your resume than being unemployed.) Remember, don't use the word "volunteer" to describe this position—work is work is work!

For example:

      1992   **Word Processing Assistant**   Episcopal Community Services

For PAST periods of unemployment, FIRST try rounding off to years rather than mentioning months, as shown on the previous page.

Then for any remaining gaps, create an accurate, dignified JOB TITLE for any period when you were not actually paid or employed by someone else, but you did ANYTHING that could be presented as "work." Be sure to label the work section "Work History" rather than "Employment History." Also incorporate any unpaid TRAINING into the Work History to fill in the gaps.

WORK HARD to find the job-title alternative that will have the most credibility in the work world! Be realistic, and at the same time don't buy the idea that certain work "doesn't count"; instead, present that work with dignity.

Some examples:

1990	**Self-Employed Handyman** (4 months)
Spring 1991	**Electronics Trainee** - San Francisco Vocational Program
Summer 1991	**Peer-Counselor/Volunteer** - San Francisco Vocational Program
1990	**Apprentice Painter** - Moe's Paint Shop, San Leandro
1976	**Full-time Parent** - Three small children
1988	**Full-time Student** - Podunk Community College
1979	**Full-time Caregiver** - Home care of elderly parent
1983	**Community Work & Parenting** - PTA; Scouts

CLINIC

Several Positions at the Same Company

Some job hunters may have changed positions or departments, but stayed at the same company. In the examples below, this is made clear without cluttering up the resume. Notice, in the first example, that we know the job hunter had two positions at Clorox; we can easily see how long she was in each position, and we can also easily see the total duration of her Clorox employment.

- TIP: Employers appreciate it when you make it EASY for them to find the information they need.

 Solutions

EMPLOYMENT HISTORY

1986-88	PRODUCTCOM, INC., San Francisco, CA
	Account Manager
1985-86	DREYER'S GRAND ICE CREAM, Oakland, CA
	Asst. Brand Manager
1983-85	THE CLOROX COMPANY, Oakland, CA
	Asst. Brand Manager 1985
	Brand Assistant 1983-84
1978-80	RICHARDSON-VICKS, INC., San Diego, CA
	Division Salesman

Another example shows the job hunter working his way up through four positions at Hewlett-Packard. We can see clearly how much time he spend in each position, as well as his total length of employment there.

EMPLOYMENT HISTORY

Current	ROSEWOOD & ASSOCIATES, Oakland (real estate services)
	Interim Office Manager/Consultant
1980-89	HEWLETT-PACKARD, Palo Alto
	Personnel Section Manager (1985-89)
	Senior Personnel Rep (1983-84)
	Personnel Rep (1981-82)
	Assoc. Personnel Rep (1980)
1979	WESTSIDE COMMUNITY MENTAL HEALTH AGENCY, San Francisco
	Research Assistant

Long, Repetitious Work History

A Work History that includes many entries plus several repetitions of the same job title may make the job hunter look like a "job hopper." The Work History below, for example, is a bit overwhelming to the reader.

WORK HISTORY

Present	**Teacher, English as Second Language**, S.F. Jewish Community Center, S.F.
1985-present	**Teacher, English as Second Language**, San Francisco Community College
1986-present	**Teacher, English as Second Language**, College of Marin, Kentfield, CA
1987-1990	**Teacher, Amnesty Classes**, College of Marin, Kentfield, CA
1979-1987	**Manager**, Greens Restaurant, San Francisco, CA
1976-1979	**Office Manager**, Green Gulch Farm, Muir Beach, CA
1975	**Bilingual Teacher**, Everett Junior High School, San Francisco, CA
1972-1974	**English Teacher**, Linguaphone School, Paris, France
	English Teacher, Air France, Paris, France
	Interpreter, American Center, Paris, France
1970-1972	**French and Spanish Teacher**, public schools, Syracuse, NY

Solution

The same information looks more compact and manageable when we:

a) consolidate the first three teaching positions

b) combine two of the 1972-74 jobs.

WORK HISTORY

1985-present	**Teacher, English as 2nd Language:** S.F. Jewish Community Center, S.F, present
	College of Marin, Kentfield, CA, 1986-present
	S.F. Community College, 1985-present
1987-1990	**Teacher, Amnesty Classes**, College of Marin, Kentfield, CA
1979-1987	**Manager**, Greens Restaurant, San Francisco, CA
1976-1979	**Office Manager**, Green Gulch Farm, Muir Beach, CA
1975	**Bilingual Teacher**, Everett Junior High School, San Francisco, CA
1972-1974	**English Teacher**, Linguaphone School, Paris; Air France, Paris
	Interpreter, The American Center, Paris, France
1970-1972	**French and Spanish Teacher**, public schools, Syracuse, NY

(Example provided by Susan Ireland)

How to Show Job Promotions

 Solution

Hinda Bodinger writes: "When I have a client who is working at a job where they have been promoted, I generally include that in the Employment History as follows":

1981-Present   Littlestone Publications, Rochester, NY
                MANAGING EDITOR (Promoted from Assistant Editor)

or

1981-Present   Bloucher Industries, South Orange, NJ
                EAST COAST SALES MANAGER (Since 1987)

"However, here is a new way I've tried, which I think is very effective":

1981-Present   Franklin Lakes Development Corporation, City, State
                SUPERINTENDENT/FIELD MANAGER
                 JOB PROGRESSION: Porter, Head Porter, Handyman, Certified Boilerman,
                Plumber, Assistant Superintendent

"This client had been concerned about being at one job for ten years (how times have changed!!) and wanted to show that he had grown in the job."

Sticky Problems

 **No Clear Job Objective**

Kim Coats of Illinois called with this problem: Her client, a factory worker for seventeen years, was laid off, did odd jobs for a while in Florida, and was then rehired by his old employer. He hates it and wants to return to Florida, but doesn't know what he wants to do. Kim didn't know what to put on his resume. HE wanted to put EVERY-THING he has done on it: shipping/receiving (his favorite), grounds-keeping, machine operation, customer service, etc.

 I advised Kim to do a separate targeted resume for EACH of the top four areas he's interested in (since the fields are so diverse), but to encourage him to conduct his job search in only ONE area at a time—starting with an all-out focus on his favorite area and trying his second choice only after he has exhausted all his leads for his first choice.

No Experience, the Catch-22: Try Volunteering

Counselor John Ellis writes: People making career transitions often find themselves in a Catch-22—employers won't hire them without experience, yet they can't get the experience until they've worked in the field.

 His solution: volunteering, to get the required experience. While people are sometimes reluctant to consider working for nothing, John convinces them they are making a wise investment in their career that will pay off.

As a volunteer, he points out, you may be able to choose work experiences that will support your career goals—while entry-level paid employees don't always have that choice. And these volun-

teer activities can appear on a resume under the heading "Professional Experience" or "Relevant Experience"—employers generally are more concerned with what you learned than whether or not you were paid. And they're often impressed by candidates who have volunteer experience, viewing them as more dedicated and responsible.

If his clients (mostly students at College of St. Rose, Albany, New York) need more convincing, he points out these benefits of volunteer work:

a) you'll gain general experience in the world of work;

b) you'll gain specific experience in a desired field;

c) you'll develop professional contacts;

d) you can learn new marketable skills, such as how to use a computer;

e) you can test recently acquired skills and knowledge;

f) you can explore new occupations or related fields, on a trial basis.

g) you can try out some ideal or fantasy career goals.

 Leaving on a Bad Note

A Colorado resume writer poses this dilemma: Her client, Ginny, was employed as a nursing student and left on a bad note. They wanted her to work a twenty-four-hour shift, and she left without notice. Then she went into truck driving for a while. (This is a true story.) Now she is on a leave of absence while she finishes nursing school, and wants to return to nursing.

Ginny says she can't put the past nursing job on her resume because she's afraid they won't give her a good recommendation. And she can't mention the truck driving because they don't know she is considering other work and may not return from the leave. The resume writer wanted to know how to handle this.

If I were advising Ginny, I'd tell her she HAS to go back and mend the fences with her nursing employer—it's too important for her future. She should go back and say she regrets the way she departed and would really appreciate their willingness to at least not give her a bad recommendation, so that she can get started in the field again. She needs to resolve her fears about what the prior employer is thinking of her and would say if contacted. (Maybe the ex-employer isn't all that angry; or maybe they aren't even in business anymore.)

Anyway, Ginny needs to clear it up before the resume can be properly written. Then, even if the WORST happens and the old employer is unsympathetic, at least Ginny will know exactly what she's dealing with, rather than being scared of what MIGHT happen.

Gap in Paid Employment

Resume writer Justine Stelling wrote: One of my clients worked in various areas of the construction industry. He wanted to change to a sales position leading to management.

The difficult part came when I asked about his latest work experience. He had not worked at a salaried job for a year because he had left his job to work on his home, which had suffered major damage in the earthquake.

The dilemma was, how to put that in a resume, keep it factual, and not have him look unstable?

 This is what I came up with for his current work history:

19xx-Present   Independent Construction/
              Remodel of earthquake-damaged
              residence.

I think this was the best solution to the problem, as all his background has been in construction anyway. And I was right: The client is delighted with his new resume.

Job Plateau

Another resume writer asks: How do I handle my client's employment history when they've stayed at one place a very long time in the same position with no advancement and only meager raises?

In that case, I'd use a functional format so you can switch the focus to the skills needed for the new job and what this worker ACCOMPLISHED on his old job that documents those skills. Also, help him examine ALL his outside activities for any additional evidence of achievements.

Downward Mobility

Pat called with this problem: Her client worked for a company that recently experienced a big management shakeup and a lot of politicking and in-fighting. After twenty years of assuming more responsible positions, her client suddenly got demoted to his old position. Now it's a year later and he wants to get out.

He was worried about showing his most recent position on the resume, since it would be obvious he got demoted. If he doesn't mention the position it will leave a one-year gap in his work record. He wants an honest resume, and this problem had them both stumped.

Here's one solution I proposed to Pat: Use a modified format that lists all the positions he held in the company (starting with the most responsible management position) without saying exactly when and for how long he held each position. (His **current** position would then be the **second** one on the list.) And omit "responsibilities included." Then group together (in another section) all his accomplishment statements for that company. It would look like this:

WORK HISTORY & ACCOMPLISHMENTS

General Widget Corp., Houston, TX, 1971-90
    Vice President, Operations
    Gen. Manager for Warehouse Operations
    Warehouse Supervisor
    Warehouseman

- List an accomplishment (relevant to the new job objective) with a little detail about specifically what he did and how it benefitted the company.
- List another (relevant!) accomplishment described in a similar manner.
- List a third accomplishment described in a similar manner. And so forth.

I am NOT suggesting that one use this format under normal conditions—but when you have a sticky problem you sometimes have to choose the lesser of two evils in order to make the best of the situation and give the client a chance at the interview.

Age Discrimination

Several resume writers asked: If the resume shows too many years of experience, it tips people off to a job hunter's age and invites age discrimination. How can you deal with this and still be honest?

 Solution: You can say, in the Highlights, "over fifteen years' experience"—when in fact there are twenty, twenty-five, or thirty years of experience—and still be honest. Then, list your most recent fifteen or twenty years of work history under a heading called Recent Work History (or Relevant Work History) instead of Employment History.

HOWEVER, if that results in having to leave off some of the BEST experience (from WAY back), then try this variation:

- Use a functional format;
- List your most recent fifteen or twenty years of work history under "Recent Work History" as above;
- Under THAT, insert an brief entry saying "Additional earlier experience in (let's say) marketing and retail sales." That would allow you to mention, in your functional/skills paragraphs, some accomplishments that occurred further back, in support of your job objective that now involves (let's say) marketing and retail sales.

 An Excessively Long Resume

Ace, a job hunter from Iowa, wrote: "Yana, I think your book is fine. Here is my resume. It is almost **three pages long!** And **no job objective** is stated! I understand this is a no-no for resumes, but I am at a loss as to how to shorten it. Can you help, please?"

Ace enclosed his resume; it had its good points, but the resume was very detailed and wordy and went way, WAY back in time.

 I wrote to Ace as follows: What you have included in three pages is actually what I've heard called a "private resume." That is, it's a detailed account of virtually everything you've done—which should really be FOR YOUR REFERENCE ONLY.

A private resume like this is a wonderful first step to get an overview of your experience. In fact,

you have gone to the second step and made sure that everything you recounted is expressed in action verbs. You have also included some results and explicit figures, such as: "tripled Marvin Company's purchase volume," "shipped 20 million bushels of grain," and "trained eight grain merchants."

The main principle of resume writing that I think you need to keep firmly in mind is this: SOME information is of interest only to you! (Sorry about that). And SOME of it will be of intense interest to someone who would like to hire a man like you for a particular job in their company. What you need to do is EXTRACT from your excellent private resume ONLY the information relevant to the particular position you're applying for. Of course that creates a dilemma: You won't be able to tell what's relevant until you zero in on (sirens and bugles) THE JOB OBJECTIVE! (Oh, drat!)

So, I would suggest that you temporarily set aside your private resume (while keeping in mind that you did a pretty impressive job on it). Spend whatever amount of time it takes to explore the areas that catch your imagination and interest. This is where a good career counselor can really come in handy. If there's a college nearby, you might get a good referral from that source. When choosing a counselor, be very careful—trust your intuition! The latest edition of *What Color Is Your Parachute?*, by Richard Bolles, has an enlightening section on selecting counselors and career centers.

A career counselor might advise you to do some homework such as going through all those "one-liners" and ranking them from 1 to 10 based on how much SATISFACTION or sense of ACCOMPLISHMENT you got from doing each one. There are also a few excellent books that would help you. One I found to be a great inspiration is called *Guerrilla Tactics in the Job Market* by Tom Jackson. You can open it up almost anywhere and feel *good* about the challenge of exploring the world of work.

Now, let's say you've zeroed in on something you'd like to do. Say you found a really neat manufacturer that has a good solid start in developing and producing farm machinery geared toward innovative and environmentally sound farming—one of the interests you mentioned. Further, let's imagine that you feel you could really get behind their products. You KNOW you could convince others to buy them, so you'd like a crack at being their regional sales manager.

Well, NOW you'd have a Job Objective. So you'd take out a fresh piece of paper and write, under your name-address-phone, "Job Objective: Regional Sales Manager for Hot Stuff Farm Equipment." Then just "follow the yellow brick road" outlined in *Damn Good Resume Guide*, selecting from your "private resume" about 15 to 20 percent (MAX!) of the material you have written that directly relates to this specific objective.

You would, no doubt, omit all details about the military service (unless relevant), and you would omit all references to skiing, golf, hunting, tennis, walking, swimming, church trustee-ing, etc. A good resume is absolutely NOT a "life history," even though you have seen many resumes over the years that looked like autobiographies. Please take my word for it: Those were NOT good resumes even then, and today they are looked upon with amusement, at best. In this competitive market, everything on a resume has to pass this test: Is it relevant?

Look again at the examples in *Damn Good Resume Guide*. Your resume should not be any more wordy than the wordiest one there. In many of those cases we started out with as much material as you have in your three-page resume. But then we cut and cut and cut until we had extracted the best, the most relevant, the most powerful.

You don't want to overwhelm your reader with volumes of information. Instead you want to knock their socks off with simplicity, focus, organization and clarity. You need to be *extremely* selective about what goes on your resume. Remember that the purpose is to get you an interview—not to REPLACE the interview! Apply that concept consistently and you'll end up with a dynamite resume.

Mature Job Hunter with Minimal Work Experience

Andrew Thompson, a charming and impeccable sixty-one-year-old British gentleman, came to me needing a resume. He was a recent graduate of Hampton College's Legal Assistant program and he wanted to get started in this field.

Here are the problems we needed to deal with to come up with a good resume:

1. Minimal paid work experience of any kind

2. Lack of a credible job title for his primary job

3. Older worker

4. Just entering a new profession with virtually no relevant work experience

Compare Andrew's old resume with his new one, both of which appear on the following pages. There is a dramatic difference in the presentation. A primary and disastrous failure of his old resume was that it left the reader almost totally mystified as to his chronological work history—dates were avoided, and the lack of explanation about his family's business would leave the reader feeling very wary and suspicious about what it all meant.

As I explored what his REAL employment history was and attempted to create a chronology, it became evident that his traditional jobs took place twenty years ago. Virtually all of the space in between involved his family's business—and he seemed to have a relatively minor role in that.

Since this, at face value, wouldn't look great on a resume, the task was to "normalize" his experience as much as possible. Without any lying or serious exaggerating, we had to give his role a respectable job title and then present what he actually DID in an impressive way. We presented "managing the assets" as an active rather than a passive function.

Usually I drop earlier job titles if the experience happened long ago. but in Andrew's case we needed to include these jobs because they contributed to an overall image of someone who DID have "standard" job titles at one point in his work history—i.e., job titles that can be verified, as distinguished from family business roles which are sometimes impossible to verify.

Since Andrew expected to present his resume mostly in person rather than by mail, people would see that he is a mature gentleman. Therefore, there was no need to avoid showing his age on the resume, although we left out the dates of his earlier degrees so as not to call any MORE attention to it. We of course left in the 1989 date of his just-completed training.

We dropped one of his degrees because he ALREADY looks somewhat overqualified, and we didn't want to convey the image of a very highly educated person seeking a relatively menial job.

(This was perhaps the truth here, but why push it?)

Instead of including an Objective, since ALL the positions he will apply for will be for Certified Legal Assistant, we linked that job title directly with his name—which appears to make him look more official. It's accurate, and it has a credible and professional look to it.

Andrew was delighted with his new resume and embarked on his job search with a good deal more self-confidence. The "old" version appears on the next page, followed by the "new" version we did together.

CLINIC

Andrew Thompson
1555 Powell Street #205
Hampton, California 94000
(415) 793-4400

EDUCATION

<u>Paralegal Certificate</u>, Hampton College, Hampton, California,
South Campus, June 1989

One year ABA approved programs with coursework in:

Legal Research & Writing	Corporate Law I,II
Legal Concepts	Probate
Contract Law	Family Law
Litigation I,II	Wills, Trusts, & Estate Planning
Real Estate Law	

<u>Bachelor of Arts</u>, University of Vermont, Burlington, VT
<u>Master of Library Science</u>, University of California, Santa Cruz
<u>Master of Arts</u>, Los Angeles University, Los Angeles
<u>Archives Certificate</u>, University of Utah, Salt Lake City

EXPERIENCE

<u>Legal</u>:

<u>Paralegal Intern</u> for the law firm of the City Attorney's
Office of Hampton, May 3, 1989 - May 31, 1989

<u>Attorneys</u>: John C. Brown, Zachariah Smith, William Reardon

Time: Approximately 89 hours

Summarized depositions, medical records, and employment
records; devised profiles of estimated earnings, losses
and estimated medical expenditures; prepared Notice of
Entry of Judgement Forms; participated in exposure
experience to Westlaw

<u>Library</u>:

<u>Bibliographer</u> in the Department of Technical Services at
the University of California, Santa Cruz

Pre-cataloged new acquisitions; forestalled duplication
of existing materials; verified the presence of journals
and periodicals

<u>Librarian</u> in charge of the Clark Hospital School of
Nursing Library, East Hampton, California

Cataloged library materials; provided reference services
to faculty and students; ordered library materials;
maintained special files of illustrated materials;
instructed students in the use of the library; prepared
special bibliographies

<u>Business</u>:

Secretary in family antique reproductions firm

Prepared inventories; handled telephone inquiries; in
charge of business correspondence for purchases;
maintained business files

ANDREW THOMPSON
- Certified Legal Assistant -
1555 Powell St., #205 • Hampton CA 94000
(415) 793-4400

SUMMARY OF QUALIFICATIONS
★ 1989 Graduate of Hampton College Paralegal Program.
★ Completed internship with City Attorney's office, earning a
reputation for high standards in teamwork and professionalism.
★ Extremely thorough in working with details, and able to extract
the most relevant points in legal documentation.

RELEVANT EXPERIENCE

PARALEGAL EXPERIENCE
As Paralegal in the Hampton City Attorney's office, working for attorneys John C. Brown,
Zachariah Smith, and William Reardon:
• Summarized depositions, medical records, and employment records.
• Devised profiles of estimated earnings, losses, and medical expenditures.
• Prepared Notice of Entry of Judgment forms.
• Participated in 9-hour introduction to WESTLAW, a computer program for law offices.

LEGAL COURSEWORK (ABA approved program)
...Legal Research & Writing   ...Legal Concepts   ...Contract Law
...Litigation I, II   ...Real Estate Law   ...Corporate Law I, II
...Probate   ...Family Law   ...Wills, Trusts, & Estate Planning

RESEARCH
• As Administrator/Librarian of Nursing School Library:
  - Researched available medical texts and made recommendations to department heads.
  - Classified books by specialized coding system.
• As Bibliographer for the University of California's Technical Services Dept.:
  - Conducted ongoing detailed cross-checking of library holdings to minimize costly
    duplication of materials.

BUSINESS EXPERIENCE
As Secretary in family-owned antique furniture reproduction business in Seattle WA:
• Handled correspondence, phones, monthly inventories.
• Researched American and British sources of quality classic reproductions.
• Following sale of the business, co-managed the proceeds and assets of the firm.

WORK HISTORY
Fall 1989	**Paralegal Volunteer**	CITY ATTORNEY'S OFFICE, Hampton CA
May 1989	**Paralegal Intern**	CITY ATTORNEY'S OFFICE, Hampton CA
1973-present	**Assets Manager**	Managing and investing assets of Stanyan Ltd.
1967-73	**Partner/Secretary**	STANYAN LTD., antique reproductions firm
1961-66	**Librarian/Administrator**	NURSING LIBRARY
		Clark Hospital School of Nursing
1960-61	**Bibliographer**	TECHNICAL SERVICES DEPT.,
		University of California, Santa Cruz

EDUCATION & AFFILIATION
Paralegal Program - Hampton College, Hampton CA 1989
M.L.S., Library Science - University of California, Santa Cruz
B.A., Liberal Arts - Univ. of Vermont, Burlington
Member, Hampton Association of Legal Assistants

6
Working with Special Populations

6

Working with Special Populations

POPULATIONS

In this chapter "special populations" refers to categories of job hunters, who for various reasons, have unique needs and circumstances—people for whom our usual approach to resume writing may not be quite adequate. They might include: the underemployed, disabled, low-income or homeless, veterans, inmates and ex-inmates, long-term unemployed, younger and older workers, students, refugees and immigrants, ethnic minorities, people with minimal work history, reentry women, high school drop-outs or others with limited education, injured workers, and so on.

The needs of these clients challenge us to come up with innovative approaches to our work. This usually calls for creative use of language to present their abilities to full advantage. In some cases this could mean translating military jargon to its civilian equivalent, or job titles from another country to their job title equivalents here.

Quite often, working effectively with these clients may involve going beyond strictly resume writing—helping clients link up with, or become aware of, educational resources and volunteer opportunities to gain work experience, for example.

And always there is the issue of self-esteem to deal with, since job hunters who are unique in any way MAY see themselves as less competitive in the job market.

Ironically, *the more these special populations of job hunters differ, the LESS they differ,* when it comes to the factors in creating a great resume! What I mean is illustrated by this experience: I recently noticed—when I put together some guidelines for volunteer resume writers who work with the *homeless*—that the exact same guidelines would work equally well for the resumes of *another* group I work with: *laid-off senior executives!* This was a sobering revelation. It seems that the principles are fairly simple and universal, but getting them across to job hunters and resume writers is NOT so simple! As you launch into this chapter, you may want to refer back to **The Five Characteristics of a Good Resume** in Chapter 1 and **What Is a Resume?** in Chapter 2.

Just a few of the special population groups mentioned above are discussed in detail in this chapter:

- the underemployed
- college students
- ex-military
- inmates
- immigrants
- the homeless

This is only intended to open up an exploration of the issues and challenges for resume writers who work with special populations of job seekers. I would like to invite readers to expand on this beginning exploration through the *Resume Pro Newsletter* (see page 407).

Pairing Your Passion and Your Skill

If you happen to be blessed with the **talents that go into superior resume writing** (see page 18), AND you have a **passion to somehow help a particular population of people**, you're in an excellent position to make a BIG contribution to that group.

In this chapter you'll see how some other resume writers, counselors, and even student volunteers are **bringing together their PASSION and their WRITING SKILLS** to work with THEIR special populations. In all these cases, professionals and nonprofessionals, agency staff and volunteers, have all seen how desperately important it is for their clients to obtain meaningful work, AND how important a resume can be in that effort.

Remember, **a resume is one of the few job-search tools that nobody considers a luxury**, so if you are good at writing, AND you have a passion to help, resume writing could be a very **accessible** and gratifying channel for your energy.

My Special Population: The Underemployed

The special population that I consider MY specialty is perhaps not considered special at all because its problem is so widespread: These are the UNDERemployed. **The underemployed means, to me, those who are not able to connect with work that uses their highest level of skill,** work that could provide them a sense of job satisfaction and accomplishment. I relate to this population very intimately because I was IN it for so many years myself! So I have a particular empathy for those folks and tend to go out of my way to be helpful and supportive to them.

People who are underemployed are typically unhappy with their current jobs. They may feel it doesn't offer enough of a challenge (it's so boring) or they have the uneasy feeling they've gotten into the wrong line of business (I should have been a . . . .);

POPULATIONS

or they may be burnt out. On the other hand, quite often they are not at all clear about what they DO want to do.

This is why I make frequent use of the information interview or draft resume, which has been described at length in Chapter 3. (There are also two more sample draft resumes in this chapter, pages 117 to 119.) Clients use it to explore career options, presenting the resume either prior to or during an information interview. This draft resume has two other pluses:

- Helping to create it often clarifies the job hunter's thinking about careers with job satisfaction.
- It is usually a simple matter to alter this draft resume later for actual job applications.

PROBLEMS OF THE UNDEREMPLOYED

The typical problems of the so-called underemployed can include:

- ability, but lack of credentials
- lack of self-marketing skills, self-confidence, or self-esteem
- lack of focus on a clear goal
- naiveté about the job-search process
- naiveté about the world of work
- being in the wrong place or being there at the wrong time
- job discrimination related to a handicap or a personal characteristic

As a resume writer, I obviously can't address ALL the job-related problems suffered by my favorite special population. But still, I CAN MAKE A LOT OF DIFFERENCE (and so could you). Of the problems of underemployment listed above, for example, at least half can be greatly minimized by an EXCELLENT resume.

DEFINITION OF AN EXCELLENT RESUME

"Well," you might ask, **"what IS an excellent resume? And what does an excellent resume DO?"** You might further ask about the problems of the underemployed, or other special populations of job hunters.

We've already gone into this (see Chapter 2), but let me restate it, because an excellent resume can make more difference to the *under*employed than to other job hunters who are simply changing jobs.

- An excellent resume is one that paints a dynamic, appealing picture of the job hunter competently and successfully at work applying his preferred skills—and targets a future job where he could apply those same skills to something he "gives a damn about."
- An excellent resume can show how a person with no credentials could nevertheless get the job done. It does this by focusing on effective actions taken and measurable results.
- Developing an excellent resume is a focusing process that results in a clear statement of job goals—which is among the first few steps of an effective job search process.
- An excellent resume can minimize the impact of negative factors such as a ragged work history.
- An excellent resume dramatically improves a job hunter's self-esteem and self-confidence. *This COULD be its most valuable function!*

On the following pages are two examples of what I call "Information Interview" resumes prepared for two of my underemployed clients. The immediate **purpose of these resumes was to begin the process of exploring some new career directions** where their preferred skills could be put to better use. They planned to take the resume along at information interviews and get feedback on how effective the resume would be in their chosen new field.

LISA Q. ACADIA
459 Truman Street
San Francisco CA 94118
(415) 234-5678

Objective: Position as investigative assistant, involving
•**Field research and interviewing** •**Report writing** •**Data entry.**

SUMMARY OF QUALIFICATIONS
- Detail oriented, able to recognize and document important details.
- Skill in formulating interview questions and drawing out information.
- Proven ability to generate clear, concise reports and summaries.
- Perseverant in seeing a project through to completion.
- Very hardworking, responsible, and willing to learn.

RELEVANT EXPERIENCE & ACCOMPLISHMENTS
RESEARCH
As Registrar's assistant in a unique college allowing students to develop their own degree programs, serving as member of Graduation Contract Committee:
- **Researched** students' graduation contracts and their overall academic record, to assure that essential liberal arts degree requirements were met.
- **Negotiated** with students on the specific coursework to meet degree criteria, with responsibility to exercise a **high level of attention and discrimination, watching for biases and conflicts of interest** on the part of students and instructors.

REPORT WRITING & DOCUMENTATION
- **Wrote very exacting contracts**, accurately summarizing the precise agreement reached between Graduation Contract Committee and student, with special attention to eliminating any possibility of ambiguity.
- Attended conferences to **stay abreast of federal regulations,** advising foreign students of their visa status, and advising veterans on their eligibility for benefits.
- Currently **write concise summary reports** of patients' condition, **observing and assessing** emotional state, family dynamics, and physical health, as volunteer for Bayside Hospice.

INTERVIEWING
- **Conducted hundreds of telephone interviews** of potential clients, as intake interviewer for a clinic specializing in occupational stress:
  -**Made initial assessment** of the urgency of the call and eligibility of the caller for clinic's services.
  -**Drew out details** from caller, to **identify the essence of the problem**.
  -**Explained clinics services,** tailoring explanations to the sophistication and emotional condition of the caller.

DATA ENTRY
- **Entered and retrieved data** (student class schedules and personal information) on Hewlett-Packard computer terminal.
- **Entered and balanced invoice data** for accounting office of real estate investment company.

EMPLOYMENT HISTORY
9/91-present	**Intake Coordinator**	CORRO CLINIC, San Francisco (by assignment through Jan Olson Personnel, Inc.)
1983-91	**Registrar's Assistant**	UNIVERSITY OF PACIFIC, Office of the Registrar

EDUCATION & TRAINING
B.A., Humanities and Fine Arts - Creighmont College, UNIVERSITY OF PACIFIC
Some coursework in political science and constitutional law.

- References available on request -

STELLA Q. RHENQUIST
993 Lincoln Drive
Blairsville CA
(123) 456-7890

Objective: Administrator/coordinator position
involving marketing, PR, development, and/or program coordination

SUMMARY OF QUALIFICATIONS
- Broad experience in program administration.
- Quick learner; thrive in a dynamic, challenging environment.
- Ability to prioritize, delegate, and motivate.
- Work cooperatively with a wide range of people.
- Committed to high standards of performance.

PROFESSIONAL SKILLS & ACCOMPLISHMENTS

As Executive Director of ARTS FOR YOUTH (AFY), developed a small arts education organization into a recognized leader in the field, doubling the budget allocation, and tripling the programming to 730 offerings per year.

Program Design & Administration
- Developed several major new programs:
  -Young Audiences at the City Arts Museum of San Jose
  -Young Audiences at the School of Science
  -Blairsville Performing Arts Programs for Schools: a series for underprivileged children.
- Scheduled and coordinated all performances and workshops.
- Directed auditioning process for a celebrity "master class" event (open to all area public schools) selecting judges, and overseeing publicity.
- Supervised the development of curriculum materials for all school and special programs, hiring curriculum writers and reviewing/approving their work.

Marketing, PR, Community Relations
- Directed brochure design and production.
- Supervised public relations campaigns for special programs. Wrote and presented a proposal accepted by a major local retailer for sponsorship of advertising during Young Audiences Week.
- Secured TV and newspaper coverage for regular and special programming through press releases and phone contacts.
- Served on panels and planning committees, acting as liaison to the community, representing AFY and its performing artists.

Budgeting & Fund-Raising
- Authored successful proposals which won funding from major corporations and private foundations, for AFY programming.
- Developed and supervised organizational budget.

Personnel Supervision
- Oversaw small staff in clerical and program support functions.
- Coordinated volunteers, successfully keeping them involved in program support.
- Monitored program evaluation process, and advised artists on improving performance in response to audience feedback.

- Continued on page two -

STELLA Q. RHENQUIST

Page two

WORK HISTORY

1991-present	Family/estate management	
1990	**Public Relations Intern***	SOUTH BAY ART ASSOCIATIONS, San Jose
1989	**Client Services Rep**	CAREER CENTERS INC., San Jose
1988	Sabbatical year studying in New York and Israel	
1984-88	**EXECUTIVE DIRECTOR** (arts education organization)	ARTS FOR YOUTH of the BAY AREA, San Jose
1981-83	**Dance Teacher**	Jewish Community Center, Pleasant Valley
1979-80	Full time student	Rogers College, Berkeley
1974-78	**Dancer/Teacher**	LILLIE MODERN DANCE CO., Berkeley

* part time

EDUCATION & TRAINING

Business/Administration Courses:
- Fund-Raising - The Fund Raising School, San Jose
- Arts Administration - UC Berkeley Extension
- Intro to Computers - Oakland Adult Education

M.A., Dance - ROGERS COLLEGE, Berkeley, CA
B.A. - HILLER UNIVERSITY, Garden Grove, NY

Working with College Students

Resume writers who live near universities and colleges will most likely find themselves writing resumes for students, who will be seeking internships during their last two years in school or regular full-time jobs after graduating. My experience is that college students frequently harbor some very conservative notions about resumes, often reinforced by very conservative (even outdated) advice from their college's counseling department or placement center. Following that conservative advice will only yield them a bland, boring, "career obituary"-type resume that is barely distinguishable from all the OTHER bland, boring resumes of their classmates. (Can't you just see all the employment recruiters going directly to sleep "without passing Go," as they screen a stack of these lifeless documents?)

Fortunately, most students are flexible and open to fresh, new ideas. YOUR task, then, is to show them that there IS an alternative, and to help them create a resume that highlights their uniqueness and their marketable assets—one that doesn't put the recruiter to sleep.

ONE APPROACH TO STUDENT RESUMES

Here is an example of a relatively simple process for doing a resume with a student who has a clear job objective. The resulting resume, for Rachael Meny, took the resume writer and student about two hours to put together.

Rachael was a junior at Mills College in Oakland, and said she wanted help with a resume to apply for an internship—possibly with the American Civil Liberties Union (ACLU) or the office of the District Attorney (DA)—and might want to modify it later for other jobs during her student years.

Following are my working notes jotted down on the computer screen as I asked questions about the position Rachael was going for. Notice that I did not *necessarily* have to know anything about the kind of work she'd be doing, other than what she was able to tell me.

By asking what the job involved, I got her to focus on her skills and experience that would be *most relevant* to the new employer and the new position.

By inquiring what else she HOPED to be doing in the new job, I got her to identify *additional* skills she might want to include.

By asking what characteristics they'd be looking for, I got her to put herself in the shoes of the employer and to present her assets from the perspective of *their* needs and priorities.

I asked Rachael, "What exactly do you think you'll be doing in this internship?" I jotted down her reply, as follows:

a) Probable Tasks for ACLU

- basic research
- filing
- computer work
- typing memos, letters
- typing up/outlining data for court cases
- prepare fliers (use graphics)
- work with the public on ACLU issues . . . set up tables at major events, give out info
- participate in training workshops for speakers
- help train the potential speakers (explain what ACLU wants covered)
- interview clients

b) Probable Tasks for DA's Office

- basic "go-fer"
- research, filing, interviews for casework
- accompanying to court and being a "go-fer"
- legal filing of documents in court
- type legal documents

Then I asked her, "What else would you LIKE to have included in the job?" She came up with:

c) I Hope They'll Let Me:

- be exposed to actual clients
- do more legal research
- get exposure to the courtroom
- prepare presentations to the public

Finally I inquired, "What characteristics will they be looking for?" and suggested that she put herself in the employer's shoes for a minute. Her response:

d) What They'll Want

- dependability
- intelligence
- ability to communicate well with others
- trustworthiness
- knowing enough about what you're doing to do a good job
- writing skills
- ability to take the initiative on tasks
- ability to complete the tasks thoroughly

Then we kept all the above in mind as we chose the activities and wording for the resume. Before Rachael left, I printed out these "working notes" and gave them to her, along with the printed-out resume, which appears on page 122.

A similar process resulted in the resume for Liz Woods, which follows on page 123. The primary difference, from the resume writer's point of view, is that significantly more time was needed to create Liz's resume—about four and a half hours. We spent an hour just to identify and prioritize her areas of interest, and then to settle on a logical job objective for this resume. Taking all the time needed at the beginning, however, pays off in a stronger and more focused resume.

For yet a third example, see "Working with a Student," back in Chapter 2 on page 20.

POPULATIONS

RACHAEL E. MENY
2923 Carmel Way
Fairfield, CA 94533

(415) 123-4567

OBJECTIVE

Internship position with a private or public law agency,
providing experience and exposure in the field of criminal law.

HIGHLIGHTS

- Strong commitment to working toward a legal system that is universally available and equitable, working within the criminal law system to accomplish this end.
- Completed extensive college coursework in law.
- Intelligent and self-motivated; maintained a 3.8 GPA while holding down several jobs and volunteering in community service.

RELEVANT EXPERIENCE

1988-90

Full-time student, Mills College
Relevant coursework:
- Law & Society •Legal Aspects of Business •Psychology & Law •Social Inequality
- Court Systems of the Metropolitan Area •Public Policy Making Process

1989-present

BAWAR (Bay Area Women Against Rape)
Crisis Counselor - 10 hours per week
- Provided hot-line counseling 4-5 times each month in four-hour shifts, involving:
  - acute listening skills
  - ability to probe and discover the problem
  - providing information on community resources
  - advising on legal procedures and rights
  - interacting with law enforcement and medical agencies.

Aug '89-May '90
Aug '90-May '91

MILLS COLLEGE
Residential Assistant
- Counseled students on academic, personal, and crisis issues.
- Assessed students' interests and developed social and academic programs; arranged for speakers and logistics of these programs.
- Provided on-site regulation and management of student residence hall.

1989-present

PACIFIC GAS & ELECTRIC
Engineer's Aide/Field Clerk
(Full-time summers '89 and '90; part-time current academic year)
- Operated both Macintosh and IBM computers, implementing a complex computer test generation program.
- Familiar with a variety of software, including:
  -WordPerfect -Microsoft Word 4 -VolksWriter 4 -SuperCalc -Dreams -Newsmaster -Labels -Ability.
- Researched apprenticeship training files.
- Scheduled instructors' classes.
- Co-developed an organizational structure for the entire office.

EDUCATION

B.A. in progress (1992) - Mills College, Oakland
Major: **Political, Legal, and Economic Analysis** • Minor: Women's Studies

POPULATIONS

LIZ WOODS

P.O. Box 3289
Berkeley CA 94703
(510) 632-0206

OBJECTIVE

Position as activities/travel organizer. Available for:
- Sales/Promotion • Customer Service • Trip Logistics Coordinating
- Excursion Guide • Trip Photography and Meals

HIGHLIGHTS

- Able to personally model the company philosophy of unlimited challenge and opportunity for fun and adventure.
- Skill and experience in land and water sports -- providing an inspiration to customers to stretch their physical and psychological limits.
- Record of achievement in sales, promotions, and customer service.
- Professional attitude; loyal and dedicated; attentive to details that count.

RELEVANT SKILLS & EXPERIENCE

SALES & CUSTOMER SERVICE
- **Sold club memberships** for Club Natique:
  - **Led tours** of the club facilities for prospective members.
  - Served as skipper's assistant on **promotional sailing events**, handling the sails and ropes, assisting with navigation, and entertaining the prospects.
  - **Conducted cold-calls.**
- **Top Salesperson** for the Rusty Pelican; consistently won monthly prizes and awards.
- **Won major prizes** for increasing **sales** of bank services.

LOGISTICS & Trouble Shooting
- **Planned short and long-term trips** for Club Natique members.
- Provided **computer system training** and workflow **trouble-shooting** for Fidelity S&L.
- Assisted in **organizing a backpacking trip** for incoming Mills freshmen.

SPORT SKILLS
- Weight Lifting • Aerobics • Jogging •River Rafting •Rock Climbing/Rapelling
- Sailing •Skiing •Water Skiing •Backpacking •Horseback Riding •Tennis

COOKING
- Prepared unique gourmet meals for parties of 10; earned reputation as an excellent cook. Provided opportunities for guests to participate in the fun of meal creation.

PHOTOGRAPHY
- **Won two awards** for photographic excellence and contribution.
- **Photographed** sporting events for yearbook.

WORK HISTORY

1990 winter	*Trip Organizer*	MILLS COLLEGE Family Athletic Program, Oakland
1988-90	*Wait Person*	THORNHILL CAFE, Montclair
1988	*Wait Person*	THE CANTINA and MESA CAFE, Oakland
1987	*Photo Assistant*	HENRY LIM PHOTOGRAPHY, San Francisco
1987 summer	*Assistant trip leader*	MILLS COLLEGE Athletic Dept., Oakland
1984-86	*Cocktail Waitress and Benefits Rep,*	PARK EXCHANGE disco/lounge, San Francisco
1984	*Membership Sales*	CLUB NATIQUE sailing club, Alameda
1981-83	*Cocktail Waitress*	RUSTY PELICAN restaurant, Alameda

EDUCATION

B.A. Fall 1991, Liberal Arts, MILLS COLLEGE, Oakland CA
A.A., Humanities, MERRITT COLLEGE, Oakland CA
Coursework •Professional Photography •Occupational/Educational Photography
Memberships •Greenpeace •Big Green Initiative •KQED •Nature/Conservation Club

COLLEGE STUDENTS ON THEIR OWN
CREATE A "DAMN GOOD RESUME"

Lauren Vogel, a student at University of Texas at Dallas, chose the functional format for her resume, shown on page 125. Her resume advisor, Allen Krause of UTD's Career Planning & Placement Center, writes: "Lauren's problem was that she had neither prior management experience in an arts organization nor a degree in Arts Management. However, she had an extensive background of educational, vocational, and leadership achievements, so that it was only a question of her organizing them in terms that were meaningful to the arts organization administrator. After creating this resume, Lauren got feedback from the General Manager of the Dallas Symphony Orchestra (where she is a percussionist). He said her resume was 'dynamite.' He also provided her with numerous contacts and she was able to start job searching in earnest."

Henry Ostendorf, a student at San Francisco State University, needed a resume to accompany his request for a funding grant, to support the work of his brainchild, the Roving Resume Writers (see page 151). Given the nature of his project, Henry knew *his* resume had better be a *damn good* reflection of the kind of work he could do! And it is; the resume is on page 127.

POPULATIONS

LAUREN VOGEL

8534 Coppertowne Lane
Dallas, Texas 75243
(214) 348-1858

OBJECTIVE: Administrative / management position in an arts organization.

HIGHLIGHTS OF QUALIFICATIONS

★ Successful manager with 12 years experience in retail percussion sales.
★ Industry reputation for professionalism, expertise, and organization.
★ Proven record in increasing sales and customer base.
★ Excellent communication skills, both written and verbal.
★ Self-motivated, goal-oriented, and extremely well-organized; work well under pressure.
★ Dedicated to highest quality work.

PROFESSIONAL EXPERIENCE

Business Management

- Managed nationally-based mail-order percussion store, monitored processing of orders and shipments, and supervised five employees.
- Developed effective and efficient method of processing a large volume of orders.
- Built a reputation for the company as a leader in the percussion industry.

Administration

- Planned, prioritized, and supervised daily operations.
- Oversaw all facets of record keeping, involving banking, accounts receivable, and accounts payable.
- Prepared daily and monthly sales reports.

Sales

- Processed mail and telephone orders quickly and efficiently.
- Advised customers on the best products and value for their specific needs.
- Established highly effective relationships with customers on all levels, from the symphony player to the beginner.
- Calculated new pricing structure when necessary.

Customer Service

- Established a reputation for highly reliable and personalized service.
- Fostered repeat business by consistently providing quick, professional service.
- Processed returned merchandise promptly to satisfy the customer's needs.
- Guided out-of-town visitors on tours through the facilities.

— continued —

POPULATIONS

Special Events / Media and Publicity

- Addressed large and small groups at various conventions and clinics.
- Attended annual percussion convention and manned exhibit booth.
- As chairman of the Percussive Arts Society (PAS) Marching Forum:
    - Established new rules and format for the competition.
    - Communicated with participants via telephone and mail.
    - Executed the planned activities as scheduled and finished events on time.
    - Followed up with appropriate "thank yous" and publicity.
- Publicized various clinics and events with mailings and followed up with articles for inclusion in industry journals and publications.

Research and Writing

- Published over 30 articles, including three cover stories for *Modern Percussionist* magazine.
- Assembled information and pasted-up the camera ready copy for a 48-page semi-annual catalog/price list.
- Composed product information letters and quotations for customers.
- Prepared letters of reference for numerous customers and employees.

EMPLOYMENT HISTORY

1978 - 1990	Vice President/National Sales Manager	Lone Star Percussion
1984 - Present	Contributing Writer	*Modern Percussionist*
1979 - Present	Extra Percussionist	Dallas Symphony Orchestra
1979 - 1988	Percussionist	Dallas Ballet Orchestra

VOLUNTEER WORK

1987 - Present	President, Board Member	Copperfield Homeowners Assn.
1988	Chairman	PAS Marching Forum
1981 - 1987	President ('84-'87), Vice Pres. ('81-'84)	Texas Chapter PAS
1983 - 1985	Board of Directors	Percussive Arts Society (PAS)
1983	Percussion Instructor	Phantom Regiment Drum Corps

EDUCATION

B.A., Music; performance emphasis: percussion - Univ. of Texas at Dallas, 1982.
    Graduated summa cum laude.

- Resume written by Lauren Vogel, student at University of Texas at Dallas -

HENRY WILLIAM OSTENDORF
704 BUSH STREET, APARTMENT 301
SAN FRANCISCO, CALIFORNIA 94108
(415) 781-1019

OBJECTIVE
Coordinator of Roving Resume Writers Project

HIGHLIGHTS OF QUALIFICATIONS
- Over four years experience organizing students and enhancing community service programs.
- Maintain a close working relationship with staff and clients of social service agencies.
- A proven leader; effective administrator and program planner.

EXPERIENCE AND SPECIALIZED SKILLS

ADMINISTRATION AND PLANNING
- Founding member and senior staff person of a regional homelessness prevention program.
- Consistently achieved goals and objectives while establishing a multi-disciplinary homelessness education project on the SFSU campus involving students, faculty and staff.
- Initiated and delegated tasks for a regional newsletter: coordinated staff work plans, production budget, and distribution for first three issues (9000 copies).

VOLUNTEER TRAINING AND SUPERVISION
- Taught peer counseling and communication techniques to 14 students at campus volunteer center
- Pioneered the Roving Resume Writers, successfully utilizing volunteer labor to assist over 120 homeless and low-income people to market their job skills:
  - -formulated workable budgets   -recruited students from 9 campuses   -developed training materials -organized resume workshops in the community   -supervised 40 student volunteers.
- Developed curriculum and trained two student teachers to facilitate public education forums on housing policy, community organizing, and the prevention of homelessness.

COMMUNICATIONS
- Qualified in computer applications including word processing and desktop publishing.
- Authored funding proposals and comprehensive work progress reports.
- Articulate spokesman, increased media attention by issuing clear, concise press releases.

WORK HISTORY

Campus Projects Coordinator	Bay Area Homelessness Program, SF, CA	1989-present
Special Enumerator	US Census 1990, Follow-up count of Tenderloin SRO's	1990
Administrative Assistant	Department of Political Science/Urban Studies, SFSU	1987-1991
Summer Research Assistant	Bradley Inman, Real Estate Journalist, Oakland, CA	1988
Intern, San Joaquin Cty Master Plan	Sedway-Cook Associates, Environmental Design, SF, CA	1987-1988

EDUCATION

San Francisco State University, SF, CA	Career Counseling MS Program (Applicant)	entering 9/92
San Francisco State University, SF, CA	BA in Industrial Design, Minor in Urban Studies	1992
Pratt Institute, Brooklyn, NY	School of Architecture	1981-1985

- Resume written by Henry Ostendorf, student at San Francisco State University -

Working with Ex-Military

Some of us may be getting more requests for help from people returning to civilian life as the military continues to cut back and close bases around the country. Below, some advice is offered to resume writers by Joe Costa, who has applied his own past military experience to helping other servicemen and women make their transition. For the past five years he has been teaching job-search techniques to military personnel separating from the service—working through the State of California, veterans organizations, and community colleges

EX-MILITARY AND THEIR RESUMES

by Joe Costa

The present world political situation coupled with the massive U.S. budget deficit is causing a reduction in our military forces. Fewer servicemen and women are being asked to remain on active duty. The groups hardest hit by this reduction in force are the first-timers and those with more than twenty years of service.

To offer the best possible assistance to these new clients, we need to take aspects of their last employment into careful consideration. They are leaving a very structured environment.

They will have looked at resume-writing books and will probably have attempted to produce their own first resume. In all probability, this first resume will be in chronological format and loaded with military terminology.

Naturally, the chronological format will work well for a few. But the majority will need to look toward a functional or combination format. Others may need to go directly to a technical format.

The next hurdle is to "de-militarize" their draft resume. They will insist that their work description code will be understood by the civilian world. Not only are the codes NOT understood outside the military, neither are the ranks, pay grades, nor job titles.

So here's a bit of advice I would like to share: When producing a resume for a member of the military, **try your best to eliminate everything that sounds military**. If it sounds military or confusing to you and you don't understand it, how can you expect a civilian personnel manager to understand it? Also please **ask each and every client to prepare a complete listing of their collateral duties**. They often forget to mention these tasks. You will be surprised by the number of jobs held down by one individual. Each one of those collateral duties is usually a separate job in the civilian sector and worthy of note in a resume.

Good Resources

It is extremely important for the client to have a resume that is in ENGLISH, not in military terminology. To **assist in demilitarizing a service person's career**, the government has linked the military jobs to the *Dictionary of Occupational Titles'* nine-digit code. These codes have been incorporated in each service's personnel manuals.

The Department of Defense also published this information in their two-volume **Military Occupation Training Data (MOTD)**. This would be handy for anyone who is helping military people transition out and helping write resumes. The MOTD is available from: Defense Manpower Data Center, 1600 Wilson Blvd., Suite 400, Arlington, VA 22209.

For **Navy** personnel, ask around on the base for a copy of Appendix F of the Retention Team Manual. That appendix will provide a listing of all enlisted ratings. It describes the tasks of the ratings and lists the corresponding civilian jobs and DOT numbers (*Dictionary of Occupational Titles*). When your client is determined to talk to you in NECs (Navy Enlisted Classifications), you'll need a copy of NAVPERS 1806E. That's the manual for NECs and you will need section II. Naval officers can best be served with the manual for NOBCs (Naval Officer Billet Codes). NOBCs describe the officer's job. That should be more than you will ever need to assist Naval personnel.

The **Army** has a like set of instructions in their AR (Army Regulations) 600 series where all the MOS's (Military Occupational Specialty) are listed. This publication has three separate sections, one for enlisted, one for warrant officers, and one for officers.

Since the **Marine Corps** classifies its personnel like the Army, using MOS's, the Corps has a breakdown of

POPULATIONS

MOS's in their FMF Personnel Manual (Fleet Marine Force).

The **Air Force** is the service with which I am least familiar. They classify their personnel using AFSCs (Air Force Specialty Code). Generally I have found that ex-Air Force personnel are very capable of giving a complete description of the tasks normally performed by someone with their AFSC.

Another Good Resource

Texas resume writer Sherry Sheegog does a lot of these resumes for ex-military personnel, and recommended this paperback book, all about job search and resumes for people leaving the military: ***Marketing Yourself for a Second Career****—A Practical Guide for Military Personnel Who Seek a Career in Civilian Life,* published by The Retired Officers Association (TROA). The author, Colonel Doug Carter, USAF-Retired, is director of TROA's Officer Placement Service.

The book includes ten real-life sample resumes that are filled with action statements and accomplishments, translating military experience into civilian language. It also contains three cover letters, three broadcast letters, and even the successful job application letter that Leonardo da Vinci sent to the Duke of Milan in 1482! (da Vinci's letter is a timeless gem and is reprinted in this book on page 177.)

To order the book, send $3 to The Retired Officers Association, 201 N. Washington St., Alexandria, VA 22314-2529.

Several examples of resumes prepared for job hunters who were leaving, or had left, military service appear on the following pages.

JOHN M. HAMMELL

207 REDWOOD CIRCLE
HARKER HEIGHTS, TEXAS 76543
(817) 287-3700

OBJECTIVE LAW ENFORCEMENT/SECURITY MANAGEMENT

QUALIFICATIONS

Twenty-two years of strong law enforcement and security management experience, including supervisory positions in security operations, criminal investigations, corrections, administration and training. Professionally challenged, not constrained, by new operating procedures, personnel, geographic location, environment and culture. Available for worldwide relocation; extensive experience in the Middle East and Asia. Excellent credentials as a decision maker, problem solver and innovator.

EDUCATION

Master of Arts in International Relations
Georgetown University
Bachelor of Science in Political Science
University of the State of New York
Bachelor of Science in Criminal Justice
University of Nebraska
Federal Bureau of Investigation National Academy Course

EXPERIENCE HIGHLIGHTS

LAW ENFORCEMENT

SUPERINTENDENT, MILITARY POLICE - Coordinated and supervised personnel management, intelligence, operations, logistics, communications-electronics activities, budget forecasting and planning for an organization of over 550 military police personnel and 228 support personnel who provide law enforcement and confinement services to a community of 125,000.

CHIEF OF POLICE - Directed all law enforcement activities involving U.S. military personnel in a 500-square-mile area, to include patrol, drug, vice and other investigations, special operations, administrative management, and coordination with foreign national police, customs service and other police agencies.

SECURITY TRAINING

PERSONAL PROTECTION - Trained and equipped the personal bodyguards of the Crown Prince of the Kingdom of Saudi Arabia.

SPECIAL OPERATIONS - Planned for, equipped, and trained counter-terror and other special forces units. Responsible for the daily security of 300 embassy employees and family members. Developed comprehensive training program for the counter-terror unit and coordinated the equipment acquisitions and mobile training teams required.

SECURITY TRAINING -

EXPLOSIVE ORDNANCE - Commanded a five-nation multinational training task force in Pakistan, providing explosive ordnance disposal (EOD) training to Afghan paramilitary personnel. Coordinated training of EOD teams, explosive detection dog teams, survey and reconnaissance teams, and mechanical mine clearance teams. Coordinated training, support and administration with the United Nations, embassies of donor nations, and non-government organizations and contractors.

FACILITY MANAGEMENT

DIRECTOR, CORRECTIONAL FACILITY - Directed the security operations, administrative management, health, welfare, training and discipline of 350+ serious offenders at a military prison facility.

SECURITY MANAGEMENT

SECURITY COORDINATOR, UNITED NATIONS - Directed the daily security operations of offices and residences of all personnel employed by United Nations agencies and their families in a 5-nation area of the Middle East. Prepared all United Nations evacuation and security plans for the Middle East.

CHIEF, ECONOMIC CRIME INVESTIGATIONS - Directed all economic crime investigations within the U.S. Army involving military and civilian employees and civilian contractors.

ADMINISTRATION

CHIEF, POLICE ADMINISTRATION - Supervisor of administration of all police records and reports; and coordinated with the United States Magistrate's Court for a community of over 75,000.

WORK HISTORY
1990/91:   Commander, Military Training Mission, Pakistan
1989/90:   Deputy Commander, Military Police
1987/89:   Program Manager, Special Operations
1983/85:   Commander, Maximum/Medium Custody
1981/82:   Security Coordinator, United Nations Agencies
1977/81:   Chief, Economic Crime Investigation
1974/75:   Provost Marshall, assignment in Korea
1972/73:   Chief, Police Administration

AFFILIATIONS

International Association of Chiefs of Police
American Society for Industrial Security
International Association of Airport & Seaport Police
FBI National Academy Association

POPULATIONS

- Resume Writer: Sherian Sheegog -

PATRICIA HEMMINGWAY
14 Lucas Rd, #A11
Kansas City, KA 00432
(201) 702-3682

Objective: Analyst position, targeting productivity or organizational development

Highlights of Qualifications
- Strong analytical skills, with exceptional attention to detail.
- Successful in establishing productive work relationships.
- Thoroughly explore all avenues and options in solving problems.
- Positive, professional attitude; committed to excellence.
- Outstanding presentation skills, both written and spoken.

PROFESSIONAL EXPERIENCE

Problem Solving / Needs Analysis
- Developed wide-ranging recommendations for cost-effective solutions:
  - decreased shop labor costs 21% through personnel reallocation;
  - improved inventory control through establishing optimum quantities for stock on hand, and a regular schedule for inventory;
  - improved personnel accountability by redefining responsibility for essential functions.
- Streamlined motor pool's administrative procedures, saving money, space and time by identifying & eliminating needless steps & computerizing the process.
- Created first-ever comprehensive picture of Presidio road facilities, quantifying and consolidating historical data, maps, blueprints and past studies.

Cost/Benefit Analysis
- Saved over $ half million for government offices:
  - gathered and analyzed cost data and documentation provided by suppliers;
  - made formal presentation to upper management;
  - recommended conversion from lease to purchase of WANG word processing and other equipment.

Presentation/Communication
- Developed highly effective presentation outlining results of a work productivity study, contributing to the adoption of over 80% of my recommendations.
- Served consistently as study team's preferred presenter, delivering all team briefings to top management, using audio visual aids.
- Delivered informational talks on study results and newly adopted procedures, to:
  - employee groups - administrative units - office personnel - managers.

Organizational Development
- Developed working knowledge of evaluation techniques:
  - work sampling   - operational audit   - group timing technique
  - engineered and non-engineered standards   - technical estimate

Language
- Interpreted negotiations and translated documents regarding the marketing of an imported French soft drink. Provided translation for technically complex quality control meetings.

- continued -

EMPLOYMENT HISTORY

1989-present	Management Analyst	U.S. ARMY, Kansas City
1988-89	Administrative Asst.	U.S. ARMY, Kansas City
1985-88	Interpreter/Tour Guide	Freelance/self employed - Kansas City
1983-85	Tour Director/bilingual	SEASONAL TOURS - Kansas City
1981-83	Sales Assistant	STRONGS & PERRY STOCKBROKERS - Kansas City

EDUCATION & TRAINING

M.A., French - KANSAS STATE UNIVERSITY, 1987
B.A., Comparative Literature - KANSAS STATE UNIVERSITY, 1985

Management Engineering courses:

- Planning & Conducting Management Audits
- Administrative Systems Analysis & Design
- Economic Analysis for Decision Making
- Work Methods and Standards
- Organization Planning
- Work Planning & Control Systems
- Human Behavior in Organizations
- Efficiency Reviews

POPULATIONS

ELIZABETH ANDERSON
4949 First Avenue
San Leandro CA 94000
(510) 700-6617

Objective: Management position in a non-profit organization.

HIGHLIGHTS OF QUALIFICATIONS
- Six years successful supervisory and management experience.
- Resourceful and self-confident; get the job done, and do it well.
- Strong interpersonal and communication skills.
- Extensive experience in design & implementation of training programs.
- Remain calm and work well under demanding conditions.

PROFESSIONAL EXPERIENCE

Management
- Established training programs:
  - Wrote and published yearly training calendars;
  - Located and scheduled instructors for weekly classes in military skills;
  - Coordinated training for personnel dispersed over 1.7 million miles;
- Planned, coordinated and conducted management conferences attended by officers from all over the country.
- Managed a small convenience store, overseeing orders and deliveries, and supervising three employees.

Supervision
- Exercised total supervisory responsibility for a unit of 22 technical security personnel:
  - Organized the unit into teams and designated the first-line supervisors;
  - Established an evaluation program, utilizing quarterly written reports;
  - Directed field operations, including planning, budgeting, travel and housing arrangements.
- Successfully planned, organized and led field training missions in a "real-world" environment, ensuring adequate provisions and operational equipment, and providing direction and supervision for 30-40 trainees for up to three weeks.

Written & Oral Communication
- Made presentations and briefings to officials to get approval and funding for operations.
- Wrote and presented information briefings to peer officers to maximize utilization of resources.
- Effectively counseled team leaders and supervisors.
- Authored award recommendations for subordinates that consistently won approval.
- Compiled and edited comprehensive activity reports from subordinate units for national publication.

WORK HISTORY

1991	Administrative Asst.	HIRE OPTIONS Career Center - Oakland
1972-90	Chief, Technical Security Branch	US ARMY - Santa Barbara
"	Battalion Plans & Training Officer	"
"	Chief, Collection Mgt. Section	US ARMY - Germany
"	Platoon Leader	"
1970-72	Student	
1968-69	Manager	PACKHARD CORP. - Springfield IL
1973-74	Admin.Asst/Bookkeeper	ATLANTA BANK & TRUST - Plains IL

EDUCATION

B.A., German - Illinois State University, Springfield IL

- Resume writer: Yana Parker -

CHARLES I. STEIN
12702 Califa Street
North Hollywood, California 91607
(818) 762-8446

A uniquely qualified Computer Systems Analyst, whose expertise includes: knowledge of Local Area Networks (LAN), Systems Selections for optimum results, hands-on familiarity with many Operating Systems & Languages, Quality Control, Program & Financial Management, plus Leadership qualities honed by six years as a U.S. Air Force Officer

SUMMARY OF QUALIFICATIONS

- ☐ A decision maker & problem solver; innate ability and knowledge to identify actual/potential problems, & to create & implement effective solutions
- ☐ Successfully plans, organizes, implements, & supervises several detail-oriented, multi-faceted projects simultaneously with minimum of supervision
- ☐ Goal-oriented; determined & motivated to succeed, however great the challenge
- ☐ Fair, patient, & "team" approach to management & teaching, instills confidence, achieves & maintains high morale, and assures highest level of productivity
- ☐ Quality & Cost Conscious; completes all projects within schedule and either within or lower than estimated budget

OUTSTANDING ACHIEVEMENTS

U. S. AIR FORCE, WRIGHT-PATTERSON AIR FORCE BASE, Ohio (1985 - 1991)

- **LAN Systems Manager**
  - ✓ Initiated, designed, installed, & managed LAN, achieving maximum benefits for 600 person organization;
  - ✓ Created & developed operating plan; established software inventory to baseline assets
  - ✓ Conceived, developed, and instructed classes in computer applications
  - ✓ Improved financial forecasting by automating tracking and report systems
- **Cost Estimator**
  - ✓ Successfully planned, acquired & managed all program finances
  - ✓ Estimated and negotiated military transports & delivery equipment
  - ✓ Automated tracking programs for funding of diverse projects
- **Project Officer**
  - ✓ Saved Government millions of dollars by cost-conscious negotiations, including aircraft purchases, transport upgrades, travel costs, computers, etc.
  - ✓ Automated program scheduling, tracking, & Proposals for Mission Support Aircraft

INDEPENDENT COMPUTER CONSULTANT (1990 - PRESENT)

- ✓ Advises corporate & private clients as to which system will best fill needs, and instructs them on complete and correct application usage

Computer Expertise:

OperatingSystems: MS-DOS, WINDOWS 3.0, MAC-DOS, UNIX, DCA 10Net
Machines: MS-DOS SYSTEMS, MACINTOSH, AT&T 3B2
Languages: BASIC
Programs: MS Excel, Word for Windows, Enable, Lotus 123, Wordperfect 5.1, Harvard Graphics, DBase III+, MS Powerpoint, Aldus Pagemaker, Superbase 4 Windows, Ami Pro

Education:

MS: Aeronautical Science (Embry-Riddle Aeronautical University, FL...1991)
BA: Political Science: (California State University, Northridge, CA...1983)

References Available Upon Request

POPULATIONS

Working with Inmates

Although I wrote the following letter to answer questions about resume writing for ex-offenders, you'll see that the advice applies to any resume: always emphasize job satisfaction, sense of accomplishment, and pride.

LETTERS

To: Dianne E. Paroli/JTPA
Commonwealth of Pennsylvania
Bureau of Corrections
State Correctional Institution
Muncy, PA

Dear Diane:

In your last letter you mentioned the problem of convincing ex-offenders that they had something to contribute to the employer. The contributions that you mentioned—being punctual, having completed a certificate program, offering some job tax credits, and federal bonding—are the kind of benefits that COULD be included at the TOP of the resume, just beneath the objective, in a special paragraph I call a "Summary of Qualifications."

Next you mention a lot of moaning and groaning from your people about having to write down every single thing for a chronological resume. Maybe if there was more of a focus on writing down things that gave the ex-offender a sense of accomplishment and pride, they might enjoy it more. They might even come up with some examples that were from sources other than their jobs, and those examples could be equally important and a whole lot more gratifying to include on their resume. And MAYBE it would even help get them a better job, in the long run. So you may want to try that approach: Ask them to "Write down everything you can think of that you EVER DID that gave you a sense of pride and accomplishment," including things that other people appreciated and said were valuable to them.

You asked about people who were working on their GEDs. My thought is that you don't need to mention the high school they attended when referring to their GED. And I agree with the people who said you don't necessarily need a zip code on your resume. The resume is really a MARKETING PIECE, it's not an official document. If they need official documents for anything, I think those should be separate.

Next, the issue of an unrealistic job objective. You cited the case, for example, that an ex-inmate wants a job as a nurse's aide or some other position that they're prevented from having by law. In that case, I think you might ask them, **"What IS it about that job that attracts and interests you?"** Help them identify all the appealing characteristics of that job. THEN the research for them would be, **"What OTHER kind of job could provide that same appeal, but WOULD be legally acceptable?"**

 One of the last things you mentioned was people having a job objective but no related training or work history, or feeling stuck in jobs like waitressing and housekeeping because that's what they've always done in the past.

What I would suggest is to have as many different possible tricks up your sleeve as you can, and try them all. For some people one thing will work, and for other people something else will work. For example, visualizing (persistently and systematically imagining every detail of being in a more ideal situation) works for some people and not for others, but I would have it available as one of the things to try. Information interviewing (making some contact outside with people who have a job similar to what you want) is another route to try. That's certainly a lot harder when people are incarcerated! But they've got to do it; they've got to make that break to the outside world.

Another of the little tricks I like to use is having my client write an imaginary letter. They pretend it is now one week  AFTER they've started some really fine job that they love, and they're writing to a good friend of theirs, describing their workday in great detail. That helps them begin to imagine themselves in the new situation, and they find it's a fun thing to do, even if they are a little resistant at first.

Assemble a whole lot of different tricks, all of which are aimed at breaking their mental pattern (believing that these old jobs are the only way to go), and have them try the different techniques until something works.

Sometimes a spiritual perspective is welcomed. For example, "unemployment" can be viewed as a kind of ASSIGNMENT from the Great Spirit. Let's say my assignment is: to make a contribution to anything positive and constructive that is going on in the world. Once I know what I could contribute, the part of it that I have to figure out NEXT is how to deliver my contribution in such a way that people perceive its value and will provide me money to live on!

Or, you could take a very practical give-and-take approach to linking the new job hunter and the world he or she will be going back to. For example, there are lots of PROBLEMS in the world to be solved, and if your client could get excited about one of those problems, and get into a problem-SOLVING mode, that would be great. Encourage them to look "out there" and begin to develop solutions to problems they'd enjoy working on, and aim for THAT as their next career.

One last observation: I've discovered that it seems to make a much more exciting and interesting resume if you take a future-oriented approach. I get my clients to look at their resume as a sort of word picture of the NEXT job rather than a word picture of their prior jobs. But of course this word picture of the future job is created out of bits and pieces (the most RELEVANT bits and pieces!) drawn from the past.

The resume starts out with the name, address and job objective, and right beneath that we might say, "Relevant Experience." And under that there usually will be three or four paragraphs, each labeled with the name of a skill area that is essential to the new job objective. Then, under each skill title, one-liners describe exactly what the person has already done that demonstrates the client's experience and skill in that area.

We end up with a word picture that describes the FUTURE rather than the past. Even though a lot of the data comes FROM the past, the way it's selected and presented changes the focus. Not surprisingly, this approach also makes the resume writing process (and the result) a lot more interesting to the job hunter because the focus is on the NEW JOB, what they want to do in that new job, and how they could show that they really CAN do it.

I also make it a rule—in describing what a person did in the past—to avoid describing experiences that the person did NOT enjoy doing. The same goes for work they enjoyed THEN but don't want to do again. Every one of the one-liners has to be something that the person ENJOYED DOING, gave them a sense of satisfaction, and is something they would like to do again in the future. Now when you limit it to that criteria, the resume gets much, MUCH more interesting!

Sincerely, Yana Parker

[*Yes, it's a name freak's find—Diane Paroli really DOES work with inmates. I didn't make it up. —yp*]

Arlene Q. Silvernail

P.O. Box 180 • Muncy, PA 17756
(717) 546-3171, Ext. 331
Leave message with Dianne Paroli, Counselor

OBJECTIVE: Automobile Mechanic

HIGHLIGHTS OF QUALIFICATIONS
- Nearly 4000 hours of auto mechanic training completed.
- Able to work well without supervision.
- Enthusiastic and committed; a go-getter who doesn't quit until the job is done right.
- Enjoy challenging work.

WORK HISTORY

Pennsylvania Department of Labor and Industry
Joint Apprenticeship and Training Council, Harrisburg, PA

Automobile Mechanic Apprenticeship   1989 -1991
Completed 3,977 of 6,000 hours.

Vehicle Repair (automobiles and trucks)
• Operated hydraulic jack, removed and disassembled units such as engines, transmissions and differentials to be repaired.
• Inspected parts for wear using micrometers, calipers and thickness gauges. Repaired and replaced parts such as pistons, rods, gears and valve bearings.
• Rebuilt crankshafts and cylinder blocks, removed faulty units from vehicles, and replaced worn and broken parts.

Brake Adjuster/Repairer
• Repaired and overhauled brake systems.
Replaced defective wheel cylinders using a honing gun. Removed and replaced brake shoe units, opened valves on hydraulic brakes to bleed air from line, replaced and repaired line and also adjusted brakes. Checked fluid in master cylinder.

Tune Up Mechanic
• Tuned engines to insure efficient operation, removed spark plugs, took compression test, set spark gap with feeler gauge, installed new plugs, inspected distributor breaker points for wear and pits, replaced or reset points. Checked ignition timing using timing light, adjusted timing. Adjusted carburetor needle setting using vacuum gage or oscilloscope, set valve tappets using gauge or dial indicator, removed fuel pump, examined battery and connections, adjusted and repaired fan belts and water pumps.

Electrician's Helper   1991 - 1992
Repaired and replaced light fixtures and switches.

Truck Driver Helper   1988 - 1989
Assisted truck driver in loading and delivery.

- Resume writer: Dianne Paroli -

COUNSELING INMATES

by John Ellis

When I counsel inmates, I always encourage them to **seek additional education.** If they did not have a high school diploma or its equivalent, I tell them to sign up for GED classes. I also stress the importance of additional education—either college study, computer training, or vocational courses. You would be surprised at the variety of free educational programs that are available to New York state inmates. Even the college programs don't cost a penny.

An Inmate's Resume

The educational pursuits help inmates to avoid those embarrassing gaps in one's employment history that incarceration can cause. Instead of writing on a resume:

1980-85   Hudson Correctional Facility, Hudson, NY

an inmate could write:

      EDUCATION
1980-85   B.S. in Education, Empire State College,
            Hudson, NY

      WORK EXPERIENCE
1980-82   Carpenter, Hudson, NY
1982-85   Carpentry Crew Foreman, Hudson, NY

Most inmates had jobs in the correctional facilities that they could also include on a resume. These jobs include clerk, cook, plumber, carpenter, recreation assistant, mechanic, and gardener. I encourage inmates to **seek jobs within the facility that will help their career plans and goals.**

Incarceration and Employers

The important thing is for an inmate to **make constructive use of their time** during incarceration. Chances are that an employer will find out about the incarceration. So instead of lying or making excuses, it would be much better for the ex-offender to say that they made a mistake, and paid their debt to society. But, most importantly, they became a better person and a better potential employee.

No Lying

I advise inmates and parolees not to lie about their incarceration, but also not to volunteer any information that is not requested. It is also very important for them to know what are legal and illegal questions during an employment interview. For example, an employer may ask about their conviction record, but not about their arrest record. If the subject of incarceration does come up, then I advise them to highlight the positive aspects, such as educational accomplishments and work experiences while incarcerated.

John Ellis
Assistant Director, Career Services
College of Saint Rose
Albany, NY

POPULATIONS

Working with Immigrants

Three professionals who write resumes as a part of their work, here discuss the issues that are unique in helping their special population: immigrants. Their observations will provide some insight and a perspective for resume writers considering working with immigrants.

Like the ex-military job hunters who need to translate their work experience into "civilian-ese," job hunters from other countries need to learn to translate each of their old job titles into its American equivalent. That is a tough assignment for newcomers.

Complicating the matter further are social and cultural transitions that can be profound. For example, in communist Russia, Ellis Orsay points out, "You were 'sent' to your first job directly after completing school—the government figured it all out for you. And then it was not uncommon for people to stay at the same job for over twenty years."

Thus, resume writers and counselors may find that they have to insert a kind of "crash course" on the American World of Work into their sessions with these clients. Otherwise, concepts such as "a resume is a *marketing* piece" will make no sense to the immigrant job hunter.

WORKING WITH RUSSIAN EMIGRÉS

by Ellis Orsay

I work with newly arrived emigrés from the former Soviet Union providing vocational counseling, resume writing, and job preparation classes at the Palo Alto, California, Jewish Vocational Service. I would like to share some of these issues with you and some of the solutions I've arrived at.

There are **three main concerns that I have as a counselor with regard to the job readiness** of the clientele I serve: skill level, how much time is available, and English proficiency.

Skill Level

My clients generally fall into the following categories:

- **Need to Upgrade.** Most of the clients I work with are highly educated and hold degrees in higher education. However, even those who were engineers or computer programmers in Russia do not have immediately transferrable skills, primarily because Russian technology lags behind that in the United States.

- **Overqualification.** If the problem is not an inadequacy in skill level, then it is overqualification. Often I help someone in their mid-forties who has twenty-odd years of experience, and a series of promotions (perhaps a former department head with several patents). But because of low language proficiency, they are faced with the likely prospect that their first job will be entry level. This is normally not a problem for most of my clients; the majority are thankful to be here and content to work their way up. But an employer certainly looks askance at someone in this age bracket who, at least on paper, has shown very little upward mobility.

- **Need to Retrain.** Finally, I work with folks whose experience just does not quite translate, like chess coaches, ballerinas, or physics and math teachers who, despite the desperate need for their services in our schools, do not yet possess the language proficiency. For these, retraining is in order. That is largely a problem to be dealt with by the vocational counseling unit.

Time Available

Before I outline how I go about addressing these problems, I must mention an element of utmost importance in this whole equation: *Time*. My task is to help these folks find their first job *in as little time as possible*, mainly because of financial constraints. They are on a four-month funded cycle after which—if employment is not found—most are eligible for a special welfare program. They are, however, quite opposed to this handout alternative.

English Proficiency

I work with people whose mastery of English ranges from zero to near-native. I speak Russian and have a good number of Russian translators who help me out when I'm in a jam. For the most part communication between me and the client isn't the issue—it's **communication in the job interview or workplace that is of crucial importance.** All my clients attend English as a Second Language (ESL) programs in their communities, and though we are thankful for them, most are overcrowded and/or not sufficiently intensive.

Remedies

- **The Resume.** When writing a resume, I am faced with a variety of challenges. One is to **accurately portray skills and qualifications** while attempting to **bridge the gap between the client's reality and what the job market/job description demands.** Normally this entails over- or undercompensating to make a fit possible. That's *on paper.*

- **The Job Developer.** I have a capable and effective job developer who is responsible for conveying the job hunter's skills and qualifications to a potential employer *in person* (or at least over the phone). We always try to directly contact employers, to establish a rapport and advocate for our clients. This direct contact method is optimum and has proven to make the critical difference, especially when a client's skill level is in question.

- **Mentoring.** We have established a mentor program where we match up clients with a professional in their field (or as close a match as possible). This gives the client much needed contact with conversational and work-specific English where expert advice is given and contacts are shared, both with the client and with our office.

- **Interview Preparation.** We also provide interview preparation classes to all our clients regardless of their language level.

- **General Help.** Our program volunteers help the clients in all sorts of ways. They provide conversational English practice and support, take emigrés to appointments or shopping, provide job leads and/or contacts.

WORKING WITH RUSSIAN ENGINEERS IN BOSTON

Across the country, we have another resume writer working with immigrants. Louis Zirin is a retired engineer who does volunteer work in the Boston area, helping immigrant Russian engineers with their job search. "Besides taking them to libraries at MIT and the Boston Public Library to show them the various newspapers and journals," he writes, "I also teach them technical English and help them write letters and resumes."

Louis advises his clients to list their accomplishments in a chronological format, and he wrote asking my views on this. I told him that I think each format has its strengths, depending on the circumstances. But more important than the FORMAT is this: Be sure it is the workers' **accomplishments** that are made prominent, not just their job duties.

Louis's engineers will be facing stiff competition, so their resumes need to be outstanding. And since the whole concept of "marketing yourself" and competing for jobs is relatively new to them, he will have to teach his Russian engineers to "think accomplishments," and to ask themselves:

- What did I do that made things more efficient and more profitable, or produced a better-quality product?
- How did I distinguish myself from someone doing mediocre work?
- What was unique about my contribution to the work?

Two of the Russian engineers' resumes appear on the following pages. Of Natalya Arkatova, Louis reports: **"Within two and a half months of her arrival, she obtained six interviews and a job with this resume"**—which is very unusual, as many Russians have not had any interviews at all. The factors in her favor were that she is a female (many companies are making an effort to hire women) and her English was very good from the start. She seemed to have a knack for describing the organization she worked at in the old USSR, which is a good talent for Russians to develop, because most American employers know very little about workplaces in Russia.

GREGORY A. TRESTMAN
17-19 West Baltimore Street, Apt. 41
Lynn, Massachusetts 01902
(617)593-3379

Objective

A position as power supply design engineer.

Summary of Qualifications

Seventeen years of experience with research, design and development of electronic power supplies for gas discharge and pulse devices such as lasers and high intensity lamps. In-depth knowledge of principles and equipment of power conversion.

Experience

1974 - 1991

DEPARTMENT OF RESEARCH & DEVELOPMENT
Tajik University, Dushanbe, USSR

As **Group Design Chief** of electronic power supplies:
• Developed new concepts for mid-capacity (0.5 to 50 kW) power supplies with high-frequency conversion sections for gas discharge and pulse devices. These concepts included the following:
— Resonant high-efficiency conversion of electrical energy.
— Non-ballast, high-efficiency power supply for gas discharge devices and charging of power capacitors with supplies of impulse power.
— Methods of increasing the capacity of power supplies by paralleling conversion sections.

On the basis of these concepts, developed:
• Stabilized power supply for an argon laser with capacity to 12 kW, efficiency 97%.
• Stabilized power supplies for short-arc xenon lamps with capacities of 1 and 3 kW and efficiency of 92%.
• Power supply for impulse gas discharge lamp with frequency range of 1 Hz to 1 KHz.

Also initiated work in the following areas:
• Power supplies for impulse discharge tubes for solid lasers.
• Power supplies for industrial CO_2 lasers with capacities up to 20 kW.
All power supplies developed utilized air cooling, are compact, and are lightweight.

Education

M.S. Degree in Physics
Tajik University, Dushanbe, USSR, 1973

Patents

• Thirteen patents concerning the conversion of electrical energy and electrical supply of gas discharge and pulse devices.

Personal

Permanent resident of the U.S. with full Immigration and Naturalization Service authorization for employment.

- Resume writer: Louis Zirin -

POPULATIONS

143

NATALYA Q. ARKATOVA

475 Park Street
Hartford, CT 06101

(302) 123-4567

SUMMARY
: Experienced **design and research Electrical Engineer** in the areas of high-voltage power systems, transmission lines and substations, electromagnetic field calculations, evaluation of environmental consequences, and safeguards of electric systems and services.

EDUCATION
: Moscow Polytechnical Institute; Moscow, U.S.S.R.
M.S., Electrical Engineering (equivalent) 1976
Concentration in Electrophysical Engineering

EXPERIENCE

1980-1991
: RESEARCH AND DESIGN INSTITUTE OF HIGH VOLTAGE POWER SYSTEMS AND ELECTRIC NETWORKS; Moscow, U.S.S.R.
One of ten subsidiaries of the National Research Institute for Power Systems, doing research for national and local power systems, large power consumers, and foreign countries.

Scientific Associate, High Voltage Laboratory 1985-1991

- Calculated electromagnetic fields and how to minimize various electric losses in high-voltage lines.
- Researched new designs of high-voltage lines to increase capacity and to reduce losses.
- Developed protective devices (electric screens) to guard high-voltage (up to 750kV) substation operating staff from impact of electric fields.
- Designed environmental protection from potential hazardous impact of electric fields near high-voltage overhead lines (330-1150kV).

Senior Electrical Engineer, Large Power System Design Group 1980-1985

- Implemented engineering designs of high-voltage power systems 110kV and above.
- Planned for future expansion of power distribution in high-voltage systems and networks.
- Performed complex electrical computations for planning system development-- power flow under normal and abnormal conditions, voltage and load limitations, voltage drop, system stability and short circuit currents.

1976-1979
: INSTITUTE OF ELECTRICAL MACHINES; Moscow, U.S.S.R.
Research Institute developing prototypes and models of engines and generators.

Research Engineer

- Tested insulation in electric engines and generators. Research of aging in insulation materials.

PERSONAL
: Fluent in English. Permanent resident of the U.S. with full Immigration and Naturalization Service authorization for employment.

- Resume writer: Louis Zirin -

POPULATIONS

WORKING WITH ASIAN IMMIGRANTS

by Rhonda D. Findling

One of the most dramatic changes occurring in the makeup of the U.S. workforce is the entrance of Asians in increasing numbers. The government's Bureau of Labor Statistics projects Asians will be one of the fastest growing groups in the labor force between 1986 and the year 2000.

In assisting any special population with their job search, it is important to learn about the history and culture of the clients we are serving. I would like to use the case of a Cambodian client with whom I worked to illustrate this uniqueness, and demonstrate the importance of learning about the specific background of our clients.

When I worked as a job developer at an agency in Oakland that served Southeast Asian refugees, a young Cambodian man, Sophal, came in wanting help finding a job in the nursing field. Sophal was just graduating from high school and was accepted to the nursing program at the local community college. He needed a job to help supplement welfare and support his younger brother and sister. He was their guardian since his parents were killed in the "holocaust" in Cambodia.

Without knowing anything about the history of Cambodia, one might assume it would be difficult to help a recent high school graduate with limited English

skills find a nursing job. My research on Cambodia revealed the following:

1) Many Cambodian refugees in the U.S. came from rural backgrounds with an education level significantly lower than their North American counterparts;

2) Most had survived the Pol Pot years in Cambodia, meaning they worked in forced labor camps and witnessed the murders of many of their own people including immediate relatives;

3) Most escaped by foot to Thailand through land-mined jungles;

4) Most lived for several years in Thai refugee camps where children went to school and those old enough to work were employed by the International Committee of the Red Cross;

5) Most lived for six months in a refugee resettlement center in the Philippines prior to being routed to a Western country, and were given language lessons relative to the country they were being sent;

6) Upon immigration, most Cambodian kids' birth dates were changed by several years (birth records from Cambodia had been destroyed, so the INS could not challenge the family's word) to allow them to get into schools here and thus "catch up" with their U.S. counterparts.

About Resumes

What does all this mean in terms of putting together a resume? For one thing, I learned that Sophal was not a teenager, but a twenty-six-year-old with nursing education and experience. While in the Thai refugee camps, he worked in the local clinic as a nurse's aide. He was trained by the International Committee of the Red Cross and given courses in basic nursing, prenatal and infant care, anatomy and physiology, and injections. I also discovered after calling the Red Cross offices in New York, that certificates for these courses, as well as letters of recommendation and verification of employment, could be faxed from Thailand to New York and then sent directly to us.

The point I want to stress in this story is that the history and background of the special population you are serving may tell you pertinent information relevant to helping your clients with their job search. Many clients, however, may not initiate talking about their past when it includes hardship or trauma, and may be modest about their achievements. Historical information will help you know what questions to ask.

POPULATIONS

Unique Resume Problems

There are, of course, problems and questions that come up when working with special population clients or clients who have such tragic or unique histories. First, **how do you account for long gaps in employment** that result from a war? While this issue is debatable, I contend that it is best to keep it very general on the resume but have the client be prepared to answer more detailed questions in an interview. The resume could have, for example, "1974-1978— held in a forced labor camp performing rice harvesting duties, during the takeover of Cambodia by the Pol Pot regime." To have survived such an atrocious and life-threatening experience shows, I feel, a certain strength of character. In addition, leaving such a large block of time off the resume could cause suspicion.

Second, **how do you translate, on a resume, the educational background** of someone from a poor country or a country whose educational system is so different from ours? My advice would be to consult with the social service providers or educators of the group you are serving. The answer to this question will likely differ from country to country.

Third, **do you include in the resume someone's years of subsistence living?** I feel the resume should try to account for any long period of a person's adult life. This situation is not much different than that of a reentry woman who spent fifteen years managing a household. Accounting for managing a farm is similar in that we can focus on the transferable skills that relate to the world of work in this country. While milking a cow may not be very transferable, supervising and organizing the work of nine children in order to provide food daily for a family of eleven might be.

Cultural Awareness Needed

While it is important to look at the unique and specific aspects of the history of the particular person we are serving, it can also be useful to be aware of the general characteristics of Asian cultures.

For instance, there are clear lines of authority in Asian cultures. Elders are viewed with great reverence, while children are expected to be obedient to parents, teachers, and those in positions of authority. Counselors and service providers may find— especially when working with younger clients—that clients answer affirmatively to ALL yes/no questions. Responding negatively is perceived as a challenge to or disrespectful of authority. It may thus be helpful to pose open-ended questions as opposed to yes/no questions, or have the client answer questions for a resume in writing. In establishing a counselor/client relationship, efforts should be made to minimize the image of the counselor as an authority figure.

Counselors may need to be more patient, alter expectations in terms of the client's willingness to reveal information, and have sessions more structured. Direct suggestions and a logical, rational approach may be better received than an effective, reflective approach.

Sophal's resume appears on the following page.

SOPHAL OEUN
222 - 35th Ave.
Oakland CA 94600

JOB OBJECTIVE

Position in a hospital or clinic as a Nurse's Aide

SUMMARY

- Four years experience as a Nurse's Aide.
- Currently enrolled in Nursing Program; previous training in basic nursing, and prenatal and infant care.

EXPERIENCE

As Nurse's Aide:

- Assisted physicians and staff with surgical procedures.
- Worked with children, performing injections for the treatment and prevention of disease.
- Provided basic nursing care for patients of all ages.

WORK HISTORY

1986-present **Student**

1981-1985 **Nurse's Aide** Khao-I-Dung Refugee Camp, Thailand

TRAINING

Nursing Program, Merritt College, Oakland, CA (beginning Fall 1989)

Related studies:
Refugee Resettlement Center, Philippines, 1986
- English as a Second Language

Through International Committee of the Red Cross, Khao-I-Dung Refugee Camp, Thailand, 1981-1983
- Basic Nursing
- Prenatal and Infant Care
- Anatomy and Physiology
- Injections

- Resume writer: Rhonda Findling-

Working with the Homeless: Tips & Ideas

I prepared the guidelines below for Roving Resume Writers (see page 151) who work with homeless job hunters. These tips and ideas were based on my assumptions that the homeless job hunter

- probably DOES have a work-history problem and we need to direct attention AWAY from that;
- MAY NOT have a long-term stable address and phone number yet;
- DOES need to get a job SOON, and therefore the job objective may oftentimes be an immediately available "bridge" job. (More about "bridge" jobs on page 149.)

CREATIVE SOLUTIONS

Probably the **functional format** will work best in most cases for job hunters whose recent work history is a bit ragged—with long periods of unemployment, only short-term jobs, unexplained gaps in the work history, or NO work history at all.

A ragged work history is a problem to be solved, not a hopeless barrier. The trick is to **be creative without being dishonest**—to give the job hunter the benefit of the doubt and to present them in the BEST possible light.

But remember, it will NOT work to tell lies on the resume because:

a) Lies undermine the self-esteem of the job hunter. They'll just be convinced that they aren't acceptable the way they really are, and that they have to hide something.

b) Lies undermine the security of the job hunter. After they get a job, they can get fired if the lies are discovered, AND they may become very uncomfortable waiting to be found out.

1. SOLUTIONS FOR A RAGGED WORK HISTORY

a) For jobs that lasted less than six months, mention the **year**, and perhaps the amount of time, but not the specific dates.

For example:

1990	**Self-Employed Handyman,** Oakland (4 months)
1989	**Short-Order Cook,** Cheezy Pizza, Berkeley (2 months)

That is HONEST, and it gives a better first impression than:

2/90-6/90	**Self Employed**
5/89-7/89	**Short-Order Cook**, Cheezy Pizza, Berkeley

b) ROUND OFF employment periods that were more than a half year.

For example:

1986	**Teachers' Aide,** Podunk School District, Marietta GA

rather than

4/86-10/86	**Teachers' Aide**, Podunk School District, Marietta GA

c) Find the job hunter an immediate short term OPPORTUNITY to get some unpaid or volunteer work experience, and PUT THAT ON THE RESUME NOW, even if they don't start until next week. This will look better on their resume than being unemployed.

For example:

1991	**Word Processing Asst.** — Damn Good Resume Service (2 months)

d) Create an accurate, dignified JOB TITLE for periods when the job hunter was not actually paid or employed by someone else, but did ANYTHING that could be presented as "work." And be sure to label the job section "Work History" rather than "Employment History."

Here are some descriptive examples:

1990	**Self-Employed Handyman** (4 mo.)
1990	**Apprentice Painter** — Moe's Paint Shop, San Leandro

1976	**Full-time parent** — three small children
1988	**Full-time student** — Podunk Community College
1979	**Full-time nursing** — Home care of elderly parent
1983	**Community Work and Parenting** — PTA, Scout Leader
Oct. '91	**Electronics Trainee** Oakland Vocational Program
Jan. '91	**Peer Counselor/Volunteer** San Juan Vocational Program

Work hard to find the job title alternative that will have the most credibility in the work world! Be realistic, but at the same time don't buy into the social stereotypes that certain types of work don't count. Instead, present that work with dignity. This will be an immense service to your job hunter.

Some reasonable job title possibilities:

Full-time Parent

Handyman (lawn mowing, odd jobs, washing windshields)

Recycling Assistant (collecting aluminum cans)

e) Incorporate any unpaid TRAINING into the Work History, to fill in gaps.

For example:

| Oct.-Nov. 1991 | **Electronics Trainee** San Jose Vocational Program |

2. SOLUTIONS FOR NO STABLE ADDRESS AND PHONE NUMBER

MARJORIE JOB HUNTER
P.O. Box 45678
[Homeless Project or Temporary Shelter's P.O. Box]
San Francisco, CA 94199

Message Phone: 123-4567
(Please leave a message with Mrs. Conrad)

JOSEPH JOB HUNTER
Golden Gate Ave.
San Francisco, CA 94123

Message Phone: 123-4567
(Please leave a message with Mrs. Conrad)

(They may not even notice that there's no street number; if they do, the job hunter could say, honestly, "I'm moving soon and not sure of the street number at my new place.")

3. SOLUTIONS FOR CREATING AN AVAILABLE ACCEPTABLE JOB OBJECTIVE

It is assumed that getting a job SOON is a high priority, and therefore the job objective may, in this case, represent an immediately available bridge job. It may NOT be the job hunter's ideal long-term job objective, but rather a position that will bridge the gap between unemployment and the ultimate better job that they want.

a) Find out, early on, what the job hunter hopes to do for work a few years down the road, when their life is more stable. It MAY be something that's available right now, or it may take several steps to get there.

b) Help the job hunter imagine a series of job goals, starting with the job they would like to have in a year or two, and working their way backward to the most immediate job objective.

Help them see how an AVAILABLE job could get them some immediate income and at the same time provide solid work experience to put on their resume later when they apply for that better job.

The bridge job needs to be appreciated by the job hunter as a critical tool for getting the job they ultimately want, rather than as a compromise or a failure. The resume writer can help immensely in making that distinction. One way is to acknowledge and affirm the long-term goals. Take a little extra time to document the skills needed to achieve those long term goals, and show how the short-term objective is a critically valuable step on the path to achieving the long-term goal.

You might even provide the job hunter with notes and ideas that could be incorporated into a future resume, and these images of future pro-

POPULATIONS

149

gress and success could provide a bit of inspiration to keep them going.

c) Assuming that this bridge job may be an entry-level position, the resume should appear appropriate—that is, not excessively formal and sophisticated. The resume should look as though the job hunter COULD have produced it by themselves—not obviously produced by someone else. In fact, it's important to teach the job hunter how to do it themselves, rather than do it for them. For now, take the position that you're doing it WITH them.

Finally, it's important that the job hunter's own words be used, rather than words and phrases that are not in their vocabulary. Have them read the completed resume out loud to be sure they're comfortable with the wording.

ROVING RESUME WRITERS

Roving Resume Writers is a local voluntary community service that I personally choose to support because I think their innovative efforts are particularly timely, and they deserve a helping hand. I asked them to introduce their program to the readers of this book, thinking that some of you may want to replicate this kind of effort in your location. Here is how they describe themselves:

Roving Resume Writers is a pilot public service/education project that matches volunteers with homeless or near homeless persons in need of a simple skill-based resume. During a skills assessment interview, the volunteer and client complete a functional resume form. Afterwards, the resume writer formats the resume on a computer or word processor, delivers the draft copy directly to the client (giving them an opportunity to make changes), and then finalizes the resume.

The project, sponsored by the Bay Area Homelessness Program (BAHP), is housed at San Francisco State University. The BAHP is a consortium of 10 Bay Area colleges and universities working in collaboration to direct university resources to the prevention of homelessness and to develop student leaders.

Roving Resume Writers was established in April 1991. The idea for a "roving" resume service came from Henry Ostendorf, then a senior at San Francisco State. Ostendorf participated in a national service event called The National Student Campaign Against Hunger and Homelessness Sixth Annual Clean-up, where he offered resumes to parents at the Hamilton Family Center (a homeless shelter in San Francisco). The same day students from 120 universities, colleges, and high schools across the nation volunteered their services at local homeless shelters and soup kitchens.

San Francisco State offers a course called Homelessness Practicum, which provides support and training to a core group of regulars in the Roving Resume Writers. Students enrolled in the course attend a weekly seminar/training meeting facilitated by employment and career counselors, desktop publishing specialists, homeless persons, and social service providers.

The response to the project has been good, with many professionals offering their expertise in the training of resume writers. Yana Parker provides on-line advice to Roving Resume Writers through their BAHP electronic bulletin board at San Francisco State.

A story on urban universities and the activities of the BAHP appeared in the college edition of *U.S. News and World Report.* For more information on Roving Resume Writers, contact Henry Ostendorf at (415) 338-1938.

EXPERIENCE OF ONE ROVING RESUME WRITER

Dear Yana: In doing resume work with homeless job hunters, I have noticed that it is important to check in with the person to give them some sense of control. How do they feel about it? Are they comfortable with the information being given? It's best to avoid referring to a 'resume format'—this may make the person feel anonymous—like they could fit into the guidelines of a form in neat little boxes. Talking with someone about life experiences and goals is more personal. You are asking them to trust you and to share possible past failures and future dreams.

The next issue is to discuss with the job hunter is how they would respond to questions from a prospective employer. Don't set them up for failure; check to see if they may be ill at ease talking about themselves in a positive manner. If the resume is a true marketing tool, then your client must also be able to follow through and "sell" himself verbally in the interview.

My last observation is that when a homeless job hunter sees the resume and how much tangible experience they actually have, it is a positive experience for them. Their self-esteem takes a leap forward when they see their professional-looking, laser-printed resume.

Josephine Loo
Roving Resume Writers

POPULATIONS

Jane Hubbard

98765 Geary Blvd.
San Francisco, CA 94121
(415) 123-4567 (message telephone)

Objective: A Clerical or Receptionist Position

Highlights of Qualification

- Over two years experience in varied positions of office work
- Three years experience in customer service and relations
- Responsible and reliable with a professional appearance and manner
- Friendly, outgoing and have a pleasant phone voice
- Strongly self-motivated, punctual and follow directions accurately

Relevant Skills and Experience

Clerical

- Paid close attention to accuracy, and worked well with numbers
- Updated records, copied and filed documents for state office
- Gained skill in word processing and accounting programs
- As employee of the dead-letter department for the U.S. Postal Service:
  - Worked with minimum supervision   - Confidentially searched for senders
  - Filled out necessary forms   - Coded and filed mail for final delivery

Reception

- Received and directed customers, as a security guard of a bank
- Answered phones and placed initial calls for political campaign
- Team-worker; cooperated well with other employees

Work History

Full-time Parent - Managed household finances 1987-1992
Security Guard - American Protective Services, San Francisco, CA 1987
Mail Clerk - U.S. Postal Service, San Francisco, CA 1986
Office Assistant - Wells Fargo Bank, San Francisco, CA 1985
Office Assistant - Cal Trans, San Francisco, CA 1981

Business Training

Academy of Stenography, San Francisco, CA 1984-1985
School of Business and Commerce, San Francisco, CA
Studied: word processing and accounting 1987

- Resume by Roving Resume Writers -

MARTIN Q. DROGAN

322 Fortieth Ave.
Rockplace, CA 94222
(512) 123-4567 or 666-3456 (messages)

Objective: Position as a warehouse worker and/or driver

HIGHLIGHTS OF QUALIFICATIONS

- Experience as a warehouse worker with a major firm.
- Sharp and creative in solving problems; great mechanical aptitude.
- Extensive experience and knowledge of warehouse operations and moving equipment.
- Hard worker, follow instructions easily, work well under pressure.
- Possess own tools and equipment.
- Volunteer experience in community service agencies

RELEVANT EXPERIENCE AND SKILLS

Warehouse/Inventory
- Supervised the loading and unloading of goods, making sure that items were handled with care and placed accurately in the warehouse.
- Prepared, wrapped, weighed, and loaded items for shipping.
- Monitored inventory paperwork and ordering, to keep warehouse fully stocked at all times.
- Operated a forklift operation extensively.

Driver/Mover
- Operated a variety of moving equipment including: dollies, safe-jacks, book-carts, tubs, piano dollies.
- Drove bob-tail truck; working towards possession of Class 1 (A) Driver's License.
- Currently employed part-time by a San Francisco moving firm.

RECENT EMPLOYMENT HISTORY

1990-Present	Mover/Installer	Fast Action Movers, Sebastopol
1990-1991	Supervisor/Cook	Haynes Family Center, Crosstown
1988-1989	Weight Trainer	Boys Clubs of America, Crosstown

OTHER RELATED WORK EXPERIENCE

2 years	Warehouse Worker	Tri-City Paper, Sebastopol
2 years	Carpenter	Solid Action Construction, Crosstown
3 years	Mover	Felix Trucking, Jump City
5 years	Construction Worker/Foreman	Pine Ridge Construction, Taylorville

EDUCATION AND TRAINING

Richardsville College, Richardsville, Psychology Major, 1975-1976
Peterson School of Industry, Crosstown High School Diploma, Culinary Arts Major, 1968-1974

- Resume by Roving Resume Writers -

POPULATIONS

Paul J. Littleson
995 Marlboro Street, Suite 915
San Felipe, CA 94000
(306) 479-5614; leave message with Marjorie Peabody

Objective: A position as a housekeeping supervisor

Highlights of Qualifications

- Over 18 years of professional housekeeping service.
- Motivated, independent, self-starter.
- Well organized, efficient and highly productive.
- Special talent for working with all types of people.

Experience and Specialized Skills

Special Projects Supervisor
- Coordinated the refurbishing of rooms in a five-star hotel.
- Supervised maintenance of various flooring surfaces, each requiring special attention.
- Planned, designed, and installed a full service hotel laundry at the Hi-Star Hotel.

Troubleshooter
- Successfully solved special maintenance problems in a five-star hotel.
- Initiated an in-house carpet cleaning program covering various types of special carpet. This program eliminated the need for the costly services of an outside contractor.
- Supervised the replacement and repair of damaged surfaces, furniture, etc.

Assisted Executive Housekeeper
- Supervised a housekeeping staff of 40 in an upscale hotel.
- Maintained a high level of quality control by paying special attention to detail.
- Designed and implemented a plan that greatly improved the productivity of a large housekeeping staff.

Education and Specialized Training

Madera Peninsula College	Courses studied: hotel department management in conjunction with Triple Treat Inn training program	1977-1978

Employment History

Lead Shelter Volunteer	Secular Community Services	San Felipe, CA	1991
Housekeeping Special Projects Supervisor	Hi-Star Hotel	Castro, CA	1988-1989
Acrylic Cleaner	Madera Atrium	Madera, CA	1986-1988
Room Inspector	Sanford Hotel	San Felipe, CA	1984-1985
Lead Housekeeping Supervisor	Red Linx Inn	Omega, NE	1982-1984
Housekeeping Advisor	Brighton Hightop Inn	Princeton, AZ	1980-1982
Housekeeping Supervisor	Triple Treat Inn	Houston, TX	1978-1980

- Resume by Roving Resume Writers -

CATHY PINKEY
306 Staple Street
Oakville, CA 90000
(317) 218-2020 ext. 712

Objective: (1) Receptionist; (2) Office Clerk;
(3) Entry Level Management

SUMMARY
* Six years office experience.
* Computer knowledge and data entry experience.
* Well organized and reliable.
* Excellent telephone manner.
* Courteous and pleasant with the public.

OFFICE SKILLS

RECEPTIONIST
* Greeted public.
* Answered phones.
* Typed with memory typewriter.
* Coordinated paperwork with MediCal, MediCare, social workers, office manager, central supply.

CLERICAL WORK
* Performed data entry and typing.
* Kept inventory of supplies and stock.
* Monitored shipping and receiving.
* Managed mail distribution.
* Handled copying, collating, filing.

SUPERVISORY WORK
* Supervised inventory and stock production.
* Trained youth for summer programs.
* Developed organizational chart for warehouse storage and supplies.
* Trained personnel in bookkeeping and accounting.
* Provided computer keypunch training.

WORK HISTORY

Data Entry Clerk   Top-Notch Temporary Services 1990-91
Receptionist   Oakville
Filing Clerk

Assistant Manager Flowers Plus Trading Co.   1988-90
Sales Clerk   Oakville
Assembly Work

EDUCATION AND TRAINING
Oakville City College
Amelia Brown Medical Assistant School

- Resume by Roving Resume Writers -

POPULATIONS

Diane Plesantte
201 Eighth Street
San Francisco, CA 94103
(415) 123-4567 (message)

Objective: A reception or medical assistant position.

Highlights of Qualification

- Developed technical expertise through on-the-job training.
- Certificate in medical assisting at BOCES vocational school.
- Sensitive, caring and professional attitude toward staff, patients, and their families.
- Friendly and outgoing, with a pleasant manner and phone voice.

Relevant Skills and Experience

Technical Expertise
- Developed skill and efficiency in the following areas:
  -taking patients' temperature   -recording pulse & respiration level
  -monitoring of blood sugar   -assisting to distribute medications
  -setting up of intravenous poles   -urinalysis testing
- Prepared patients for X-ray and physical examinations.

Administration
- Recorded daily vital signs in patients' medical records.
- Operated busy switchboard and fielded calls.
- Office management skills include:
  -ten-key calculator by touch -accurately type 68 WPM
  -PC-DOS programs including WordPerfect
- Serviced accounts and processed receivables for marketing firm.

Patient & Family Services
- Communicated with families about patients' daily condition.
- Assisted elderly clients in a wide variety of tasks in home settings.
- Advocated for patients' rights and needs; referred clients to local agencies.
- Assisted clients in scheduling medical appointments.

Work History

Marketing Assistant	Carasel Marketing, San Francisco, CA - 1992
Receptionist	YWCA, Portland, OR - 1990-91
Health Assistant	Fireside Homes-Tara Corp, Portland, OR - 1988-90
Nurses Aid	River Mead Manor, Portland, OR - 1987

Education and Training

Certificate training for Alzheimer's Disease, MLK High School, Portland, OR 1989
Nurses' Aide and Health Assistant Certificate, BOCES Vocational School, NY
Graduate, John F. Kennedy High School, NY

- Resume by Roving Resume Writers -

ALICE Q. HAU
102 Fifth Street
Lobster Point, CA 94000
(514) 134-6666 (Message)

Objective: **A position as a cook.**

HIGHLIGHTS OF QUALIFICATIONS

- Over 30 years cooking experience.
- Skilled in American-style cooking; some knowledge of French and Italian cuisine.
- Catered for large and small parties.
- Completed cooking training program.
- Responsible, efficient and flexible.

RELEVANT EXPERIENCE

1987-1991   **Cook and Housekeeper**
Mr. and Mrs. Gerome Friday
Planned, prepared and shopped for all family meals;
served as cook and assisted host for parties of up to 16 people;
performed general housekeeping.

1983-1986   **Cook and Housekeeper**
Mr. and Mrs. Frederick Jones
Prepared family meals; planned, cooked and served for
parties; managed general housekeeping and child care.

1980-82   **Child care**
Mr. and Mrs. Coopers
Provided primary care for children; prepared light meals.

1976-1979   **Cook and Housekeeper**
Mrs. Jeannine Crisp
Performed all cooking and housekeeping.

EDUCATION: High-School Graduate
Studied at Paul Peter's Cooking School

POPULATIONS

102 Fifth Street
Lobster Point, CA 94000
(514) 134-6666 (message)

March 23, 1992

Father John Martinelli
St. Ignatius Rectory
101 St. Ignatius Way
Redondo, CA 94402

Dear Father:

My resume is enclosed and I am writing to apply for the position as cook in your rectory. I have over 30 years of cooking experience, including meal planning, preparation and serving. I am a native English speaker and a member of the Catholic Church. I am interested in a live-in position and am available to start immediately.

I look forward to speaking with you and learning more about the position.

Sincerely,

Alice Hau

- By Roving Resume Writers -

ROVING RESUME WRITERS' FORMS

On the following pages are some of the basic recruiting materials, guidelines, and working forms currently in use by the Roving Resume Writers. These are included because they may inspire and assist volunteers in other communities to develop a similar program.

- Information for Student & Community Volunteers
- Volunteer Guidelines
- Flier
- Job Seeker's Resume Worksheet
- Skill-Based Resume Form (resume writer's worksheet)

POPULATIONS

ROVING
RESUME WRITERS

Information for Student and Community Volunteers

What We Do: Roving Resume Writers is a public service/education project that matches trained volunteers with the working poor or homeless persons in need of a simple skill-based resume. Regularly scheduled events held at community agencies, shelters, and job programs provide volunteers an opportunity to work one-on-one with a job-seeker to clarify their employment objectives, skills and work experience. During a 1-2 hour skill assessment interview the volunteer and job-seeker complete a skill-based resume form. After the event the volunteer formats the resume on a computer or word processor (at home or school), mails a draft copy directly to the job-seeker (giving them an opportunity to make any changes), and finalizes the resume once it is approved by the job-seeker. The process (including interview and follow-up) takes between 2 and 5 hours depending on the volunteer's interview skills and resume-writing savvy.

Who We Are: Roving Resume Writers are both students and professionals who volunteer on a short-term basis. They have different skills, personal interests and schedules, but all want to be part of the solution to homelessness. While many volunteers have had limited exposure to homelessness, all consider themselves to be good listeners. They find that homeless people are a diverse population and generally have simply fallen upon difficult times and are unable to "pull their lives together" without help. Volunteers learn while lending a hand. As the volunteers choose the events they attend, they are given the opportunity to work with people facing different and distinct situations. Volunteers have worked with homeless parents, persons in substance abuse recovery, battered women, veterans, the HIV infected, and runaway youth.

Our Training: All volunteers attend a two-hour basic training session. This meeting outlines volunteer responsibilities, resume formats, listening techniques, and sensitivity to homeless issues. The meeting also provides volunteers an opportunity to explore suitable solutions to specific situations they might encounter when preparing resumes. All volunteers are requested to acquire a copy of the Damn Good Resume Guide, by Yana Parker (Ten Speed Press). This easy-to-understand how-to guide containing resume examples (available in libraries or for $6.95 at bookstores) has proven invaluable to the project.

The Project's Early Success: Roving Resume Writers was established in April 1991 at San Francisco State University. Since this time volunteers have assisted over 120 job seekers in need of resumes at agencies including: Central YMCA, Employment Development Department, Episcopal Sanctuary, Family Living Center (Santa Clara), General Assistance Advocacy Project, Glide Memorial Church, Hamilton Family Center, Richmond Hill Family Manor, Salvation Army Gateway, South of Market Multi-Service Center, Swords to Plowshares, and the United Way Job Finders Network. Student volunteers have been recruited from: City College of San Francisco, Hastings College of the Law, San Francisco State University, Santa Clara University, Stanford University, U.C. Berkeley, University of San Francisco, and Saint Ignatius High School.

For More Information, Training, and Event Schedules Call: Henry Ostendorf, Coordinator of Roving Resume Writers at (415) 338-1938.

A Project of California Campus Compact and the Bay Area Homelessness Program
1600 Holloway Avenue, San Francisco, California 94132 (415) 338-1938   1992

POPULATIONS

Roving Resume Writers
Volunteer Guidelines

PRIOR TO EVENT

1. Attend training meeting and/or review the *Damn Good Resume Guide* by Yana Parker, Ten Speed Press. The guide illustrates skill-based resume writing techniques and format. Receive event notification in mail and RSVP to Henry Ostendorf at 338-1938 as soon as possible.

2. Arrive at Roving Resume Writers event 45 minutes early.

3. Meet other volunteers and the host agency's coordinator.

4. Participate in event briefing and have questions answered.

DAY OF EVENT

5. The coordinator will pair you off with a job-seeker in need of a resume.

6. Introduce yourself as a volunteer and explain the steps necessary to prepare a "damn good resume."

7. Review the job hunter's filled-out worksheets; clarify the job objective and the skill areas that are relevant to the job objective. (Refer to examples or guide-books if needed.)

8. Working with the job hunter, create "one-liners" describing past work experiences that illustrate or support the skills. Write this information on the "Skill-based Resume Form." Use technical terms or language relevant to the job being sought.

9. Clarify work history and educational history and clearly write these on the resume form.

10. Double-check that all information is complete and clearly written.

AFTER EVENT

11. *Lay out the resume on a computer at home or work. (Call the job hunter directly for any clarification or if you need more time to complete the resume.)

12. Return a draft copy (dot-matrix is fine) to the client within one week, with a letter asking them for any needed corrections.

FOLLOW-UP

13. Follow up this letter with a phone call two to three days after you send the draft resume; perhaps they have questions or need further assistance.

14. If needed, make final corrections and return the final resume.

* If you do not have access to a computer, another volunteer will complete the resume. In this case, it is paramount that the form be completed fully and contain precise "one-liners." Problems or omissions should be clearly explained on the resume form for the next volunteer.

POPULATIONS

POPULATIONS

162

Roving Resume Writers
Job Seeker's Resume Worksheet
- To be completed by the job-seeker BEFORE the resume writing workshop. -

JOB SEEKERS, PLEASE READ:

☞ If you would like a job-search resume, one of our Roving Resume volunteers will help you write a "Damn Good" one.

☞ A resume is a way to help market your job skills on paper. Resumes are written with one specific job in mind, but they can be updated or modified each time you learn a new skill or look for a different job. Some people have two or more different resumes, one for each kind of job they want to apply for.

☞ You can think of your resume as a friend who introduces your skills, training, and experience to an employer. Resumes help you get job interviews because they tell why you would be good for the job.

☞ Fill out these pages as completely as you can. They will assist you in talking about your skills and experience. If you have a job in mind, or know of a job similar to the one you want, bring along a description or a classified ad. This will help in preparing your resume.

☞ Plan on spending about 2 hours with the volunteer resume writer. Together you will decide what you want to include on your resume and how to word it. Afterwards, the volunteer will finish it on a computer and return it to you as soon as possible.

A Volunteer will be available to meet with you on_____ at _____

Your Name_____

Current Address_____

City_____ **Zip**_____ **Phone** (   ) _____

(Use your current address even if you will be moving soon. You can use a message telephone if you're sure you'll get the messages.)

Personal Information

Start by listing things that you are really proud of, or like, about yourself.

☞ This list should help your resume writer get a feel for who you are; but remember, not everything will be used in this version of your resume.

Some people feel funny making this sort of list because they were taught to be modest and not to brag about themselves. But a resume isn't a place to be modest or shy. Your "Damn Good Resume" will catch people's attention because it will tell them just how valuable you could be as an employee.

_____

_____

_____

_____

_____

_____

_____

_____

_____

_____

_____

_____

_____

_____

_____

_____

Resume Focus

☞ Considering your skills, your experience, and the job market, **what kind of a job would you like to find with this resume?**   (Other versions of your resume can be completed at a later date.)

• _____

List the reasons that you'd like this kind of work, and why you'd be good at it.

(example)   •<u>a telephone sales or customer service job</u>

     1. <u>I have about 3 years experience in sales, I like the work, it's easy for me</u>

     2. <u>I enjoy working in an office because I can interact with others</u>

1. _____

2. _____

3. _____

4. _____

5. _____

6. _____

7. _____

Job Skills and Work History

☞ **List your work history.** (Include self-employment and any volunteer or unpaid work; even though you didn't get paid to do something, it could still count as experience on your resume.)   Begin with your present or last job or work situation and work backwards. Continue writing on the back of the page if you run out of space.

(example) Position or Job Title <u>Cashier</u>

    Company <u>McDonald's Restaurant</u>   **City** <u>Chicago, Ill</u>   **Years** <u>Summer 1991</u>

    • **What were your primary responsibilities?** working in the front of the restaurant, greeting customers, taking orders, packing food, operating an electronic cash register.

    • **What work related things did you do best at this job?**
- <u>I always kept a smile. (It was a temp job and I was saving money for my move)</u>
- <u>I got along very well with my co-workers and enjoyed training new employees.</u>

A. Position or Job Title_____

Employer_____ **City**_____

Years_____

    • **What were your primary responsibilities?**

    • **What three work-related things did you do best at this job?**

• _____

• _____

• _____

POPULATIONS

B. Position or Job Title_____

Employer_____ City_____

Years_____

- What were your primary responsibilities?

- What three work-related things did you do best at this job?

- _____
- _____
- _____

C. Position or Job Title_____

Employer_____ City_____

Years_____

- What were your primary responsibilities?

- What three work-related things did you do best at this job?

- _____
- _____
- _____

D. Position or Job Title_____

Employer_____ City_____

Years_____

- What were your primary responsibilities?

- What three work-related things did you do best at this job?

- _____
- _____
- _____

POPULATIONS

E. Position or Job Title_____

Employer_____ City_____

Years_____

  • What were your primary responsibilities?

  • What three work-related things did you do best at this job?

  •_____
  •_____
  •_____

F. Position or Job Title_____

Employer_____ City_____

Years_____

  • What were your primary responsibilities?

  • What three work-related things did you do best at this job?

  •_____
  •_____
  •_____

Education, Training and Military Experience

School or Institution (example)	Courses studied, Diplomas, Degrees, Rank	City/State	Years Attended
American Red Cross	CPR Training Certification	Las Vegas, NV	2 weeks (1990)
TrainCo Business College	Courses studied: receptionist skills	Chicago, IL	1987
Illinois National Guard	Reservist, requisitioning assistant	Chicago, IL	1977–1980
_____	_____	_____	_____
_____	_____	_____	_____
_____	_____	_____	_____
_____	_____	_____	_____
_____	_____	_____	_____
_____	_____	_____	_____

ROVING
RESUME WRITERS

SKILL-BASED RESUME FORM
(to be completed by resume writer during interview)

Host Agency_____ Date_____ Volunteer_____ Phone_____

Where should this resume be sent when completed?
In care of who?_____ (case manager, friend, etc.)
Address_____
City_____ Zip_____

Number to call if additional info is needed from the job-seeker this week _____

Volunteer who will finish this resume on a computer if different from above_____

Header

Name_____

Mailing Address_____

City_____ Zip_____ Phone ( )_____

(Employer must be able to contact client or leave a message for them at this address and telephone number)

Job Objective_____
(Example: An entry-level position in telephone sales and/ or customer service.)

Highlights of Qualification

Example of "Highlights":
- Over 3 years experience in sales and customer service positions
- Pleasant telephone voice and manner
- Career oriented, accurate, follow instructions with ease
- Successful record of persuading customers to buy

- _____
- _____
- _____
- _____
- _____

POPULATIONS

167

Relevant Skill Areas and "Action Oriented One-Liners"

skill _Effective Sales Techniques_

- *Assisted* customers in identifying needs and successfully promoted suitable in-stock items
- *Suggested* alternative selections and additional impulse purchase items
- *Provided* customers with information about product effectiveness and warranties
- *Enlisted* the help of immediate supervisors to help close difficult sales
- *Returned* telephone calls to prospective customers to follow-up potential sales

skill _____

- _____
- _____
- _____
- _____

skill _____

- _____
- _____
- _____
- _____

skill _____

- _____
- _____
- _____
- _____

Work History

Example:

Cashier	front of house operations	McDonald's Restaurant	Chicago IL	1992
Temp work	reception/sales positions	All Work Inc,	Chicago IL	1987-1991
Temp work	packing/filing/warehouse	Ready Men and Women	Chicago IL	1985-1987
Sales staff	housewares, furniture sales	Jackson Sales Company	Chicago IL	1974-1977

Position	**Company/City**	**Dates in years**
• _____		
• _____		
• _____		
• _____		
• _____		

Education and/or Military Training

TrainCo Business College, Chicago — Courses studied: receptionist skills, word processing — 1987
Jones Commercial College, Chicago — Graduated with merits in: business skills, accounting — 1972-1974
Metropolitan High School, Chicago — 1970-1972

School or Program/City	**Courses studies/degrees/certificates**	**Years Attended**
• _____		
• _____		
• _____		
• _____		

7
Cover Letters, Etc.

7
Cover Letters, Etc.

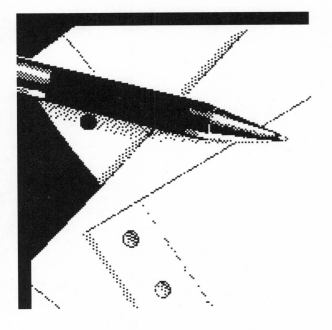

Most professional resume writers provide their clients with at least this one additional service related to the job hunt: help with the writing of cover letters.

What Is a Cover Letter?

A "cover letter" is simply a letter or note that must *always* accompany a resume whenever the resume is NOT delivered by the job hunter, in person, directly to the employer. For example:

1. When the resume is sent by mail along with a request for an in-person interview—in any case where the job hunter can't make this request verbally, such as when responding to a blind ad.

2. When a resume is being sent after an interview, at the request of the employer. Then the letter might serve two purposes—as a cover letter and as a thank-you letter.

How I Handle Cover Letters

Many of my clients request that I help them write a letter to go along with their resume, and we do that at the end of the resume session.

Typically, they will want me to help write a "generic" cover letter that they can send, along with a resume, each time they apply for a job. And I always refuse, because I don't believe in generic cover letters.

"Then what can I DO?" they wail, "I can't write a separate letter for EVERY job I apply to, can I?" "Well, yes," I reply, "That's exactly what you

should do." Since I won't be on hand every time they send a resume, yet I believe they shouldn't write generic letters, my solution is this: I help them write one customized cover letter for one of the job openings they will apply for (the one currently most appealing) so they understand how to do it correctly. Then, on their own, they can use that first letter as a model for writing the remaining *customized* cover letters they need.

To prepare for writing this first (model) customized letter, I ask them:

- Why do you want to work for that particular company?
- What do you know about the company, and how did you hear of them?
- What do you know about the position you're applying for?
- How could you help that particular company reach its goals?

Obviously, the answers to these questions would be very different for each different company they consider. And that is why each cover letter—as well as each resume—has to be customized. Remember, a generic cover letter *feels* generic to the receiver, and results in a very lukewarm response. We want our clients to generate intense interest on the part of the employer, and the only way to do that is to *show* intense interest!

Cover Letter Guidelines

When you apply for a job by mail, your resume should always be accompanied by a good cover letter. And, like the resume, a good cover letter is not easy for most people to write. The secrets to success are much the same as with the resume:

- Relevance
- Appropriateness
- Clarity
- Brevity
- Sincerity and warmth
- Uniqueness

Here are some guidelines for writing a good cover letter:

1. Be sure to **address your letter to someone who has the authority** to hire you. Try to use their name and title. When it's *impossible* to get that information, use their functional title—"Dear Manager." You may have to guess—"Dear Selection Committee"—but *never* say "To whom it may concern" or "Dear Sir or Madam"!

2. Show that you **know a little about the company** and that you can see THEIR point of view (their current problems, interests and priorities).

3. **Sound enthusiastic and interested** in this line of work or this company. If you have a good idea that might help the employer resolve a problem currently facing his industry, offer to come in and discuss it.

4. Try to be **professional** but still **warm and friendly**. Avoid using generic phrases like "enclosed please find" and "Dear Sir or Madam." This is a letter to a real live person!

5. **Set yourself apart** from the crowd. Identify at least one thing about you that's unique—perhaps a special gift for getting along with all kinds of people. Mention some unusual skill that goes beyond the essential requirements of the position—something that distinguishes you, and is relevant to the position. (Then, if several others are equally qualified, there's some REASON to pick YOU.)

6. **Be specific** about what you are asking and what you're offering. Make it clear which position you're applying for and just what experience or skill you have that relates to that position.

7. **Take the initiative about the next step** whenever possible, mentioning just what you intend to do next. For example, "I'll call your office early next week to see if we could meet soon and discuss this job opening." Or, when you're exploring for unadvertised jobs that may come up: "I'll call your office next week to see if we could meet soon to discuss your company's needs for help in the near future."

8. **Be brief**—a few short paragraphs, all on one page.

All this is recapped in a Cover Letter Template and Cover Letter Example on the following pages.

Your Name
Street Address
City, State, Zip

Today's date

Mr. Hiring Person
HP's Job Title
HP's Company
Company Street Address
City and Zip Code

Dear Mr. Hiring Person,

In the first paragraph, tell how you heard about the job opening* (or about the company, if this is not an advertised job but rather one you are trying to discover or create by making direct contact). Mention the actual job title, and say that you're sending a resume that shows how you're qualified for that particular job.

*[*Try, try, try! to find somebody who personally knows the Hiring Person, and ask if you may say in your cover letter "Bill Smith suggested I write to you directly." A NAME the Hiring Person recognizes helps tremendously in getting you noticed.]*

In the second paragraph show some enthusiasm and interest in the company, and appreciation for their products. If you know of a problem or opportunity facing the company, mention it—without in any way criticizing the company. Give an example of something you could do to help resolve the problem or help take advantage of the opportunity.

[The best example would be something similar that you did for a previous employer to improve the situation.]

In the third paragraph, tell how you will follow through. "I'll call your office early next week to see if we could meet soon and discuss this job opening."

[Or, if you're exploring for unadvertised jobs that may come up: "I'll call your office next week to see if we could meet soon to discuss your company's need for help in the near future."]
[Or, if you're answering a blind ad in the newspaper, and CAN'T call them—just end on an upbeat note and provide a phone number with an answering machine where you can be reached.]

Sincerely,

Joseph Job Hunter

Enclosed: resume

SAMPLE COVER LETTER

The example that follows beautifully illustrates the principles outlined in the Cover Letter Guidelines. And *more*: it shows how you can create a unique letter that can still be customized to send to several different employers—as long as they are in the same field.

Resume writer Jeff Lewis of Sherman Oaks, California, explains, "I interweave into the letter something unique about the job hunter's life, and then set up the letter so they can insert the name of the company in at least two locations in the letter. I also impress upon them the importance of targeting the letter to precisely the right person in the company."

Notice how lively this "generic" cover letter is compared with most letters you've seen. Besides being a gifted writer, Jeff has developed a unique method of interviewing his resume clients; he taps into their passion for their work, often leading them to discover more fully their work-related assets and accomplishments. *This is the art we should all strive to master!*

Your Name
Street Address
City, State, Zip
Phone Number

Date

Name & Title
Company
Street Address
City, State, Zip

Dear Mr. _____ ,

If January's issue of Money Magazine is only partially correct, Phoenix will soon take its place among the top five or six expansion-oriented cities in the country. With a projected increase of forty-six thousand white collar jobs within five years, and a state-wide population increase of another half million people within eight years, Arizona's marketing opportunities in general, and [Name of Company's] in particular are poised to take major leaps forward that will make past advances appear to have been nothing more than baby steps. With my diverse marketing accomplishments, coupled with my forever being "turned on" by challenge, growth, and being "where the action is," there's no question where I'm going to hang my hat.

Which brings me to this letter and my reason for contacting you. I believe that I can be as beneficial to your goals as you can to mine. The enclosed resume describes some of my achievements in creative product development, media placement, and market penetration. I'm aware that some of [Name of Company's] interests have included [Product(s), Service(s), or Whatever], and I think you'll agree that my track record with [Name the item or items from the resume] is evidence of my expertise in this (these type(s) of project(s).

If, having read the above and the enclosed resume, you agree that [Name of Company] and I could be mutually advantageous to each other, I'd like the opportunity of discussing it in greater depth, in person. Since I'll definitely be relocating to the Phoenix area, I'm planning a trip there in the near future to explore several items of interest to me. I'd be most pleased if a meeting with you could be held during this visit.

I'll phone you on [Day & Date] between [Hours] to see if you're interested, and when would be most convenient.

Sincerely,

Your Name

Fun with Cover Letters

To insert both humor and historical perspective into this discussion, I've included the following gems:

- Two Fascinating Letters
- Where There's a Will There's a Way
- Unforgettable Student Cover Letters

Two Fascinating Letters . . .

Notice how these letters, written centuries ago, demonstrate what works and what doesn't work in employer/employee communications—principles that are universally and everlastingly valid. —yp

The following two letters were actually used in applying for jobs. (They're both in the public domain—share at will.)

The first letter was written by Franz Schubert when he applied for the post of Assistant Conductor at the Imperial Court of Vienna in 1826.

The second is a petition from Leonardo da Vinci to the Duke of Milan, written in 1482, for a job that seems to have been a combination of chief engineer, Minister of Defense, and artist in residence.

As you might suspect, Leonardo, with his **emphasis on achievements and his eye on the Duke's needs, got the job.** Schubert's letter—bland and unexciting—was not even acknowledged by his most gracious Emperor.

from *Marketing Yourself
for a Second Career*
by Col. Doug Carter

FRANZ SCHUBERT'S LETTER

Your Majesty!
Most gracious Emperor!

With the deepest submission the undersigned humbly begs Your Majesty graciously to bestow upon him the vacant position of Vice-Kapellmeister to the Court, and supports his application with the following qualifications:

1. The undersigned was born in Vienna, is the son of a schoolteacher and is 29 years of age.

2. He enjoyed the privilege of being for five years a Court Chorister at the Imperial and Royal College School.

3. He had received a complete course of instruction in composition from the late Chief Kapellmeister to the Court, Herr Anton Salieri, and is fully qualified, therefore, to fill any post as Kapellmeister.

4. His name is well known, not only in Vienna but throughout Germany, as a composer of songs and instrumental music.

5. He has also written and arranged five Masses for both smaller and larger orchestras, and these have already been performed in various churches in Vienna.

6. Finally, he is at the present time without employment, and hopes in the security of a permanent position to be able to realize at least those high musical aspirations which he has ever kept before him.

Should Your Majesty be graciously pleased to grant this request, the undersigned would strive to the utmost to give full satisfaction.

Your Majesty's most obedient and humble servant,
Franz Schubert

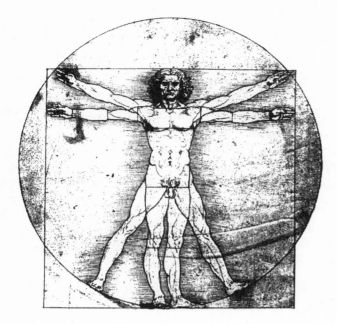

LEONARDO DA VINCI'S LETTER

Having, most illustrious lord, seen and considered the experiments of all those who pose as masters in the art of inventing instruments of war, and finding that their inventions differ in no way from those in common use, I am emboldened, without prejudice to anyone, to solicit an appointment of acquainting your Excellency with certain of my secrets.

1. I can construct bridges which are very light and strong and very portable, with which to pursue and defeat the enemy, and others more solid, which resist fire or assault, yet are easily removed and placed in position, and I can also burn and destroy those of the enemy.

2. In case of a siege I can cut off water from the trenches and make pontoons and scaling ladders and other similar contrivances.

3. If by reason of the elevation or the strength of its position a place cannot be bombarded, I can demolish every fortress if its foundations have not been set on stone.

4. I can also make a kind of cannon which is light and easy of transport, with which to hurl small stones like hail, and of which the smoke causes great terror to the enemy, so that they will suffer heavy loss and confusion.

5. I can noiselessly construct to any prescribed point subterranean passages either straight or winding, passing if necessary underneath trenches or a river.

6. I can make armoured wagons carrying artillery, which shall break through the most serried ranks of the enemy, and so open a safe passage for his infantry.

7. If occasion should arise, I can construct cannon and mortars and light ordnance in shape both ornamental and useful and different from those in common use.

8. When it is impossible to use cannon I can supply in their stead catapults, mangonels, trabocchi, and other instruments of admirable efficiency not in general use. In short, as the occasion required I can supply infinite means of attack and defense.

9. And if the fight should take place upon the sea, I can construct many engines most suitable either for attack or defense and ships which can resist the fire of the heaviest cannon, and powders or weapons.

10. In time of peace, I believe that I can give you as complete satisfaction as anyone else in the construction of buildings both public and private, and in conducting water from one place to another.

11. I can further execute sculpture in marble, bronze, clay, also in painting I can do as much as anyone else, whoever he may be.

12. Moreover I would undertake the commission of the bronze horse, which shall endue with immortal glory and eternal honour the auspicious memory of your father and of the illustrious house of Sforza.

13. And if any of the aforesaid things should seem to anyone impossible or impracticable, I offer myself as ready to make trial of them in your park or in whatever place shall please your Excellency, to whom I commend myself with all possible humility.

WHERE THERE'S A WILL, THERE'S A WAY:
How One Job Hunter Gave Her Resume and Cover Letter a Unique Helping Hand!

by Bryan Howard

So you have a resume: Now what? For many job-hunters, this step represents the climax of finding employment. In fact, a great many excellent resumes never find their way to an employer's desk or, if they do, they become lost amid a hundred others, all vying for "the job."

Here's how Tessa O'Hara (our not-so-fictitious heroine) goes about short-circuiting the competition. Having prepared a customized cover letter to accompany her resume, and knowing that the odds of landing a newspaper advertisement are slim, Tessa maps out a strategy designed to get an interview for a classified ad that reads:

> "Wanted: A Girl Friday (everyday) to assist the Public Relations Manager at the Lord Nelson Hotel. Bilingualism preferred. Address CV to Mr. Taylor at 161 Elgin St. by noon on 22nd."

Let's say that today is Tuesday the 19th. Tessa decides to hand deliver her resume to the hotel, but with a slight difference. On her way there, she wraps her resume in a broad silver ribbon, buys a single long-stemmed yellow rose, and confronts the concierge with a special request. (Now, now, we're talking about resumes!)

Within minutes, the obliging hotel staff produce a silver tray embellished with lace cloth; Tessa's vased rose tastefully accompanies her ribboned resume. A small card attached to the rose stem says simply: "Look no further."

While she is there, Tessa learns the name of the hotel's head receptionist: an elderly lady by the name of Ms. Perry. The very next morning, she calls Ms. Perry and plants seed number 2. This time, Tessa asks Ms. Perry to convey a message to Mr. Taylor. (He is in a meeting and cannot answer his phone.) The message is simply that Tessa O'Hara called to confirm her interest in the position of "Girl Friday."

Later that same day, Tessa tries to contact Mr. Taylor again, but he is "very busy" and is not taking calls right now. Undaunted, our intrepid Tessa writes a short note to Mr. Taylor, using a very plain card. She writes:

> "Dear Mr. Taylor:
> You really are a very busy man! I have been trying to contact you for two days now, and agree that you do indeed need a "Girl Friday." Please allow me the opportunity of a brief interview at your earliest convenience.
>
> > Yours in service,
> > Tessa O'Hara"

Today being Thursday the 21st, Tessa once again visits the Lord Elgin Hotel, card in hand. This time, the card is delivered in the same distinctive fashion as before (rose optional).

By now Mr. Taylor has received so many messages, his colleagues are intrigued by his extraordinary mail, and the silver tray has become a trademark of a Tessa Someone who seems to be so pleasantly persistent that he cannot but add her name to his list of interviewees.

Far-fetched? This is the exact strategy of a young lady I know who not only landed the job, but was appointed Special Events and Publicity Manager within a month of having been hired.

You can work the same magic for yourself! As you can see, there's really no magic involved at all—it just takes a bit of creative marketing to set yourself apart from the masses, and a few extra phone calls and "thank you's" to get the results that a stand-alone resume could never achieve.

**Bryan Howard
St. Albert, Ontario,
Canada**

UNFORGETTABLE COVER LETTERS BY COLLEGE STUDENTS

by Drema Howard

Many times critiquing student resumes and cover letters is fairly routine. There are, however, a few whose ingenuity and humor have placed them in my "too-unusual-to-forget" category. I think your readers may enjoy hearing about some of my favorite ones.

- An architecture student had his heart set on working at a particular firm in England. This firm was one of only two in the world that designed a unique type of structure the student was interested in designing.

  Recognizing how competitive the screening process would be, the student decided his resume would have to stand out from all the others. He placed a well-written resume between two 8 x 11 half-inch thick pieces of glass and secured each corner with pewter screws. He made a special box to house his resume and air mailed it to the president of the firm. He was granted an interview and offered the exact job he wanted.

- An elementary education major worked as a magician in her spare time and had built a number of her student-teaching lesson plans around magic tricks to teach the day's lesson. Rather than a formal resume, she offered employers a portfolio that included pictures, student letters, and a "lesson in magic." She tied her avocation of magic and illusion to the classroom with a well-illustrated introductory letter about the "magic of education." She was offered an interview from every employer who received her portfolio.

- After eight months of unemployment, an agriculture graduate scheduled an appointment to talk about his inability to obtain an interview. A quick scan of his resume indicated the reason. At the top of his resume he'd listed personal data. Beside the category of HEALTH, he'd stated: "SCHIZOPHRENIC, BUT BETTER NOW."

- A chemistry major included only one reference in her credential packet—it was written by the student. The reason was spelled out in the beginning of her letter: "I write this letter of reference for myself because no one knows my skills, abilities and talents better than me. Only I know what I can offer and how great a job I will do for whoever hires me."

Drema Howard
University of Kentucky
University Career Center
Lexington, KY

Other Job-Search Letters & Issues

Resume writers may also be asked to help the job hunter write other kinds of letters, or provide advice about the job-search process in general. Here are some pointers you can pass along to your clients:

- **Thank-you letters** are not just a courtesy —although they are that, too—but serve to make one more important contact with the employer. Because so few job hunters remember to send thank-you letters, the few who DO stand out favorably in the employer's mind.

   A guideline and an example for thank-you letters are on pages 181 and 182.

- **Recommendation letters,** also called reference letters, are written FOR the job hunter, not BY the job hunter—and are written by someone who is willing to put in a good word for the job hunter. Such a letter is generally needed ONLY under special circumstances when it would be impossible or inconvenient for the potential employer to contact the job hunter's personal and professional references by phone.

   Very few people write a good recommendation letter because they don't know what to say. To write an adequate letter, they need to know the job hunter's objective, as well as the overall impression he is attempting to make on the potential new employer. The job hunter can make the letter-writer's job MUCH easier by providing the information outlined on the Letter of Recommendation Worksheet and Guide on pages 183 and 184. The results will be far more effective.

- **References** are generally provided only AFTER they are requested—usually after a job interview that went well. An appropriate format for a list of references is on page 186.

   It is sufficient (and even optional) to say "References available on request" at the bottom of a resume.

- **Salary history requests** are an extremely sticky issue! Employers frequently ask for this information (even insist on it) prior to an interview, yet it is NEVER in the job hunter's best interest to provide the information at that time—if ever.

Here are some sources of sound advice on this issue:

- *What Color Is Your Parachute*, by Richard Bolles, page 20 in the 1992 edition: "IF the ad requests or even demands that you state your salary requirements, some experts say ignore the request; others say, gently dance around it . . . others say if you want to meet it head-on, state a salary range. . . . The overall iron-clad rule, however, is: if the ad doesn't mention salary requirements, don't you either. Why give another excuse for getting your response screened out?"

- *Sweaty Palms: The Neglected Art of Being Interviewed* (revised), by H.A. Medley. See pages 163-78 on how to handle salary questions when you are actually AT the interview.

- European job-search expert Daniel Porot insists: "The party that mentions money first, loses." He advises job hunters to delay discussing the specific salary until the last minute, and then to turn the question back to the employer so that the employer has to name a dollar amount first.

Thank-You Letter Template
Always send a thank-you letter
immediately after a job interview.

Your Name
Street Address
City, State, Zip

Today's date

Name of new employer
(or whoever interviewed you)
Their job title
Name of company
Company address

Dear _____

In this paragraph, **thank the interviewer** (or express your appreciation) for the chance to meet with them to discuss the job and see the premises (use the term "meeting" rather than "interview" if it seems appropriate). Make some reference to your positive impressions of the company.

In this paragraph **offer some new information** or additional reason for the employer to be interested in you for that job—perhaps a "goodie" that you didn't mention in the interview. (You might even link this new information to a problem or opportunity the company is experiencing.) Repeat the job title you are applying for, and show continued interest in it.

In the last paragraph, let the employer know (graciously) that you expect to hear from him again and **plant the idea in his mind of making a phone call to you.** Make it clear you're willing to come in and discuss the job further.

Sincerely yours,

Your Name
Your work phone: (xxx) 123-4567
Your home phone: (xxx) 321-7654

Geraldine JobHunter

990 Grove Street
Middletown NY

October 18, 19xx

Martina Bosserio
Manager, Product Development Dept.
Widget Corporation
1520 Widget Drive
Metropolis NY

Dear Ms. Bosserio,

I enjoyed the opportunity to meet with you and have a brief tour of Widget Corporation. The high level of creative energy among your staff, as well as their personal pride in the company's products, was obvious and very gratifying to see.

In addition to the information I shared with you in our meeting, I thought of another project I worked on that reflects the kind of contribution I could make as a member of Widget's product development team. The details of that project (the proposal and the final report, both of which I authored) are enclosed for your review.

As soon as you're through interviewing the other candidates, I'd appreciate hearing from you, and of course I'd be pleased to meet with you again, if necessary, on fairly short notice. I can be reached at home in the evening as well as at my office during the day.

Sincerely yours,

Geraldine JobHunter
office: (xxx) 123-4567
home: (xxx) 321-7654

The job hunter can make the task easier for the person writing a letter of recommendation if they provide this Letter of Recommendatiom worksheet (after filling in the blanks) and the Letter of Recommendation guide on the next page, along with a copy of their resume.

Letter of Recommendation • Worksheet

Date when the letter is needed_____

Name of potential employer who gets the letter _____

Job title and company (if known) _____

1. In the first paragraph, state that this is a letter of reference for _____

(job-hunter's name) _____ who is seeking a position as/in

(the job title, or kind of work sought)_____

2. In the second paragraph state your RELATIONSHIP to the job-hunter — supervisor, colleague, long-time personal friend, teacher, etc. — and how you happen to know the job-hunter — for example, the nature of the work or projects or other experience that you shared, and how LONG you've known the job hunter.

Relationship _____

Nature of the work or project _____

Length of time known _____

3. In the third paragraph, mention several of the job-hunters SKILLS, TALENTS, ABILITIES, and describe one or two primary ACCOMPLISHMENTS that you believe would be interesting to the new employer because they demonstrate the skills needed for the work NOW being sought by the job-hunter.

A skill or ability important to the new job _____

A skill or ability important to the new job _____

A skill or ability important to the new job _____

An accomplishment that illustrates those skills _____

An accomplishment that illustrates those skills _____

(Note: The job hunter may point out some accomplishments she'd like mentioned, but the Reference Person is the one who actually writes the description of the accomplishment.)

4. In the last paragraph, if you are willing to be called by the new employer, state how you can be reached for more information.

- Letter of Recommendation worksheet -

Provide each of your reference people a copy of this guide.

Letter of Recommendation Guide

This is what needs to be included in a good letter of recommendation (also called a letter of reference):

1. Name, title, and company of the party to RECEIVE the letter, if known.

Use "To whom it may concern" only if you don't know the recipient's name or the letter must be generic. Do TRY to get the actual name from the job hunter.

2. Job title of the position being sought by the job hunter.

If unknown, or it must be somewhat general, then refer to the OVERALL TYPE of work (management, sales, marketing, nursing, teaching) the job hunter is seeking.

3. A few accomplishments of the job hunter.

Describe accomplishments that are familiar to you, either because you both worked together at the time or you supervised the job hunter during that time. These accomplishments should clearly illustrate skills (abilities, talents) needed for the person's new job. Include one accomplishment that "says it all," if possible.

Sample Letter of Recommendation:

> To: Miriam Slater, Director
>   East Bay Main Career Center
> From: Yana Parker, Principal
>   Damn Good Resume Service
> Re: Susan Ireland, Resume Writer
>
> Dear Ms. Slater,
>   I'm pleased to have been asked to provide a letter of reference for Susan Ireland and I believe she is very well qualified for your position of In-House Resume Writer and Workshop Leader. Susan completed a full-year apprenticeship with me and has distinguished herself as a professional in this field. She is very resourceful in resolving the resume-writing problems presented by job hunters, who come to us for help with an amazingly wide range of "sticky" career issues.
>
>   Very early on, Susan proved she has what it takes when I called upon her to take over my resume business while I dealt with a death in the family. She rose to the challenge and earned my respect for both her courage and her inherent good business sense, as well as the sensitivity she applied to the writing of our clients' resumes.
>
>   Susan has co-taught six resume workshops with me, handling both the workshop design and the classroom presentation to my satisfaction, and I am confident that she is now ready to lead these workshops entirely on her own.
>
>   Please feel free to call me if you would like to discuss Susan's qualifications in more detail. I can be reached at (510) 123-4567.
>
>   Sincerely,
>   Yana Parker

(Thanks to James P. Carr of Dallastown, Pennsylvania, for suggesting this recommendation letter guide. –yp)

Your clients will probably ask for advice about using or not using references. Here's what to tell them—or copy this whole page as a handout.

IN REFERENCE TO REFERENCES

by Claudia Jordan

References can play an important role in the job search. Careful consideration and preparation of references not only aids in cinching the job after an interview, but may uncover new opportunities as well.

References can be a strategic job networking source if used wisely and considerately. I advise my clients on the use of this little-known but effective method, and I include preparation of a list of references as part of my resume services package. Here is what I tell my clients:

First, make a list of your professional references—previous supervisors are best—and your personal references. Then call each one, briefly describe the kind of work you want to do, and ask them to be your reference. Most people will be glad to help and are flattered by your request. If there is a negative response, now is the time to discover it and mend your fences. If that is impossible, drop that reference and use the others.

Next, write a thank-you letter to each reference, enclosing your resume. Reiterate your objective, and ask them to let you know of any new developments or opportunities in the field. Your references are an extra set of eyes and ears in the job market—they are also in a position to refer you to others. Hint: Never ask your reference for a job! Don't put them on the spot or you will lose their assistance.

(One job seeker, who had recently relocated from out of state, followed these principles. Two weeks later, an ex-employer contacted her, explained the company was expanding to her location, and offered a position over the phone! She had not known of the expansion nor had the company known of her move.)

Preparing your references in advance can pay off in a big way. At the conclusion of the interview, hand the employer a list of your references. It's convenient for the employer—no fumbling for names and phone numbers, no dealing with corporate switchboards. It adds to your professional polish and you KNOW you will receive glowing reviews!

Simply follow these steps to write a list of references.

a) Make sure your name and phone number appear at the top of the page.

b) Use the heading "References" or "Professional References."

You could add another section called "Personal References" only if the Professional Reference section is sketchy or your personal reference has an impressive title, is well known, or is somehow associated with your job objective.

c) List your references in the order of importance. Employers are most interested in speaking to the people you worked with, usually your boss.

d) Here is how each reference should look:

Supervisor: Mr. Thomas Buckley
Vice President, Operations
ABC Manufacturing, Inc.
6002 Sterling Drive, Suite 111
Phoenix AZ 85354
(602) 996-3951

e) If one of your references has changed companies since your tenure, list their current position and company. Also insert a line (enclosed in parentheses) stating something like "formerly Vice President of XYZ Manufacturing" so the potential new employer will understand.

f) A minimum of three references and maximum of one page should do it.

The list of references should be presented AFTER an interview, not with a resume in the mail. The employer will not perform background checks until after hiring interest is evident.

Claudia Jordan
Phoenix, AZ

Your Name
Street Address
City, State, and Zip
(415) xxx-xxxx

REFERENCES

Relationship* and Name
Title
Company
Address
City, State, and Zip
Work Phone
Home Phone (optional)

Relationship* and Name
Title
Company
Address
City, State, and Zip
Work Phone
Home Phone (optional)

(example)
Supervisor: John J. Williamson
Director of Marketing
Widget Corporation
123 Fourth Avenue
Metropolis NY 12345
Office: (123) 456-7890
Home: (234) 567-8890

For example:
Supervisor
Long-time Friend
Colleague
Minister
Client
Teacher

Job hunters often seek help from a resume writer just before they apply for a specific job, so one of the next challenges they may face is filling out a job application form. You might think this a cut-and-dried matter, but there's more to it than meets the eye, as Joe Meissner explains below.

You can do your client a service by providing them a copy of this article and recommending they read it carefully before filling out an application blank.

JOB APPLICATIONS:
Filling in Those Blankety-Blank Blanks!
by Joe B. Meissner

Regardless of how you come to the attention of a prospective employer—letter/resume, college placement, networking, referrals, or just dropping into a personnel office—sooner or later every interested employer (and some not so interested) is going to ask you to complete a company application form.

Lengthy job application forms may seem to request information already supplied, but much can hinge on the way they are handled.

"Many corporations have a psychological climate that subtly dictates an employee must let himself be a bit victimized by the bureaucracy in order to fit in. What better way to test this trait than by making an applicant fill out an application form before anyone talks to him?" says David Noer, President of Human Resources Services Company, in his book, *How to Beat the Employment Game: Secrets of the Personnel Recruiter* (published by Chilton).

Since virtually every job applicant comes armed with a resume providing pertinent information about themselves, filling out an application seems like a waste of time. A good resume pinpoints accomplishments and specific qualifications for a given job. Application blanks,

on the other hand, often ask questions that seem irrelevant.

But most companies require application forms and, since you can't avoid completing them, you might as well learn to accept them and do them well. Part of acceptance comes with understanding. There are good reasons that justify employers' insistence on the ritual forms.

The Company's Viewpoint

Most companies feel that, even though you have presented them with a resume, you should still fill out their standardized form—which is designed specifically to obtain the information the company needs to know.

According to Damian A. Fitzroy, formerly College Recruitment Supervisor for Bechtel Power Corporation, "The typical graduate's resume does not give us enough information to make a screening decision; application forms fill in blanks that a recruiter needs filled."

Furthermore, according to Fitzroy, an application form is not just used for screening. "It is used in most firms for permanent company records and administrative purposes and, after hiring, becomes a part of your personnel file. Much of the information, though irrelevant for hiring, is nonetheless important in the company's scheme."

Other reasons for formal applications lie in a company's desire to protect itself. Having a filled-out form on record can be evidence against discrimination charges. An application is the company's way of formally proving that your qualifications and desire to work were on file.

Another purpose of the application is to encourage applicants to be honest. Most standardized forms have statements which say, in effect, if the applicant lies on the form, he or she will be subject to dismissal.

Applications may also relate to expenditure approvals connected with employment interviews. In many cases, one or more authorized "okays" are

required to spend money to fly in out-of-town applicants. It is easier to secure these approvals on the signed application form than by attaching an approval to a resume, maintains human resource expert David Noer.

Moreover, applications may be used instead of resumes to provide a preliminary evaluation of your abilities as a potential employee. In the area of screening, a formal application blank provides a simple test of your ability to spell, write, and give factual answers to questions. If required before you are interviewed, it also gives the interviewer additional insight about you before the interview begins.

Says Fitzroy, "Information given on application forms is not useless information; it helps the candidate by helping us to make better employment decisions."

For all these reasons, it is prudent for a job seeker to take application forms seriously. The way you fill out those seemingly "routine" application blanks may very well determine whether or not you get an interview.

Helpful Hints

As an outplacement consultant who has advised hundreds of job seekers over the past twenty-one years, I've learned that if you follow these basic rules when confronted with an application blank, you will be more efficient in your job search and more attractive as an applicant.

- Avoid completing an application form in an employer's office. Ask to bring it in the next day, or send it back later in the week by mail.

- Don't touch an application blank with pen, pencil or typewriter until you have made a photocopy. Work on the copy and keep the original clean until you are ready to fill it out in final form.

- Read every question carefully before answering and follow all instructions to the letter. The way you fill out a form, no matter how mundane it may seem, can speak volumes about you. Remember, the form represents you to people who have never met you. If it is untidy, incomplete, or inaccurate, you will be judged accordingly.

- When you complete the occupational history section on a form, you may want to amplify the data by referring the reader to the achievements listed on your resume. Many applications seem to highlight liabilities while leaving little or no space for achievements. (I sometimes think they are designed by sadists!)

- In every case (barring exceptions discussed later), fill out everything called for on the application, leaving no blanks. Every employer must have its own record and it is to your advantage to fill out each form completely. You may have written the same facts 100 times before, but to the employer who is seeing you for the first time, the information is new and important.

  Ask Denny Ward, formerly Chevron's Manager of Professional Employment. "A recruiter has no time for additional phone calls to clarify a point," he says. "If necessary data is missing from an applicant's form, the recruiter will simply bypass the application and go on to the next person."

- If a question is not applicable to you or your field— for example: "What is your rate of taking shorthand?"—simply indicate "N/A" (not applicable), but do not leave a space blank.

- Be extremely careful with your facts; they probably *will* be checked out. Make sure that information on your application does not contradict anything on your resume. Dates, schools, degrees, and employment—all must correspond exactly. Often the consistency of the information reported is as important as the information itself.

- Always strive to have your application forms typed. If you are not a good typist, hire one who is. (If you've had somebody else type your resumes, keep that person on call.) A sloppily typed form that is difficult to read will obviously make a bad impression.

- Remember to sign your name.

- When mailing an application, attach a brief written cover letter of thanks. Never pass up an opportunity to sell the employer on your skills and interest in the company.

- Because of the broad nature of standardized forms (they are generally designed for everyone from the janitor on up), always attach a copy of your resume. Although the application form is for the record, in many cases I have seen an interviewer defer to a well-written resume over a cumbersome standardized application.

Exceptions and Sticky Stuff

In most cases, heeding the advice given above is all that's needed to handle application forms properly. But most cases aren't all cases, and sometimes company policies or personal factors may mandate some changes in procedure.

- If a form states, "complete in your own handwriting," or if you are forced to fill out a form in an employer's office, do so only after you have first made a scratch copy. (Ask for an extra form.)

- If you do expect that you will have to fill out a form in the employer's office, bring white-out to correct possible slips in penmanship. Be sure to take along relevant information, such as names, addresses, grades, dates, phone numbers, so that you can accurately provide the data requested.

- Although applications should be filled out completely and honestly, you do want to avoid giving negative information. If a form requests information on a problem area, you may want to avoid answering on the form and explain later in the interview. This is risky, but there is rarely enough space for a long explanation on an application. When asked why you left the space blank you can explain by saying, "I did so because I knew I could answer the question better in person."

- Another tactic is to put the problem in a more favorable light: Rather than stating that you left school because of weak grades, you could explain a year's gap in your academic and work record by truthfully saying that you took time off to travel.

- Occasionally you might be justified in denying that a problem ever existed. If you spent a few hours in the hoosegow after a fraternity prank a few years back, there is no reason to bring it up.

- On most applications you are asked why you left previous jobs. "To return to school" or "To accept a more responsible position" are good

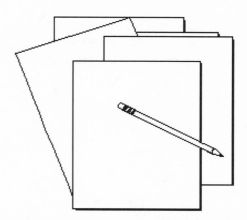

reasons to explain quitting (or even terminations), even when the de facto reasons are more complex.

- Phrasing can make a big difference in how negatively or positively your answers will be interpreted. To the question about why a person left his last job, one candidate may reply, "Laid off," while another says, "The cancellation of a government contract caused a cutback in my department." Which sounds better to you?

- A little tact and initiative never hurts. When asked why he wanted the job, one candidate replied, "You have a good reputation for job security, your products sell well, and I like your benefits program." Another said, "I think your R&D department is the best in the industry, but it isn't number one in thermal systems. I have the skills to help you reach that plateau." The latter obviously won the recruiter's interest.

Application Blanks Deserve Respect

Application blanks are one of the necessary evils of job hunting. They may not get you the job, but careless disregard of them may assure that you will not get it. Remember to treat them with respect. Which leads to this final tip:

- Keep copies of all your completed forms. You will discover, after you have done three or four, that applications are very similar. They ask for a lot of detail and sometimes require you to compose essays or provide other forms of creative expression. By being able to refer to applications you already have filled out, you won't have to reinvent the wheel when all those questions reappear.

Joe B. Meissner
San Francisco, CA

My clients always seem to have a lot of questions about the job search that aren't directly related to resume writing. Informally, I share with them what I know, refer them to good resources, and sometimes **provide a few pertinent handouts as goodwill "freebies."**

Here is a concise tip sheet that you could give to your clients in the same spirit, when it seems appropriate.

TIP SHEET

Job Finding In Tough Times
(Or in Good Times)

Work smarter, not harder, while conducting your job search. Don't just answer the want ads. Remember that hundreds or thousands of other people are seeing the same ad at the same time. This is NOT the crowd you want to be in.

Do play the numbers. Remember that 85 percent of the new jobs will be with *smaller* companies (fewer than 25 employees) and 80 percent of ALL jobs are never advertised.

Apply for a job with a good smaller company BEFORE they place the ad. How? This is the "smarter" part:

1. Choose a few companies you respect and would like to work for.

2. Then, be a sleuth: for each company, find out what kind of job titles have been advertised in the past year. How? Through your public library, on-line computer service, business library, or employment office library. (No crowds here!)

3. Pick one or more job titles that are similar to the kind of work you're looking for.

Next, a very critical task—don't avoid it:

4. Find a contact person in one of the companies who most attracts you. How? Ask around, and ask around, and ask around, and ask around. Start with your next-door neighbor, if you have to, or your brother-in-law, or a friend—just find *somebody* who knows *somebody* in that company.

5. Once you obtain the name of somebody in that company, ask THEM to identify a person who works in the department you want to be in.

6. Talk to THAT person about: a) what's happening in the department—its current problems and opportunities; and b) who actually does the hiring for that department.

7. Apply directly to the hiring person with a cover letter that talks about the current problems and opportunities the department faces and what YOU can do to help. Mention the name of your contact person. (You will have already asked permission to mention the name, right?)

Send a resume that documents your achievements—meaning those achievements that are most relevant to the problems and opportunities of that company (or department).

In your cover letter, state that you will follow up with a phone call in the next few days.

8. Follow up with that phone call and request an appointment to come in and talk about *their* opportunities and problems, and how *you* can help.

This is too logical, folks. Hardly anybody will do it! Therefore, when YOU do it, you will stand out in a crowd of hundreds, even thousands.

8

More on Resume Design

8
More on Resume Design

Altering the Physical Appearance

The physical appearance of a resume can make or break its effectiveness. A mediocre resume that LOOKS good can get more attention than it deserves, while an otherwise excellent resume may be passed over simply for lack of physical appeal—just like people!

If you can produce terrific-looking resumes, two parties benefit:

- Your client gets more attention from potential employers.
- You can justify a higher fee for your resume-writing services.

Playing with the graphic elements of resume writing can be lots of fun. Of course, having a standardized graphic layout is more efficient in terms of your time and productivity, but if you can find or make the time to experiment, learning new graphic techniques will be rewarding.

There are many **ways to change the physical appearance and appeal** of a resume, dramatically or subtly, and the most obvious are:

- choice of font (type style)
- distribution of white space
- the use of bold and italics
  (Avoid the use of underlining in a resume.)

On the following pages you will see some of these effects illustrated.

First, on pages 195-199, the same resume (Lorrie Shippman) appears in a variety of **different fonts**. Notice that the choice of font can dramatically influence the available white space, or how crowded a page looks and how readable it is. Surprisingly, 10-point type size can be fine in one font and barely readable in another! This is caused by the design variations of each individual letter in a particular font, as well as the leading (white space *between each line*). When there is not enough white space, the reader rebels because it's difficult to read.

Also notice that some fonts have a very businesslike look to them, while others are more artistic. If you venture out into the world of fonts, be sure to **choose a font that is appropriate** for the specific resume. Artistic fonts, for example, don't cut it in the banking world!

Next, on pages 200-203 some graphic do's and don'ts are illustrated, where the same Lorrie Shippman resume is shown suffering from the following design errors:

- crammed-together text
- a funky, inappropriate font
- text all in italics

Page 203 illustrates the effective use of bold and italics to strengthen a resume.

On pages 204-205 you can see how a densely packed resume was improved by better distribution of white space.

LORRIE SHIPPMAN
7855 West End Avenue
Lafayette CA 94549
(510) 999-8745

This is Courier font.

Objective: Position as a research assistant, legislative advocate,
        and/or press aide with a public policy organization.

Highlights of Qualifications
* Strong communication and research skills.
* Successful in promoting an organization and generating funding.
* Willing and able to handle a wide variety of tasks.
* Creative, resourceful, and thorough in developing a project.

EMPLOYMENT / RELEVANT EXPERIENCE

Current   Current Affairs Research Intern   - KQED PUBLIC TV, San
Francisco CA

COMMUNICATION & RESEARCH SKILLS
* Investigated program topics for "Express" show and "MacNeil/Lehrer
  Newshour" involving extensive library research and interviewing.
* Negotiated with government and private agencies for data and film footage.
* Summarized research and prepared informational packets for producers.
* Pre-interviewed studio guests. Wrote position papers for show moderator.

1985-86   Assistant Director - ASUCD STUDENT FORUMS, University of
California, Davis

PROGRAM DEVELOPMENT - MEDIA/PUBLICITY
* Collaborated on the planning, promotion, and production of 30 public
  lectures (total audience 32,000). Speakers included Geraldine Ferraro,
  author Alice Walker, physicist Edward Teller.
  - Corresponded with prospective speakers and scheduled appearance dates.
  - Organized event logistics: seating, security, decor.
  - Coordinated and scheduled publicity; prepared advertising budget.
* Conceived and produced a comprehensive TV program on AIDS which was tied
  in with community AIDS Awareness Week.
  - Won funding of $2,000 for the project through written and oral
    presentations.
  - Wrote press releases, PSAs, advertising copy; worked with graphic
    artists on design of promotional materials.
  - Secured media coverage and re-broadcasting of the event on community TV.
  - Earned commendations from university administration and City of Davis.

FUND-RAISING - COMMUNITY RELATIONS
* Successfully won support and funding from campus and civic
  organizations through a variety of means:
  - Met with organizational directors to present program ideas and
    needs, securing donations of services: catering, limousine
    services, publicity.
  - Coordinated and promoted fund-raising receptions attended by civic
    leaders, generating significant funds for ASUCD and broad media
    coverage.

EDUCATION
B.A. Economics, cum laude, University of California, Davis 1986
Education Abroad Program - Tokyo, Japan, Summer 1986

LORRIE SHIPPMAN
7855 West End Avenue
Lafayette CA 94549
(510) 999-8745

Objective: Position as a research assistant, legislative advocate,
and/or press aide with a public policy organization.

Highlights of Qualifications
* Strong communication and research skills.
* Successful in promoting an organization and generating funding.
* Willing and able to handle a wide variety of tasks.
* Creative, resourceful, and thorough in developing a project.

EMPLOYMENT / RELEVANT EXPERIENCE

Current   Current Affairs Research Intern - KQED PUBLIC TV, San Francisco CA

COMMUNICATION & RESEARCH SKILLS
* Investigated program topics for "Express" show and "MacNeil/Lehrer Newshour" involving extensive library research and interviewing.
* Negotiated with government and private agencies for data and film footage.
* Summarized research and prepared informational packets for producers.
* Pre-interviewed studio guests. Wrote position papers for show moderator.

1985-86   Assistant Director - ASUCD STUDENT FORUMS, University of California, Davis

PROGRAM DEVELOPMENT - MEDIA/PUBLICITY
* Collaborated on the planning, promotion, and production of 30 public lectures (total audience 32,000). Speakers included Geraldine Ferraro, author Alice Walker, physicist Edward Teller.
  - Corresponded with prospective speakers and scheduled appearance dates.
  - Organized event logistics: seating, security, decor.
  - Coordinated and scheduled publicity; prepared advertising budget.
* Conceived and produced a comprehensive TV program on AIDS which was tied in with community AIDS Awareness Week.
  - Won funding of $2,000 for the project through written and oral presentations.
  - Wrote press releases, PSAs, advertising copy; worked with graphic artists on design of promotional materials.
  - Secured media coverage and re-broadcasting of the event on community TV.
  - Earned commendations from university administration and City of Davis.

FUND-RAISING - COMMUNITY RELATIONS
* Successfully won support and funding from campus and civic organizations through a variety of means:
  - Met with organizational directors to present program ideas and needs, securing donations of services: catering, limousine services, publicity.
  - Coordinated and promoted fund-raising receptions attended by civic leaders, generating significant funds for ASUCD and broad media coverage.

EDUCATION
B.A. Economics, cum laude, University of California, Davis 1986
Education Abroad Program - Tokyo, Japan, Summer 1986

LORRIE SHIPPMAN
7855 West End Avenue
Lafayette CA 94549
(510) 999-8745

Objective: Position as a research assistant, legislative advocate,
and/or press aide with a public policy organization.

Highlights of Qualifications

* Strong communication and research skills.
* Successful in promoting an organization and generating funding.
* Willing and able to handle a wide variety of tasks.
* Creative, resourceful, and thorough in developing a project.

EMPLOYMENT / RELEVANT EXPERIENCE

Current   Current Affairs Research Intern - KQED PUBLIC TV, San Francisco CA

COMMUNICATION & RESEARCH SKILLS

* Investigated program topics for "Express" show and "MacNeil/Lehrer Newshour" involving extensive library research and interviewing.
* Negotiated with government and private agencies for data and film footage.
* Summarized research and prepared informational packets for producers.
* Pre-interviewed studio guests. Wrote position papers for show moderator.

1985-86   Assistant Director - ASUCD STUDENT FORUMS, University of California, Davis

PROGRAM DEVELOPMENT - MEDIA/PUBLICITY

* Collaborated on the planning, promotion, and production of 30 public lectures (total audience 32,000). Speakers included Geraldine Ferraro, author Alice Walker, physicist Edward Teller.
  - Corresponded with prospective speakers and scheduled appearance dates.
  - Organized event logistics: seating, security, decor.
  - Coordinated and scheduled publicity; prepared advertising budget.
* Conceived and produced a comprehensive TV program on AIDS which was tied in with community AIDS Awareness Week.
  - Won funding of $2,000 for the project through written and oral presentations.
  - Wrote press releases, PSAs, advertising copy; worked with graphic artists on design of promotional materials.
  - Secured media coverage and re-broadcasting of the event on community TV.
  - Earned commendations from university administration and City of Davis.

FUND-RAISING - COMMUNITY RELATIONS

* Successfully won support and funding from campus and civic organizations through a variety of means:
  - Met with organizational directors to present program ideas and needs, securing donations of services: catering, limousine services, publicity.
  - Coordinated and promoted fund-raising receptions attended by civic leaders, generating significant funds for ASUCD and broad media coverage.

EDUCATION

B.A. Economics, cum laude, University of California, Davis 1986
Education Abroad Program - Tokyo, Japan, Summer 1986

LORRIE SHIPPMAN
7855 West End Avenue
Lafayette CA 94549
(510) 999-8745

Objective: Position as a research assistant, legislative advocate,
and/or press aide with a public policy organization.

Highlights of Qualifications

* Strong communication and research skills.
* Successful in promoting an organization and generating funding.
* Willing and able to handle a wide variety of tasks.
* Creative, resourceful, and thorough in developing a project.

EMPLOYMENT / RELEVANT EXPERIENCE

Current   Current Affairs Research Intern - KQED PUBLIC TV, San Francisco CA

COMMUNICATION & RESEARCH SKILLS

* Investigated program topics for "Express" show and "MacNeil/Lehrer Newshour" involving extensive library research and interviewing.
* Negotiated with government and private agencies for data and film footage.
* Summarized research and prepared informational packets for producers.
* Pre-interviewed studio guests. Wrote position papers for show moderator.

1985-86   Assistant Director - ASUCD STUDENT FORUMS, University of California, Davis

PROGRAM DEVELOPMENT - MEDIA/PUBLICITY

* Collaborated on the planning, promotion, and production of 30 public lectures (total audience 32,000). Speakers included Geraldine Ferraro, author Alice Walker, physicist Edward Teller.
  - Corresponded with prospective speakers and scheduled appearance dates.
  - Organized event logistics: seating, security, decor.
  - Coordinated and scheduled publicity; prepared advertising budget.
* Conceived and produced a comprehensive TV program on AIDS which was tied in with community AIDS Awareness Week.
  - Won funding of $2,000 for the project through written and oral presentations.
  - Wrote press releases, PSAs, advertising copy; worked with graphic artists on design of promotional materials.
  - Secured media coverage and re-broadcasting of the event on community TV.
  - Earned commendations from university administration and City of Davis.

FUND-RAISING - COMMUNITY RELATIONS

* Successfully won support and funding from campus and civic organizations through a variety of means:
  - Met with organizational directors to present program ideas and needs, securing donations of services: catering, limousine services, publicity.
  - Coordinated and promoted fund-raising receptions attended by civic leaders, generating significant funds for ASUCD and broad media coverage.

EDUCATION

B.A. Economics, cum laude, University of California, Davis 1986
Education Abroad Program - Tokyo, Japan, Summer 1986

LORRIE SHIPPMAN
7855 West End Avenue
Lafayette CA 94549
(510) 999-8745

Objective: Position as a research assistant, legislative advocate,
and/or press aide with a public policy organization.

Highlights of Qualifications
- Strong communication and research skills.
- Successful in promoting an organization and generating funding.
- Willing and able to handle a wide variety of tasks.
- Creative, resourceful, and thorough in developing a project.

EMPLOYMENT / RELEVANT EXPERIENCE

Current   Current Affairs Research Intern - KQED PUBLIC TV, San Francisco CA

COMMUNICATION & RESEARCH SKILLS
- Investigated program topics for "Express" show and "MacNeil/Lehrer Newshour" involving extensive library research and interviewing.
- Negotiated with government and private agencies for data and film footage.
- Summarized research and prepared informational packets for producers.
- Pre-interviewed studio guests. Wrote position papers for show moderator.

1985-86   Assistant Director - ASUCD STUDENT FORUMS, University of California, Davis

PROGRAM DEVELOPMENT - MEDIA/PUBLICITY
- Collaborated on the planning, promotion, and production of 30 public lectures (total audience 32,000). Speakers included Geraldine Ferraro, author Alice Walker, physicist Edward Teller.
  - Corresponded with prospective speakers and scheduled appearance dates.
  - Organized event logistics: seating, security, decor.
  - Coordinated and scheduled publicity; prepared advertising budget.
- Conceived and produced a comprehensive TV program on AIDS which was tied in with community AIDS Awareness Week.
  - Won funding of $2,000 for the project through written and oral presentations.
  - Wrote press releases, PSAs, advertising copy; worked with graphic artists on design of promotional materials.
  - Secured media coverage and re-broadcasting of the event on community TV.
  - Earned commendations from university administration and City of Davis.

FUND-RAISING - COMMUNITY RELATIONS
- Successfully won support and funding from campus and civic organizations through a variety of means:
  - Met with organizational directors to present program ideas and needs, securing donations of services: catering, limousine services, publicity.
  - Coordinated and promoted fund-raising receptions attended by civic leaders, generating significant funds for ASUCD and broad media coverage.

EDUCATION
B.A. Economics, cum laude, University of California, Davis 1986
Education Abroad Program - Tokyo, Japan, Summer 1986

LORRIE SHIPPMAN

7855 West End Avenue
Lafayette CA 94549
(510) 999-8745

Objective: Position as a research assistant, legislative advocate,
and/or press aide with a public policy organization.

Highlights of Qualifications

- Strong communication and research skills.
- Successful in promoting an organization and generating funding.
- Willing and able to handle a wide variety of tasks.
- Creative, resourceful, and thorough in developing a project.

EMPLOYMENT / RELEVANT EXPERIENCE

Current   Current Affairs Research Intern - KQED PUBLIC TV, San Francisco CA

COMMUNICATION & RESEARCH SKILLS

- Investigated program topics for "Express" show and "MacNeil/Lehrer Newshour" involving extensive library research and interviewing.
- Negotiated with government and private agencies for data and film footage.
- Summarized research and prepared informational packets for producers.
- Pre-interviewed studio guests. Wrote position papers for show moderator.

1985-86 Assistant Director - ASUCD STUDENT FORUMS, University of California, Davis

PROGRAM DEVELOPMENT - MEDIA/PUBLICITY

- Collaborated on the planning, promotion, and production of 30 public lectures (total audience 32,000). Speakers included Geraldine Ferraro, author Alice Walker, physicist Edward Teller.
  - Corresponded with prospective speakers and scheduled appearance dates.
  - Organized event logistics: seating, security, decor.
  - Coordinated and scheduled publicity; prepared advertising budget.
- Conceived and produced a comprehensive TV program on AIDS which was tied in with community AIDS Awareness Week.
  - Won funding of $2,000 for the project through written and oral presentations.
  - Wrote press releases, PSAs, advertising copy; worked with graphic artists on design of promotional materials.
  - Secured media coverage and re-broadcasting of the event on community TV.
  - Earned commendations from university administration and City of Davis.

FUND-RAISING - COMMUNITY RELATIONS

- Successfully won support and funding from campus and civic organizations through a variety of means:
  - Met with organizational directors to present program ideas and needs, securing donations of services: catering, limousine services, publicity.
  - Coordinated and promoted fund-raising receptions attended by civic leaders, generating significant funds for ASUCD and broad media coverage.

EDUCATION

B.A. Economics, cum laude, University of California, Davis 1986
Education Abroad Program - Tokyo, Japan, Summer 1986

LORRIE SHIPPMAN
7855 West End Avenue
Lafayette CA 94549
(415) 999-8745

DON'T choose "funky," inappropriate
type fonts for a resume.

Objective: Position as a research assistant, legislative advocate,
and/or press aide with a public policy organization.

Highlights of Qualifications
- Strong communication and research skills.
- Successful in promoting an organization and generating funding.
- Willing and able to handle a wide variety of tasks.
- Creative, resourceful, and thorough in developing a project.

EMPLOYMENT / RELEVANT EXPERIENCE

Current Current Affairs Research Intern - KQED PUBLIC TV, San Francisco CA

COMMUNICATION & RESEARCH SKILLS
- Investigated program topics for "Express" show and "MacNeil/Lehrer Newshour" involving extensive library research and interviewing.
- Negotiated with government and private agencies for data and film footage.
- Summarized research and prepared informational packets for producers.
- Pre-interviewed studio guests. Wrote position papers for show moderator.

1985-86 Assistant Director - ASUCD STUDENT FORUMS, University of California, Davis

PROGRAM DEVELOPMENT - MEDIA/PUBLICITY
- Collaborated on the planning, promotion, and production of 30 public lectures (total audience 32,000). Speakers included Geraldine Ferraro, author Alice Walker, physicist Edward Teller.
  - Corresponded with prospective speakers and scheduled appearance dates.
  - Organized event logistics: seating, security, decor.
  - Coordinated and scheduled publicity; prepared advertising budget.
- Conceived and produced a comprehensive TV program on AIDS which was tied in with community AIDS Awareness Week.
  - Won funding of $2,000 for the project through written and oral presentations.
  - Wrote press releases, PSAs, advertising copy; worked with graphic artists on design of promotional materials.
  - Secured media coverage and re-broadcasting of the event on community TV.
  - Earned commendations from university administration and City of Davis.

FUND-RAISING - COMMUNITY RELATIONS
- Successfully won support and funding from campus and civic organizations through a variety of means:
  - Met with organizational directors to present program ideas and needs, securing donations of services: catering, l imousine services, publicity.
  - Coordinated and promoted fund-raising receptions attended by civic leaders, generating ignificant funds for ASUCD and broad media coverage.

EDUCATION
B.A. Economics, cum laude, University of California, Davis 1986
Education Abroad Program - Tokyo, Japan, Summer 1986

LORRIE SHIPPMAN
7855 West End Avenue
Lafayette CA 94549
(415) 999-8745

*Objective: Position as a research assistant, legislative advocate,
and/or press aide with a public policy organization.*

Highlights of Qualifications
- *Strong communication and research skills.*
- *Successful in promoting an organization and generating funding.*
- *Willing and able to handle a wide variety of tasks.*
- *Creative, resourceful, and thorough in developing a project.*

EMPLOYMENT / RELEVANT EXPERIENCE

Current   Current Affairs Research Intern - KQED PUBLIC TV, San Francisco CA

COMMUNICATION & RESEARCH SKILLS
- *Investigated program topics for "Express" show and "MacNeil/Lehrer Newshour" involving extensive library   research and interviewing.*
- *Negotiated with government and private agencies for data and film footage.*
- *Summarized research and prepared informational packets for producers.*
- *Pre-interviewed studio guests. Wrote position papers for show moderator.*

1985-86   Assistant Director - ASUCD STUDENT FORUMS, University of California, Davis

PROGRAM DEVELOPMENT - MEDIA/PUBLICITY
- *Collaborated on the planning, promotion, and production of 30 public lectures (total audience 32,000). Speakers included Geraldine Ferraro, author Alice Walker, physicist Edward Teller.*
  - *Corresponded with prospective speakers and scheduled appearance dates.*
  - *Organized event logistics: seating, security, decor.*
  - *Coordinated and scheduled publicity; prepared advertising budget.*
- *Conceived and produced a comprehensive TV program on AIDS which was tied in with community AIDS Awareness Week.*
  - *Won funding of $2,000 for the project through written and oral presentations.*
  - *Wrote press releases, PSAs, advertising copy; worked with graphic artists on design of promotional materials.*
  - *Secured media coverage and re-broadcasting of the event on community TV.*
  - *Earned commendations from university administration and City of Davis.*

FUND-RAISING - COMMUNITY RELATIONS
- *Successfully won support and funding from campus and civic organizations through a variety of means:*
  - *Met with organizational directors to present program ideas and needs, securing donations of services: catering, limousine services, publicity.*
  - *Coordinated and promoted fund-raising receptions attended by civic leaders, generating significant funds for ASUCD and broad media coverage.*

EDUCATION
B.A. Economics, cum laude, University of California, Davis 1986
Education Abroad Program - Tokyo, Japan, Summer 1986

LORRIE SHIPPMAN

7855 West End Avenue
Lafayette CA 94549
(510) 999-8745

DO add bold and italics appropriately, for emphasis.

Objective: Position as a research assistant, legislative advocate, and/or press aide with a public policy organization.

Highlights of Qualifications

- Strong communication and research skills.
- Successful in promoting an organization and generating funding.
- Willing and able to handle a wide variety of tasks.
- Creative, resourceful, and thorough in developing a project.

EMPLOYMENT / RELEVANT EXPERIENCE

Current   *Current Affairs Research Intern* - KQED PUBLIC TV, San Francisco CA

COMMUNICATION & RESEARCH SKILLS

- Investigated program topics for "Express" show and "MacNeil/Lehrer Newshour" involving extensive library research and interviewing.
- Negotiated with government and private agencies for data and film footage.
- Summarized research and prepared informational packets for producers.
- Pre-interviewed studio guests. Wrote position papers for show moderator.

1985-86   *Assistant Director* - ASUCD STUDENT FORUMS, University of California, Davis

PROGRAM DEVELOPMENT - MEDIA/PUBLICITY

- Collaborated on the planning, promotion, and production of 30 public lectures (total audience 32,000). Speakers included Geraldine Ferraro, author Alice Walker, physicist Edward Teller.
  - Corresponded with prospective speakers and scheduled appearance dates.
  - Organized event logistics: seating, security, decor.
  - Coordinated and scheduled publicity; prepared advertising budget.
- Conceived and produced a comprehensive TV program on AIDS which was tied in with community AIDS Awareness Week.
  - Won funding of $2,000 for the project through written and oral presentations.
  - Wrote press releases, PSAs, advertising copy; worked with graphic artists on design of promotional materials.
  - Secured media coverage and re-broadcasting of the event on community TV.
  - Earned commendations from university administration and City of Davis.

FUND-RAISING - COMMUNITY RELATIONS

- Successfully won support and funding from campus and civic organizations through a variety of means:
  - Met with organizational directors to present program ideas and needs, securing donations of services: catering, limousine services, publicity.
  - Coordinated and promoted fund-raising receptions attended by civic leaders, generating significant funds for ASUCD and broad media coverage.

EDUCATION

B.A. Economics, cum laude, University of California, Davis 1986
Education Abroad Program - Tokyo, Japan, Summer 1986

JAMES R. SMITH
38 Winter Street
Charleston, SC 05046
(858) 465-9876

OBJECTIVE: A senior management position in transportation, distribution, or operations where experience, education, and mature judgment will accomplish corporate goals.

SUMMARY *Over twenty years of progressive achievements in transportation, air terminal management, distributions, and relocation services, creating a blend of executive and operations management experience. Specifically:*
- pioneered international transportation movement programs for personnel and cargo;
- implemented management control systems ensuring productivity;
- conceived and instituted massive equipment maintenance programs;
- managed personnel in planning and executing air movement of cargo and passengers.

Personal Profile: A problem-solver and decision-maker in fast-paced business environments; assertive yet diplomatic management style that yields results; equally effective in individual, group, or executive settings; energetic and committed.

**PROFESSIONAL
ACHIEVEMENTS**

Directed worldwide logistics and transportation of passengers and cargo for one of the nation's premier employers of professional and technical personnel.
• Ensured effective operational capability of 40 military air terminals worldwide.
• Earned commendation for direction of 450 people and management of $16.6 million equipment budget, producing cost savings and increased efficiency.
• Developed and implemented programs reducing equipment down time by 50% under a 12% reduction in force and $232,000 budget cutback.
• Planned and directed installation of specialized computer hardware that increased surveillance by 30% on cargo movement through airlift system.
• Established hazardous material handling procedures, reducing mishaps by 40%.
• Increased cargo load factors by 8% and passenger processing time from 14 to under 5 hours on international flights.
• Coordinated commercial truck and rail transportation of 4,400 personnel and 2,250 tons of classified Department of Defense documents, under accelerated schedules.

Managed the Domestic Operations division for a progressive corporate relocation company, procuring $10 million in annual services.
• Renegotiated van line contracts ensuring quality service and equitable revenue splits.
• Developed and implemented computer programs to expedite claims, and track permanent and in-transit storage lots, resulting in decreased risk management costs.
• Mediated situations with shippers, van lines and airlines, move coordinators, and risk management teams, significantly reducing claims and short tempers.

EXPERIENCE **Corporate relocation services** MANAGER OF DOMESTIC OPERATIONS
1989-present Solutions to Moving, Charleston, SC

1986-1989 **Air Transportation** CHIEF, INSPECTOR GENERAL
1985-1986 **Cargo and Requirements** DEPUTY DIRECTOR
1983-1985 **Cargo Operations** CHIEF
1981-1983 **Vehicle Transportation** COMMANDER
United States Air Force (1967 to 1989), Lieutenant Colonel

EDUCATION CENTRAL MICHIGAN UNIVERSITY, M.A.
GROVE CITY COLLEGE, B.A.
Northwestern University: Advanced Studies in Transportation Management/Operations

REFERENCES Professional, personal, and career references provided upon request.

- Resume writer: M. Lea Cabeen -

JAMES R. SMITH

38 Winter Street
Charleston, SC 05046
(858) 465-9876

AFTER: It is more readable, with a change of font from Times to Palatino, and the addition of white space between the statements.

OBJECTIVE   A senior management position in transportation, distribution, or operations.

SUMMARY

Over twenty years of progressive achievements in transportation, air terminal management, distributions, and relocation services, creating a blend of executive and operations management experience. Specifically:

- Pioneered international transportation movement programs for personnel and cargo.
- Implemented management control systems ensuring productivity.
- Conceived and instituted massive equipment maintenance programs.
- Managed personnel in planning and executing air movement of cargo and passengers.

Personal Profile: A problem solver and decision maker in fast-paced business environments. Assertive yet diplomatic management style that yields results. Equally effective in individual, group, or executive settings. Energetic and committed.

PROFESSIONAL
ACHIEVEMENTS

Directed worldwide logistics and transportation of passengers and cargo for one of the nation's premier employers of professional and technical personnel.

- Ensured effective operational capability of 40 military air terminals worldwide.
- Earned commendation for direction of 450+ people and management of $16.6 million equipment budget, producing cost savings and increased efficiency.
- Developed and implemented programs reducing equipment down time by 50% under a 12% reduction in force (RIF) and $232,000 budget cutback.
- Planned and directed installation of specialized computer hardware that increased surveillance by 30% on cargo movement through airlift system.
- Established hazardous material handling procedures, reducing mishaps by 40%.
- Increased cargo load factors by 8% and decreased passenger processing time from 14 to under 5 hours on international flights.
- Coordinated commercial truck and rail transportation of 4,400 personnel and 2,250 tons of classified Department of Defense documents, under accelerated schedules.

Managed the Domestic Operations division for a progressive corporate relocation company, procuring $10 million in annual services.

- Renegotiated van line contracts ensuring quality service and equitable revenue splits.
- Developed and implemented computer programs to expedite claims, and track permanent and in-transit storage lots, resulting in decreased risk management costs.
- Mediated situations with shippers, van lines and airlines, move coordinators, and risk management teams, significantly reducing claims and short tempers.

EXPERIENCE
1989-present

Solutions to Moving Inc., Charleston, SC
Corporate relocation services   *Manager of Domestic Operations*

United States Air Force, 1967-1989, Lieutenant Colonel

1986-89	**Air Transportation**	*Chief, Inspector General*
1985-86	**Cargo and Requirements**	*Deputy Director*
1983-85	**Cargo Operations**	*Chief*
1981-83	**Vehicle Transportation**	*Commander*

EDUCATION

M.A., Central Michigan University
B.A., Grove City College
Advanced studies in **Transportation Management/Operations**, Northwestern University

REFERENCES   Professional, personal, and career references provided upon request.

- Resume Writer: M. Lea Cabeen -

Experiment with Graphic Techniques

Here are some **other ways to increase the effectiveness of a resume by manipulating its appearance**:

1. **Change the position of headings**. Compare flush left, indented, and centered, all of which create different effects. When everything is flush-left there is a danger of achieving an imbalanced look.

- *Tip: You can turn the resume upside-down* (so you aren't distracted by the words) and see if it looks fairly well balanced on the page.

2. **Vary the type size** to call attention to the organization of the material and create variety and interest. The job hunter's name also could be considerably larger than anything else on the resume—or the first letter of the first and last names could be larger than the rest. The headings called "Objective," "Summary," "Experience," "Education," etc., could be larger, all in caps, or bold—or all three.

3. **Highlight the key words** in bold throughout the resume, especially to call attention to accomplishments. But do this sparingly. Overemphasis results in NO emphasis.

Experiment with the Basic Layout: Two- and Three-Column Resumes

After you have some experience under your belt, you could liven up your workday by trying some radically different resume layouts. For example, **try laying out the resume text in two or three columns** instead of the usual format. This technique results in a more efficient use of the space, so you can get more material on a page without a crowded appearance. (See templates and examples on pages 207-214.)

Since this is a departure from tradition, you'll need to make sure the resulting document still conveys the immediate message: *"This is a resume."*

YOUR NAME

Your street address
City, State, and Zip
(415) xxx-xxxx

Objective

Position as Director of Whatever

Education

University of So-and-So, Podunk City
B.A., Basket Weaving, 1989
Relevant Coursework
Credentials

Highlights

- Number of years experience in work* at all relevant to the objective above.

- Credentials or education or training, relevant to this objective.

- A key accomplishment** that shows you're a hot candidate for this job.

- A strength** or characteristic** of yours that's important to you and relevant to this job.

- Something else the employer should know — a skill**, a trait**, an accomplishment**

*including unpaid work
** reflected in the details under
"Relevant Experience" *of course*

Relevant Experience

199x-present   COMPANY NAME
Job Title

A two- or three-line overview of your essential role in this company, including the kind of products or services you dealt with.

- An accomplishment from THIS job, illustrating a skill needed in the NEW job.
- Another accomplishment from this job, illustrating a skill needed in the new job.
- Another activity from this job, illustrating a skill needed in the new job.

198x-xx   COMPANY NAME
Job Title

A two- or three-line overview of your essential role in this company, including the kind of products or services you dealt with.

- An accomplishment from THIS job, illustrating a skill needed in the NEW job.
- Another accomplishment from this job, illustrating a skill needed in the new job.
- Another activity from this job, illustrating a skill needed in the new job.

198x-xx   COMPANY NAME
Job Title

A two- or three-line overview of your essential role in this company, including the kind of products or services you dealt with.

- An accomplishment from THIS job, illustrating a skill needed in the NEW job.
- Another accomplishment from this job, illustrating a skill needed in the new job.
- Another activity from this job, illustrating a skill needed in the new job.

197x-xx   COMPANY NAME
Job Title

A two- or three-line overview of your essential role in this company, including the kind of products or services you dealt with.

- An accomplishment from THIS job, illustrating a skill needed in the NEW job.
- Another accomplishment from this job, illustrating a skill needed in the new job.
- Another activity from this job, illustrating a skill needed in the new job.

YOUR NAME
Your street address
City, State, and Zip
(415) xxx-xxxx

Objective
Position as Director of Whatever

Highlights

- Number of years experience in work* at all relevant to the objective above.
- Credentials or education or training, relevant to this objective.
- A key accomplishment** that shows you're a hot candidate for this job.
- A strength** or characteristic** of yours that's important to you and relevant to this job.
- Something else the employer should know — a skill**, a trait**, an accomplishment**

*including unpaid work
** reflected in the details under Relevant Skills and Accomplishments, *of course*

Education
University of So-and-So, Podunk City
B.A., Basket Weaving, 1989
Relevant Coursework
Credentials

Relevant Skills and Accomplishments

ONE MAJOR SKILL *(that is directly relevant to the job objective stated above)*

- An accomplishment that illustrates this skill (including where this occurred).
- An accomplishment that illustrates this skill (including where this occurred).
- An accomplishment that illustrates this skill (including where this occurred).

ANOTHER MAJOR SKILL *(that is directly relevant to the job objective stated above)*

- An accomplishment that illustrates this skill (including where this occurred).
- An accomplishment that illustrates this skill (including where this occurred).
- An accomplishment that illustrates this skill (including where this occurred).

ANOTHER MAJOR SKILL *(that is directly relevant to the job objective stated above)*

- An accomplishment that illustrates this skill (including where this occurred).
- An accomplishment that illustrates this skill (including where this occurred).
- An accomplishment that illustrates this skill (including where this occurred).

A SPECIAL KNOWLEDGE-AREA (essential to the objective named above)

- An accomplishment illustrating/documenting this special knowledge (including where this occurred).
- A list of equipment or processes you're familiar with, consistent with expertise in this area.
- A list of courses or trainings you took that shows your expertise in this area.

Work History

1990-present *Job Title*
Company and city (+*another line of explanation if needed*)

198x-xx   *Job Title*
Company and city

198x-xx   *Job Title*
Company and city

197x-xx   *Job Title*
Company and city

J. RICHARD NORTON

1365 Corona Street, #6
Denver, Colorado 80218
(303) 861-8058 (home)
(303) 894-4027 (work, evenings)

Macintosh/PageMaker designer-editor with magazine and advertising agency experience is ready to be your one-man SWAT team, on-call for overflow work or handling a desktop publishing crisis

SUMMARY

Can follow, imitate, or create design styles; has a stick-to-it, finish-the-job attitude; responsible and independent; able to develop design alternatives and recommendations; creative, detail-oriented, flexible; wants to put out best-product-possible-within an articulated budget; has excellent knowledge of English language mechanics, punctuation, and spelling; quickly learns and rapidly adapts and incorporates new software skills into jobstream; exercises humor when under pressure.

SKILLS INVENTORY	**Desktop publishing** **Editing, writing, and copywriting** **Project planning and implementation** **Proposals, presentations, and marketing**
SOFTWARE PROFICIENCIES	**Aldus PageMaker 3.01/4.01** **Aldus Persuasion 2.0** **Aldus FreeHand** **Apple File Exchange** **Claris FileMaker II/FileMaker Pro** **Claris MacDraw II/MacDraw Pro** **Claris MacWrite II** **Microsoft Word 4.0** **Microsoft Works 2.0** **Microsoft PowerPoint** **A variety of other DTP and WP software**
ADDITIONAL SKILLS	**Mature, reliable, independent** **Creative, resourceful problem-solver** **Combines design sense with editorial eye** **Trained in people skills and group work** **Rapid and eager learner**

ACCOMPLISHMENTS

Prepared winning proposals, design work, and promotional materials for national choral festival (Denver 1992) and for international festival chorus project (Vancouver 1990).

Donates professional services and time in design, public relations, and marketing for cultural, educational, community, civic, religious, and political organizations.

Involved in peer counseling/crisis intervention; selected to lead training groups to prepare volunteers; undertook additional undergraduate training in psychology and counseling.

Participant/board member in community choral and instrumental music organizations for ten years; edited national newsletter for organization of community bands.

ACADEMIC

Bachelor of Arts in Journalism (News-Editorial Sequence)
University of Wisconsin; additional complete major in English
A.A. in mental health (psychology and counseling) in process, Montgomery College, Takoma Park, Maryland (course work complete, one fieldwork placement still needed); Citizens Mental Health Advisory Committee; Phi Theta Kappa.

WORK EXPERIENCE

DENVER, COLORADO (1988-PRESENT)

Macintosh Coordinator, Kinko's Copies, (Auraria Store) (1989-present)
Weekend typesetting production and management of full- and self-serve desktop publishing and word processing services; customer training, instruction, troubleshooting, and problem solving.

Design Director, Great Bear Studios (Consulting) (1988-present)
Owner/operator of small full-service graphic design and production studio, focussing on small-business and home-office support, marketing, copywriting, and Macintosh training.

Technical Document Specialist, Harding Lawson Associates, (1989-present)
Production word processing of scientific/environmental reports for consulting firm on MS-DOS-based system using WordPerfect 5.1.

WASHINGTON, D.C. (1976-1988)

Typesetter, Hanley-Wood Publications, Inc. (1986-1988)
Production typesetting of two monthly national trade publications (*Builder* and *Remodeling* magazines), using XyWriteII+ as front-end to ATEX system.

Evening supervisor/legal secretary, Hogan & Hartson (1983-1985)
Coordinated off-hours secretarial support for 400+ person law firm; production word processing, including WP as front-end to typesetting.

Editorial project director, Page-Bennett Associates (1981-1983)
Copywriting, research, design, paste-up and advertising/production coordination for a 4-person public relations firm; major focus in bookselling, catalogs, non-profit organizations, and events promotion.

Legal systems analyst, Informatics, Inc. (1978-1980)
Design, implementation, and documentation of RECON IV data bases; market research and intelligence; user hotline support and training; proposal writing, editing, and production supervision.

Technical abstractor/proofreader, Informatics, Inc. (1977-1978)
Abstracting and indexing of technical information in chemistry, biology, legislation, medicine, public policy, and the environment; abstracting French, Spanish, and Italian language technical articles; general clean-up of on-line bibliographic data bases.

Production proofreader, National Geographic Society (1976-1977)
Proofreading, quality and specification review, and final release authorization for *National Geographic* and *World* magazines and numerous books published by the Society.

ANCIENT HISTORY

Journalism and English teacher, Norwalk, Ohio (1974-1976)
Including supervision, fundraising, design, and quality review of yearbook; teaching writing, editing, design and hands-on production of monthly student newspaper. Both were award-winners.

Reporter/Editor, Madison, Wisconsin (1973-1974) Supervised all arts and entertainment coverage of six-person cultural staff; edited, reported, and reviewed movies, theatre, and special events for UW weekly campus newspaper.

REFERENCES AND WORK SAMPLES AVAILABLE UPON REQUEST

- Resume writer: J. Richard Norton -

DAVID W. DOWLER

1365 Corona Street, #6
Denver, Colorado 80218
(303) 861-8058 (home)
(303) 650-8850 (voice mailbox)

I have pursued a variety of responsible clerical, sales, and customer-service positions while having a parallel career as a musician, musical director, voice coach, and theatrical director...

I now seek reliable, secure employment while I (finally!) finish a degree-granting, part-time college-level program.

SKILLS INVENTORY	Customer service
	Information services
	Account administration
	Reproduction, binding, DTP
	Sales presentations & account management
	Administration of licenses and permits
	General secretarial; data entry
	Retail sales

DATA/WORD PROCESSING; OFFICE EQUIPMENT	Computer literate
	Experienced in IBM/DOS and Macintosh environments
	IBM System 36/WP, MIS
	Microsoft Word; Claris MacWrite II
	A variety of other word processing, account tracking, and desktop publishing software packages
	Xerox 9500; Kodak Ektaprint 225
	WP typing speed: 65 wpm

ADDITIONAL SKILLS	Mature, reliable
	Works well with people of all ages
	Quick learner
	Skilled in resolving conflicts and misunderstandings
	Skilled in sign language (manual communication for the deaf)

ACCOMPLISHMENTS

Elected to boards of directors of church-related, performing-arts, and music organizations.

Organized and taught continuing-education course in beginning sign language via University of Missouri at Kansas City.

Involved with the direction, production, or musical production of over 50 stage musical productions and over 35 dramatic productions.

Have dealt with wide variety of people, from seniors to children, in community drama activities.

ACADEMIC

Re-entry student; seeking to complete B.A. degree

Central Missouri State University, Warrensburg, MO
Have earned 95 credits towards Bachelor of Fine Arts, concentration in Musical Theatre, including courses in Acting, Directing, Makeup, Music Theory, Orchestration, Opera Theatre, Oral Interpretation.

WORK EXPERIENCE

Key Operator, Night Shift—(1/89-11/89)
Kinko's, Kansas City I Store, Kansas City, MO
Quickly became expert in operation of sophisticated xerographic units, binding machines, laser typesetting; fulfilled production needs of a constant-deadline situation; assisted Managers in orientation and training of new employees in all phases of store operation.
Hired as a temporary employee, I was made permanent after three weeks and offered a position requiring mechanical expertise, ability to work unsupervised, and a stick-to-it, get-the-job-done attitude.

Manager, Package expediting service—(11/88-1/89)
The Shipping Dock, Kansas City
Specialized in packaging and freight in response to customer needs, from gift wrapping to UPS shipping; supervised/scheduled volunteer staff of 12; became expert in UPS regulations. Responsible for balancing register each night and making bank deposits.

Sales Manager/Customer Service —(4/84-8/88)
Kansas City Convention Center, City of Kansas City
Responsible for clerical and word processing support of busy 3-person convention center sales office, handled both phone and public contact; after internal reorganization, functioned as a part-time Sales Manager, booking events, quoting rental rates, filing paperwork to confirm events. Responsible for depositing checks and some contract writing. Group sales ranged from conventions of 250 to 5,000 persons.

Secretary/Health Permit Processor —(10/83-4/84)
Health Department, City of Kansas City
Prepared required reports for federal, state, and local health agencies; processed applications for Food Establishment Health Permits. Answered routine phone queries regarding regulations and referred technical questions to authorities.

Clerk/City Earnings Tax —(9/82-10/83)
Revenue Division, City of Kansas City
Sort mail for division of 40, processing quarterly tax returns (up to 10,000 pieces daily); filled phone requests for city tax forms; data entry of tax returns.

Senior Accounting Clerk —(11/80-1/82)
Truman Medical Center, Kansas City, MO
Data entry of patient accounts posted to outpatient billings; collected charge slips from hospital departments, divided charges to appropriate member of 4-person pool; performed regular data entry quality control checks.

Secretary to Director, Student Information —(9/79-12/79)
University of Missouri, Kansas City, MO
Personal secretary to Director; processed incoming mail requests from prospective students about University programs, regulations, procedures; supervised two student employees; (this was a long-term temporary assignment).

- Resume writer: J. Richard Norton -

CHORAL/CONDUCTING RÉSUMÉ
DAVID W. DOWLER

5810 E. 10th Street
Kansas City, Missouri 64126
(816) 241-3625 (h)
(816) 444-0500 (w)

SKILLS INVENTORY	**Choral conducting** **Instrumental conducting** **Section leader** **Rehearsal accompanist** **Composition** **Vocal arrangement** **Instrumental arrangement**
VOICE PART	**Baritone (G→G)**
INSTRUMENTS	**Piano (formal study, 7 years)** **Flute** **Clarinet** **Saxophone** **Violin** **Viola**

Principal organizer and ofttimes performer for choral and instrumental community musical groups

Heartland Men's Chorus, Kansas City, MO
Interim Conductor, 11/88-2/89
Associate Conductor, 5/88-present
Conducted Christmas concert on two weeks' notice, shepherded chorus through hazardous period between permanent directors. Other duties include Bass Section Leader, Rehearsal Accompanist; Charter member, 7/86

Metropolitan Community Church of Greater Kansas City, Kansas City, MO
Director of Music, 1982-85; 1987-88
Choir Director, 1982-85; 1987-88
Responsible for coordinating church music program for congregation of 200, choir of 25; scheduled and coordinated rehearsals, and performances of choir, accompanists, and vocal soloists.
   Major works conducted include the Fauré *Requiem*, Britten's *A Ceremony of Carols*, Sloan and Braman's *O Come Let Us Adore Him*, Red and Courtney's *Celebrate Life*, Hayes' *Come and See His Glory*

MAGIC, Kansas City, MO (1984-1985)
Conductor, 1984-1985; **Instrumentalist**
Size of ensemble ranged from 5 to 15.

LGBA
Guest Conductor, Fall 1985
Conducted festival massed bands of 150 instrumentalists at annual national conference, Dallas, TX

ACADEMIC
Central Missouri State University, Warrensburg, MO
Earned 95 credits towards Bachelor of Fine Arts, concentration in Musical Theatre, including courses in Acting, Directing, Makeup, Music Theory, Orchestration, Opera Theatre, Oral Interpretation.

MUSICAL THEATRE	**Musical director of over 50 productions, including—**

Most recent credits
   Director, *She Loves Me*
   Music Director, *Music Man* (cast of 70)
   Music Director, *L'il Abner* (cast of 50)
      (Cameo as Mayor Dawgmeat)
   Music Director, *Some Enchanted Evening* (Rodgers and Hammerstein review, cast of 5)
   Music Director, *Handsome and Girdle* (opera parody, cast of 7) (Première)

Original Compositions
   Truckin' (Première) (also musical director)
   Wildcats in Petticoats (Première) (also musical director)

Arrangements of Existing Music
   Hanged in Their Own Family Tree (Première)
      Contemporary melodrama
   Ten Nights in a Bar-Room (Première)
      Music of Stephen Foster

Conductor/Music Director
   Guys and Dolls; Music Man; Oliver

Music Director
   Aesop's Falables; Dames at Sea; The Fantasticks; Godspell; Handsome and Girdle (premiere); *I Do! I Do!* (2x); *It's a Zoo in There!* (premiere); *Li'l Abner; Man of La Mancha; Oh, Coward; Old King Cole; Once Upon a Mattress; You're a Good Man, Charlie Brown*

Assistant Musical Director
   Applause; Fiddler on the Roof (3x); *Gypsy* (2x); *Kiss Me, Kate* (2x); *Oklahoma!* (2x); *Where's Charley?*

ENSEMBLE AFFILIATIONS

Bell Road Barn Players/J. David Theatre, Riverside, MO
Community, non-Equity Theatre. Production staff of 8 to 10, part-time/volunteer.

Missouri Theatre Ensemble, Higginsville, MO
Professional, non-Equity Dinner Theatre. Resident company of 7-14 members, production staff of three.

Anderson Schoolhouse Theatre, Sidney, IA
Professional, non-Equity Theatre. Resident company of 8-15 members, production staff of four.

Peanut Playhouse/Popcorn Playhouse Osage Beach, MO
Professional, non-Equity theatres. Resident companies of 6 to 8 members, production staffs of three.

ADDITIONAL EXPERIENCE

Private Study in Musical Directing/Conducting with David Richards, former Musical Director/Conductor for Rich Little

Additional private study in voice and conducting

Pit Orchestra
Anything Goes, Applause, Bye Bye Birdie, Chicago, Company, The Fantasticks, Fiddler on the Roof, Guys and Dolls, Gypsy, Jesus Christ Superstar, Mame, My Fair Lady, Oklahoma!, Once Upon a Mattress, Seven Brides for Seven Brothers, Some Enchanted Evening, You're a Good Man Charlie Brown, et alia...

- Resume writer: J. Richard Norton -

JANET E. LEWALLEN

P.O. Box 200203
Denver, Colorado 80220
(303) 355-9941

SEEKING/OFFERING

Position as a travel agent in a friendly service-oriented office that appreciates my established clientele—

- *Proven ability to handle a wide variety of details involved with successsful sales of FIT, tour packages, and group travel*
- *Proven adaptability and flexibility in being able to orient to new surroundings and procedures quickly, efficiently, and professionally in capacity as a Temporary Travel Agent*
- *Proven ability to establish and keep a broad base of clientele and to serve their travel needs successfully*

SKILLS INVENTORY	Customer service
	Detail-oriented
	Resource and research specialist
	Manager and organizer
	Clear written and oral communication
	Sales presentations & account management
DATA BASE TRAVEL COMPUTER SYSTEMS	Computer literate
	Experienced in IBM/DOS environment
	Special travel industry applications: SystemOne CRS; APOLLO; PARS CRS
	Account tracking
ADDITIONAL SKILLS	Mature, reliable
	Works well with people of all ages
	Quick learner
	Skilled in resolving conflicts and misunderstandings
	Exercises humor when under pressure

ACCOMPLISHMENTS

Through involvement in social, and political organizations, I have served in a variety of positions including Boards of Directors, officers, and committee chairs.

Learned travel industry from the ground up, with no prior experience or training in the industry.

Enjoy reputation as a knowledgeable and skilled, client-responsive travel agent.

ACADEMIC

Bachelor of Arts, *cum laude*
Morningside College, Sioux City, Iowa
Sociology major; Psychology and Social Work Minor
Who's Who Among Students in American Universities and Colleges; President, Alpha Kappa Delta, National Sociology Honorary; President, Sociology Club

WORK EXPERIENCE

Travel Trade Temporaries, Littleton, Colorado
- **Independent Contractor – 4/90 to Present**

On-call assignments as a domestic travel agent to handle agencies' overflow work; have successfully completed assignments with both SystemOne and APOLLO agencies, including Professional Travel Corporation, Carlson Travel Network, and Master Travel, as well as a number of smaller agencies.

Journeys, Denver, Colorado – 11/88 to 8/90
- **Travel Consultant**
- **Office Manager**
- **Outside Sales Agent**

Was hired as agent for 3-person office, then promoted to Manager when owners moved to Los Angeles; when financial considerations of the agency forced personnel reorganization, continued on as outside sales agent until agency folded on good terms with ARC.

Focus: Leisure, group, and corporate sales, both domestic and international; agency specialization in Mexico; utilized SystemOne CRS through an IBM PC.

The Travel Junction, Wheat Ridge, Colorado
- **Travel Consultant** } 6/90 to Present
- **Outside Sales Agent** } 6/87 to 11/88

With no prior professional experience or specialized training in the travel industry, was originally hired to do outside sales; with increasing skills as a service-oriented, client-concerned agent, learned the travel business from the ground up and was promoted to a full-time position after only three months. Utilized PARS CRS prior to agency conversion to APOLLO. [Have reassociated with agency as an outside sales person since Journeys folded.]

Focus: Promoted leisure and group travel, primarily domestic; through my successful service-oriented approach, I developed a number of personal and small-business accounts which followed me when I moved to my next position.

Denver Women's Chorus
- **Trip Manager – 1/87 to Present**

Responsible for arranging biannual trips for 100-member group, including transportation, lodging, and all other logistics. Responsible for record-keeping, monitoring budget, and cost accounting.

Have organized successful group trips to Seattle and Washington, D.C.; currently arranging June 1991 trip to Boston and New York City for 150 travelers.

- Resume writer: J. Richard Norton -

SALLIE YOUNG
Impressions by Sallie • San Jose, CA
(408) 978-7278

Objective: Your Resume Writer.

HIGHLIGHTS OF QUALIFICATIONS

♦ Creative idea generator
♦ Finely tuned sense of the English language and its usage
♦ Flair for graphic design
♦ Pride in achieving the best possible results
♦ Thrive on helping clients get the results they want

EDUCATION

B.A., Journalism
San Jose State University

3rd Degree
School of Hard Knocks

TECHNICAL SKILLS

♦ Type 90 wpm in MicroSoft Word on Macintosh SE.
♦ Can operate any Mac word processing or desktop publishing program.
♦ Also have IBM and Atari capabilities.
♦ Can produce final copies with print shop-quality results.

PROFESSIONAL EXPERIENCE

Writing & Editing

♦ Penned dozens of interesting and lively features from interviews of amazingly diverse people during five-plus years as a professional reporter.
♦ Discovered gold mine of bright bits to write about people, programs and occupations, through informational interviewing, to publish in district newsletters and local news media during five-plus years in school district public information.

Graphic Design & Layout

♦ Created graphic design and layout of posters, flyers, programs, brochures, booklets and resumes for a family-owned print shop.
♦ Conceived ideas in a variety of media, on a limited budget, for newsletters, flyers, programs, manuals, full-color brochures and other publications for public school districts.

Resume Results

♦ Crafted several resumes that will be published in "Resume Round-Up: A Nationwide Sampler of Successful Resumes," compiled by resume guru Yana Parker, published by Ten Speed Press, to be released in January 1992.
♦ Fashioned dozens of resumes for family and friends throughout the past 15 years that secured interest, interviews, and ultimately, jobs.

WORK EXPERIENCE

Present	Proprietor	Impressions by Sallie, San Jose, CA
1991	Freelance Writer	*Los Gatos Weekly-Times, Metro, South Bay Accent Magazine*, Santa Clara County
1990	Reporter	*Los Gatos Weekly-Times*, Los Gatos, CA
1987-89	Staffperson	Santa Clara County Supervisor Dianne McKenna's Office, San Jose, CA
1989 (Fall)	News Editor	*Spartan Daily*, San Jose State University San Jose, CA
1989 (Spring)	Reporter	*Spartan Daily*, San Jose State University San Jose, CA
1987	Freelance reporter	*Indio Moneysaver*, Indio, CA
1984-87	Public Information Specialist	Desert Sands Unified School District, Indio, CA
1983	Reporter	*Palm Springs Desert Sun*, Palm Springs
1981-83	Public Information Technician	Bakersfield City School District, Bakersfield, CA
1980	Graphic Artist	Hall Letter Shop, Bakersfield
1978-79	Reporter	*Yuma Daily Sun*, Yuma, AZ

- Resume writer: Sallie Young -

A B B Y

2775 Custer Drive, San Jose, CA 95124
(408) 978-7278

Objective:
Position as Graphic Designer's Assistant or Pasteup Artist

Highlights of Qualifications

- Creative and artistic sense in graphic design.
- Learn quickly; interpret information accurately.
- Enthusiastic, energetic; excellent at working in a team setting to meet deadlines.
- Three years' experience in graphics design and layout.
- Working knowledge of pasteup techniques, mechanicals, ruling and assembly of type.

Education
Degree Pending
Academy of Art
San Francisco
A.A.,
DeAnza College
San Jose

Design Experience

GRAPHIC DESIGN

- Created calligraphy for businesses and individuals; as free-lance calligrapher:
  ~ selected character styles appropriate to the assignment;
  ~ produced original and adapted designs for ornamentation and borders;
  ~ Designed and produced Book of Records for Pyramid Productions, involving calligraphy of 300 names of customers and officers, and ornamentation.

- Designed logos for community group, retail store, and professional therapists.

- Designed successful brochure for Narendra Bulow, bodywork therapist, choosing type, colors and materials consistent with desired image.

PASTEUP

- Pasted up brochure of services for Surfaces Beauty Salon, involving calligraphy, photo reduction and pasteup.

- Pasted up mail order catalog for Emerald Priestess retail store.

- Pasted up many flyers for community organizations and small businesses.

Employment History

1986-Present, Student and Graphic Artist, Academy of Art, San Francisco (free lance)

1985, Receptionist, About Face & Body salon, San Francisco

1985, Graphic Designer, Emerald Priestess, books and crystals, Berkeley

L O N G

- Resume writer: Sallie Young -

9
Starting Up Your Business

9
Starting Up Your Business

BUSINESS START

Getting Advice Before You Start

If you're thinking of getting into the resume-writing field, **talking with someone who has already started a resume business** could be very helpful.

However, other resume writers MAY be reluctant to talk with you if they think you'll become their competition. We'll get around that problem in this chapter by **listening in as several entrepreneurs candidly relate their experience in starting a business**.

To start off, **I'll tell you how my Damn Good Resume Service came into being**.

Yana's Business Start-up Story

First, a bit of background. In all my adult life (until 1979) I had only two jobs that I truly enjoyed:

a) my first "real" job, as *inspector in an electronics plant*—which I loved because **I could earn enough** to support my family, and **it was an exciting learning environment** (I learned how to read blueprints and use tools such as a microscope, a micrometer, calipers, etc.)

b) and a job as *Community Worker (liaison) in a state employment office* in Albany, New York, where **my experience alone qualified me to do a professional-level job**, and there was lots of **opportunity and encouragement to apply innovation and initiative.**

BUT—the Big But—both of these great jobs disappeared when massive layoffs were necessary. I moved to California, hoping to get a fresh start, but it was Recession Time, during the early 1970s, and soon I was humbled enough to accept a clerical job in a downtown San Francisco engineering firm. (Grateful to get it, by then!) Later on, TRW bought up this small firm, put in place some intolerable working conditions, and effectively eliminated my job. So once again I found myself very vulnerable to the whims and fortunes of big business and government.

One day, while searching for an appropriate job, I noticed a sign in an empty storefront: Montclair Business Service. I checked around and learned that it had recently gone out of business. My mind clicked into action: "I can CREATE my own job! I have a great typewriter, the rent is due, I'm broke, and here is this service that no longer exists. I'LL do it!"

And so Parker Business Service was born, specializing in typing, fliers, resumes, and anything else I could do with my brains and my typewriter. I made up some fliers and distributed the first batch at the supermarket parking lot.

Over the next few years I struggled to keep my business going, and periodically **had to take some short-term jobs with a "temp agency" to make ends meet**. For a while I even worked full time at the local university, and ran my resume business on nights and weekends.

During this struggle, **I engaged a financial advisor** to help me figure out what it would take to make my business actually flourish. He pointed out one way to increase my income: to charge a small fee for the "freebie" packet of material I was giving to new clients. I upgraded the packet, and gave it a title—"Damn Good Resume Guidelines"—and a $2 price tag.

To make a long story short, that little packet quickly evolved into a small book, the *Damn Good Resume Guide,* and then Ten Speed Press discovered and published it. So now my fledgling **resume business had led me to a lucrative spin-off**: authoring books!

Soon I was able to phase out the temporary job, initially cutting back to a four-day week, then to half time, and finally to zero time, all the while rebuilding my business to a full-time operation (now called Damn Good Resume Service), and ultimately publishing a second book, and then a third book.

Over the years **my business has been transformed from resume writing to TEACHING resume writing** through books, newsletters, workshops, and software. With this level of diversity, my homemade job now provides all the satisfaction I enjoyed in those two all-time-favorite jobs from which I was laid off. Where will it all go from here? Who knows!

Lessons Learned

Here are just a few of the lessons I'd like to share from my experience of starting a business:

1. **Begin with whatever services are most marketable**, so you can get a foothold and have á base from which to be more creative, BUT don't lose sight of your long-term goal.

Start out slowly—with minimal financial investment—so you aren't risking your security. Figure out how much time you can afford to give yourself to learn, and pace your business development. Put the timing down in writing, so you don't panic when progress seems slow. Then you'll realize that you are still on track.

2. **Learn to write resumes!**

Get immediate hands-on experience. Don't wait. Find some people RIGHT NOW to practice on. Do their resumes for free, but act as if you were being paid for each resume, so you'll find out what the issues are when writing professionally. This experience will have two benefits:

- You'll get past the scary "I-don't-know-how" phase.
- You'll begin to establish a word-of-mouth client base.

You could create an internship with a career center; volunteer to do some resumes (with supervision) for their clients as a way to gain direct experience.

Do some research; read, read, read everything you can find about resumes. Look at all the resume books in the bookstores and pick out just the best for your own reference library. New ones appear all the time, and a *few* of them are worth buying, such as these two I just discovered:

Just Resumes, by Kim Marino (200 examples) published by John Wiley & Sons, Inc., 1991

No Pain Resume Workbook, by Hiyaguha Cohen, published by Business One Irwin, 1992

3. **Set your initial fee.**

Call around (just as your clients will be doing) and find out what other people charge. Try at the same time to get a sense of the value of each service (is it a "factory" or do they provide personalized, skilled services?) and, for starters, price yourself in the middle. In the beginning, I charged MORE than local word processors and somewhat LESS than the more pricey career counselors.

Start out charging a little less than what you expect to charge in six months when you are more skilled; but charge enough so you can afford to do it at that rate. Estimate the minimum weekly amount you need to make as a trainee (full time) and how many resumes you could produce in a week. You'll have to try it, really, to find

out—it depends on your work style. (More on this in Chapter 11, All About Money.)

4. **Don't give up** if it doesn't happen to work at first. You can retrench, get a temporary job, and try again.

5. **Get help when you need it**.

Determine what you need from other people in terms of your professional development, make a list, and find out who is best at providing each thing.

Assemble—at least in your mind!—a team of advisors, people you meet with individually, or even as a collaborative team, to give you advice. These might include:

- a word-processing tutor
- a resume-writing mentor
- a business-development advisor

6. **Network with related services**.

Assemble (in your mind) your team of directly affiliated **services**. For example:

1) Who will you send your clients to for laser printing and making copies?

2) Who will help your clients with other job-related advice, like interviewing skills, job-search information, and skill assessment?

Go and visit these service people, tell them what you're doing, leave them some business cards, and tell them you'll be sending clients. Finally, tell them you'd like them to send you clients. Write a thank-you note when they send someone.

7. **Get smart about the career scene.**

Learn about the "whole enchilada" of job hunting. Your clients will expect you to know about related things—so use some of your time to explore the same resources THEY will be exploring. You'll need to know where these resources are, and you'll want those resource people to know about YOU.

Some of those important related resources are:
- Business libraries
- Career centers (private, public, university)
- State employment services
- Agencies that have a career sideline (Jewish Community Center, college reentry programs, etc.)
- Bookstores with a great "Careers" section

8. **Develop your uniqueness**.

When you are unknown, you need something to distinguish you from the fifteen other resume-writing services nearby.

What's in it for the client if they choose you? How will you be different? Make your advertising and marketing pieces reflect this uniqueness.

9. Look for ways to **combine your special skills and interests**, which might lead to a profitable spin-off or niche market.

LETTERS

I get lots of letters and telephone calls from people asking for help or advice on getting started. This first letter from Lisa Gessner of Glen Gove, New York, pretty well covers all the classic questions of a new resume writer, and my classic responses.

The Classic Questions of a New Resume Writer

Dear Yana: I am interested in possibly writing resumes for profit, not necessarily under the aegis of a company. I would offer resume-writing services and perhaps other related services too.

In recent months, I have purchased a Macintosh II desktop publishing system, in the hopes of supplementing my income with freelance writing. I have also realized that I enjoy writing resumes (with the aid of the *Damn Good Resume Guide*) and cover letters, and that I am good at it. I am considering offering services on a part-time, professional basis. However, I have many concerns.

First, and foremost, should I advertise? I will be working out of my home. Do I want to take the chance of inviting virtual strangers (after a phone interview) into my house, especially if I am home alone?

Hint in responding: I live on Long Island, which is not the safest place to reside. I am not able to open an office at this time. My thought is that I should generate business cards and network like crazy. I would feel more comfortable with doing work for friends and acquaintances of friends and working on a strictly

referral basis. At the moment, I'm not looking to make a lot of money, but I'm wondering if I'll make any money this way.

Lisa

Dear Lisa: I have worked out of my home for over ten years and so have my associates. We all started out with the same worries, and none of our fears have materialized. The people who make and keep appointments are generally NOT the same people that would hassle you or burgle your apartment.

You probably need to advertise SOMEWHERE in the beginning, as it takes a substantial time for client referrals to build up significantly. If advertising in the Yellow Pages is a bigger step than you want to take right now, I'd recommend putting a SMALL ad in a local newspaper (even a weekly publication) and keeping it there consistently. Repetition is the key in advertising. —yp

My next question is: what services should I offer? I have a printer that produces excellent copy, so I could just offer basic typing, formatting, and printing of already-existing resumes; minor updating would also fall into this 'no sweat level.' However, I'm prone toward the creative process as well, [such as]: writing and editing, which involves more time and sweat. I realize that by charging by the hour I can earn more money, but I'm afraid of one major drawback: What if my client doesn't get a job with their new resume? Does anyone work on a satisfaction guaranteed basis? Is it possible to do so? Does that mean providing career counseling and/or job search capabilities? And should I then offer to write cover letters, and how is this done in an expedient manner? For example, the client sees an ad in Sunday's paper and wants a cover letter done for Monday. What if this isn't possible from my perspective? —Lisa

Lisa: To start with, focus on the actual resume writing (that's where the money is.) Nobody works on a "job guaranteed" basis! Remember, the purpose of a resume is to get an *interview*, and getting the *job* involves much more than just a good resume. You have no control over all that, nor any responsibility for it. You should, however, follow up on some of your clients to see if, generally, their resumes are working to get interviews.

Timeliness, however *is* very important. Remember, by the time a person realizes they need a resume, they oftentimes need it now, RIGHT now. Find out, first, how urgently they need the resume, and if they need it "anytime in the next month or so," then arrange your schedule so you keep some quick-turnaround time available for people who DO need their resume immediately. I have even rescheduled clients who didn't need the work done immediately in order to accommodate a client who did. —yp

To confuse me even further, a friend suggested that I offer a whole resume package: resumes, cover letters, business cards, letterhead, envelopes, etc. I love designing, despite my lack of formal artistic training, but I'm afraid of the wear and tear on my printer. Could I design the peripherals for clients, put the material on a disk, and have them go to a print shop? —Lisa

Lisa: Certainly! You could visit one that's near your home, ascertain that they do high quality work, and then make an agreement with them: you'll send clients regularly if they'll take good care of them. You may even choose to have a charge account with the copy center and include the copying cost in your total resume package.
—yp

I am designing my business card now. Is it okay to list 'resume service' and then pick and choose the extent of the services I want to perform, depending on the client's needs and my time? (I intend to continue working at a full-time job.) Is this a legitimate starting method, or will the inconsistency jeopardize my prospective clientele? —Lisa

Lisa: It's a viable way to start and won't get you in trouble with clients. If you pick and choose, then it would be wise to network with other reliable tradespeople who could provide the related services you don't offer. —yp

Making the transition from a full-time job to successful self-employment is definitely possible. The way I did this was to first make myself relatively indispensable at my full-time job (so I had some negotiating clout), then request (persuasively) one day off a week to pursue my own interests. I made it clear that a) I would get my work done in the remaining four days, and b) I would probably have to leave altogether if my request wasn't granted! About six months later, after my business built up somewhat, I similarly negotiated a half-time position and helped hire and train another person to job-share with me. About a year after that, I was able to quit my job and go full-time as an independent resume writer.

Stories of Business Start-ups

Here are the real-life business experiences of several other aspiring resume writers, largely in their own words excerpted from correspondence with the author and/or from the *Damn Good Resume Writer Newsletter.*

JEFF'S STORY: PART I

Jeff, a sixty-year-old man from Los Angeles, looked for new work for almost two years after losing his job. Despite a great background, he kept hearing, "You're overqualified; we couldn't pay you enough."

He started looking for a way to create his own job, and saw an ad in the local newspaper: RESUME BUSINESS FOR SALE.

He checked it out and learned that the owner wanted over $80,000. He knew that even spending $20,000 would wipe out his family's savings. Still, he was attracted to the resume business.

Jeff found my book, the *Damn Good Resume Guide,* which mentioned "advice for would-be resume writers," So he called to talk the matter over. I urged him not to spend anything on buying the resume business because it was very unclear whether he'd be getting anything worth a significant investment.

I thought Jeff could put together a business by himself for much less money. He could get equipment, advice, and the training he needs—from several different sources, and he would have the flexibility to choose the best of each.

I also felt he should not increase his anxiety level by going way out on a limb financially. Besides, how much is an existing resume business worth? Most revenue is generated by new business, not from past clientele.

A few weeks later, Jeff came up to Berkeley for an all-day consultation. We talked about all aspects of the business and I showed him my office, filing systems, resource library, and computer equipment. Jeff went home with five hours of tape-recorded advice, enthusiastic to get started. He still had a lot of hard work to do, anxieties to deal with, equipment to buy and master, and new skills to learn.

JEFF'S STORY: PART II

Later, Jeff wrote a letter to readers of the *Damn Good Resume Writer Newsletter*:

ADVENTURES OF AN UNEMPLOYED SIXTY-YEAR-OLD

Here's a brief professional background, which might explain why I turned to resume writing as a business at the ripe young age of sixty-two.

After a lifetime in entertainment both on- and off-stage, as performer and promotional writer, I became involved with trade associations through writing promotional, educational, PR, editorial, and business texts as well as planning, directing, and supervising conventions and trade shows. In December 1987, I found myself an unemployed sixty-year-old with talents not in great demand in Southern California and a bank account that held its head in shame. The next two years took a terrible toll on me and my family.

While searching for a business which could benefit from my skills without needing much cash, I saw an ad for a resume service for sale. Since promotional writing is the art of using as few words as possible to convince the reader to accept your point of view, it seemed that resume writing wasn't that different from what I had already been doing.

Some research resulted in two observations: 1) This business was a godsend for me and, if successful, I could eventually branch out into other areas of promotional writing; 2) Why go into debt to buy someone else's resume company, since most business comes from future promotion rather than past jobs? I could probably start my own company with a much smaller investment and no debt.

Turned on by two of Yana's books, I phoned her for an honest opinion and later flew to Berkeley for the most constructive seven-hour session I've ever spent with anybody. I left with what I needed the most—the feeling that I can and should do this thing, enough basic information to get me started, and the confidence that I can make it work. Result: I have leased an office and will soon open my new company, **A Better Resume**.

(Jeff also wrote about his new computer equipment, See page 239 in the next chapter.)

SEVEN MONTHS LATER: HANGING IN THERE

I can't believe I've been "in business" for over seven months, and that I'm still surviving. (Well—trying to!)

Although I wouldn't exactly say that I'm setting the resume-hungry world on fire, I am holding my own and making overhead expenses (barely). But word is spreading (however slowly), clients are sending me referrals (a slow drip but gradually developing into an anemic trickle), and I'm even beginning to get referrals from several executive search firms. In fact, one executive had me do HIS resume (surreptitiously, of course).

I'm not following the crowd. I have developed my own procedure, which is based on a deep and thorough introspective analysis of the client as both human being and professional. My concept: We're the sum total of our total environment since childhood. This has a profound effect on the type of worker we are and, therefore, the accomplishments we've achieved. My relationship with the client is very personal, and the two comments I hear most often are: "Jeff, I feel like I'm with my shrink!" and "I don't understand. You're a total stranger. Why am I telling you things I've never told to another soul?"

Breaking the Rules

I'm breaking all the rules. I end with "objective" rather than start with it, since I've often found that the objective prior to the probing analysis has changed somewhat by the time we're finished. Therefore, at the end of our "session(s)" (yes, if needed, sometimes I give two or even three), we finally get to the "Tomorrow"

section. It's incredible how, after reliving and analyzing one's life, so many perspectives for the future change from what they were before the session. The fact is, I don't always use an "objective." In some cases I substitute an opening statement when I think it will be more advantageous—opening up more possibilities by stating who the client is and what their talents are rather than what they're looking for. Sometimes I don't use years, and once I even left out employers.

I don't follow anyone else in town in substance, look, or procedure, so I don't compete with them in price. A client looking strictly for price isn't interested in the personal service offered by "a better resume." I've raised my fee twice—starting with $125, then raising to $150 and now to $200. (These rates include the session(s), one-page resumes, and twenty copies on expensive but not ostentatious paper.)

Happy Clients

It seems to work. My clients are happy, seem to have higher self-esteem when they're finished, and sometimes even say that I'm not charging enough. They send me all kinds of goodies; my last, an artist, presented me with a magnificent original photographic art-work that has won several awards. Most important, I feel good about what I'm doing, even though my wife is convinced that, because of the hours I devote to each client—which obviously limits the number of clients I can handle—bankruptcy is just around the corner. Well, perhaps it is, but at least I'll know I did what I believed in.

Jeff Lewis
A Better Resume
Sherman Oaks, CA

SUSAN'S STORY

This is the story of how I got started as a resume writer. In May 1989 I met Yana Parker at a resume workshop she gave at the Berkeley YWCA. Looking back now, I see that I really got my money's worth ($5) out of that class! Before the session, I got her book from the library and made an attempt at writing my own resume. To tell the truth, I thought I knew what I wanted to do: to "work with people." I was a little embarrassed to find out that was not nearly focused enough to create a good resume. I needed to know exactly how I wanted to work with people. I needed a job title. In spite of that, Yana liked my resume.

I defined my job title and used that resume to get a position as a secretary at an electronics firm. Two months later I realized how much I hated it. The only thing on the job that excited me was acquiring Macintosh computer skills. I had never worked on a computer before and this gave me plenty of word processing experience and some composing opportunities.

At this point, when I was totally depressed about this paper-shuffling job, I finally admitted to myself that I didn't like it and I needed to find something else. I asked myself, "What do you really want to do?" The answer came very spontaneously: "I want to work with Yana Parker as a resume writer. And I want to manage a resume-writing office."

And so the idea was born. It took me two months to gather the courage to write a letter to Yana. In that letter, I said exactly what I hoped for and figured the worst she could do was say "No."

Two days later I got a call from her; she said she was interested. She was dealing with a family medical crisis and could use assistance with the business. We made arrangements to get together the next night to discuss the possibilities.

The upshot of the meeting was that she needed to go to Arizona for a short time and would leave my name and number on her answering machine for prospective clients. (I later learned that she figured I couldn't get into TOO much trouble in a few weeks' time!)

So I went into it cold turkey! Without any training from my new mentor, I was called upon by job seekers to write their resumes. I scheduled my first appointment two weeks in advance. In those two weeks, I sought out every opportunity to get experience; I did as many friends' resumes as possible for free.

Finally, the day came when I had to perform as "the professional resume writer." I was surprised at how well it went. Of course I was nervous and tried my best to hide it. I remember feeling very self-conscious that someone had paid me to think. And that they were sitting there, watching me think! Why, they were probably more intelligent than me! But the magic was not in what I thought or wrote. It was in what we composed together as a team. It was a wonderful process of bringing out the best, most inspiring aspects of the client's life and documenting them. In the next few months I saw people come into my home in confusion and insecurity, and leave with self-confidence and self-esteem. And this all came from recording the absolute truth! There was no need to fabricate or exaggerate. Each one had valid experiences to feel proud of. People would come to life when they talked about what they loved doing. They started talking a little faster and a little louder when they spoke about their accomplishments. That's how I would know we were on to something.

Yana came home and we got together to review my resumes. Her critiques were extremely helpful and overall she was pleased with my work. We decided to embark on a year-long apprenticeship program.

Susan Ireland
Dynamite!! Resumes
Kensington, CA

CYNTHIA'S STORY

In establishing my career after college, I spent a lot of time reading resume books and talking to recruiters, headhunters (i.e., executive search firms), counselors and the like, trying to get at the best way of representing myself in a resume. Apparently, I had success with my methods, because I was always able to land the interviews I really wanted. I was also able to successfully cross industries (e.g., go from manufacturing to banking to consulting to telecommunications).

I soon realized my resume was promoting my skills well enough so that I wasn't being pigeonholed according to my previous job title; instead I was being evaluated for the skills that I had become effective in. I found myself helping many friends and acquaintances with resume writing/creating. I became more and more aware of the difficulties that both those with college degrees and those without had in accurately representing themselves when seeking employment.

My brother noticed that I spent a lot of time doing this and suggested that I start a business. He encouraged me to attend a class on new businesses for young entrepreneurs. In this program (sponsored by Youth Entrepreneurial Services, or YES, located in Berkeley, California) we had to develop a full business plan. This included a marketing plan, cash flow analysis, etc. This plan really allowed me to focus on what I wanted to do. It also gave me confidence that I could do it! However, one of the program administrators told me that he thought I couldn't make any money from this type of venture. Well, I've never been a person who could accept "can't" easily—in fact, his words continue to challenge me to be successful!

In that vein, I work hard to provide the best personalized assistance to the client, whether it is a small business developing a profile or an individual beginning a job search. I put a lot of effort into bringing the true person within out into the limelight. In addition to resume creation, seminars on resume writing, job search, and interview techniques, I provide cover letters, biographical sketches, and advertisement/resumes for

small businesses. All services include one-year storage on my own diskette filing system, professional tips as applicable, two laser print copies, and up to 100 high-quality photocopies.

I believe that I do an excellent job with my clients and seminars. Clients have taken their resumes to recruiters and received flattering comments about their quality. One agent of an executive search firm said I have the Midas touch, which he described as the ability to take a variety of information and focus it—to the point. Yet the most restricting factor, I think, is myself. One of your readers wrote a letter saying how hard it is to work on the business when you come home from a full-time job. This is so true!

Marketing my part-time business as a full-time employee is my most difficult task. Most of my present clientele have been obtained through personal contacts, referrals, and the seminars and career fairs that I attend, but I have a difficult time following up some of the leads. I have lost some potential clients because they wanted a resume in a day, and I was just too tired to make the extra effort!

To be honest, I have lost clients because I have taken too long to respond with an appointment. So, in an effort to make the best use of both the client's and my time, I often ask for current resumes via mail so that I can assess the time it would take me to complete them. I do not do four-hour marathon sessions with my clients when I create resumes (because of my full-time employment). I usually work on a resume over the space of a week. The clients who don't need resumes immediately could easily go longer.

Financially, I cannot give up my full-time job, but I truly want to give my resume business a good go of it. Although the income I've received hasn't been significant, I would describe the business as moderately successful so far.

**Cynthia Mackey
Winning Strategies
Oakland, CA**

Peeking Into Other Offices

Most resume writers love to talk shop, and those who are thinking about getting into the business would do well to take a peek and listen in on these **revealing conversations about the day-to-day practice of resume writing**.

From the letters and phone calls I've received, I'd say 90 percent of resume writers start off on a part-time basis with a home-based office. Many became resume writers as I did—pretty much by accident, discovering this outlet for their talents while on their way somewhere else!

In some of the samples that follow, the resume writers have written a **brief profile** of themselves specifically for this chapter. In most cases, though, I have simply quoted from their **letters** directly, or summarized a **phone conversation.** You will note that the issues of money, equipment, and time continually crop up.

Following these "peeks" into other offices, this chapter closes with some advice from Linda Marks on making the transition from full-time employment to becoming successfully self-employed.

DISCLAIMER

Please note that I am not personally endorsing the work of any particular resume writer by including their name in this book. —yp

Dear Yana: After my son was born, I read about a mother of four who had a home-based typing business. Hating housework and thriving on the company of other people, I thought a home-based business might be just what I needed. This seemed especially enticing since I wanted to stay home with my son. Because of my past secretarial experience and my interest in computers, I decided on a word-processing business. I did a little research (very little) and dove in head first (or is it jumped in feet first?). I grossed approximately $0 the first two months. After doing the research I should have done initially, I decided to add resume counseling to my list of services.

I received two appointments within a week. Armed with no degree, no experience, and a very nervous stomach (but I did have the *Damn Good Resume Guide*), I greeted my initial client— a university grad with an engineering degree. I was just beginning to feel as cool as I imagined myself looking, when he stated (as he sat down at my kitchen table), "I planned to do this resume myself, but this job is so important I decided I needed a professional."

I have since set up a nice office in the basement, learned a great deal about resume writing and running a business, and have met a lot of interesting people. I still get a nervous stomach now and then, but I feel good about my work.

My engineering grad called a few weeks ago for a revision. The resume I wrote for him had helped to land the job he wanted. He had since returned to school and is on the hunt again. After taking another look at my very first project, I redid the entire resume for the price of a revision. This made him happy all over again.

Vicki Law-Miller
Scribbles to Script
Montrose, CO

Dear Yana: I am a truck driver by trade, and I like to write as a hobby, which is why I purchased my computer to begin with. Close friends and relatives have started coming to me for help with their resumes because they know I have a computer and like to use it.

I was told about your book by a computer applications instructor while attending a word-processing class. I purchased the book and I am very pleased with the results.

I have been amazed by managers' reception of the resumes prepared using your methods, and I have discovered that a great amount of satisfaction lies in helping people move ahead in life. There is just one small problem: I am helping everyone but myself!

After reading and using your book, and enjoying the results garnered from the methods learned in it, I've decided that maybe I am missing my calling, and would like very much to learn more about starting my own resume service here in Detroit. I feel there is a good market for the service here and in neighboring areas, such as Ann Arbor and Ypsilanti, which are growing at a near out-of-control pace. It would please me very much if I could earn a living doing something that enables me to derive such a degree of pleasure.

By the way, the computer I've been using is a very simple D model Leading Edge with dual 5.25 drives and a very basic software package. I have almost none of the graphics capabilities of your Macintosh, which proves to me that the writing style means more to managers than a lot of the fancy stuff other resume services offer.

Doug Zeiger
Mt. Clemons, MI

Dear Doug: Go for it! You are already a writer; just make sure you keep your spell checker and grammar guidebook close at hand. I'd also recommend looking at all the resume books available; many of them are terrible, but a few are good—for example, *The Perfect Resume* by Tom Jackson. —yp

Kelly Bow, of Caldwell, Idaho, is in one of the fastest growing areas of the U.S., with big employers coming into the city. Boise is a half hour away.

Kelly has a sixteen-month-old baby and another is due very soon. She and her husband started **The Information Marketplace** a few months ago, originally focusing on software consulting but now specializing in resumes. They have essentially no competition.

She charges $40 for a resume and it takes her about two to three hours (sometimes four to five hours). Her strategy has been to charge minimally to attract business. I pointed out that she is not paying herself very much and she should experiment with raising her rate to at least $75. If she establishes herself as the BEST resume service in the area she won't have any trouble making money.

I advised Kelly to reconsider the name of her new business, now that she has switched the focus to resumes. If the key word, "resume" appeared in the name of the company, that would help potential clients find her.

Kelly Bow
The Information Marketplace
Caldwell, ID

Judi Robinovitz, of East Brunswick, New Jersey, is a published software author and technical writer. She started her business, **Resumes That Work!**, after revising a neighbor's resume that was poorly prepared by a professional. Equipped with the *Damn Good Resume Guide*, WordPerfect, a laser jet printer, and a scaleable font cartridge, Judi began marketing her talents.

After a probing interview to reveal her client's most rewarding accomplishments, Judi synthesizes the facts and her impressions into a resume designed to create just the right impression. Judi is a perfectionist who prides herself on both the content and physical appearance of her resumes. Many of Judi's clients have hired her to write individual cover letters and follow-up letters as well.

Judi keeps in touch with her clients throughout their career search, and is proud of the fact that all of them have quickly gotten interviews using her resumes. Her business has blossomed to include additional staff and computer training/consulting (aptly named Computer Solutions). She also conducts resume workshops and seminars.

A while back Judi wrote: "I called your office about four or five months ago to get some insight into the resume business. I have since started, and I want to share some of my ideas with you.

"I started advertising, primarily in college newspapers, about two months ago. I also advertise in a local weekly newspaper and in my synagogue's bimonthly newsletter. I've just begun to display fliers on college bulletin boards.

"I've volunteered my services to two colleges to do free student seminars on resume writing, but they've turned me down ('turf' problems with their career counseling staff seems to be the reason). I plan to try again, volunteering my services to our local library, aiming more at professionals. I truly adore public speaking—almost as much as I love to write!"

Judi Robinovitz
Resumes That Work!
East Brunswick, NJ

Oliva Gorey wrote in April: "Last fall I started a part-time resume writing business, working out of my home, evenings and weekends, and have met with moderate success.

"I have a computer-equipped office and have written approximately thirty-five resumes. The first ten I did for friends at no cost to develop the necessary skills. I am presently using a double-disk, Leading Edge computer, color monitor, and Panasonic P1124, twenty-four-pin, letter-quality printer. I started out using a program called 'The Resume Kit'; however, it had limitations so I am presently using WordStar 4000 (a word-processing program).

"My service includes a one-hour or longer interview, a draft if requested, and a final package of twelve copies of the resume, matching letterhead and envelopes, and several 'Tip Sheets' on writing a good cover and thank-you letter. The resume is stored on a disk and each client is entitled to two updates free of charge."

Oliva G. Gorey
Ideal Resume Service
Portland, ME

Nancy Rosenberg of Babylon, New York feels that a resume service makes an excellent home business. Nancy, the owner/operator of **The Right Resume,** began part-time after the birth of her daughter, Alison. She now limits her work to four jobs a week (sometimes she has to turn work away) and also conducts resume-writing workshops for local libraries and other organizations.

Currently, her office is a corner of the dining room in her small condominium and consists of a word processor, desk, and bulletin board. Overhead is, of course, very low, but the tradeoff is the

inability to write off all of her rent, telephone, and utilities expenses.

Nancy doesn't feel her professional image has suffered from running her business alongside her young family. "Many clients have raised families and are very intrigued by the way I combine my work and home life. Also, I keep my prices very competitive because I can't offer extras at this point. I deliver a 'plain vanilla' package which includes a resume on plain paper suitable to go to the printer and one other copy (a sample on good-quality resume paper)."

When her daughter enters public school in two years, Nancy plans to expand her operation to full time and look for an "office to share" in the local downtown area. She would also like to teach resume writing in local colleges and adult continuing education programs.

Nancy Rosenberg
The Right Resume
Babylon, NY

Dear Yana: After talking with other resume writers, I settled on my service fee, charging $15 an hour for straight word processing/typesetting, and $20 an hour for creating/updating resumes. This is still subject to change, however, depending on my competition survey results.

Since I also intend to advertise at local colleges (using fliers), I am going to charge a "student discount" rate of $15 an hour for creating/updating resumes. I know my rates are low, too low for my area, but until I get my feet under me, I'm comfortable with these rates.

So far, I'm dragging my heels a bit about creating and posting my fliers, and spreading the word via my business cards. I find it extremely difficult to work on the Mac at work eight hours a day (even though the editing, layout, and design I do there is fun) and then come home and work on my Mac for another two hours at night.

I thought it would be different, that I'd rush home each day to do all the important stuff I have to do to get my resume service going. I know that if I plan to support myself during the time I'm home raising a family, I'd better get my a__ in gear, soon."

Lisa Gessner
Glen Cove, NY

Dear Yana: The most practical way to put my computer equipment to work was to begin creating resumes. After studying your book, the *Resume Catalog*, I created my first resume. It was for a friend, it was free, and it landed an interview and a job as a legal assistant. I then conceived **Dataco Resume Service**.

After talking with you by telephone, you sent me my first paying client. He had read the *Damn Good Resume Guide*, liked what he saw, and wanted a resume that looked like one in the book.

Dataco Resume Service operates with an IBM clone, WordPerfect 5.1, RightWriter (the grammar and style checker), Bitstream's FaceLift that provides seven font styles in point sizes from 2 to 500 using two key strokes. It's all brought together with a Panasonic KX-P4420 LASERPARTNER.

Calvin Baird
DATACO Resume Service
Hialeah, FL

Dear Yana: I work out of my home, as **Schneider Word Processing**—and there's a downside to that: Sometimes people don't consider you "professional" if you work at home. But I have discovered a plus: Some people like the confidentiality of going to a quiet neighborhood rather than to a public office building to have their resume prepared.

I do a broad scope of work, from term paper typing to complicated desktop publishing (I really enjoy the variety) and I consider myself quite capable in the English department (grammar, spelling, vocabulary).

I am surprised at the prices that are quoted in your newsletter. I don't come close to those figures, partly because I'm not sure of myself and afraid of losing business, and partly because this area of the country can't support it.

I charge by the hour for consultation, and by the page for the actual typography. Over time, I am working out the bugs in the way I conduct business. As I get better, I am getting more confident about charging for the actual time it takes to produce that one- or two-page resume.

I enjoy my setup: an IBM compatible, WordPerfect 5.1, Bitstream Fonts (plus a few others), a laser printer and a fax machine. I am not the least bit interested in using a resume software program (no apologies).

I have several ideas about what I would like to put in a handout to give clients well before our meeting. My problem is that there IS no "well-before-our-meeting!" The procedure I usually use goes something like this: Once a customer calls, we make an appointment, they come in, and we proceed with the consultation (I ask them on the phone to bring at least the basic information written down). After that first meeting, I work on my own to create their resume. They come in again and if necessary, we fine-tune it right then, and the customer leaves with the resume. I don't really have an opportunity to send them a handout with tips, ideas, and "seeds." Most of them are in too much of a hurry to wait for something to come in the mail before we meet.

My clients are mostly blue-collar workers, women reentering the work force, or low-end sales and business people. The majority have no concept of what a resume and cover letter should be and are not in the frame of mind to try to understand. This is one reason I want to put something in writing. I'm hoping it will save me time explaining certain basic theories and policies, over and over. Also, the written word often carries more clout.

Chris Schneider
Schneider Word Processing
Mobile, AL

Dear Yana: I began my business full time in February of 1991. I had a slow start, but things are now picking up. The name of my business is *A Scribe to Greatness*. This is a play on words that many people appreciate, and others just say, "Huh?"

First and foremost, I consider myself a professional writer and consultant. My college training has been in psychology, technical writing, counseling, and personnel management. This formal training is augmented by ten years in retail/personnel work, crisis counseling, and real estate sales. This diversified background is an advantage when working with the average career explorer.

My business is located in a college town (there are two state universities in Denton). I offer professional writing, typing, word processing, resumes, personal interview coaching, and full-color photographic business cards. I find that after helping a client in his/her career search, I often provide them with distinct business cards! Most of my business is resumes and word processing right now, but I have begun a direct mail campaign to secure other writing assignments as well.

For me, the most effective advertising medium has been the Yellow Pages. I went all-out with a color display ad. The advertising contract included the equal-dollar amount in free advertising elsewhere in the book. The phone book has been out for only one week and my phone has been ringing steadily with requests for all types of work.

I printed and distributed 1,500 fliers—all I got was blisters on my feet and a sunburn.

I have had success with my newspaper ads—but I don't run them under "Resume Service"—I run them under "Help Wanted." My most effective ad reads: 'A resume should be a personal marketing statement about you. Let me help you stand out from the crowd—A Scribe to Greatness."

I was so pleased with the results from this ad that I used the same statement in my Yellow Pages ad. Our local paper also runs a "Who's Who in Business" and I have a contract ad running under "Professional Writing."

I have found that my greatest competition is a local mailbox rental storefront that also does direct mailings, word processing, and resumes. Their fees for the same service that I provide are almost three times as high. I have priced my service along the same lines as the local word-processing services.

One service that I offer that makes a difference is free pickup and delivery. I work out of my home, and had the usual fears about letting strangers into my home. I find that I can meet prospects in their home or a neutral location (such as Denny's for coffee), go over a questionnaire I use for initial information gathering, and arrange for a later meeting.

I write and design on an IBM-compatible computer. (Hyundai Super 286 C, with a VGA Color Monitor, one 5 1/4 inch disk drive, one 3 1/2 inch disk drive, plus 4 meg. hard drive). I use a Epson twenty-four-pin dot matrix printer that features eleven fonts. I hope to add a laser printer soon, as well as a graphic scanner. I have a fax number, but no machine. (I have an arrangement with a local public fax service. This saves me money: I have access to faxing without the expense or upkeep of the machine.)

Some of my customers prefer the "typed look" for their resume. It gives the appearance that they did it themselves. So I also use an IBM Selectric (industrial type) typewriter. One customer gave me the job because she had a twelve-page application that needed to be typed and no one in town still used a typewriter (other businesses told her that their computer didn't do forms). So you see, "old faithful" still has a purpose!

Rene Stelzer
A Scribe to Greatness
Denton, TX

Phyllis Pechman of Iowa City, Iowa, started her business, **Pechman Professional Services**, nine years ago as a word-processing service. She worked out of her home for the first few months (till the distraction of her teenagers drove her out!). "I initially called it a secretarial service but discovered that was a big mistake and changed it."

Before long, a local community college called and asked her to teach word processing. Gradually Phyllis built a business that is unique in her area. She has grown to a company with a staff of eleven (eight teaching classes and three doing resumes). The classes include word processing, telephone techniques, and how to purchase a computer. Class size is limited for lots of one-on-one attention. They also do computer installation, consulting, and ongoing training for businesses.

Half of Phyllis's business comes from corporations, the other from students and professional people. Student resumes cost $200, resumes for professionals are around $250 (since the latter often take a lot more time, she is reconsidering this price). Each resume comes with a "satisfaction guarantee."

The Pechman resume process is: a) a two-hour interview, b) writing and typing the resume, c) a follow-up appointment for any small changes (typically around ten minutes, but sometimes longer). Phyllis also offers practice in job interviewing using videotape.

She uses WordStar 2000+ on an IBM. "Everybody around here is IBM or IBM compatible. WordStar 2000+ is relatively easy to train people in."

One-third of her business comes from the Yellow Pages, one third from advertising in the daily college newspaper, and one third from word-of-mouth.

Phyllis Pechman
Pechman Professional Services
Iowa City, IA

Note: Addresses and phone numbers are on page 399.

Making the Transition

The majority of us entrepreneurs make a *gradual* break from working full-time for someone else to full-time SELF-employment. This can be a stressful transition, fraught with potential failure, and it calls for every talent we possess, plus some we *don't* yet possess! Over ten years ago when I was making this transition myself, I was helped by Linda Marks who was then on the staff of New Ways to Work, a San Franciso nonprofit that promotes work-time options. Now Linda herself has made that transition, and is an *independent* consultant helping people write "win-win" proposals to present to their employers when they want to negotiate a part-time or job-sharing arrangement. She also advises career counselors and resume writers on preparing *joint resumes* and cover letters for job sharing. I asked Linda what she would advise aspiring entrepreneurs, and here are her tips on how to make the transition easier.

FROM FULL-TIME EMPLOYEE TO FULL-TIME SUCCESSFUL ENTREPRENEUR

by Linda Marks

You've decided you want to gradually phase out of your full-time job and, when there's enough money coming in, become a full-time resume writer. Here are some ideas to make it happen:

1. **Present your employer with a solution instead of a problem.** Don't say "I want to reduce my work schedule" without adding "and this is how the rest of the work will get done." Write down the tasks and responsibilities of your position and determine what you can realistically accomplish with a reduced schedule. Then propose a way to get done what you can't. Some possibilities are:

- **Delegate.** Ann, an operations manager for a software company, wanted to reduce her schedule to four days a week. She looked at the tasks and responsibilities of her job and found that about 20 percent of it was personnel-related. She identified a secretary in the company who was college-educated and bored because she didn't have enough work to do and presented a proposal to her employer that was "win-win-win": Ann would get to work four days a week; the secretary would get to do the personnel-related tasks in addition to her secretarial work (and make more money); and the company would get to keep Ann, get all the work done *and* save money. It was a winning proposal.

- **Use freelancers.** Peter, an attorney/ entrepreneur, proposed to his law firm that he reduce his hours and call in a contract attorney on an hourly basis to do any work he didn't have time for. Since the firm's work load was down, the firm saved money on Peter's salary and the proposal was accepted.

- **Job share.** Amy, who works as a manager for a professional association, tried working three days a week after her second child was born but found herself attempting to do a full-time job in part-time hours. She proposed sharing her job with someone else. She knew the association had difficulty recruiting top people, so she attached the resume of her next-door neighbor, who was highly qualified to job share with Amy, to her proposal. It worked.

2. **Put yourself in your employer's shoes.** How will what you propose benefit your employer?

- He/she will keep your skills and experience at least a bit longer.
- You'll be able to train your replacement over an extended period of time.
- Your proposal might save money.

- Part-timers and job sharers use less sick leave and have lower absenteeism rates.
- With job sharing, an employer gets two people's ideas and energy, a wider range of skills in one position, greater flexibility in scheduling, and trained coverage for vacations, sick leave, and crunch periods.

3. **Be prepared to answer your employer's concerns about your reduced schedule:**

- "It will cost more" (for benefits, overhead, paperwork).
- "Part-timers (and job sharers) aren't serious about work."
- "If we let you do it, everyone will want to."
- "What if you're needed and aren't here? "
- "How will you keep informed?"
- "Managers can't work part time."

4. **Above all else, don't apologize for wanting a reduced work schedule.** Be positive and optimistic, and make it happen. Get your employer to work with you on your "phase out," and, with luck, someone else's "phase in." GOOD LUCK!

Linda Marks
Work Options Consultant
San Francisco, CA

10
Computer Equipment

10
Computer Equipment

Oh! It's So Confusing! . . .

Your **computer or word processor** is going to be your **most expensive and most important piece of equipment**, followed up closely by the **printer** that goes with it.

Yes, you could certainly *get by* with an *excellent* typewriter, and you could certainly *start* your business with a typewriter. But you will have to move up to the current technology sooner or later, in order to develop and keep a competitive edge, or you'll lose your clients to those who can deliver a more impressive resume product.

If you don't already have a computer, then this chapter will introduce you to some of the issues you'll want to consider before you buy your equipment. A few words of consolation: **It IS confusing — very confusing. There are too many choices, and none is perfect**. The computers that are easy to learn are overpriced. The affordable choices are harder to use. It's a dilemma!

Your best bet, to prepare for making a difficult choice of what to buy, is to **find several people who use their computers the way you will be using yours**—primarily for word processing. If you plan to do high-end, pricey resumes, then talk to people who do desktop publishing or page layout on their computers. **Find out what SOFTWARE they think is best** and then **find out what HARDWARE will run that software**. Ask them LOTS of questions—such as "WHY do you like this one better than that one?"

For now, we're going to use the word "computer" to refer to EITHER a computer or a word processor.

(A machine called a dedicated word processor does only word processing, acting like an automatic typewriter. A computer does MANY things besides word processing, and it needs a separate software program for each of those functions.)

The question of IBM vs. Macintosh comes up over and over again. Here's my hit on this comparison: IBM's advantage is that it's a lot cheaper and there are more programs available. Mac's advantage is that it's very easy to learn and use, and it is more powerful in in the area of graphics. Whatever route you go, realize there's a giant gulf between them and it's tough to switch from one to the other!

In this chapter, **I'll start off first with MY Macintosh story**, and then you'll find articles

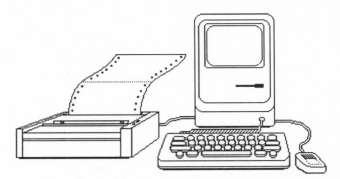

and letters from other people about their computer experience and tips. You'll notice that IBM clones, also known as DOS-based computers, outnumber Apple Macintoshes by an overwhelming margin, largely because they are less expensive.

Yana's Computer Tales

In 1984 I bought my first computer, a tiny (128K) Macintosh, and the honest truth is that **buying it was a totally emotional decision**—there was no rational decision making going on here *at all*! I didn't even know anybody who owned their own personal computer. I had tried out the other major brand (minimally) at my "temp" job and felt intimidated by its complexity. The ads said the Mac was easy to learn, and fun, and that was what appealed to me. Also there was a special-purchase discount for staff, so I closed my eyes and said, "Yes, yes, I want it."

It has been a love-hate relationship ever since. I wince every time my associates tell me what they paid for their IBM-clone equipment, compared with what my Apple equipment costs. Yet I've never wanted to trade machines with them! I am very resistant to reading manuals (you could even say **I HATE to read manuals**!) and the Mac is the best choice for someone with that attitude.

Since 1984, I've moved up from the 128K Mac, to a 512K Mac, to a 1 meg. MacPlus, to a 2 1/2 meg. MacPlus, to a 4 meg. accelerated MacPlus, and finally taking a BIG leap to an 8 meg. Mac IIci equipped with a thirteen-inch inch color monitor and a twenty-one-inch two-page black-and-white monitor. Over the same time period, I have had only two printers: a dot-matrix Apple ImageWriter for the first two years, and then an Apple Laser-Writer II-NT, which is an excellent, trouble-free workhorse of a machine. My equipment is definitely fancier (and pricier) than what you'd need for simple resume writing, but now I am producing books, software, and all my own marketing and training materials, so I can justify this indulgence!

The **large monitor** has been among my all-time favorite pieces of optional equipment. Macs come with fairly small screens, and it was heavenly to graduate to a screen where I could see the whole resume at once.

Choosing software for the Mac is easy because several basic programs are runaway-first-choices in their category. I simply **go for the best-known programs**, using Microsoft Word for word processing, Aldus PageMaker for page layout, and Claris FileMaker Pro for my databases of clients and resumes. I use Hypercard for cataloging clip art.

If you don't have a computer yet, and you are a person with a creative or artistic bent, you are going to love having this tool at your fingertips!

Two tips to keep in mind when you go shopping:

a) **Keep your investment affordable**; don't get heavily in debt for your computer, but . . .

b) **Buy the best equipment you can possibly afford and be sure that it's expandable** to meet your future needs.

Other Computer Stories . . .

BUT FIRST SOME ADVICE ON HOW TO CHOOSE RATIONALLY:

HOW TO CHOOSE YOUR COMPUTER SYSTEM

by Lynn Desker

For individuals thinking of starting their own resume business, the perennial question arises: Which computer system will I choose for my business? I am using the following approach to determine which computer system I need for my business.

1. Determine what you ideally want the computer to accomplish. For example I would want a computer system that can:

- Manage databases and generate mailing lists.
- Account for income and expenses of multiple small business units.
- Generate computer-scored career tests for the Myers-Briggs Type Indicator & Strong Interest Inventory.
- Produce expense tracking reports for myself and my clients.
- Produce newsletters and fliers for marketing and promotion purposes.
- Produce resumes that are ready for the client to mail to target employers.
- Generate correspondence.

2. Prioritize the requirements of your computer system based on your business goals and strategies. Which niche is YOUR niche? Are the individuals you deal with clients or customers?

I intend to focus primarily on career issues of professionals and self-employed individuals. This translates into a system that allows me to write business plans for myself and my clients, generate spreadsheets for budget forecasts, and produce monthly profit-and-loss statements. I also require a good database management system to generate mailing lists for my current and potential clients.

Therefore, I would rather have a computer system that has a business emphasis (read IBM) over a more creative system (read Apple/Mac).

An alternative strategy would be to buy a Mac specifically for the resume business if I were con-

COMPUTERS

vinced I could generate the income to pay for this investment.

Or I could get an Amiga, which supposedly allows the user the advantages of both the IBM and the Mac. What are the disadvantages? Is it twice as confusing?

3. Find out what software packages are available, and the advantages and disadvantages of each package.

4. Ask the individuals already using a computer in their work (in the same or similar industry), and not in competition with you (different geographical area?) for their experiences with their software packages and systems. Good, bad, or indifferent?

5. Determine what complimentary services are provided by other organizations in the vicinity. For example, many copy centers provide desktop publishing services using the Mac. This is useful information for clients who want to produce copies of their resumes for more than one potential employer. Some copy centers provide similar services for both the Mac and IBM. They also provide file conversion services from IBM to Mac and vice versa.

Will you be using these options in your service strategy? What would your customers/clients prefer?

6. Determine what support services you will need to overcome initial anxieties of using the computer system.

Ask yourself how familiar you are with any computer system. If you have never had any previous computer experience, the vendor's support and training services become crucial.

Can you get training in essential software packages from other sources, e.g., community colleges?

7. What is your budget for getting a computer system?

8. Design a decision-making grid to help you determine what your most appropriate computer system and software package options are.

9. Evaluate your hardware and software choices by examining the possibility of renting a similar system from a hardware vendor.

Alternatively, you may have a friend who will allow you the use of their system over the weekend. Check it out! Does the system perform as you had anticipated?

What else needs to be figured into the decision-making grid? Go back to step one to figure out what needs, if any, have been previously omitted.

Lynn Desker is a recent graduate and is developing her private practice in Singapore.

Every resume pro can tell you stories about the computers in their lives—and what works for them and what doesn't. What they have to say may help you make up your mind if you are contemplating a purchase or a upgrade.

Macintoshes in Resume Writing

SUSAN IRELAND'S MACINTOSH

Dear Yana: I have a Macintosh SE with a 20 meg. hard drive, an external 90 meg hard drive, a Mobius two-page monitor, and a LaserWriter II-NT printer. Having used Microsoft Word 4.0 to write hundreds of resumes and create marketing pieces, and Quicken to monitor my business activities, I find my setup works really well for me. I especially enjoy the easy-to-learn features of the Mac.

If my clients are "Mac-literate," I often provide them with their resumes on disk as well as hard copy, encouraging them to understand what I've done on the computer so they can make updates, changes, and different versions themselves. And I show them some of the ways I manipulate space, fonts, and graphics in the document.

Here are some Microsoft Word 4.0 tricks I commonly use:

1. To customize the space between lines: create and select a full space between the lines; press "command/M"; replace "AUTO" in the highlighted box with "-3"; click on "OK"; and watch the size of the space change. Try different numbers and notice the space increases as the number increases. This is a wonderful tool for creating just the right amount of white space on the paper while keeping the resume to one or two pages.

2. With some fonts, the bold print (in headings, for example) has exaggerated gaps between words. To

correct this, select the space between the words and reduce the point size of that space.

3. Using all caps (such as acronyms, the name of a company, etc.) or several numbers in a row (such as the year) can have an OVERSIZED effect. If that isn't the look you want, or you desperately need the space, you can reduce the size of those letters or numbers by one point. It will save space and make it look "normal" in comparison with the upper and lower type.

4. I like to use two fonts within a resume. Using Helvetica for the main headings and Times or Palatino in the text gives a nice effect. Helvetica provides a bolder bold, and the Times and Palatino are easier to read and more space economical.

5. Using style sheets is a wonderful way to keep your formatting flexible and cut down on writing time. It's worth the effort it takes to learn how to create them.

Susan Ireland
Dynamite!! Resumes
Kensington, CA

A Mac Limerick:
HARD AND SOFT, WHERE?

Of all the computers I use,
The Mac is the one that I choose.
    Atari's not strong;
    The Wang is all wrong;
IBM didn't pass my reviews.

With my Mac SE, I create
Résumés that excite and elate.
    My juices are stirred
    In Microsoft Word-
4, it doesn't exacerbate.

I like to add graphical style
to documents which I compile:
    That's why I adore
    Using PageMaker 4
It's great for a desktop-publishophile.

With PostScript® and fancier gear
The jaggies will all disappear.
    Mega-dots per inch
    Mean quality's a cinch
With hundreds of fonts, *de rigueur*.

When lines, shades, and fonts aren't enough
(Some clients want showier stuff)
    I use Freehand 3
    To twist and skew. See?
Designs that really look buff!

With all this stuff I've produced,
My copies could sure use a boost;
    A laser print finishes
    What dot matrix diminishes,
Which is why I pickt what I choost.

Sallie Young
Impressions by Sallie
San Jose, CA

JOAN COUSINS' MAC

Joan Cousins of Pittsfield, Massachusetts, is a career counselor who does resumes on the side. She said she found that it was an important service for a career counselor to provide.

She recently got a Macintosh, is using Microsoft Word and finds it hard to get used to, after being familiar with a DOS machine. "There is practically NO crossover of skills between them," she says.

Joan writes that she bought a GCC Technologies laser printer, "which is made to work with the Mac; they have a good reputation, are cheaper than Apple, and produce excellent quality. It's not Postscript, but you can upgrade to Postscript for $900."

Before deciding to buy it, she took the features list to a local Mac dealer and asked his opinion; he said "You're better off with the GCC." It has these fonts: Chicago, Courier, Geneva, Helvetica, Monaco, Times, and Calligraphic.

Joan Cousins
Career Counselor
Pittsfield, MA

So that's a bit about Macintoshes, but, as I said before, the majority of resume writers work on IBM-compatible (DOS-based) computers.

IBM Compatibles in Resume Writing

A "COMPATIBLE" SYSTEM

Dear Yana: For resume development I use an AT-class IBM-compatible computer with a hard drive and a laser printer. The laser printer does an excellent job, but I have also used dot matrix printers for resumes, and photocopies of the dot matrix (twenty-four-pin) resumes have turned out very well. The photocopier blends the dots together in each character so it is difficult to tell that it is dot matrix.

The software that I use is Sperrylink and Microsoft Works word processing programs. I like Microsoft Works much better because I can use a mouse with it and it also is much more user-friendly. It has spreadsheet, database, and communications programs included in it.

To polish up the resumes I use Ventura Publisher desktop publishing program. This program is very powerful and useful but it is expensive and it takes awhile to learn. I have also used First Publisher and Publish It desktop publishing programs, which are easier to learn, but they are not as flexible as Ventura Publisher.

John Ellis
Assistant Director, Career Services
College of Saint Rose
Albany, NY

A DIFFERENT "COMPATIBLE" SYSTEM

Dear Yana: Here's what I use:

Software:

- Microsoft Word (I had been using WordPerfect 5.0 and was frequently frustrated. I switched back to 4.2 and was happier, but I'm learning Word and really like it a lot!)

- PageMaker (We just got it and so far I am still intimidated to use it, but I will when I have a project that warrants it.)

Hardware:

- IBM 386 Computer

- HP LaserJet III printer

Hinda Bodinger
Career Planning Techniques
Bayside, NY

CLONES: A LOW-COST OPTION

Dear Yana: I've done much reading, studying, asking questions and soul-searching regarding quality, functionality, adaptability, and price. At first I was gung ho about the Mac IIci (Yana, you're gonna hate me!) and the II-NT laser printer.

Then the Hewlett-Packard LaserJet III came on the market with quality as good as the Mac II-NT printer at half the cost. This was followed by Microsoft Windows 3.0, which enabled an IBM compatible user to enjoy the ease/fun of graphic menus without paying Mac's prices.

The next step was even more exciting. I learned that good IBM clones are as functional as IBMs. I further discovered that top-quality hardware with similar IBM components under proprietary names can be purchased from reputable computer mail-order houses offering full warranties, constant free support, on-site service, and more for even less money.

Result: I've just ordered a Gateway 2000 386 VGA system with 25 Megahertz, 4 Megs RAM, 110 Meg ESDI drive, a full keyboard, a VGA fourteen-inch color monitor with high resolution, plus MS DOS 4.1 and Microsoft Windows 3.0. I've already picked up the HP LaserJet III printer. Also, I was about to purchase WordPerfect until a close friend and computer whiz suggested a program called AMI Professional, made by Samna. It's gotten rave reviews by all the top computer magazines, and I can't wait to learn how to use it.

Jeff Lewis
A Better Resume
Sherman Oaks, CA

CYNTHIA'S IBM

I have read many of the articles describing the different systems that your readers have. I'd like to describe mine. I have used the IBM PC system for many years. Within the last three years, I have been introduced to the Apple Macintosh system at my full-time job. The advantage of the Mac is the relative ease with which you can do everything. You can buy a system, set it up, and begin using software all in the same day. In fact, some software, such as Microsoft Works, can be purchased and used for virtually every need of a small business—all in one package. This is where the standard IBM system falls short. Sometimes it can be exasperating just setting the system up. In addition, you may need to buy more than one software package.

Enter Microsoft's software version of the Mac, Windows 3.0. This software simulates the MAC environment by creating all sorts of windows and icons (small pictures representing the action or software to be used). It also allows you to do multitasking (i.e., run one software application while using another).

Why, you might say then, would someone purchase an IBM "simulation" instead of the real McCoy? I chose to purchase this type of system (IBM using Microsoft Windows) for two major reasons: cost and maintenance. Being the low-budget outfit that I am, it was important to keep my costs down on my initial equipment purchases.

Since I am somewhat familiar with using both systems, speed is also important to me, especially in a graphics intensive environment. Where does speed come into play with graphics? For each graphic the computer shows you, there is a programming command that must be executed first. The faster the system, the faster the command processing, and the faster the display to you. The Mac SE systems (including the SE 30) are slow (in my opinion). The cost to purchase the next system up, the Mac IIci, was prohibitive to me. [There are now other Macs available between the SE and IIci. —ed.]

I was able to purchase a top-of-the-line IBM clone system (clone meaning not IBM-made, but compatible with their products), with a 386 processor at 16 Mhz (one of the fastest systems available), plus a monochrome monitor, 40MB hard disk with 5 1/4-inch and 3 1/2-inch floppy-disk drives, 2Mb RAM, modem, mouse, and HP LaserJet IIP for less than $3500!

I am extremely happy with my system! It is very fast, and, in the Windows environment, there is an enormous amount of software available for costs rivaling the Mac (if

not lower). Many of the same interactive software packages (i.e., spreadsheet, word processing, and database management) are also available.

Cynthia Mackey
Winning Strategies
Oakland, CA

 NANCY'S PC

Dear Yana: I finally purchased a PC and love it! It is an IBM-compatible 386SX with 2 meg. of RAM, 42 meg. hard drive, a high density 5 1/4-inch disk drive, a 3 1/2-inch disk drive and a VGA color monitor. The printer is a desktop LaserJet —the NEC SilentWriter2, Model 90 with 2 meg. of memory and Postscript. I am using WordPerfect 5.1 and having a great time exploring its capabilities. Interestingly enough, some of my clients still want their work on my [old] word processor. It does a nice, professional-looking job, and can give the appearance that the resume was prepared by my client. This makes it more "personal." I guess I won't be retiring my old word processor for a while after all!

Nancy Rosenberg
The Right Resume
Babylon, NY

 KEEPING UP WITH SOFTWARE CHANGES

Learning the ins and outs of our software is not only good business practice, but for most of us, it's something we enjoy. But finding time to experiment is a challenge. Try these time management tricks:

- Schedule (and keep) regular appointments with yourself to learn new or seldom-used features.

- Photocopy instructions for interesting tips, tricks, and shortcuts and stick them on your copy stand. When you're stuck on hold or a customer is late for an appointment, choose one and run through the keystrokes. If the tip seems worth remembering, keep it on the stand for a few days and practice it until it becomes familiar.

Reprinted from:

Keyboard Connection
Glen Carbon, IL

WORDPERFECT MADE SIMPLE

Dear Yana: You and many others who appear in the newsletter seem to favor the Macintosh. Well good news for those using the IBM clones with WordPerfect who might feel intimidated. (It can get a bit frustrating.) There is a program called PERFECTLY SIMPLE that takes over and runs WordPerfect for you. No need for tutors, manuals, or classes. Why, even I can run it! Here's where to find out more:

PERFECTLY SIMPLE, GR Technology Inc., 3565 Ridge Meadow Pkwy., Ste. 101, Memphis, TN 38115, (800) 525-4423.

As for technical help, Mike Smith is the greatest.

WordPerfect corporation distributes the Bitstream Fontware 3.0 Installation Kit. It comes with three font faces, Bitstream Charter, Swiss, and Dutch. Each of the fonts comes in roman, bold, italic, and bold italic in point sizes from 6 to 36. Much more than enough for the resume writer.

Also, I've added a laser printer KX-P4420, by Panasonic. Its great!

Calvin Baird
DATACO Resume Service
Hialeah, FL

WORDPERFECT TIPS

Dear Yana: While these tips are especially appropriate for WordPerfect with a LaserJet printer, I'm sure they have applicability to other word-processing systems:

- Turn kerning on.
- If you need to squeeze more on a page, consider reducing the line spacing from single space (1) to 0.9.
- For better readability, leave a bit of additional space between major bullets (advance down 0.08 inch).
- Use a "Scotch Rule" below the name—the proportions for the thin line, space, and thick line are 1:2:4 (e.g., 0.013 inch, 0.026 inch, 0.052 inch); the rule can also be drawn with the thick line first, or as a double rule of thin line, thick line, thin line.
- Use small caps to print the person's name.

- Keep the side margins as close to 1 inch as possible.
- Make sure your bullets are in good proportion to the rest of the typeface.

Judi Robinovitz
Resumes That Work!
Vero Beach, FL

"C" IS FOR CONSERVATIVE

Dear Yana: Ottawa being a Federal Government town, most of my jobs have to be capital "C" for Conservative in format.

I rely almost exclusively on my daisywheel printer, and only rarely am I required to format a resume using a laser printer. The farmed-out cost for laser printing varies all the way from 12 cents a sheet to $4! All I do is enter the required type styles on my floppy disk, indicate which printer is to be used, and the sub-contractor produces a laser-printer copy in seconds. At these prices, I doubt whether I'll ever need a laser printer of my own.

WordPerfect 5.0 or 5.1 appears to be standard software used in Ottawa, so that's exactly what I opted for as well. I have recently offered my services to the Federal Government as freelance writer and word processor. I will be doing the same job—lobbying with the Provincial Government.

Bryan Howard
St. Albert, Ontario

Resume Software Packages

I asked readers of the *Damn Good Resume Writer Newsletter* whether they have used any resume software programs, and to report on on their experiences with them. I also asked what features they'd like to see in a good program. Here are some of their responses:

RESUME MAKER

Dear Yana: Yes, I have used ResumeMaker by Individual Software, Inc. DID I HATE IT? No, it had a very attractive photo on the box, coupled with descriptive text that made it seem very desirable. DID I LIKE IT? No. First, it's menu driven, which is not bad, but each menu offers several options with a description box explaining the highlighted option. Each option superimposes another menu, with options, on top of the preceding menu.

Finally you come to a menu with three options: Opening Statement, Experience, Education. If you choose "Opening Statement" this might correspond to "Highlights of Qualifications" and up pops an "information card". This is a "paragraph field" which allows unlimited information. BUT it doesn't tell or show where you are on the page. To find this out you have to back out through the superimposed menus to the main menu, select "Make a Resume", then choose "View a Resume". This brings up a full page view of the resume. The type is too small to read, so there are two options, view top half or view bottom half, which is useless because the "View a Resume" screen can't be edited.

This program features three fonts that look as much alike as their names sound: Evergreen, Redwood, and Sequoia. One redeeming feature is a glossary of action verbs, along with the spell-checker and thesaurus.

What would I want a resume program to do?

- Write everything on one screen, which can be edited;

- A variety of fonts available at one or two key-strokes;

- Spell-checker and thesaurus.

Hey! With the exception of the glossary, I just described Word Perfect!

Calvin Baird
DATACO Resume Service
Hialeah, FL

RESUME KIT

About resume software programs—I've tried Resume Kit by Spinnaker.

Things I Like:

- The built-in font variety and font sizes.

- Resume layouts/formats.

- The ease of changing fonts and layouts/formats.

- The ability to change category boxes.

- Built-in help system.

Things I Dislike:

- Lack of flexibility.

- Limited number of employment records can be entered (and kept together).

- Built-in word processor did not have the same fonts as resume.

- Limited space for names and addresses (some can be long).

- Not being able to delete and replace text elsewhere.

I am sure that there is more, but I have not used the program because I have more control with my word-processing software. By using word processing, my only limitations are myself and my equipment. I may not have given the program a fair shake, but I didn't like the limitations the program put upon me. I use the program occasionally, as the output is nice!

Marty Hughes
Accu-Pro Data Management
Hayward, CA

COMPUTERS

RESUME KIT: ANOTHER VIEW

Dear Yana: In regard to resume computer programs: we have used Resume Kit and have not been altogether pleased with it. The disadvantages are that it's too hard to reformat or make changes, different fonts can't be lined up well, you can't see on the screen the entire document you're working with, there's no right justification, and only two bullets are available.

The advantage (and the one thing we liked) is the variety of fonts and type styles it has.

I, for one, would like to see a computer program that has several (boilerplate) formats all ready to go and one would only assimilate and input the information. In fact, we have several samples that we can pull up and fill in as the need arises. I also would like to have a program that has some new ideas and slants (we seem to get into a rut now and then), different fonts, layouts, etc.

May Nolan
Paper Chase Secretarial &
Temporary Services
Oak Harbor, WA

SOFTWARE LIMITATIONS

Dear Yana: In your last newsletter someone wrote in and asked about good resume-writing software. We have looked at a number of packages over the years and have not been all that satisfied. Many have limitations in printers they support or in character formatting that limit their usefulness for final design. We have a few in our catalog that we liked but they are all designed for institutional rather than individual use and are, therefore, somewhat more expensive.

A software program called The Perfect Resume, based partly on Tom Jackson's book of the same title, is quite good and we carry the institutional version. A personal version is available through many retail outlets and is less expensive, but I believe it limits the number of people who can use it —not a useful feature for most resume writers.

I do think that some resume software could be useful to your readers. One use is to have their client complete the fact-based section on their name, address, skills, experience and other data that the better

programs collect quite efficiently. The resume consultant can then interview the job seeker to refine the content and format it on a word processor if the program's formatting is not sufficiently advanced. That could save time, impress the client (if it is handled well), and result in better resumes.

Mike Farr
JIST Works, Inc.
Indianapolis, IN

Style Sheets as an Alternative to Commercial Software

Dear Yana: Yana, you asked for opinions about computer programs for resumes; what I'd like to see are prefabricated style sheets made on a popular word processing software package. I think this would be better than the programs that are out there; from what I have heard they are quite inflexible.

I am a Microsoft Word user on an IBM clone; for the resumes that I create I have style sheets that are made up for the typical formats that I use. For instance, in one style sheet I may have the name and address centered in boldface—rather than use several speedkeys to obtain the desired results, I have "programmed" my style sheet to do both functions with one speedkey. In another style sheet, I may want to fit more on a page so I have my style sheet "programmed" to print a smaller typeface.

Style sheets not only save keystrokes, they can also be used to make changes throughout a document. If you have all job titles set to look a certain way and then you decide that they would look better another way, all you have to do is edit the job title style sheet entry and all the job titles will change automatically.

If other readers think this is a good idea, I would be glad to work with MS-DOS Word users to create some style sheets that would be useful for the job hunter and resume professional.

Debbie Salzman
FlexForce Consulting Group
Irvine, CA

COMPUTERS

Yana's Alternative to Resume Software

As to the resume packages in general: Frankly, I haven't heard of ANY that were considered really satisfactory. I looked over the potential for developing something myself, and concluded that an actual software "program" unfortunately has the effect of LIMITING the job hunter's options for designing a resume—and God knows we need MORE flexibility rather than LESS, to allow for reality. (It is typical, for example, to have a work history that does not readily fit into tidy little boxes on a computer screen.)

The **Self-Teaching Resume Templates** I have put together for use with standard word processing programs are my answer to the need for software-based guidelines that DON'T box the user in. (For details, see page 409.)

11
All About Money

11
All About Money

Money, money, money—everybody wants to talk about it! "**How much should I charge for doing a resume?**" and "**How much can I expect to earn in this business?**" are two of the questions I hear most frequently from beginning and would-be resume writers. They'd like a simple straightforward answer, yet it's not a simple straightforward question. The answer I have to give is: *"It depends."* It depends on a lot of factors, and we'll cover most of them in this chapter.

How Much Should You Charge?

The factors that influence the RATE you can charge for resume writing include:

a) Your definition of "doing resumes," or in other words, **what service you're actually offering**. The primary skills you could be using are:

- counseling and problem solving
- creative writing and editing
- word processing and page layout

If the nature of your service is *primarily* word processing, you can charge approximately what word processors charge in your area. If your work involves significant counseling and problem solving, your rates can approximate that of career counselors, who charge considerably more than word processors. If you are highly skilled in all three areas—counseling, writing, and word processing/page design—you can reasonably charge top dollar for your services.

b) **Your location**. Rates are significantly higher on the East Coast and the West Coast than in the central states. Rates are much higher in large cities than in small towns, and they're higher in communities with a relatively large population of white-collar workers.

c) **Your target market**. College students, for example, simply can't pay top dollar (usually), while business executives expect to pay hundreds for a good resume. In between the extremes there is a very wide range of expectations and willingness to pay what *you* might consider reasonable rates.

Fee Setting for Beginners

Here is my basic advice about fees, for beginning resume writers:

Realize that sometimes, especially when you are learning, it will take you an absurd amount of time to create one particular resume, and if you figured strictly by the hour, you would probably lose all your business because your fees would be unrealistic from the job hunter's point of view. As one new resume writer described it (after noting the fees that some other resume writers reported), "I did a resume for my daughter, and I kidded her that at $40 an hour, she owes me $560." Well, that's what learning is like, in the beginning. And sometimes you DO spend extra time for a special friend or a relative.

Generally, you need to be aware of the local fee structure; but you should simply ignore what other resume writers are charging if they advertise $10 and up. That is meaningless. How far up is up? What can they possibly be doing for $10?

You should be charging more than typists charge because you are using skills that command more money. On the other hand, when you're still learning, you have to charge a lesser rate than you will when your skills improve, and what that rate IS depends very much on the wage levels in your locality. As a highly skilled resume writer, I'm charging about 75 percent of the hourly rate of career counselors in my locality.

I know that doesn't entirely answer the question, but there isn't a hard-and-fast rule about this because it depends, too, on WHAT your clients are GETTING for their money, and what the general population expects. Over the long haul, you'll get a sense of the "right level" by how often you're hearing "Wow, this is expensive" or "Wow, that was worth every penny."

Four Ways to Set Fees

1. per resume

2. per page

3. per hour

4. sliding scale

- **Pricing by the resume**

Some people charge by the resume and are quite comfortable with that. In order for this approach to work, though, you would have to be pretty consistent in the amount of time spent on each resume.

- **Pricing by the page**

Although it's a common practice, I don't think that pricing by the page is a good option for several reasons:

1) You are asking your clients to decide on the length of resume they need, and as you've found out, they are not in a position to know whether they need one page or two pages. (And *forget* three-page resumes!)

2) You create the impression that writing a one-page resume is less work and takes less time than two pages. In fact, a two-page resume is easier to do; it takes a lot of disciplined writing and sharp prioritizing to do an excellent one-page resume, and that does NOT mean it takes less time—quite the contrary.

3) You create the impression that "more is better"—that two or three pages are more valuable and therefore more costly than one page. In fact, an excellent one-page resume is a gem; it is worth MORE than any three-page resume, which would undoubtedly be padded with excessive detail and irrelevant data.

- **Pricing by the hour**

Pricing by the hour isn't a perfect solution either, but it's my choice. I let my client know ahead of time that it USUALLY takes about three and one-half hours, but it may take more, or less. If they are very anxious about the cost, I MAY modify this by promising them that we won't go over a certain top amount, even if it takes more time. Or, if I see, midway through the session that it is likely to take a long time, I stop and renegotiate the fee before we proceed.

I charge for every minute that the client is with me in person, and I do all my resume work with them at my side. I don't charge anything for the preliminary talk we had on the phone, and I limit that talk to about fifteen minutes. I DO charge for the time I waited, if a client is late for their appointment.

- **Pricing by sliding scale**

Personally, I have not had any good experience with sliding-scale pricing. I am not comfortable negotiating with people about what they can "afford," given the vastly different attitudes people have about money.

In practice, what I actually do on occasion is slice a little off the billable TIME (but not the hourly RATE) when a lesser fee seems justified. Then the client is usually grateful, and I haven't messed with my hourly rate.

Letters and Calls About Fees

Now, once again, I'll turn to my letters and phone calls for input from others in the field.

 NEW YORK CITY

Nora S. has been running a business in Manhattan for a little over a year, and called to discuss the issue of fees for services. She has been charging $25 per hour for editorial services and sometimes feels like "something is wrong here" when she works so hard for a client and ends up with very little. Her husband thinks she doesn't charge enough.

She spends about two and a half to three hours on a resume for a person who is relatively new in the job market. It takes her up to six hours to do a resume for someone with twenty years of work experience, but she actually charges for only three to three and a half of those hours.

I told her she should charge more per hour, given that her locale in New York City is at least as affluent a setting as San Francisco. I recommended she immediately raise her rates to at least $35 or $40 per hour and estimate a job at around $120 to $130.

SEATTLE

Mary F., a resume writer in Seattle, called with a concern about fees. She has been charging $50 per resume, regardless of the time involved, and I all but insisted that she increase it immediately to $85, at *least*. She countered with $60 and I kept pushing!

I asked her to begin keeping careful notes about how long it actually takes her to develop a resume and to record her process as she goes along. (She had been avoiding looking at that; she thinks the whole process takes her around four to five hours.)

Mary works in two or three sessions. In the first session she interviews the client and looks over their old resumes. After preparing a draft, she meets with the client a second time to review the draft, and the next day has the final version ready for them.

A lot of her clients have been college students, but she's moving away from that because "they are always out of money."

Mary has been meeting people in coffee shops and other locations for THEIR convenience (although she has no problem with them coming to her house), and I told her she didn't need to do that since she is not paying herself for the travel time. She thought she needed to accommodate her clients in order to attract business, but I pointed out that resume writing is a necessity people willingly pay for, and she doesn't need to go that far out of her way to attract them.

LETTERS

CYNTHIA'S PRICING

Dear Yana: Pricing is an ever-changing issue with me! My brother (a computer consultant) always tells me not to be afraid to charge for the work I do. I don't know why it seems that resume writing should be a low-cost item. Many potential clients have declined my services when I tell them my prices.

Currently I charge $30 per hour, and I'm considering raising it to $40 per hour. This fee applies to resume writing (layout or format changes from a client's original and/or simple changes, and printing) and resume creating (interviewing the client, determining their job objectives, determining the most effective resume format, layout, and printing).

For cover letters I charge $10 for each different letter (i.e., major changes within the text of the letter). If the letter is basically the same, but the address changes for a different employer, that cost is $10 for the initial, and $5 thereafter. For my new idea of job-support groups, I plan to charge $10 per person without a guest speaker, and $15 per person with a guest speaker. I plan to give the extra $5 per person to the speaker as sort of a honorarium.

Cynthia Mackey
Winning Strategies
Oakland, CA

FEE CHANGES THAT WORKED

Dear Yana: My business has really picked up and is turning more and more to corporate- and executive-level resumes. I have set a general scale of $100 for students (I often waive this one), $120 to $140 for entry-level applicants, $150 to $175 for professionals, and $250 for executives. I include a cover letter, as I like to tie it together with the resume. What is astonishing is that I get less static about these prices than my old $65 to $80 range.

I did go through a transition when I changed pricing and lost some referral business in the early fall—people who thought I was going to charge $65. But my new clients are actually referring more new business than the original clients. Or maybe I'm getting better. I am anticipating a great year; at least I'm ending well in 1990.

Mary Ann Finch-Vandivier
Pacific Beach Resume Service
San Diego, CA

A HIGH VOLUME SERVICE; NO HOURLY RATES

Dear Yana: The focus of Resume Righters is management clientele. Our office is in the financial district in San Francisco, and our operation is five years old.

After the initial two years of taking any paying resume job that came along, it is a real pleasure to be able to decline a project because the client is rude, or the career move is impossible, or we are simply too busy to meet the client's time constraints.

We gross a quarter million dollars per year, and we only do resumes and cover letters. We have chosen not to diversify, as my own analysis indicates that the dollar-per-hour for resumes exceeds every other job we have ever accepted.

"We bid our jobs based on a no-obligation first meeting, and we work on a satisfaction-guaranteed basis. We do not give a quote of any sort over the phone. It is impossible for the potential client to see the high quality of our work over the telephone, and it is impossible for us to assess the client's project over the telephone.

Although I do not explain the formula to my clients, I bid jobs based on three criteria: a) the estimated length of writing time, b) the difficulty of the writing, and c) the value to the client. Obviously, a student seeking a first career job cannot pay the same as an executive vice president seeking a CEO position, even though I may spend the same amount of time writing each of these projects.

You will note that, in our case, this removes the concept of an hourly rate for our services. We decline hourly jobs, preferring to bid projects on a one-fee, satisfaction-guaranteed basis. Clients are also comfortable knowing in advance exactly how much it

will cost them to reach satisfaction. We ask for the full amount in advance, but we will accept a 50 percent deposit if the client prefers. We absolutely do not do any work "on speculation."

Rates for our resumes would be $145 for a college student, $165 to $195 for a typical business resume, and around $245 for an executive. We print twelve copies, stationery, and a master copy, and we keep all client projects on file and in the computer for five years. We charge for updating; the formula for estimating updating fees is "roughly proportional to how much is changed."

I see no relationship between the amount of time spent on a resume, or the amount of time spent with the client, and the value of the project to the client. If a client can get a $20,000 raise with a product from this office, it makes no difference whether it took one of our writers thirty minutes or two hours to write it.

Since our clientele are mostly career-motivated business people, we do not have to do a lot of hand-holding. As a matter of fact, if a client has no clue what he or she wants to do next, I will usually decline to work with them, as career counseling is not my area of expertise.

Don Asher, President
Resume Righters
San Francisco, CA

MONEY

Letters on Other Money Issues

Many resume writers are uneasy about discussing money matters with their clients. My correspondence with several of my readers covers some of those basic money concerns, including the all-important matter of getting paid for work done.

HOW DO I TALK WITH MY CLIENTS ABOUT MONEY?

Dear Yana: As I complete my second month in business, I am reevaluating my present pricing structure. I started out charging fixed prices for different styles/lengths of resumes. I've discovered that there are some clients with whom I am able to finish in one to two hours, and there are others I spend almost an entire day on. While I realize the nature of this business involves having "hard" clients and "easy" ones. I am not at all comfortable with two people paying the same price for a product regardless of the time I've spent. Charging an hourly rate would solve the problem of this injustice to both the client and to myself. Any ideas about how to explain a time-priced structure to my clients?

Kim Coats
A Better Resume Service
Moline, IL

Here is my open reply to Kim and to anyone else with similar concerns:

I would explain it something like this (insert your own typical hours and your own hourly rates):

"Dear Kim: I can tell you *approximately* what it will cost, but the exact amount depends on just how long it takes us. Most of the time, we get done in three to four hours, and I charge $35 an hour. So the average cost is about $120. If we get done earlier, of course it would be less—but if it takes longer, it will cost more than that. I can only tell you what's typical."

If they are still uneasy with that, you could add:

"I can't *guarantee* you how long it will take, but if you will just be sure to get here on time, we can buckle right down to it and try our best to keep it as short as possible. You can help by bringing in your job history clearly typed up (or an old resume), and by deciding beforehand just what your job objective is. Bring in some ads or job announcements that describe the kind of job you want."

Be sure to ask your client what their job objective is, because if they're vague about it, that's a strong clue that this could be one of those time-consuming (expensive) resumes!

Another approach when they are uneasy about money is to ask if it would help to be able to pay in two or three installments (postdated checks). But don't bargain with them about your rates. Many, many times, clients have called me back in a few days to make an appointment, after initially insisting that they couldn't possibly afford $120. If you describe your service in such a way that it is clearly valuable to them, the client will find a way to make it work.

To help them comprehend the value, I take the time to describe just how I work, explaining that my process includes:

- Clarifying the job objective;
- Determining just what skills that entails;
- Identifying and describing the key accomplishments that illustrate those skills;
- Helping the client discover and articulate how they are unique and could stand out in a crowd of applicants;
- Coming up with creative solutions to any sticky problems.

Then I encourage them to shop around and ask the other resume writers to describe how they work, and then make up their own mind which service seems right for them. (I even give them some good questions to ask the competition!) Sometimes I ask the potential client if they need help with any particular problem on their resume, and then I tell them how I would approach that problem. I suggest that they ask the other resume writers how they would approach it. My willingness to provide this information often dissolves their hesitation, and they make the appointment.

Sure, some people are totally out of touch with reality about what professional services cost, but you'll learn not to let that bother you. Just remind them, "You get what you pay for, and I think my rates are in line with the quality of work I do."

HOW DO I KNOW IF THE PRICE IS RIGHT?

Dear Yana: Of the clients I have worked with, I experienced some difficulty with several of them regarding prices. My pricing structure is based on whether the client wants a one-page, two-page, or three-page resume, and whether they want a cover letter. I also offer to do references, salary histories, and follow-up letters. Each piece is priced separately, and I'm finding that many people want the least expensive thing available. Subsequently, many people are choosing a one-page resume, when they actually need a two-page.

My average sale is about $50 and I know from the experience of having worked for a resume office that was part of a national chain, that this price is very competitive in this area. So I don't feel I am out of the ball park. I don't feel confident as a business person. When I mention an approximate price to a client, I find myself bargaining with them if they flinch at all. Maybe time will tell whether this will contribute to my sinking or swimming.

I have been flexible on pricing with a few, only because I was afraid of them walking out the door. I realize the importance of being assertive, but it is hard to let people walk out when it's such a triumph to get them to walk in. Am I just too hungry?

Illinois is very different from the Bay Area; there are many rural and blue-collar workers who don't understand the importance of a resume. The only reason they are shopping for one in the first place is that the factories and industries won't consider hiring anyone without seeing a resume first. Resumes never used to be required. Now quite a few people see the resume as a necessary evil. Many think they just need to have *something* to get in the door. It is very hard to impress upon these people the importance of doing it right.

Kim Coats
A Better Resume Service
Moline, IL

Dear Kim: First, about the "necessary evil" image of resumes in your town. Here's an opportunity to do some educating and marketing all at once. You could develop an informative flier that describes what a good resume is and how it can benefit the client. Maybe even have some real-life stories and some provocative graphics to get the points across, making it an interesting read. Then make the flier easily accessible to your potential clients.

Now about your pricing issue: First of all, review my basic strategy on page 248. Then come back here and read on.

The Bottom Line on Pricing

DON'T BARGAIN

Pricing can become a can of worms! It is important that you DO NOT BARGAIN with your client. No matter what fee you set, some clients will be outraged at how expensive it is and others will be amazed at what a bargain it is. You can't change that—it has more to do with *their* economic level and expectations, than with your realistic/unrealistic, fair/unfair rates. Remember, a can of beans costs the same no matter who comes into the store to buy it. And you are not running a social service agency if you are in business for yourself. You cannot make it your problem that they are short of money—or pretty soon *you* will be running out of money too!

If your business is slow taking off, or flounders for awhile and you are really hungry, consider a temporary part-time job to cover essentials so you can approach your own rate-setting with more confidence, rather than peddling your services at bargain rates.

DO COMMUNITY SERVICE CONSCIOUSLY

If you want to help needy job-hunters, then decide in advance just how much of your time you can afford to give away free for a good cause. Then you can have X number of "Free Scholarships" available each year, and give them out as appropriate.

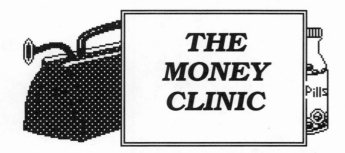

THE MONEY CLINIC

RUBY'S QUESTIONS ABOUT MONEY

A New Jersey resume writer (we'll call her Ruby) called with these questions about fees and getting paid:

Q. How should I handle a client who hasn't called and come back for her draft resume, and keeps stalling? (She owes me some money.)

A. I told Ruby to **find out what's going on with the client**. Call and ask specifically, "What's going on?" and then listen carefully. Is it that the client is unhappy with the work done, or worried about money, or distracted by other things in her life, or what? Then Ruby can **devise an effective strategy that takes into account what's going on with the client**. This may require clearing up misunderstandings, arranging payments over time, or rescheduling the work—but the client will be more cooperative if she feels that you understand and have listened to her.

Q. How should I handle a situation with a student who kept asking for more and more changes on his resume, including major rewrites and layout changes that took a lot of time, and then resisted paying when the cost totalled $200? He told me that he ended up not using the resume, but that it did help him get a lot clearer about his skills. Also, he got a good internship without directly using the resume.

Even his mother called, protesting that her son didn't realize how expensive it was going to be. They eventually DID pay, but I want to avoid such a hassle in the future.

A. I told Ruby, of course, the student has to learn to deal with the real adult world, and **you don't have to take care of him**. On the other hand, don't get too far ahead of your clients with your investment of time and energy; keep checking back with them to make sure they WANT what you're doing. Be sure to **get paid as you go**

along, rather than in one big lump sum at the end (which can shock a client).

Q. I'm not getting enough business. I'm charging $55 per hour; is that too much?

A. I suggested to Ruby that maybe $55 per hour IS too much for right now, to check on what her local competitors are getting, and **consider backing off to a lower rate**. Also, when it seems necessary, she can offer clients the option of spreading the cost over three payments, but get all three checks up front, two of them post-dated.

P.S. From Ruby

Dear Yana: All's well that ends well . . . My client who hadn't paid her bill for several months after receiving her drafts has now paid me for the drafts, another consultation to make corrections, and an advance payment for final touch-ups and printing! In fact, she was the one who suggested paying in advance! All of her problems were related to the discovery that her father was terminally ill, and some mild criticism of my drafts by her friends. Our "correction" session was a matter of her "wordsmithing" my drafts: for example, changing *large* to *substantial* (but calling me that night to change it back!). She didn't want any major changes; however, she did want more white space. Against my better judgment, I increased the font size from 10 points to 11 points, which had the effect of spreading out an already lengthy resume into three pages (ouch!). But, that's what she wanted.

Also, I'm getting much more positive feedback to a $45 hourly rate than to a $55 hourly rate, and I thank you for the suggestion.

MONEY

Getting Paid

DON'T GET BURNED—MAKE YOUR MONEY POLICIES CLEAR AND STICK TO THEM

How do you make sure you get paid? The best strategy is to make your money policies clear from the start. From your very first contact with your clients, be sure to discuss your policies on rates, payment, fees for late or missed appointments, corrections and/or revisions. Then **get an affirmative response** on your money arrangements before you begin.

Consider accepting credit cards for payment, which could make it easier to stick with these rules.

Four general rules to avoid payment hassles:

1. Make sure payment expectations are clear in advance of doing the work.

2. Get paid immediately, in full, when the work is done.

3. If more than one session is required, get paid in full for each session as you go.

4. Don't hand over even a draft until you've been paid.

HOW DO YOU HANDLE A CLIENT WHO DOESN'T PAY?

Here is an example of the problem: Janet is a new resume writer in Berkeley. During the second week of work, one of her clients, a student, informed her at the end of the resume session that he didn't have any money and would have to pay later. Janet was angry that he waited until the last minute to tell her he wasn't able to pay.

Here's what I would advise, to head off such money problems with clients:

- **Make sure your client agrees** to the money arrangements before you begin. Ask questions like, "Do we have an agreement on the price now?" or "Is that still okay with you?" (If Janet had done this, she could have found out on the phone that the student was unable to pay, and either cancelled the appointment or renegotiated the job.)

- In cases of apparently genuine hardship, **have some options available**. My favorite is, "You can pay in three installments, one-third when we do the resume, one-third two weeks later, and one-third four weeks later." They say "Fine." Then I add, "*I will need to get all three checks before you leave*, one dated that day and the other two dated two and four weeks ahead. That way I won't have to bill you or chase down the other two payments." And clients always find this a reasonable requirement. (Sometimes it motivates them to write the whole check and be done with it!)

On the following pages, several readers share their tips on getting paid.

TELL THEM, THEN
TELL THEM AGAIN

Dear Yana: On the issue of getting paid for services, I have found that my life has been made easier not only by mentioning my standard fee for service during the initial telephone contact, but also by getting the prospective client's address in order to send a confirmation of our appointment.

As you see from the sample (below) this letter gives me an opportunity to restate the fee and to make clear the ground rules before our first actual face-to-face meeting.

Sheldon Roth
Tarzana, CA

Dear _____

This is to confirm your appointment for career counseling services at (time) on (day) the (date) of (month).

The office is located approximately one-half block East of Reseda Boulevard on Ventura. Parking is available in the rear of the building at $.60 per half hour until 5:00 P.M., when it is free. There is also metered one-hour parking at the curb but please note that cars are towed after 4:00 P.M.

The usual length of each session is one hour. The fee for this service is $60 per session and is payable after each session. Billing arrangements are not available. Fees will be charged for missed appointments and for appointments not cancelled with 24-hour notice.

I am looking forward to working with you to help you attain the highest level of work satisfaction.

Sincerely yours,

Sheldon Roth

THE 50 PERCENT DOWN
POLICY AND OTHER IDEAS

Dear Yana: I have had the experience of never being paid by a client. That prompted me to let new customers know, when they call or inquire, that there will be a deposit required prior to beginning work. It is expected at the time of the interview, and if for any reason it is not paid, we do not continue until it is paid.

We have a form ready for our clients. (We point out that we don't want to waste their valuable time.) The form spells out just what the process entails, gives some helpful information that will save time for all of us, and provides a space for them to jot down notes while waiting for their counselor.

This makes it easy for us to collect a deposit of half the total cost of the resume, ensuring that even if they don't return, we have been paid for some of the time we've invested.

I have never had anyone refuse to pay or be put off by the request. If they need to wait for a payday, we simply make an appointment on or after that date. I've had clients forget checkbooks, in spite of our reminders, but they willingly go get money or a check. This has worked well for us and in 99 percent of the cases customers do come back.

Our fees start at $35 for one page, typed "as is." Complete resume service, including career counseling, ranges from $75 (maximum time of one hour) to an executive resume for $250, which involves executive paper (special stock), and intensive career counseling on job campaign management and all that it entails. We also provide several brochures and aids.

May Nolan
Paper Chase Secretarial &
Temporary Services
Oak Harbor, WA

WHAT DO YOU DO WHEN A CLIENT SHOWS UP LATE—OR NOT AT ALL?

Do you charge them for just the time you spent with them, even if you had to wait forty-five minutes? Or, do you compute your fee from the time they were *supposed* to show up? (That's what I do—at least most of the time.) And what about no-shows and people who arrive without their checkbooks or wallets?

Here's what some writers have shared about the subject.

NO MORE LATE ARRIVALS

Dear Yana: About dealing with the issue of late arrivals, here is an idea that works beautifully for me.

Before each new client arrives, I send them a sheet on "How to Make the Most of Each Session." Item #1 states:

Arrive five minutes early to center yourself and collect your thoughts. Have your check completed so that we may begin promptly and not lose your time in business transactions.

People like this approach. They feel their time is respected by giving them guidance on how best to use their hour.

Michelle Jurika, M.A.
Career & Personal
Development
Oakland, CA

WHAT ABOUT NO-SHOWS?

Dear Yana: What about policies regarding clients who are no-shows or are late for appointments? I have a lot of trouble with this. Because I run a home business, I feel my clients think I'll just continue washing the dishes if they don't show up, so it doesn't matter! I would really like to know what has worked for other resume writers and if they have lost clients by having policies.

Nancy Rosenberg
The Right Resume
Babylon, NY

Dear Nancy: You might try this solution. Confirm appointments in writing, including your cancellation and no-show policy. (See Sheldon Roth's example on page 255). You also need to develop a policy that compensates you fairly for the lost business. One idea might be to bill for late cancellations (less than 24 hours notice) or no-shows at half your usual rate. Another approach would be to get a deposit up front as May Nolan does (see May's letter, page 255). Whichever policies you choose, they should respect your time as a professional, no matter where you happen to have your office. —yp

THE CLIENT (AND RESUME) THAT GOT AWAY

Dear Yana: I ran into a few problems with handling payments. In the beginning, I found I needed to meet with the client twice—once to do a rough draft and again, a few days later, to fine-tune it. In some cases, I would mail the first printout to the client, we would discuss it on the phone, I would redo it and mail the finished version to them. Then they would pay me by mail.

This worked in all cases except one. In that one case, the woman never returned my calls, never came for her follow-up appointment, and never paid me. That taught me!

I now collect the money at the first meeting and almost always complete the resume during that first three-hour session. Any additional meetings require further payment. This not only ensures proper payment, but relieves me of having to keep track of who has paid and who hasn't. It's very straightforward and no one questions it.

Susan Ireland
Dynamite Resumes!!
Kensington, CA

MORE LESSONS LEARNED

Monique R., a resume writer in Northern California, reports that she, too, had one bad experience with a client who didn't pay.

"I had a bad gut feeling from the beginning, and decided not to work with him much longer. Next day, I left the completed work in my outside mailbox, as we agreed, along with the bill. He never paid, and I had to go to small claims court."

Here's what Monique said she learned:
- Don't give people the finished product until they have paid you.
- Don't work with a person if you get a bad feeling about them in the initial phone contact.

The "Proof Copy" Solution

It's not always possible to have your clients proofread their resume at your office. Some clients may prefer to review their resumes at their own leisure. How can you accommodate your clients and still make sure you get paid?

Consider printing final draft resumes on paper stock clearly labeled "PROOF COPY," as shown in the example below. Depending on your equipment and software, you can either design and print your own proof copy stock or have a special supply made at a commercial print shop.

The benefits? Clients actively participate in creating and proofreading their own resume, but they must pay the balance of your fee before receiving a corrected final copy.

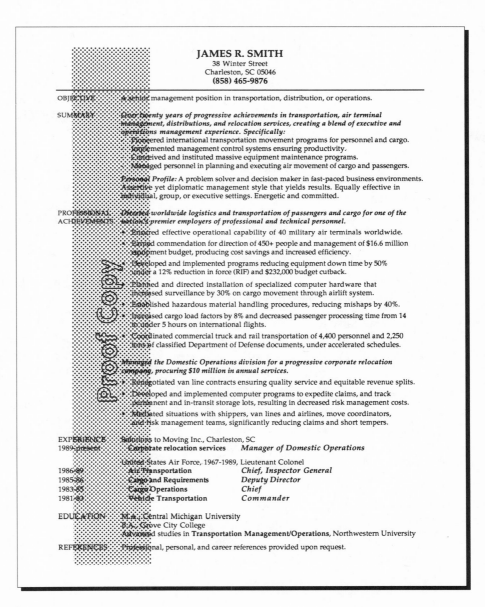

LETTERS

We'll wrap this up with two more money-related letters:

CUTTING COSTS

One way to balance income and outgo is to minimize your operating costs (without sacrificing quality).

Bryan writes:

When my resume writing business was still a fledgling operation, I managed to cut start-up and operational costs by:

1. Leasing downtown office space on an hourly basis.

2. Leasing a beeper with live-voice customized answering.

3. Including printing and laser printing companies in my supporting literature, in return for price concessions for myself and my clients.

Bryan Howard
St. Albert, Ontario
Canada

FEES FOR SEMINARS

Dear Yana: Recently I was asked to give a seminar to a group of resume writers for a local church. Their job is to help members of their church write resumes. This brings up a very difficult issue of how much to charge for seminars. The short thirty- to sixty-minute seminars that I do for the Urban League and similar organizations I conduct for free, mainly because I use these as a marketing tool, and they require minimal effort now that I'm experienced at it.

But when I am requested to conduct two- to four-hour sessions, I don't really know how to charge but I don't want to sell myself short! I haven't been in this field very long either, so I don't feel I could charge

what a more experienced person charges. Can you or any of your newsletter readers please give me some advice?

Cynthia Mackey
Winning Strategies
Oakland, CA

Dear Cynthia: When I'm asked to do a local workshop, the first question I ask is, "Who will be at the workshop, and will they be paying a fee to attend it?" Essentially, if the sponsor charges, then I charge. But if it's a free community service, and it's convenient to my home and I have time in my schedule, then I may do the workshop free.

But let's say you are asked to do a workshop for a profit-making corporation or some group who puts on workshops and charges money to the attendees. Then you might negotiate a fee that would at least equal what you could have been earning at your usual work, considering all the preparation time, travel time, and actual on-site work time—as well as the cost of any materials you might prepare and bring to the workshop. When you figure all this in, some "opportunities" don't look so attractive after all.

On the other hand, some invitations to do a workshop that pays you nothing can be worth accepting if you could benefit indirectly. For example, you might get a lot of free publicity through their public announcements of the workshop. Or you might get some referrals to do future work for individuals who attended the workshop. (Find out how many will be attending.) Or you might simply want that organization's name on your own list of groups you have worked with, for public relations and promotional purposes.

Another factor, of course, is your own level of experience and expertise. The more you know, the more you are worth. The better you are known, the higher the fee you can command. When I am asked to do a kind of presentation I've never done before (or do it for an organization that is new to me), I call around to my local colleagues in the field and ask their advice. It only takes a few calls to get a sense of what is the appropriate fee to ask. —yp

How Much Can You Earn?

We're going to turn now to the matter of making a living wage. Unless you're doing resume writing as a hobby—or on a strictly volunteer basis—the real money question is, can you make a living doing this? To answer that question, you need to go far beyond the issue of fee structures and collections.

The factors that influence the TOTAL INCOME you could earn include:

a) The **rate** you charge, of course, but in addition—

b) Your **productivity**, which involves your energy level, your efficiency, and the amount of time you allot to your business—i.e., full time or part time.

c) **Local market conditions**, including wage trends and the overall economy.

d) The **reputation** you develop. (More about this in the beginning of Chapter 12.)

e) Your business talent for effective **marketing** and for controlling **expenses**.

For two different analyses, we turn now to N. Victoria Sisson and Susan Ireland (with an assist from *Running a One-Person Business*, by Claude Whitmyer *et al.* (Ten Speed Press).

TRANSLATING "SALARY" TO CLIENT FEES

by N. Victoria Sisson

Undoubtedly the biggest question that resume consultants struggle with is, "How much should I charge?" Even consultants who have been professional resume creators for several months, or even years, can be plagued with this question.

In truth, there are several answers. The one that follows is one that is easy to adopt and will provide a fair return to the resume creator. There are only five steps:

1. Review your own professional and educational history—your own resume if you will. Based on education, experience, technical skills, and any other factors that make up your resume, figure out what you would make if you were working for someone else. Not necessarily an owner of a resume business, but any business or corporation that would pay you a salary. Let's assume that you have determined that you could reasonably expect to earn $24,000 a year as an employee.

2. If you can make $24,000 a year working for somebody else—8 hours a day, 5 days a week, 50 weeks a year (to simplify, we will assume a two-week unpaid vacation)—that's 2,000 hours. They would be paying you $12 an hour. Now you have to increase that amount to take into account the fact that you can't bill out 40 hours a week. It's very difficult to bill out more than 30 hours a week. So you should divide by 3/4 (if you divide 12 by 3/4, the amount would be $16 an hour).

3. To that figure you must add your profit margin and your overhead. Assume you determine that 20% is fair profit.

$$\$16 + 20\% \text{ profit} = \$19.20.$$

4. We will assume that your costs (advertising, rent, supplies, telephone, postage, public relations, etc.) total

approximately $9,000 per year (or $5.80 an hour). Your fair hourly rate, then, would compute to $25 per hour ($19.20 + $5.80).

5. Your final step is to decide whether you want to charge an hourly rate or a flat fee. Many clients prefer a flat fee; they are more comfortable if they are in control of the amount of their expenditure.

Experience has shown me that the average resume takes approximately four hours—from initial interview to the delivery of the final product. Thus, I am comfortable with a general rate of $100 per resume. This formula can work for you if you have launched a career as a professional resume creator.

However, this may be the first time that you have ever written a resume for anyone; or it may be the third or the tenth. Basically, you are still learning, and using your clients as guinea pigs. You could take the position of charging nominal fees while gaining valuable experience and getting your business started.

This is one of the most difficult decisions that you, as a consultant, must face. Remember, however, that if you are talented enough to consider resume writing as a career, then you deserve to get paid for it.

Whatever your goals for your business, learn your craft and don't sell yourself short. Be honest and fair while having a realistic viewpoint of what the traffic will bear.

N. Victoria Sisson
Richardson, TX

DETERMINING AN HOURLY RATE

by Susan Ireland

When I started writing resumes I charged $25 an hour, and a resume would cost my clients between $75 and $100. As I got better, not only did the quality improve but it took me less time to complete the task. When I realized I was getting paid less to do faster, better work, I knew it was time to raise my rates. I increased my hourly fee to $30 an hour with a $100 minimum per resume.

I was diligent about maintaining my records of income and expenses, but what I didn't have a handle on was exactly how these totals related to my profit. How did the volume of business actually affect my yearly profit or salary? (Note the definition of "salary" in the box below.) Was I charging enough to make the income I wanted to make, or was I just making ends meet? How much business did I need to make the salary I wanted to earn?

I got the answers to these questions by using the following worksheet adapted from *Running a One-Person Business*. Although this exercise was designed to figure out what the hourly rate should be, it also demonstrates how overhead and income affect the

A definition of "salary": Throughout this discussion, the term "salary" is defined as income used to live on. The term "profit" is used to mean money that is set aside for retirement, to purchase a home, or to put in a savings account for future use. Salary and profit are two separate figures. I think of my business as my employer and expect it to provide me with the same benefits good employers provide their employees: a pension plan, medical insurance, disability insurance, and a paid vacation. You'll notice all of these items are listed in the worksheet and are independent of salary.

profit. This was an eye-opener for me. After doing this exercise, I realized what my daily overhead is and how many billable hours I need to work to make that amount. With each additional billable work-hour my profit margin increases greatly. This knowledge gives me a realistic sense of how my business is doing and what its potential is, and helps me set concrete goals.

Knowing that the market will bear only so much for an hourly rate, I have two alternatives for reaching my salary goal: I can increase the volume of business or I can decrease my expenses. By considering these two variables, I came up with a formula (and goals) to satisfy my financial requirements. I now charge $40 an hour and work approximately 25 billable hours per weekgiving me a salary I feel comfortable with.

The following instructions and worksheet are excerpted from pages 46 and 47 of *Running a One-Person Business*.

SETTING FEES FOR PROFESSIONAL SERVICES

This exercise will help you figure out the minimum fee to charge your clients. The calculations are based on how much income you want to earn, how many days you wish to work, your anticipated expenses, and how much profit you would like to set aside in addition to salary and business expenses.

Each line of the worksheet is numbered to correspond to the instructions below. Following these instructions will make it easier to complete the form. The blank form explains all the entries and calculations you should make.

The FIRST STEP is to fill in the blanks for:

Yearly Salary (1),
Days worked per month (2a),
Days worked per year (2b), and
Desired percent profit (3).

There is no magic formula for answering these questions. They are simply personal choices that you must make. How much money do you need to spend on your personal lifestyle? How hard and how often do you want to work? How much of each dollar you bring in would you like to set aside for the future?

In the SECOND STEP you need to calculate your EXPENSES (4).

The blanks on the form may or may not represent some or all of your expense items. They are provided to stimulate your thinking. Be sure to include any additional items that may apply to your business.

The THIRD STEP is to add up the columns to get TOTAL EXPENSES (5).

The FINAL STEP is to make a few calculations and fill in the:

Daily overhead (6),
Daily salary (7),
(Minimum) revenue requirement (8),
and Daily profit (9).

Now fill in the "Required (Daily) billing rate" (10) by adding up (6) through (9). This is your "day rate," or what you should try to make per day.

If you want to know your "Equivalent hourly rate" (11), divide the "Required (Daily) billing rate" (10) by the number of billable hours worked per day."

Susan Ireland
Dynamite!! Resumes
Kensington CA

Here's an example of how one resume writer used this worksheet. Notice that she has made allowances for a paid vacation, medical insurance, disability insurance, and a business profit (which she might apply towards business expansion or a retirement plan), all of which are in addition to her basic salary. (Her office is in her home.)

Worksheet for Calculating Fees

1.   Yearly salary $30,000   (Basic salary you wish to earn)

2a. Days worked per month   20   (Number of days per month you wish to work)

2b. Days worked per year   240   (Line 2a x 12)

3.   Desired percent profit   15%   (Percent profit you want, above salary)

4.   EXPENSES (Fill in the lines below for your expenses)

Operation Overhead

Office Expenses

	Monthly		Yearly
Rent (16% of my rent)	$90.	x 12	$1080.
Phone & utilities	30.	x 12	360.
Paper	40.	x 12	480.
Postage	25.	x 12	300.
Other supplies	60.	x 12	720.
Computer	45.	x 12	540.
In-house printing	65.	x 12	780.
Other		x 12	
SUBTOTAL	$355.		$4260.

Support Services

	Monthly		Yearly
Marketing	$200.	x 12	$2400.
Outside printing	20.	x 12	240.
Consultations	30.	x 12	360.
Workshops	50.	x 12	600.
Commissions	200.	x 12	2400.
Books	20.	x 12	240.
Profess. meetings	10.	x 12	120.
Membership dues	12.	x 12	144.
Other		x 12	
SUBTOTAL	$542.		$6504

MONEY

Additional Expenses (including benefits)

	Monthly		Yearly
Automobile (use)	$10.	x 12	$120.
Vacation	200.	x 12	2400.
Miscellaneous	60.	x 12	720.
Medical insurance	125.	x 12	1500.
Disability insurance	48.	x 12	576.
Other			
SUBTOTAL	$443.		$5316.

5.   TOTAL EXPENSES (Add the yearly expense
                 figures and put total here)   = __$16,080__

6.   Daily overhead   __$67__   (Total yearly expenses ÷ line 2b)

7.   Daily salary   __$125__   (Line 1 ÷ line 2b)

8.   (Minimum) Daily revenue needed   __$192__   (Line 6 + line 7)
      (i.e., without profit added)

9.   Daily profit (above salary)   __$19__   (Line 3 x line 1 ÷ line 2b)

10.   Required (daily) billing rate   __$211__   (Line 6 + Line 7 + Line 9)

11.   Equivalent hourly rate   __$42__   (Line 10 ÷ number of billable hours/day)
                                                 (estimating 5 billable hours/day)

RECAP
$30,000 Desired basic salary
$ 4,500 Desired profit above salary
$16,080 Expenses, including benefits (vacation and insurance)
$50,580 TOTAL gross income

SO WHAT'S THE BOTTOM LINE HERE?
This resume writer concludes that she must gross $50,580 per year, or $211 per working day, to pay expenses and provide herself a basic salary of $30,000 plus standard benefits plus a 15% business profit. If she computes her fee by-the-hour and works 5 *billable* hours each working day, she must charge $42 per hour to generate the desired income.

Worksheet for Calculating Fees

1. Yearly salary _____ (Basic salary you wish to earn)

2a. Days worked per month _____ (Number of days per month you wish to work)

2b. Days worked per year _____ (Line 2a x 12)

3. Desired percent profit _____ (Percent profit you want, above salary)

4. EXPENSES (Fill in the lines below for your expenses.)

Operation Overhead

Office Expenses

	Monthly		Yearly
Rent		x 12	
Phone & utilities		x 12	
Paper		x 12	
Postage		x 12	
Other supplies		x 12	
Computer		x 12	
In-house printing		x 12	
Other		x 12	
SUBTOTAL			

Support Services

	Monthly		Yearly
Marketing		x 12	
Outside printing			
Consultations		x 12	
Workshops		x 12	
Commissions		x 12	
Books		x 12	
Profess. meetings		x 12	
Membership dues		x 12	
Other		x 12	
SUBTOTAL			

Additional Expenses (including benefits)

	Monthly		Yearly
Automobile (use)		x 12	
Vacation		x 12	
Medical insurance		x 12	
Disability insurance		x 12	
Miscellaneous		x 12	
Other		x 12	
SUBTOTAL			

5. TOTAL EXPENSES (Add the yearly expense
          figures and put total here)   = _____

6. Daily overhead   _____   (Total yearly expenses ÷ line 2b)

7. Daily salary   _____   (Line 1 ÷ line 2b)

8. (Minimum) Daily revenue needed   _____   (Line 6 + Line 7)
      (i.e., without profit added)

9. Daily profit (above salary)   _____   (Line 3 x line 1 ÷ line 2b)

10. Required (Daily) billing rate   _____   (Line 6 + Line 7 + Line 9)

11. Equivalent hourly rate   _____   (Line 10 ÷ number of billable hours/day)

12

All About Marketing

12
All About Marketing

MARKETING

We Are in the Marketing Business

Marketing is much more than advertising, just as a good resume is much more than a simple work history. In fact **a resume writer is, in one sense, in the marketing business**, because our task is to create excellent "marketing pieces" for individual job hunters.

Many resume writers, however, cringe at the thought of marketing THEMSELVES. "I just want to do my work," they say; "I like my work but I hate having to market my business."

I will have to admit that this was my attitude about marketing when I started out. I viewed marketing as some mysterious process, a fancy word for advertising, and a distasteful necessity of self-employment.

Then one day a few years ago, when my business (as both resume writer and author) was well established, a colleague commented, "You know, you are very good at marketing yourself. You've *positioned* yourself as an expert in the field." Well, I thought that was very flattering, but it also made me think: "What? ME good at marketing?! *What have I been doing* to give that impression?" (I figured it would probably be a good idea to discover what it *was*, and then *keep doing it!*)

As I pondered this question, I realized that a major component of marketing is the **professional reputation** you develop—in other words, your **overall public image** as seen by both job hunters and by anyone else who might refer a job hunter to your services. This is important, because **the more solid a reputation you build, the less you have to bother with advertising**, and the more your **marketing becomes effortless.**

This is not to say that advertising is unnecessary—in the beginning it is crucial. Self-employed people have reported that their business TRIPLED overnight after their Yellow Pages ad appeared!

But while **advertising** helps job hunters FIND you (especially when you're still unknown), it is your **reputation** that sets you apart from all the others and helps job hunters decide you're the one they want to hire.

Your Unique Marketing Style

Marketing, like resume writing, is yet another opportunity for creative self-expression, which explains why it can be so much **fun** while at the same time it serves a practical function.

You can develop your own unique marketing style that is consistent with your personality and values. One way to do this is to **think through the overall message about yourself and your service** that you'd like to convey to the public. Then you can keep an eye out for every opportunity to reinforce that message.

I have to admit that I didn't **create a professional image** very consciously, but hindsight tells me this is what I did, and it worked very well to promote my business.

The professional image I created (consciously or unconsciously) was partly determined by **the quality of service I would have liked from others**. For example, once when I went for career counseling years ago, I came away frustrated and disappointed, and thought I'd wasted a lot of money. What I really wanted, and didn't get, was *a feeling that I was being listened to,* and that the counselor could see me as a unique individual and tailor the counseling to my specific needs.

Instead of getting what I wanted, I felt I was being led through some standard, routine processes that had little to do with my immediate situation, and did nothing to relieve my anxiety and confusion about the job hunt. Remembering that painful experience, I vowed to do better with MY clients.

I thought about the overall message I wanted to convey, about the service I provide and the way I relate to my clients, and these are the **key words** that went through my mind:

Key words, on the business side . . .

- timely service, efficient, fast results
- generosity, providing an excellent value, even a bargain
- realism, practicality, appropriateness in the real world
- creativity, solving tough problems
- artistry, making the product look great

Key words, on the personal side . . .

- sensitivity, tuning in to the client's immediate needs
- listening carefully, attentiveness
- optimism, believing they can make it
- professionalism, high standards
- teamwork, empowering the client
- compassion, inspiration, caring about the results

This **overall message** about my **attitudes and values** shapes my **reputation** almost as much as the actual product, the resumes created.

We're Marketing ALL the Time!

The overall message just described—your professional identity, so to speak—gets conveyed in many ways:

1. When you **describe your service** and the way you work, in your initial phone conversation with a would-be client.

2. When you create the **wording of an advertisement** of any kind.

3. When you **write an article** that appears in a newspaper—both what you say and the way you say it.

4. When you give a **presentation to the public.**

5. In many other ways that are illustrated in this chapter.

Since marketing is HAPPENING all the time, whether we're doing it consciously or not, and since our REPUTATION is being created all the time whether we like it or not, it's worth taking the time to pay careful attention to it.

What are YOUR values and attitudes and intentions about your work? Are you getting your message across effectively? Are you creating the professional reputation you want?

This chapter will give you lots of new ideas for marketing yourself, and hopefully a fresh new perspective on the meaning of marketing. *Enjoy*!

GRAND OPENING!

What Is Marketing?

"Marketing" is anything that makes you known and ultimately brings you paying clients. Here are some of the marketing tools I have used—a few items on the list date back to my desperate early days (I no longer put fliers on windshields), but almost all the others are part of my continuing marketing plan.

1. Put fliers on windshields in the supermarket parking lot (on day #1 of my new business!).

2. Leave my business cards and fliers at copy centers, career centers, beauty shops, laundromats, supermarkets, colleges.

3. Place a small ad on the back page of the weekly paper.

4. Write articles for career center quarterly newspapers.

5. Give my clients some cards and fliers on their way out.

6. Give free talks on resumes at the YWCA, schools, libraries, colleges.

7. Write a successful book.

8. Write another one.

9. Talk on the radio. (There's a publication to advertise your availability: *Radio/TV Interview Report*, 135 E. Plumstead, Lansdowne PA 19050; 215-259-1070.)

10. Make sure my business name and phone number are on everything I give away.

11. Give away a lot of things (with my name and phone number on them).

12. Publish a newsletter (like *Damn Good Resume Writer Newsletter*) for my clients and the career-development community.

MARKETING

13. Send postcards/letters to my friends and clients, reminding them of me and asking for referrals.

 14. Send postcards to my clients, thanking them when they send me a referral.

In evaluating marketing methods, cost effectiveness is a primary consideration. As one of my readers described her experience: "My 'Mother of All Resumes' ad hit Sunday in the classifieds. I spent over $120 on classified advertising that week and got exactly $120 in business."

So before you launch yourself into a flurry of marketing activities, do a little research (read the rest of this chapter, for one thing). Then make a list of marketing activities you'd like to consider, and rank them according to cost effectiveness.

Open Advice for Any Beginner

KNOW HOW YOUR CLIENTS FOUND YOU

An important factor in marketing and advertising is keeping track of where your business is coming from. I keep a spiral notebook by the phone and start taking notes as soon as a business call comes in. The second question I ask (after "How can I help you?") is "How did you hear about me?" I jot down the answer and later transfer it to the 4-by-6 file card I keep on each person who makes an appointment. Then, once a month or so, I tally up the sources of referrals and focus more time and money on those sources that are working best for me.

Calculate what you spent on advertising last month, and how many people came in from each type of advertising. Then ask yourself if it was worth it, and drop the low-yielding ads. Eventually, you may not need to advertise at all because you'll get enough business through referrals. I send thank-you postcards to people who have sent new referrals, and possibly to offer them some kind of reciprocal service.

STAND OUT FROM THE CROWD

Be sure your business cards have a little zip to them. You could add one or two lines of small type saying something that would distinguish your service from every other resume service. (What's special? Are you more economical or faster, do you give more personal service, or do you have snazzier equipment? What can you do to help the potential client choose you or distinguish between you and other similar services?)

GET YOUR FRIENDS TO HELP

Word-of-mouth and direct referrals are the most valuable promotion. People trust the word of their friends and acquaintances far more than they trust advertising. So, do everything you can to get other people to keep your name out there. In the beginning, you might want to compose a letter to everybody you know—friends, relatives, neighbors, acquaintances, past clients, just everybody—and simply tell them how they can help you and that you want them to! Tell them what you've been doing and that you want them to recommend you when a friend or relative needs a resume. You might even include with your letter a sample of one of your best resumes (after getting permission from the job seeker or making the resume anonymous), a few business cards, and maybe even a flier that they could post for you (at the supermarket, laundromat, or library—give them some ideas).

Maybe you could even throw a party to launch or promote your new service, and make people more aware of it. (It could be a potluck so it wouldn't break your budget.)

LISTEN TO PEGGY GLENN

Go to a good bookstore and look at books on marketing. One of my favorite authors on this subject is Peggy Glenn. She has written several paperbacks for entrepreneurs, sharing her own very successful experience, and her books are a gold mine of practical ideas.

REPEAT, REPEAT, REPEAT

Now—about advertising in newspapers. This is a very expensive way to go, but it may be necessary in the beginning. The key to advertising is repetition. It doesn't have to be an expensive ad, but it needs to be there every week—the same little ad in the same place, week after week. It registers in people's minds by appearing repeatedly. Then when the time comes that they need a resume writer (or a friend of theirs needs one), they'll go to the paper and know just where to find you. I have not used the Yellow Pages—by the time I thought I could afford it, I didn't need it! — but I hear from other small businesses that Yellow Page ads have that same effect: When they need you, they know just where to look.

AFFILIATE WITH ALLIED SERVICE PEOPLE

I would recommend that you affiliate with business people who could help promote you. Think about the other services people need when they're job hunting: they tend to go to copy centers (getting their resumes printed), to bookstores and libraries (looking for guidance), to employment offices (looking for leads), to newspaper offices (placing ads). You can think of more places job hunters go—to laundromats to do their laundry, for example!

Now, make sure your fliers and your business cards are available in all those same places whenever possible. Talk to the owners of the copy shop, for example, and tell them about your business, offer to send your clients there to get their copies made, and ask them to refer their customers to you to get their resumes written.

Three More Marketing Concepts For Resume Writers

1. CREATE A "NICHE MARKET"

People sometimes increase their job satisfaction and their income by creating what is called a "niche market"—they are making good money providing a product or service that somehow falls through the cracks and isn't being handled by other practitioners—either because the others don't know how to do it or they don't like to do it.

For example, your clients will often ask you for help with something other than a resume:

- a cover letter;
- a complex application form;
- ideas for handling job references.

Notice which of these client requests most appeals to you. If you find, for example, that you love to write cover letters, then maybe you could develop a sideline in business letter writing. If you find yourself doing a lot of counseling, you may want to get even more skilled in coaching people for job interviewing or helping them with in-depth skill assessment and long-term career planning.

And notice which services other people hate to do or usually don't have the skill for. If it's something you can do, then you may have discovered a lucrative "niche market."

And while you're at it: *market!*

You could also be prepared with some written advice for your clients. (After all, you're a writer!) You could develop some carefully written handouts for your clients on various subjects related to the job search.

Be sure your name and phone number appear on every piece of paper you give out, and you will find that these "giveaways" eventually generate new clients and repeat business.

2. DEAL POSITIVELY WITH SEASONAL UPS AND DOWNS

An occupational hazard of self-employment is the uneven pace at which work projects become available. Sometimes it seems like the flow of new clients has come to a dead halt, and this is the time you could panic if you aren't prepared to deal positively with this unwelcome "opportunity."

Here's one way to get ahead of the game and minimize your stress when the work slows down. Outline *now* some business development projects you want to get done if you "ever get the time." Figure out (and write down) what resources or materials you will need to have on hand in order to proceed with the projects.

Now, set the projects aside until the first day you have a no-show client or the first day your appointment book has a blank page. Then you'll be prepared to take advantage of it and you'll be glad you have a day off to get these things done. It's only when you don't have a paying client or anything *else* productive (income-related) to do that day, that you feel bad about a day off.

Some Good Projects When Business Is Slow:

- Design a new flier.
- Design a new business card.
- Develop or expand your mailing list or marketing database.
- Do telephone networking to generate referrals from other professionals, such as therapists, educators, and tradespeople.
- Conduct a phone survey on any number of matters:
  —practices of your competitors;

—current expectations of employers regarding resumes;

—pricing, availability, and quality of related services that your clients may ask you about.

- Develop a follow-up system for contacting prior clients for feedback on their resume's effectiveness AND to determine their needs for additional work. See, for example, Vicki Law-Miller's evaluation form on pages 304-5 toward the end of this chapter.

- Do some of those follow-ups.

- Upgrade old resumes. Go through your notebook of client resumes. If you see one that could use some graphic improvements, pull it out and "spiff it up" with a sharper type font or more perfect spacing. Send it to the client, free. Sometimes they'll respond by calling in a "thank you" and a request for an update—for THAT you get paid. In any case, they're pleased and impressed. You have made yourself visible again and they are reminded of you and therefore more likely to refer another new client.

3. TRANSFORM YOUR MISTAKES INTO MARKETING OPPORTUNITIES

 If you EVER discover an error in a resume you've done in the past, immediately correct it and send several free copies to the client. You might at the same time endear yourself (and be forgiven) by upgrading the resume in terms of its overall appearance—or even just printing it out in two or three different fonts for them to choose from.

No matter what else happens, you'll feel better about it and the client will be impressed with your professionalism, integrity and generosity. (DO YOU THINK THE "RESUME MILLS" DO THIS?!)

If a long time has passed since you originally wrote the resume, the client may NOW be reminded that they wanted to call you for help with an update, a variation for a different position, or some entirely new project.

> *Hot Marketing Tip from Daniel Porot, job-search expert in Europe: Focus on your "USP" (Unique Selling Point). Position yourself on a SMALL TARGET and be the MONOPOLY in that area.

TIPS FOR A SUCCESSFUL RESUME BUSINESS
by Claudia Jordan

Designing top-notch resumes for our clients is our common goal. A successful resume business entails excellence in writing and much more. Apart from the writing aspect, let me share some key concepts, methods, and ideas that have helped me tremendously.

1. Send your **business flier** to everyone who calls. Hand it out at seminars, organizations, and networking meetings. Send it to trade schools and any other place you can think of.

2. Cultivate **outstanding customer service!** Send a thank-you note to each client when you're finished and especially to people who referred another person. After four to six weeks, I call my clients and ask them these questions:

- How is your resume working?

- Have you had any interviews?

- What methods are you using to get your resume out?

- Are you still satisfied with your resume?

- Do you think any changes are necessary?

Why do I call my clients? First I offer suggestions. Then, if we determine a change would be more effective (such as a minor rewrite, different objective, or multiple targeted resumes), I bid a reasonable price for the work. If you are not doing this, you are like the salesperson who was never heard from after the sale was made. Give your clients superb service and they will be YOUR "salespeople" by giving you referrals.

MARKETING

Note: Referrals are HALF of my business and this marketing method is FREE.

3. **Volunteer**. Give seminars, be involved, participate in networking groups or organizations that interest you. In many cities there are organizations for unemployed professionals—a perfect place to give a volunteer or paid seminar. This is a great way to hone your public speaking skills, market your service, and get referrals. Contact your local unemployment bureau or check the phone book for information.

4. **Use handouts** as an effective marketing tool. My favorites are: (a) a flier describing my service with a sample resume on the back, and (b) tip sheets on interviewing, writing a cover letter, and conducting a job-search campaign. These are well designed, well written, one page in length, and they ALWAYS state my business name and phone number. Sprinkle these handouts liberally with quotes from books and articles, being sure to name the sources. Many people come back to me for help in these areas.

5. **Don't turn away potential business.** Many people call and want a resume typed or updated even after hearing the benefits of creating a targeted resume. I used to refer these people to a typing service, but then I thought I might change their mind by meeting them in person and showing them good resume samples. Sometimes this works and sometimes it doesn't. These typing jobs pay well, but it still bothers me to produce what I consider an inferior resume. At any rate, I did my best to help them and earned some extra money.

TIPS FOR BEGINNING RESUME WRITERS

1. Choose three people with different problems and write their resumes—free. This helped me develop techniques, gain confidence, and receive referrals from my "guinea pigs."

2. Glean key information from your peers. **Interview three resume writers** or career counselors who are your competitors. Check out the phone book and newspaper advertisements and call all of them, as a customer would. This is what your customers go through! Note techniques, price structure, marketing methods—anything of value to you. Then look at how you can improve your marketing, telephone, and in-person presentations to increase your business.

3. **Learn as much as you can** about the job-search industry—it will increase your business as well as your

knowledge! As resume writers, we are naturally a creative breed. Expand that gift of creativity to all aspects of your business. There are many ways to grow and branch out from resume writing. Find your niche and follow your heartstrings to success.

**Claudia Jordan
Phoenix, AZ**

More Strategies for Getting Noticed: Readers' Tips

 ALTERNATIVES TO ADVERTISING IN THE NEWSPAPER

Dear Yana: Regarding advertising my resume business, I have concluded that the best forms of advertising are the Yellow Pages and personal referrals. I have tried newspaper ads, but with the cost of advertising today it does not appear to be worthwhile.

As for pricing my services, whenever we are asked over the phone, we are very candid with people. For instance, if someone asks what the cost of creating a resume would be, we simply tell them that the price begins at $150 and could increase depending upon complexity. That seems to be a fairly good answer and satisfies most people. However, my experience has told me that regardless of any price that we quote, most people are going to shop around. Therefore, my best marketing tool is the time my able staff or I spend on that initial contact; we are always terrific on the phone and do a good job of selling our services!

**Robert Davidson
Executive & Professional
Resume Service
Norwood, MA**

MARKETING STICKERS

Dear Yana: Here is something you might be interested in as a marketing tool. I took my Yellow Pages ad and had it reproduced as a 2-by-4-inch sticker. I put one on each folder I give my clients with their finished work inside. One day I went over to Mariner Medical and noticed my folder in the window of the Marketing Manager's office (which faced the outside). She had her work file there, and my folder was right in plain view. Talk about free marketing!

Justine Stelling
Resumes Plus
Foster City, CA

NETWORKING WITH
OTHER PROFESSIONALS

Dear Yana: I am in my second week of business and although it seems to be starting out slowly, I am just thrilled about writing resumes for my own clients. I get a great deal of satisfaction from composing an effective resume for someone who desperately needs the help.

My biggest obstacle is advertising my new service. My business opened in March, but the Yellow Pages do not come out until November. So far, I have been advertising seven days per week in the major newspaper and five days per week in three smaller local papers. I also created fliers and posted them around the five area colleges.

This week I wrote an introductory letter outlining my services to fifteen employment agencies and to the placement offices at the five colleges. I offered the opportunity to trade referrals with the employment agencies. I offered a 20 percent discount to upcoming graduates through the college placement offices. I welcome any new, unusual suggestions.

Kim Coats
A Better Resume Service
Moline, IL

Dear Kim: Some ideas that come to mind:

When you are introducing yourself to employment agencies and placement offices, expect resistance. (You may be treading on their turf or they may mistrust a total stranger.) Having some GOOD EXAMPLES of your work is critical, especially examples covering their client population (e.g., student resumes for the college placement

office). Contacting them repeatedly will eventually take you out of the "stranger" category.

(To everybody ELSE: Check your local Yellow Pages deadline immediately!) —YP

CLAUDIA'S MARKETING TIPS

Dear Yana: Thank you so much for your suggestion of making a flier that answers the typical questions people ask when they inquire about my service, and includes a sample resume on the other side. I've created one that's proved very effective in getting people motivated to use my service. I mail it to people who call me but don't make an appointment, to people who cancel appointments or don't show up, and to people who are on the fence (currently employed but thinking of changing jobs). It helps show how my service is different, and what a good resume looks like, and it keeps my name in their minds so they'll call ME when they're ready. And, of course, I give it to my customers to give to their friends or to call me if they need more help.

Here are some of my marketing results. I have been in business two months and have kept accurate records on where my business comes from. Fifty percent is from newspaper ads and 50 percent from referrals. In the major newspaper in Phoenix, I run a small ad in the Sunday paper. In two local newspapers, I am listed under the Business and Service Directory (the only resume service!). So far, the major newspaper is best, but the others have only been running two weeks. Surprisingly, people travel as much as fifteen to twenty miles to use my service (as a result of the newspaper ads!).

Claudia Jordan
Phoenix, AZ

(Note: The front side of Claudia's flier appears on page 287 in this chapter.)

SEMINARS:
STAND UP AND BE NOTICED

Dear Yana: Here's my experience with conducting seminars as a marketing tool. My biggest seminar to date was the Urban League's Career Fair held in Oakland. I spoke on "How to Find a Job." To prepare, I pulled from my own experience and from books and articles on the subject. I also put together a short, two-page handout outlining important job-hunting considerations. My first time out, there were approximately thirty people in the audience. The next year (my second time at the Urban League's Career Fair), I was amazed (and delighted) when our room was packed with more than one hundred people!

The seminar went very well. At least ten people came up to thank me, and I received two thank-you letters in the mail! What was even more exciting was the potential business that this free seminar (I didn't charge the Urban League) generated! As people entered, I had them sign a guest list. Of course, I have added their names to my mailing list. Besides potential resume clients, the audience also included local trainers and coordinators from different organizations. These contacts have led to other marketing opportunities. For example, one man from a career development center wants me to speak to his department. Another woman invited me to a special network luncheon—for free! Recently, I spoke to a vocational skills training class at the West Berkeley Health Center.

I give most of these seminars free of charge. They require minimum investment (in fact, I have done them often enough that now I have established topics and handouts to support them — all I have to do is make copies and speak). My goal is to increase my presence in the community so that more people become familiar with my business. I'm hoping that this investment will pay off in increased credibility and a solid, loyal list of clientele!

Cynthia Mackey
Winning Strategies
Oakland, CA

P.S. This seminar was held months ago and I am still getting phone calls for seminars and resumes!

HOW TO DEAL WITH THE CUT-RATE COMPETITION

One resume writer, May, wrote for help with this problem: A competitor has recently entered the picture, and copies everything she does. This makes it more difficult for May to attract customers, especially when potential clients say, "But the guy down the street says he'll do it for $25."

To help distinguish her service from others, I advised May to give each inquiring job hunter a short list of questions to ask the competitors, such as:

1. Can I speak with the person who will actually be writing my resume?

2. Can I talk to that person for a few minutes about what strategy they'll use for dealing with my unique problem?

3. How much actual time will I be spending face-to-face with my resume writer?

Then she can tell potential clients to see how much of that information the competitor is willing to provide WITHOUT insisting that they come to the office in person (for the hard-sell or bait-and-switch "closing").

May could also write an article for the local newspaper entitled "How to Choose a Resume Service" or "Tip-offs to the Rip-offs"—something along that line. Later she can put an ad in the paper offering a free copy of the article—i.e., free help in choosing a writer, WITHOUT the client having to come in.

Another tip May could offer job hunters for identifying low-budget and/or low quality resume services: They give you a long form to fill out where you list your job history and all your accomplishments. Then they essentially word-process it. You are, in effect, writing your own resume but THEY get paid for doing it.

SHOW THEM YOUR STUFF: A PROFESSIONAL PORTFOLIO

The following is a good idea from the *Keyboard Connection*, a national newsletter for independent word-processing professionals.

(For subscription information, write P.O. Box 338, Glen Carbon, IL 62034 or call 618-667-4666.)

Whether you are new to the business or a seasoned professional, it is never too late to organize a portfolio showcasing samples of your best work. Backing up your qualifications with examples provides visual proof of the capabilities of your equipment and the brains behind it—you!

Your samples book might include a collection of letters, resumes, forms, and graphic displays demonstrating a variety of typefaces, layouts, and presentations. Since resume formats are often influenced by content, seeing a variety of layouts and styles may reaffirm a client's confidence in your ability to tailor information into a professional-looking resume. When prospective clients ask about her qualifications, one resume writer introduces her work by showing prospects her own resume, which doubles as a sample resume in her collection.

Exhibit your samples in clear plastic protective covers assembled in a three-ring binder or magnetic photo album, or frame and mount them on the wall. Organize your book for quick reference to illustrate the fine points of your equipment and technical expertise. Let your samples book remind you, too, of what a good job you're doing—and give yourself a pat on the back!

Marketing Idea: Create a Good Newsletter

If you like to write and you have a tendency to collect and organize information, then creating a newsletter may be a natural project for you to explore.

Newsletters have two serious drawbacks that put off most would-be editors:

1. They are time and labor intensive.

2. They can be expensive to produce.

So you'd almost HAVE to enjoy doing it to get past these two disincentives.

Probably the main reason I do a newsletter is that it is a great outlet for creativity and self-expression. That makes it FUN, so any other benefits are a bonus. Another reason is that I want to INFLUENCE my profession. For me, it's not enough just to produce—I also want to "make waves," to challenge some of the stuffy conservative ideas that still exist in career development. I want to have stimulating dialogues with my peers, and I want to be a help and support to others. I want to experiment, too—to try out a theory that we can improve the relationship between employer and employee by helping upgrade their communications, beginning with their very FIRST exchange: the resume and interview.

There are a great many possible functions of a newsletter. A good newsletter can:

- Create a sense of community among its readers, reinforcing the interests and concerns they share and providing a forum for dialogue.
- Establish the editor (or creative team) as a central figure in that community—one who visibly contributes to its existence and vitality, and takes a leadership role.
- Create a sort of public "bulletin board" for the community that can be used freely (with reasonable restraint) by the editorial team.

MARKETING

GUIDELINES FOR A SUCCESSFUL NEWSLETTER

1. Don't wear out your welcome with excessive self-advertising; give others enough of the space so they don't feel used. On the other hand, you DO get generous coverage in exchange for providing the newsletter. It just needs to seem a fair exchange to all parties.

2. Give a bit more than is expected—more pages, more pictures, more entertainment, more data, whatever.

3. Take a strong stand. Don't be wishy-washy. Be FOR something, with passion. Champion a cause.

4. Be open to disagreement and controversy. A newsletter that never ruffles any feathers is boring.

5. Be aware of basic communication rules that apply to this medium. This is not a scholarly, scientific journal. While it can and should stimulate thought and learning, it needs to offer short, easy-access bits of information. It can promote serious deep thought by repeatedly presenting the same subject in a lot of different ways.

6. Excite and entertain the reader; make the newsletter visually appealing and leave lots of "breathing space."

7. Include some hard data, not just fluff.

8. Include names and phone numbers, so the community is immediately visible and people can identify with it and interact LATERALLY. Provide readers the option of immediate, direct access to each other—not just through you the editor. (You don't want to create barriers.)

9. Make a clear, honest, and easy-to-find statement about the purpose of the newsletter. Make it worthwhile to you and worthwhile to them.

10. Be realistic (savvy) about your expectations of the reader. If, for example, you want feedback and input from readers, you have to do much more than you would imagine to get a response. The fact is, they have lots of other priorities and interests. To get a response, you have to be: (a) persuasive, (b) loud, (c) persistent, (d) patient, (e) clever! Cajole, bribe, beg, harangue—whatever it takes, it takes! But it's worth it—a participatory newsletter is much more fun for everybody than a one-person soapbox.

11. Provide something useful and UNIQUE—something the reader can't get ANYWHERE else.

12. Offer good value; in fact, irresistible value.

13. Risk giving away what you THINK is all you've got to say. The challenge will stimulate your creative thought and renew your resources.

14. Dare to reflect your own personality. Take a chance. Remember, there's no shortage of conservative, boring, minimal-appeal newsletters out there. Better that yours should be talked about (and occasionally ridiculed) than be ignored.

15. Consistently invite participation of your peers and others you respect. They don't have to always agree with you; a different opinion can stimulate dialogue.

16. Thank and encourage readers and contributors. (But don't take offense at a lack of response; remember, inertia is the NORM. It doesn't necessarily mean disinterest.)

Promotional Idea:
Talk on the Radio

Here are ten questions that radio talk show hosts have asked me when I appeared as their guest.

1. What's the real purpose of a resume? (And what are the side benefits of writing one?)

2. What's the main difference between a good resume and a mediocre one?

3. How do people do a traditional resume, and what's wrong with that? Is there any one right way?

4. What are the rules? What are the do's and don'ts?

5. Why do some resumes work and some don't?

6. What are the different kinds of resumes?

7. What information should definitely be included or not be included?

8. If there was ONE thing you could do or add that would improve your resume, what would it be?

9. How did you get into this business? How long have you been doing it?

10. How do you find a good professional to help you with a resume? How is a professional helpful?

GETTING ON THE RADIO

Here's one way to get on the radio that worked for me. Develop an ad (like the one below) and distribute it to local radio stations. I have used a version of this technique to promote my books nationwide. This generated quite a few guest appearances for me on radio stations around the country.

EXPERT SAYS A JOB RESUME SHOULD LOOK MORE LIKE A BILLBOARD

A good resume is more like a billboard than like a phone book—it delivers a powerful message in just a few seconds. In the *Damn Good Resume Guide* (new 1989 edition), resume expert Yana Parker replaces outdated myths with these four key concepts: A resume is a marketing tool, not a personnel document; it focuses on the future, not the past; it summarizes accomplishments, not job duties; it documents skills you enjoy using, not tasks you had to do.

Contact: Yana Parker

Availability: Northern California and via Telephone (510) 658-9229

SAMPLE QUESTIONS TO FEED THE INTERVIEWER

• Why do people agonize so much about writing a resume?

• Do resumes have to be so dry and boring?

• Doesn't EVERYBODY lie a little on their resume?

• What's the fastest fix for a less-than-perfect resume?

MARKETING

Recently I conducted a workshop for resume writers—which included a brainstorming session on marketing ideas. Here are some of the participant's tips. (This also points out the value of networking—or schmoozing with others in the field.)

Tips from a Marketing Workshop

- **JUSTINE**: Join the local Chamber of Commerce, and get your promotional material into their package. Foster City has a Welcome Wagon scheme to get a package of promotional materials from doctors, dentists, and other service providers to residents new to the area.
- **LYNN:** Create a mailing list from your workshop participants. All prospects will be qualified buyers. You'll need to follow-up to convert participants to potential clients.
- **LIONEL:** Network with bankers and CPAs.
- **SUE:** Target client base/special interest groups, e.g., gays, minority groups. Then look at magazines and publications that focus on these groups.
- **CYNTHIA:** Set up a booth at a Career Fair to introduce your service. Take copies of resumes you have written as evidence of work you have done. Offer a free critique of resumes to introduce your service.
- **JUSTINE:** Advertise "Rush jobs welcome!"
- **DAVID:** Offer adjunct services to therapists, hypnotherapists, massage therapists, and groups for women in transition.
- **SUE:** Set up "rainbow marketing" with other businesses interested in the same target market, and send fliers, catalogs, promotional materials, etc. This cuts down on postage costs, which can be shared among several people.
- **CYNTHIA:** Fee exchange/barter for clients who have limited financial resources. They can distribute your fliers and promotional

material to new markets, e.g., college societies. The president and staff of one society are affiliated with other societies, and could provide you with free publicity.
- **YANA**: My favorite marketing piece was a two-sided flier—like a mini-newsletter. It asked and answered the typical questions of a potential client (how long it takes, what it costs, how I work, etc.). On the flip side was a sample of my work, i.e., a successful resume I wrote.
- **PAT:** Get your client to have their resume critiqued by an independent third party to verify that the quality of services is satisfactory.
- **ROBERTA:** Create a handout list of services for users and target groups, and include yourself on the list.
- **TOM:** Give workshops to church groups and organizations, with all or part of your fee going to the sponsor. Ask participants for their names and addresses to add to your promotional mailing list. Check the Yellow Pages for "Organizations," and find out which ones would be receptive to your doing a workshop on resumes.
- **EVE:** I have a flier that features an article about my business that appeared in the local newspaper, and this helps establish my credibility with new clients.
- **LIONEL:** Design a business card with a miniature resume on the back. (Make it clear they need to turn the card over for details.)
- **SUSAN:** Follow up on your existing client base. Send postcards to remind previous clients about possible salary increase negotiations. Develop a niche for writing ads in the personal sections of various newspapers.

Even More Tips on Marketing

- Create a flier for different types of workers. Use different graphics so you're sure to relate to each targeted audience.
- On your business card, make your name and phone number big enough to be read at a distance.
- Give at least three business cards to each client, and ask them to give two of them to their friends.
- Start a support group for your clients. This helps them in their job search, gives them another reason to recommend you to their friends, and makes them a part of your "team."
- Get listed in future editions of job search publications. Contact the publishers to see when their next edition is coming out.
- Join or create a "leads club" with other professionals.

TELEPHONE TRACKING SHEET

Dear Yana: On the following page is a chart that I use to track phone calls I get from potential clients. I keep this sheet on a clipboard near the phone so that each time the phone rings I can make a record of the call. I'm particularly interested in where the caller heard about me and what results from the conversation. I always hope it's an appointment.

Notice that I also have a box to note whether or not the appointment was kept. After a client has had their resume written, I go back to the sheet and check the "Kept Appt." box. I like to monitor this so I can see the attrition rate—this helps me pace my appointments more realistically. And if one publication seems to be drawing flaky people, I stop advertising through that paper.

The chart serves as a concise means of evaluating my marketing, as well as aiding in daily organization.

Susan Ireland
Dynamite!! Resumes
Kensington, CA

MARKETING

Telephone Tracking

Caller's Name	Date	Publica-tion #1	Publica-tion #2	Publica-tion #3	Client Ref.	Other	Inquiry	Phone Consul.	Made Appt.	Kept Appt.	Comments

**V. I. P.
RESUME
SERVICE**

A Two-Step Marketing Strategy

In the following article, Susan Ireland describes how she evaluated her place in the market and created a marketing action plan.

STEP ONE
DEFINING MY MARKETING POSITION

After reading *Guerrilla Marketing* by Jay Levinson (Houghton Mifflin Company), I took the following steps to clarify my business position in the market. I defined the highlighted topics below as clearly as possible to come up with a concise statement, "My Position in the Market." This became the key element in creating my marketing plan.

My Strengths:

1. I offer one-on-one consultation that allows me to work with the client to:

- carefully phrase each line, creating a personalized resume to handle each situation.
- customize the format (chronological, functional, or hybrid) for each individual.

2. I'm available to produce a resume in one appointment, start to finish. (It usually takes three hours per resume.)

3. I skillfully resolve difficult problems such as how to deal with gaps in work history, minimal education, layoffs, etc.

4. I use a Macintosh computer and laser printer for excellent graphics and quality printing.

5. I create a resume with a concise job objective, making it focused and powerful.

My Weaknesses:

1. Officially, I offer only the resume writing service (no career counseling or job placement).

2. I have a low advertising budget, limiting the size and quantity of ads I can place.

Who Are My Competitors?

1. Large resume companies.

2. Individual professional resume writers.

3. Job hunters who write their own resumes.

4. Resume how-to books.

Strengths Of My Most Serious Competitors:

1. Well established.

2. Well publicized.

3. Advertise fast turn-around (however, most take two to three days; some take one day; only one writer in my area offers same-day service—I offer three to four hour turn-around)

4. Advertise that they do resume work for all professions (so do I).

5. Make unrealistic promises of more money, advancement, new jobs. (Resumes can't do that; they get interviews!)

6. Most are cheaper. Those that are more expensive don't tell the client over the phone what it really costs.

7. Professional-looking documents. (So are mine.)

Competitors' Weaknesses:

1. Impersonal service—most writers meet with their client for twenty minutes, at most one hour. My clients stay with me throughout the process.

2. Limited offering of formats. They don't offer anything except chronological; most discourage the functional format.

3. Don't deal effectively with clients' weaknesses, i.e., gaps in work history, etc.

4. Often don't use a job objective or use one that is vague and wordy, making the resume less focused.

Target Market:

1. Professionals (both men and women).

2. Women reentering the workforce.

3. Job seekers who have been laid off.

Approximate breakdown of current clientele:
66 percent: women (of which one-third are reentry)
90 percent: have an income of more than $35,000

Trends Of The Economy:

1. Heavy layoffs.

2. Unemployment rate is increasing.

3. Companies are not expanding, resulting in:

- low pay raises
- fewer promotions.

What Are My Goals?

1. A twenty-five-hour work week doing resume writing with clients individually. (That's seven clients per week. Since I average two cancellations per week, I need to generate nine appointments per week to ensure I meet my quota.)

2. Two workshops per month for which I am paid.

3. Occasional workshops for no pay.

4. Co-op referral service with personnel agency that generates income.

5. Sub-writers to do my overflow—at 20 percent commission. Would like to generate enough business to keep one other person busy full-time (seven resumes per week).

Summary Of My Position in The Market:

The purpose of this marketing plan is to draw enough clients to write seven resumes per week, to refer seven clients per week to sub-writers, and to give one paid workshop every two weeks.

The target market will be professionals of all ages, both sexes, and all occupations, including women reentering the workforce. This will be done at the lowest possible marketing cost.

To accomplish this, I will position the service as one that produces personalized, high-quality, powerful resumes for job seekers who want one-on-one consultation and professional-looking results, and who feel comfortable hiring a writer to achieve this. These

clients want efficient service; that's why I offer full production in one three-hour appointment, and make revisions over the phone. I specialize in resolving problems such as dealing with gaps in the work history, layoffs, etc.

Work is done on a Macintosh computer, which offers customized formats and graphics, and is printed on a laser printer for excellent master copies. My service also includes writing cover letters, producing letterheads, and providing valuable job-search leads and information.

Marketing consists of referrals from career centers and personnel agencies, advertising in newspapers, client referrals, submitting articles to newspapers, appearances on radio/TV talk shows, and workshops at career centers, community organizations, and corporations (provided for free and for pay). In next fall's edition of the Yellow Pages, I'll have a display ad as well as a listing.

This position statement is something I read frequently to make sure everything I do for my business is relevant to this position. It's like having a clear job objective on my "business resume." Having defined my marketing position, I was ready to draw up a marketing plan that outlines exactly how I'm going to achieve the goals stated above.

STEP TWO
CREATING A MARKETING PLAN

After defining my position in the market, I went about creating a marketing plan. I started by making a list of all the marketing I had done and was currently doing. Then I did some serious reading and brainstorming to come up with another list of more things I could do.

The following is a compilation of those two lists, written in the present tense. This doesn't mean I'm presently doing them all, but it does mean that they are all part of an ongoing plan. For example, I may not be able to afford to advertise in all the publications at once, but I know that they are read by my target audience, so I'll experiment with advertising in them, one by one, until I've refined the list and have a plan that is cost effective.

I keep my plan handy as a checklist to make sure my marketing is always in progress and on target. My goal is to always be doing as much as I can do well.

1. Advertise in newspapers, such as:

- Community papers on classes and services

- Smaller periodicals

- Job and career papers

- The major city newspaper

- College newspapers

2. Take out a listing and a display ad in the Yellow Pages. [Note: For more on using the Yellow Pages, see pages 274-75.]

3. Be associated with career counseling centers to:

- Be available for resume writing on a referral basis.

- Be available to give workshops.

- Attend workshops for networking.

- Refer my clients to appropriate career centers for assistance.

- Be listed in their files as a resume-writing resource.

- Introduce myself at meetings for college career counselors.

4. Establish and maintain referral relationships with other resume writers.

- I am listed with my resume mentor as a writer doing her style of resumes. She receives a commission on these referrals and I have agreed to provide material for her books.

- I stay in touch with other career-development professionals in the area and exchange referrals.

- I work with career counselors who specialize in outplacement services for companies. I do the resume writing aspect of their service.

- I regularly attend workshops for resume writers. This is an opportunity to exchange cards and information about each others' services.

- I keep my name in the minds of other writers by writing articles for newsletters.

- I nurture my relationships with other professionals in the field by sharing valuable marketing information I get from my own business development and software we all need and enjoy.

- I network at other career development events.

5. Encourage referrals from previous clients. Establish an ongoing relationship that goes on after the initial resume writing session. (Contact clients four to six times throughout the year.)

- As client leaves my office after a session, I give them:

  Three of my business cards—one for them and two to give to their friends.

  An informative, functional handout such as a book-mark with job-search information on it.

  A "certificate of value" to give to new friends and relatives as an endorsed referral. (This might look like a coupon that the client would sign and pass on to a friend. The value of the coupon might be for ten extra free copies of their resume, fifteen minutes free, or one free cover letter.)

  A questionnaire I have created to help me track my marketing effectiveness.

- Offer to do simple revisions for free or for a small charge.

- Give lots of free information; establish myself as a valuable resource for job-hunt information.

- Call clients periodically to see how their resume is working and to give advice.

- Occasionally send a personal letter accompanied by job-search or job-related information.

- Create a newsletter.

- Send a postcard to clients eighteen months after they have their resumes written, suggesting I help them with a request for a salary increase.

- Put on special events such as workshops, receptions, and support groups for previous clients, asking them to invite friends.

6. Network with other professionals, such as:

- Word processors

- Therapists

- Bodywork people

- Any professional dealing with people in transition.

7. Offer resume critiques at job fairs, either in conjunction with a personnel agency, career-development center, or independently.

8. Provide up to ten minutes free telephone consultation to any job seeker. (Advertise this to encourage initial phone inquiries.)

9. Put on resume-writing workshops for which I may or may not get paid. Be sure to pass out useful handouts with my name and phone number on each page, as well as business cards. Keep a list of participants for mailings. Places to give workshops are:

- Independent classes offered through publications

- Colleges

- Career-counseling centers

- Churches

- Corporations—as part of outplacement programs

10. Reprint articles and ads that worked. Multiply their effectiveness by using them as fliers.

11. Solicit long-distance clients by advertising (if not too expensive) in and writing articles for national publications. Long-distance resume writing usually requires the client placing a call to me that lasts approximately two hours, my faxing the draft to them, another half-hour discussion on the phone, and one more fax for approval.

12. Be on TV/radio talk shows.

[Note: See "Talk on the Radio," page 279.]

13. Establish referral relationships with a few personnel agencies. The agreement between each agency and me is:

I conduct initial screening (which is part of the resume-writing session anyway) to determine the client's skills, integrity, and work style. After the resume is completed (not before) and IF I feel comfortable recommending them, I mention my contact at the agencies and offer to send their resume to the agencies for them. I make a few notes to accompany the resume, which I mail to the agency. The client contacts the agency in a few days, and from there on each agency works directly with the client. If the client (who now becomes the "candidate" at the agency) gets a job through the agency, I get a pre-arranged percentage of the placement fee.

The agencies recommend me to candidates who need resumes.

If an agency participates in job fairs, I offer to help staff their booth, give resume critiques, and pass out my cards.

14. Join professional organizations for human resources personnel and attend their meetings. This enables me to network with personnel management from companies who might be looking for resume-writing services (either private consultations or workshops) as part of their outplacement services, as well as keeping me in touch with what these resume reviewers are looking for in resumes (good for my professional development).

15. Write articles (include an action photo) for local publications whose readership is my audience. I have a list of "publications I will submit articles to" handy, so I'm always in the process of writing a piece.

16. Be on the review panel of The Job Forum, a service provided by the Chamber of Commerce one night a week for job seekers. The panel is made up of executives who give their time to coach job seekers.

Susan Ireland
Dynamite!! Resumes
Kensington, CA

Sample Marketing Materials

If the definition of marketing is **anything that gets you known and generates business,** then marketing materials are the **physical items that support that process,** for example:

- advertisements
- business cards
- fliers
- brochures
- newsletters
- follow-up letters
- handouts, etc.
- even (or especially!) the resumes you create!

One of my own favorite items of marketing material is what I call my Bookmark Mini-Guide, a 3-by-8-inch cardstock item printed on both sides. (See page 325.) It's small enough to function as a bookmark, yet it contains a complete outline of the steps for creating a "damn good resume" all on ONE side; the flip-side carries five provocative concepts to jar people's thinking. Plus, *of course,* a one-inch paragraph that *informs the reader of my phone number,* my publisher's phone number, and the three books I've authored. I give these bookmarks away free, by the hundreds. This is an **inexpensive way to create a marketing piece that people won't throw away** because it contains valuable information in a compact form.

Incidentally, the Bookmark Mini-Guide fulfills another more subtle function: It conveys to the reader a sense of my skill level, as well as some clues to the way I might work with a client. This kind of information in a marketing piece **helps the reader decide whether they would want to hire me as their resume writer.**

The other marketing materials presented in this chapter came almost entirely from resume writers and counselors who contributed to the *Damn Good Resume Writer Newsletter.* **Notice how these items convey an image** of the resume writer, and perhaps you will get some good ideas for what YOUR marketing materials should look like.

Here's what I liked about these examples:

- good business names
- logos repeated on different marketing items
- efficient use of double-sided pieces
- creative, eye-catching graphics appropriate to the client population
- marketing and educating effectively combined.

JOSEPH C. ROPER, President
94 STATION ST.
HINGHAM, MA 02043
(617) 749-2970

A-SCRIPT™

- RÉSUMÉ WRITING
- COVER LETTERS
- SKILLS ASSESSMENT
- JOB SEARCH PLANNING
- INTERVIEW TECHNIQUES
- CAREER REFERENCE LIBRARY
- LASER TYPESETTING
- LIFETIME DISK STORAGE

OFFICES IN MARBLEHEAD, HINGHAM & BOSTON

CA
Career Advantage

(415) 223-9417

Career Counseling
Workshops
Resumes
Job Search Strategies

Michelle M. Carroll
Career Development
Specialist

3802 North Ridge Drive
Richmond, CA 94806

CAREER PLANNING TECHNIQUES

(718) 631-3635

HINDA C. BODINGER

69-16 229th Street • Bayside, NY 11364-3119

---

editorial services
- freelance writing
- resume service

Lisa A. Gessner

(516)759-2388

computer services
- desktop publishing
- Macintosh tutoring

Barbara K. Shough, M.S.
Career Assessment
Resume Preparation

Career Development Institute

690 Market Street, Suite 404
San Francisco, CA 94104

(415) 982-2636

Resumes • Cover Letters • SF-171's

Resumes By
ROBBIE MILLER KAPLAN
Author of *Sure-Hire Resumes*

(703) 255-3388

P.O. Box 1623
Vienna, VA 22183

WINNER'S CIRCLE

PROFESSIONAL
RESUME SERVICE

BOB F. REECE
Managing Partner

P.O. Box 10387
Winston-Salem, NC 27108

Tel 800/476-3963
919/777-3415
Fax 919/777-3603

Justine Stelling
RESUMES PLUS

1291 E. Hillsdale Blvd.
Suite 209
Foster City, CA 94404

415
573-1657

MARKETING

WORKLIFE SOLUTIONS

A resume writing service -- to help land your next job!

WHAT'S UNIQUE ABOUT THIS SERVICE?
Your resume will be a personalized marketing tool for your next job --NOT a dull record of your past. (see the sample on the back)

WHY SHOULD I USE THIS SERVICE?
You'll have an outstanding resume which will...
 -present you at your very best
 -highlight your abilities
 -clearly define your objective
 -capture the attention and respect of the employer
 -create the desire to meet you
 -is sharp and professional
 -show how you're qualified for a new kind of work

You will get full credit for all of your past experience...
 -skills you used as a volunteer
 -extra work you did on the job
 -projects you did on your own
 -relevant knowledge and skills you gained in any way

WHAT IS INCLUDED?
 -Twelve printed resumes plus a Master Copy
 -List of your references on matching stationery
 -Handouts with tips on
  ...interviewing
  ...writing cover letters
  ...how to conduct an effective job campaign

WHEN DO I GET A FINISHED RESUME?
Same day resumes are available. Leave with a finished resume after a 3 to 4 hour session.

CAN WE SOLVE TOUGH PROBLEMS?
Yes! I can show you how to:
 -target your next job or several objectives
 -present your abilities for a change of career
 -bridge a gap in your work record
 -present a patchy job history to your best advantage
 -minimize lack of experience
All without lying or exaggerating.

HOW DO I GET STARTED?
 -Call for an appointment.
 -Bring a list of your work history and education, or an old resume.

HOW MUCH DOES IT COST?
It depends on how long it takes and the scope of your project. Call for an estimate or free consultation.

WHAT OTHER SERVICES ARE OFFERED?
 -resume critique and update
 -cover letters and after interview letters
 -self assessment
 -self-marketing techniques
 -job search workshops

Claudia Jordan
996-5334

289

Personnel
Resources
Inc.

Professional Resume Service

Gilda Weisskopf, Manager
444 Great Mills Road
Lexington Park, MD 20659
301-862-9093

> *A newsletter for job seekers . . .*
> Summer 1991

THE BEST PERSON FOR THE JOB IS NOT NECESSARILY THE PERSON WHO IS HIRED.

THE PERSON HIRED IS MOST OFTEN THE ONE WHO IS BEST PREPARED.

GAINING A COMPETITIVE EDGE . . .

A resume cannot guarantee you a job. A resume helps you get an interview, but even that cannot be guaranteed. Today's economic situation makes the job market extremely competitive. Companies are downsizing, government contracts are more competitive, and highly qualified candidates are more plentiful.

So how can you gain that competitive edge? Be prepared. Your first step is to create a quality resume. There are no specific *rules* for writing a resume, but here are some guidelines you can follow:

- ☛ Make sure your name, address, telephone number are on the top of the page.
- ☛ Limit size to preferably 1 page, but no more than 2. If you have a second page, put continued on the bottom of page 1 and your name and telephone # on page 2.
- ☛ **Proofread. Proofread. Proofread. Typos are deadly!!!!** Have someone else proof it for another review.
- ☛ Keep to the relevant. Hobbies/interests take up valuable space for describing skills and accomplishments. A first review takes about 20 seconds, so keep to the relevant.

- ☛ Focus on *accomplishments*, not just your job description. Which sounds better?
  Processed insurance claims.
          or
  Processed 100 insurance claims daily with less than a 2% error rate.
- ☛ NEVER, EVER tell a lie. If you state that you had "less than a 2% error rate," it must be verifiable.

WHAT TIME IS YOUR INTERVIEW?

Runzheimer International management consulting firm in New York City reports that the time of your interview is more critical than you might think. Research indicates that 55.8% of the last candidates to get interviewed get the job. Only 17.6% of applicants that are interviewed first get the job.

So what can you do? Tactfully ask if you can be scheduled for a later time, especially if you think you might be among the first candidates to be interviewed.

Other bad times: Mondays and quitting time.

Source: Executive Female, March/April 1991

RESUME MIXTAKES

This is hard to believe, but Robert Half of Robert Half International reports that he has actually seen the following statements on resumes.

"Six munts ago, I couldn't spell executive. Today I are one."

"Do not mind occasional overtime work, but desire a 30-hour work week."

"Size of previous employer: Twenty-three floors."

And here's our favorite:

"My firm currently employs 20 odd people."

And they say that kids say the darnedest things!

Source: Meetings & Conventions, October 1989

PREPARING FOR THE OPEN-ENDED INTERVIEW QUESTIONS

Most of us often get butterflies before an interview. If you are one of the self-confident people who doesn't, you are truly lucky. But if you are one of those who get nervous, your best method of eliminating (or at least controlling) the nervousness is to be prepared.

The following is a list of questions that are often asked during an interview. Prepare your answers -- use a tape recorder; rehearse your answers out loud as you are driving your car; at least practice in your mind how you would respond to each question.

✔ What are your career goals?
✔ Where do you want to be in five years?
✔ What are your strengths? Weaknesses?
✔ What do you think of (company you now work for)?
✔ Can you work under pressure?
✔ Tell me about yourself.
✔ What type of position are you looking for?
✔ Why do you think you'd like this job?
✔ Do you like routine work?
✔ Why should we hire you for this job?
✔ Did you have any frustrations in your last job?
✔ What are your special abilities?
✔ What do you know about our company?
✔ What are your outstanding achievements?

?? WHY INTERVIEWS GO WRONG ??

Did you get the feeling that something didn't go quite right with your interview? The following is a list of the most common reasons an interview goes wrong:

❑ Poor personal appearance.
❑ Lack of eye contact.
❑ Unable to communicate adequately.
❑ Arriving late without calling.
❑ Being rude.
❑ Being too familiar or casual.
❑ Unclear purpose.
❑ Indecisive.
❑ Unprepared responses.
❑ Critical of past employers.
❑ Too many excuses.
❑ Too aggressive.
❑ Too timid.
❑ Lack of interest.

Justine Stelling
Secretarial Service

Price List and Description of 5 Basic Resume Services

1. SIMPLE RESUME - WORD PROCESSING ONLY

No changes. Word processed "AS-IS".
Additional laser originals available at 75 cents per page.

$30

2. FORMATTING AND WORD PROCESSING

Change print format by adding bold or large print, underscoring, or other enhancements not on current resume. Includes 4 laser originals.

$60

3. CONSULTING, FORMATTING AND WORD PROCESSING

COMPOSING: For clients who have never had a professionally written resume.
REWRITING: *Current or outdated* resume.
REDESIGN: From chronological to functional for better presentation of background and skills.
             Includes 4 laser originals.

$90

4. CONSULTING ONLY

$30 per hour - 1/2 hour minimum

5. EDITING/REPRINTING EXISTING RESUME IN COMPUTER

$30 per hour - 1/2 hour minimum

SERVICES WE OFFER AT NO CHARGE

FAX resume to and from your office for review
24 Hour Nite-drop and Pick-up at our office for clients who also work 9-5
Laser Printing - Disc Storage

YOU CAN ALWAYS RELY ON OUR CONFIDENTIALITY

OFFICE TELEPHONE 573-1657   FAX 573-1924

1125 E. Hillsdale Boulevard, Suite 114 • Foster City, California 94404 •   573-1657

MARKETING

Behr Business Services
473 Fourth Avenue
Redwood City, CA 94063
(415) 365-9199

JOB-WINNING RESUMES

Resumes are the marketing tool of the job-hunting process. Even though they are indispensable, they are incredibly hard to write for oneself. First, you have to learn *how to write a resume* before you write it. Hopefully you don't have to write many, so how do you become proficient? Instead of going through all that pain, turn to someone who can create *your* unique resume, one that sounds like *you*, at a price you can afford.

Call Eileen Behr at Behr Business Services to discuss your resume needs and how best to develop your job-winning resume.

Pricing:

Full Resume Assistance - You come in and together we talk through all your work experiences, skills, accomplishments, achievements, job objective and skills necessary for the new job. This takes about one hour. I then develop the resume, print **five copies** on resume grade paper and store the original skills analysis and resume on disk for one year, making it available for future updates or revisions for different job objectives. - $125.00

Basic Resume Assistance - (I expect most people to be in this category.) When you call for an appointment, I describe what information I will need to create a resume, and you do some homework before coming in. The homework is to write down your work history, skills, accomplishments, achievements and job objective info. With this head start, we only need a 15-20 minute appointment. Again, I do my work and produce **two copies** of the resume on resume grade paper and store everything for a year for future needs. - All this for $70.00

Formatting Assistance - There are people who can write a good resume but just need it typed properly and printed professionally. With this service I provide **two copies** on resume grade paper and the resume stored on disk for a year. - $25.00

PROFESSIONAL RESUMES
SURPASS THE COMPETITION WITH THE IDEAL RESUME!

- 1 Hour Consultation
- Writing & Editing
- Layout & Design

Weekend & Evening Appointments
TELEPHONE: 774-5231

| I |DEAL
| R |ESUME
| S |ERVICE

- Cover Letters
- Computer Storage
- Letter Quality Printout

* STUDENT DISCOUNTS *

-IDEAL RESUMES-
Giving you an edge on the competition!

"Complete Resume Package"
Resumes
Letterhead/Envelopes
Job Search Information

*Laser Printed
*Computer Storage

STUDENT DISCOUNT

Evening & Weekend Appointments

774-5231 (P.M.)

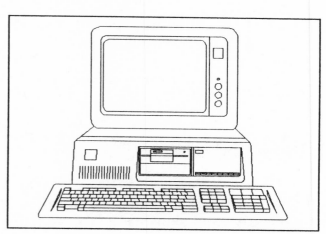

Professionally Prepared Resumes By An Experienced Writer
-IDEAL RESUME SERVICE-

MARKETING

Professionally Prepared Resumes | I |DEAL| R |ESUME| S |ERVICE By Appointment 774-5231

Professionally Prepared Resumes | I |DEAL| R |ESUME| S |ERVICE By Appointment 774-5231

Professionally Prepared Resumes | I |DEAL| R |ESUME| S |ERVICE By Appointment 774-5231

Professionally Prepared Resumes | I |DEAL| R |ESUME| S |ERVICE By Appointment 774-5231

Professionally Prepared Resumes | I |DEAL| R |ESUME| S |ERVICE By Appointment 774-5231

A PROFILE OF CROSS EXECUTIVE SERVICES

Know more . . .   Do more . . .   Be more . . .
So reads the sign that hangs above the desk of Denise Cross, owner and operator of Cross Executive Services. "These words are my inspiration to consistently offer my clients a level of service that beats anything they might have expected from a resume writing service."

Denise initially started C.E.S. in 1987 as a home-based desktop publishing/word processing service. She soon found that resume formatting was a large part of her business. With most of her early clients being family and friends whom she knew very well, she noticed that their resumes in no way reflected them or their interests. "Helping people develop and write resumes was a natural extension of the typesetting and formatting services I was already providing. But if I was going to offer this as a service, I wanted to make sure I was offering my clients the best techniques available. So I began to research every aspect of resume development and production."

The result was the blend of a myriad techniques in writing, design, type selection and paper selection and an attention-getting resume that she markets as *The Mother of All Resumes.* "I've invested a lot of time, money and energy into my quest for the *perfect resume* and I suspect I'll invest even more to keep myself in the forefront of resume development."

As for resume writing as a business, "I love what I'm doing. I find it tremendously rewarding to be able to help people help themselves."

Software
Ami Professional *(word processing software)*
Microsoft Windows
Soft Type font generation software
Adobe typefaces

Hardware
386 PC-compatible with:
-- 4 mb RAM
-- 100 mb hard drive

-- 3.5" floppy drive
-- 5.25" floppy drive
-- 80 mb tape backup

Hewlett Packard Laserjet Series II printer with:
-- Additional 2 mb memory card
-- Adobe Postscript emulation cartdridge.

CES *Cross Executive Services*

715 Silver Spur Road, Suite #204 ☎ Rolling Hills Estates, CA 90274 ☎ (213)544-7171 ☎ FAX (213)544-7172

APPROXIMATELY

90,000 HOURS

OF YOUR LIFE

WILL BE SPENT

AT WORK...

SO WHY NOT MAKE THE MOST OF IT?

A-SCRIPT WORD CENTERS

Career Services Since 1981
94 Station Street
Hingham, MA 02043
(617) 749-2970
OFFICES IN MARBLEHEAD & HINGHAM

A-SCRIPT WORD CENTERS

Career Services Since 1981
94 Station Street
Hingham, MA 02043

MORE FACTS YOU SHOULD KNOW

A survey of ten million job seekers by the Bureau of Census revealed that for every 100 who use:

- classified ads in the newspapers, 76 out of 100 *don't find a job.*

- private employment agencies, 76 out of 100 *don't find a job.*

- Federal/State Employment Service, 86 out of 100 *don't find a job.*

- school or college placement office, 78 out of 100 *don't find a job.*

WHAT DOES WORK?

A-Script's carefully designed and proven job search process, allowing you to:

- *identify* and/or clarify your strengths and marketable skills

- *design* an effective job search / networking strategy

- *develop* an effective resume and marketing letter

- *follow-through* in a persuasive, effective manner

A-SCRIPT has offices on both the North Shore and South Shore of Massachusetts, and has been one of the leading specialists in resumes and career services since 1981.

We have helped more than 6,000 people market themselves in today's increasingly demanding job market.

We are not a placement service. We work for YOU and are committed to helping you find a rewarding career.

SOME FACTS YOU SHOULD KNOW

- There is a great mobility in the job market. The average working person under thirty-five is out looking for a new job every *year and a half*. Those over thirty-five change jobs every *three years*.

- Eighty-five percent of all executive hiring is via the hidden market.

- The very best way to find a new job is through networking.

- The very worst way to find a new job is through newspaper advertising.

- The first reading of your resume will last under twenty seconds.

- No matter what you do beforehand to get you to the interview, in those thirty to sixty minutes during the interview all will be lost if you are not THOROUGHLY PREPARED.

A-SCRIPT provides complete career development services in a painless manner in a friendly environment. Experienced counselors, the majority with Master's Degrees in Counseling or English, are available to help you choose which of our services will be most useful.

Resume Writing -
- Full resume and cover letter composition and editing services

Printing-
- Choice of either laser typesetting or word processing (typing)
- Lifetime disk storage for easy access and updating

Counseling -
- Skills and Self Assessment
- Career Counseling
- Job Search Strategies
- Networking
- Interview Counseling (interview simulation/role playing)
- Salary Negotiations

Testing -
- Utilization of a variety of well-reputed tests and personal preference inventories as supplemental reinforcement whenever necessary

Reference -
- Library Research Information
- Information regarding specialized career seminars, internships, etc.
- Reference books

Hot Line -
- A-Script's "stand-by-you" policy encourages you to call us with questions during your job search

---

IF YOU ARE:

- Sure of your career skills and direction but want assistance with your resume, job search strategy or interviewing technique.

- Making a career change and want to identify your skills and abilities in order to market yourself effectively.

- Unsure of your vocational interest and need to evaluate your abilities and preferences.

- In need of personal or career counseling to function more effectively at work.

- Deciding whether to launch your own business.

- Re-entering the job market.

A-SCRIPT CAN HELP YOU!

297

MARKETING

298

Plan Ahead for May 16, August 15, & November 14

Resume Wizardry 101

Eighth in a series of **Damn Good** Professional Development Workshops on excellence in resume writing for
• Career Counselors • Educators • Business Writers • Entrepreneurs

SATURDAY, May 16
10:00 am sharp — 3:30 pm

In **Oakland** at Merritt Peralta Health Education Center
400 Hawthorne, just off Telegraph between 31st & 34th Streets

Workshop Leader: *Yana Parker*
Author of . . .
• *The Damn Good Resume Guide*　　• *The Resume Catalog*
• *Resume Pro: The Professional's Guide*　• Resume Software

Resume Wizardry we'll cover in this workshop:

• How to disappear GAPS in the client's work history.
• How to upgrade the POOR IMAGE of an underemployed client.
• How to make a job hunter look good, despite NO EXPERIENCE.
• How to handle a client who is totally UNFOCUSSED.
• How to deal with a client's UNREALISTIC JOB GOALS.
• How to transform a resume for a MAJOR CAREER CHANGE.
• AND . . . How to make your resume work EASIER and more FUN.

$85 $75 if you register and pay by May 1

For Information and Registration
call (510) **658-9229**

What People Said They Liked About Earlier Workshops •Well organized yet casual and free-flowing presentation.
• Lots of new ideas. •Lighthearted approach, straight forward explanations. • A LOT of great handouts.
• Real-life practical solutions. • Responsiveness to people's needs. • "I enjoyed myself and made great contacts."

MARKETING

Resume Preparation/Interviewing Skills Workshop

STRATEGY

Plan now to attend the 1 1/2 day workshop available to all employees interested in seeking ways to successfully prepare for a job interview and how to write a resume.

What other participants are saying ...

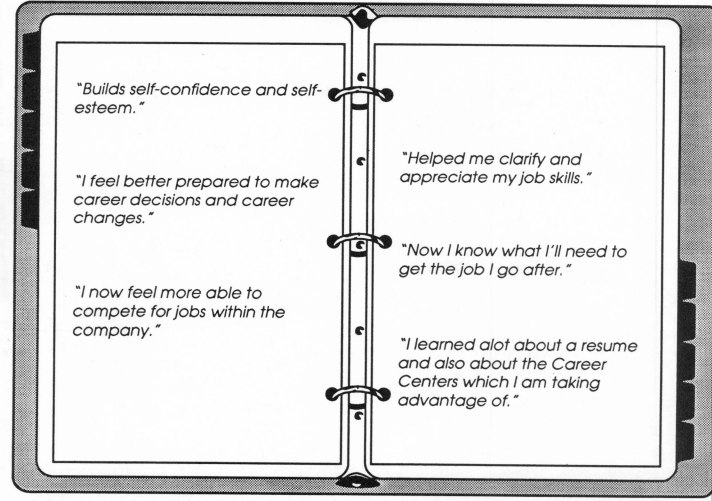

"Builds self-confidence and self-esteem."

"I feel better prepared to make career decisions and career changes."

"I now feel more able to compete for jobs within the company."

"Helped me clarify and appreciate my job skills."

"Now I know what I'll need to get the job I go after."

"I learned alot about a resume and also about the Career Centers which I am taking advantage of."

Don't delay!

To schedule or to obtain more information please call one of the Employee Career Centers.

MARKETING

300

Need a New Job?

Then you need to write a good resume!
Learn how by attending the

FREE
RESUME WRITING
WORKSHOP

Saturday, March 2nd
10:00 a.m. - 12:30 p.m.
Jones Memorial Methodist Church
Instructor - Susan Ireland

Don't underestimate your skills and strengths. You'll be surprised at how good your experience looks on paper and how good *you'll* feel going to those interviews!

This workshop will cover:

- Resolving difficult problems, such as gaps in your work history, minimal education, and being laid-off or fired.
- Carefully phrasing each line, making it a personalized resume to handle your unique situation.
- How to use your resume to get the best results.

To register, call Susan Ireland at 387-8238.

Worklife Solutions

5039 E. Paradise Drive   (602) 996-3951   Scottsdale, AZ 85254

* HOW TO CONDUCT A SUCCESSFUL JOB CAMPAIGN *

1. **Define your objective.** Know what kind of work you most enjoy and perform the best. A targeted job campaign will be more successful.

2. **Write an effective resume.** Focus on your qualifications for the type of work you want to do NEXT. Show where you are headed, not where you've been.

3. **Prepare your references.** Call or visit each person, ask them to be your reference and explain your objective. Ask them to let you know of any developments in your field.

4. **Research.** Make a list of potential employers and research each company, narrowing it down to a manageable size. You can find this information at the library--ask the reference librarian for assistance.

5. **Network.** Prepare a brief presentation describing the type of work you want to do. Make your presentation to everyone you know and meet; ask them if they know anyone who does this kind of work or is employed at a company that does this kind of work. Meet with as many people as possible and gather information about new developments in your field; the goals, problems, and challenges of potential employers; and names of people who would hire for your position. Do NOT ask for a job!

6. **Set up job interviews.** Use the contacts you have made to arrange a meeting (don't use the word interview) at target companies with The Person Who Has The Power To Hire You. Or, mail your resume and/or a well written letter of introduction, using your research. In your follow up phone call, aim for a meeting regardless of job openings.

7. **Give impressive interviews.** Develop your strategy, discuss WHY you want to work for that particular company, WHAT you can do for them, and HOW you will fit in with the company. Sell the employer on what YOU can do for THEM; aim for a job offer.

8. **Send a follow up letter** regardless of how the meeting went. Reiterate your interest in the job, the company, more discussions, or key points of the meeting.

9. **Use a combination of job hunting methods.** Don't overlook the want ads and placement services, but only spend 10-15% of your time here.

The success of your job campaign is dependent upon your strategy and the time and energy you invest. Remember, **YOU** are responsible for finding your job and no one else will devote as much care and attention as you do.

MARKETING

Worklife Solutions

5039 E. Paradise Drive   (602) 996-3951   Scottsdale, AZ 85254

"He or she who gets hired is not necessarily the one
who can do that job best; but the one who knows the
most about how to get hired." --Richard N. Bolles

HOW PEOPLE FIND JOBS

The outplacement firm of Drake Beam Morin, Inc. surveyed its candidates from 1981-1987 and reported these findings:

68% found their jobs through personal contacts.

15% through a search firm's activities.

9% by answering classified ads.

8% by sending a mass mailing of their resumes and/or letter.

_____

The Department of Labor surveyed thousands of job holders and reported these findings:

48% found their jobs through friends or relatives.

24% found their jobs through direct contact with employers--going to them and asking them for a job.

13% used a combination or other methods.

6% through school placement services.

5% succeeded through help-wanted ads.

4% used public or private employment agencies.

DID YOU KNOW.....

Two-thirds of job openings are in companies with less than 20 employees.

80-85% of all jobs are not advertised--in newspapers or with agencies.

Chances are 3 out of 4 that you will find a job through your own efforts.

MARKETING

Scribbles to Script

Please help me rate my services

Be honest with your answers, this is the only way I will be able to successfully serve you and future clients. Any and all comments and criticisms are welcome.

If you mark 'Fell Below Expectations', please offer a short explanation of how you feel I could have done better.

1. My preparation for the interview:

Excelled Expectations   [   ]
Met Expectations   [   ]
Fell Below Expectations [   ]

_____

_____

2. My rapport with you as a client:

Excelled Expectations   [   ]
Met Expectations   [   ]
Fell Below Expectations [   ]

_____

_____

3. Did I ask the appropriate questions and cover all the bases?

Excelled Expectations   [   ]
Met Expectations   [   ]
Fell Below Expectations [   ]

_____

_____

4. Do you feel the resume represents you appropriately?

Excelled Expectations   [   ]
Met Expectations   [   ]
Fell Below Expectations [   ]

_____

_____

5. Overall appearance of the resume:

Excelled Expectations   [   ]
Met Expectations   [   ]
Fell Below Expectations [   ]

_____

_____

5. Overall service:

Excelled Expectations   [   ]
Met Expectations   [   ]
Fell Below Expectations [   ]

_____

MARKETING

6. What do you feel is my strongest feature/weakest area?

    _____

    _____

7. Would you return if you were in need of any of the services Scribbles to
    Script has to offer?   [   ] yes   [   ] no

8. Are there any additional services you would like to see Scribbles to Script
    offer?_____

    _____

9. Where did you hear about Scribbles to Script?

    _____   _____

10. Scribbles to Script is now offering word processing (WordPerfect) lessons and
    PFS: First Choice software lessons. Are you interested in taking these
    lessons? [   ] yes   [   ] no

11. I periodically interview personnel managers and employers in the area for
    their response to the resumes I have done for clients. This helps me to keep
    up with trends in the market and also helps me to know what it is the
    employers want to see on a resume. Please sign below if I have your
    permission to use your resume for such an interview and as an example to
    other resume clients.

    _____   _____
    Signature   Date

Any further comments or suggestions:

_____

_____

_____

_____

_____

_____

_____

        I THANK YOU FOR YOUR PATRONAGE AND HELP IN RATING MY SERVICES!

    I have enclosed a rate sheet in the folder with your resume, if I can be of
any further assistance to you, please feel free to contact me at any time. I
keep all resumes stored indefinitely, therefore a change or update is fast, easy,
and very cost effective.

MARKETING

Thank-You Postcard

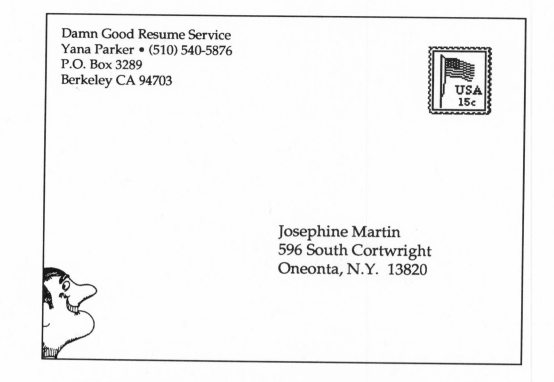

Damn Good Resume Service
Yana Parker • (510) 540-5876
P.O. Box 3289
Berkeley CA 94703

USA 15¢

Josephine Martin
596 South Cortwright
Oneonta, N.Y. 13820

October 5

Dear Josie,

Just wanted to let you know I appreciate your referring your friend, Marjorie Townsend, to me. We completed her resume today and she is quite pleased with it.

I trust you are still enjoying your new job with Atlas Co. Stay in touch -- and let me know when you need help with your application for a promotion!

Sincerely,

Yana Parker

13

Diversifying Your Business,

a.k.a. "Wearing Many Hats"

13

Diversifying Your Business, a.k.a "Wearing Many Hats"

Resume writing, all by itself, can keep you happily occupied for a very long time, thanks to the fascinating variety of clients you work with and the endless challenges of solving their resume-related problems.

Sooner or later, though, you will probably diversify, for several reasons:

a) to increase your **income**;

b) to add **variety** to your workday, both intellectual and physical;

c) to incorporate more of your **interests**, talents, and priorities into your career.

Fortunately, resume writing just naturally generates spin-off activities. You don't even have to go looking for them; they will come to you. If you're writing cover letters, or if you find yourself wearing the hat of a job counselor at times, you're already moving into spin-off territory.

Take a peek here at what other resume writers have done to develop additional services; it may inspire you in your efforts to attract more clients, increase your income, and add variety to your workday.

 Yana's Spin-offs

My own resume business presented a spin-off opportunity very early on: authoring a book on the subject of resume writing. (Although I *did* vaguely intend to write a book someday, I had an entirely different subject in mind.) The fact is, I had no idea my career would take this direction when I started out, but I'm certainly glad it did!

Other spin-offs of resume writing that I currently enjoy include:

- **Income-producing spin-offs**

1. **Conducting all-day workshops** for professional resume writers and counselors.

2. **Training** corporate career-center managers on how to critique resumes (so they, in turn, can train their staff).

3. Outplacement work: **conducting resume workshops** for laid-off employees, on contract.

4. **Training** nonprofit agency staff in resume writing.

5. **Conducting resume workshops** at job fairs, career centers, annual conventions of professional associations.

6. **Developing software** on resume writing, for the general public.

- **Volunteer spin-offs**

1. **Conducting resume workshops** at self-help job clubs such as Experience Unlimited, sponsored by the state employment office

2. Serving as **technical consultant** to a student volunteer group that writes resumes for the homeless

3. **Conducting resume research** with specific populations, such as teenagers and children.

4. **Publishing a networking/educational newsletter** for the resume-writing community nationwide. While not strictly a volunteer activity (since the publication does cost something to subscribers) it isn't exactly income-producing either (in fact, it doesn't break even), but indirectly it contributes to my overall career and to my job satisfaction.

You can see from the lists above that **teaching or training** is one of the other skills, besides resume **writing**, that I enjoy using—so inevitably I'm attracted to spin-offs that use that skill.

What other skills might YOU be using if you diversified YOUR business?

Other People's Spin-offs

In the *Damn Good Resume Writer Newsletter* we gathered correspondence from other resume writers on how they were diversifying their business, and these letters are reprinted here to stimulate your thinking about other "hats" you might enjoy wearing.

DIVERSIFYING

LETTERS

TARGETED JOB SEARCH HELP

Dear Yana: My primary business is creating resumes aimed at immediate worklife goals. I identify the client's objective, their best abilities and qualifications, and the employer's needs. Then I present these facts in a result-oriented, easy-to-read style that will capture the attention and respect of the employer. A tailored cover letter and follow-up letters, for after the interview, are equally important parts of the package.

Other services I offer include business proposals for the job search, research, consulting, and job-campaign management. Job search workshops and seminars are available and can be designed specifically for a business or organization.

The resume is only one important part of the job search strategy. A powerful resume combined with a targeted job search using the most effective methods is a sure winner!

Claudia Jordan
Phoenix, AZ

24-HOUR SERVICE

Dear Yana: My new brainchild is a twenty-four-hour resume and cover-letter mail service anywhere in the nation. The client simply calls me up and requests a mailing of the resume to the location. I guarantee to mail it within twenty-four hours. I am thinking of charging $10 plus the cost of mailing if overnight or any other special services are requested.

I also will be offering support groups for those searching for employment. In these groups we will discuss different topics at each meeting that can be of value in improving the job search. I will occasionally try to obtain a guest speaker to reiterate a particular point. These sessions will initially be held once every two to

three months, with the eventual goal of once every month.

Cynthia Mackey
Winning Strategies
Oakland, CA

ALL KINDS OF WRITING

Jan Hurley started her business in June 1990 writing resumes and cover letters; she has since added assistance with federal job applications forms (SF-171s), and other job-search assistance, and serves clients both locally and nationwide.

Jan writes: "I do all kinds of writing: poetry, magazine articles, and fiction (I've just finished the plot outline for a novel). I also type term papers for college students and letters for business people—it does bring in some cash!

"My freelance adventure comes after working for the U.S. Forest Service for twelve years. The outdoor work was great, but the bureaucracy wasn't. Now I love working out of my home."

Jan Hurley
J. Wolff Enterprises
JFH Resumes
Silver City, NM

INDIVIDUALIZED JOB SEARCH

Dear Yana: I worked for a consulting firm before starting my own business. Now I provide self-directed career guidance, resume preparation, interview training, individual and group career counseling, and network development. I feel that the job search should reflect one's individuality while maintaining an appreciation of the employers' perspective.

My services are very flexible and individualized. The first session, usually free, consists of a diagnosis and some preliminary ideas of goals and how to proceed. Some clients I see just a couple times, others I work with extensively.

I am a former college placement counselor with a master's degree in management and organizational behavior, and a bachelor's degree in English.

Julie Benesh, M.S.
Career Consultant
Champaign, IL

DIVERSIFYING

WRITING MEDICAL RESUMES

Dear Yana: We've had some excitement lately! The University of Iowa Medical College (which is one of the nation's highest-ranked medical facilities) called us and asked us to write resumes and personal statements for students in medical school. They are also interested in our videotaped mock job interviews.

We are feeling excited and hoping this goes well. We quickly contacted our printer and designed a flier directed to medical students.

I might mention that medical resumes are the easiest resumes to write. (Law resumes would be similar.) However, it is important that the writer be somewhat informed about the medical profession. (We are fortunate to have a doctor's wife on staff who will be writing these resumes.)

Right now we are in the process of building a library of medical books that will help us write personal statements, and clarify the process of entering medical school and obtaining residency. It's been fun.

Phyllis Pechman
Pechman Professional Services
Iowa City, IA

Earlier, Phyllis resported that she has diversified beyond resumes and office services into:

- job interview coaching via videotape
- community college teaching
- business skill training
- What a great composite career!

DATABASE TO LINK EMPLOYERS AND JOB HUNTERS

Dear Yana: I have been in the business of professional resume preparation for a short time now, primarily in the health care field. I have been considering expanding my area of expertise to include distribution of resumes of former clients to potential employers.

This service will utilize an electronic database that will enable the employer to locate potential employees who meet their specific employment criteria. It will, on the other hand, allow job seekers the opportunity to receive wide exposure, thereby increasing their chances for successful employment.

Marcus Kirkland
Fresh Start Publications
Taylor, MI

STUDENT SERVICES; TAX PREPARATION

Clara Carter has a business called Scholarship Resource Services in Patterson, New Jersey.

In addition to resume writing, Clara's professional services include:

- Consultation on student scholarships and financial aid.
- Income tax preparation using the MacInTax computer program. Clara writes, "MacInTax is GREAT; it takes care of everything."

Clara Carter
Scholarship Resources Services
Patterson, NJ

OTHER WRITING SERVICES

Dear Yana: The last few months have been a little slow in the resume-writing department. But without solicitation on my part, some other interesting projects have come my way. I've been asked by clients to write:

- business proposals
- grant proposals
- letters of recommendation
- fliers
- brochures
- personal profiles in response to ads in the Personals columns.

For all of these projects, I've incorporated the resume style of using bullets with short statements. Most statements begins with an action verb in order to create dynamic, concise, and easy-to-read documents.

As a means of supplementing my income, I've also been doing some mail merge projects for clients who are sending out large mailings of their resume to targeted employers.

Another fun twist to my resume consulting has been the "long-distance client." I've done a few resumes for clients living in Hawaii or New York. In these cases, we usually spend about two hours on the phone (I work at the computer during the conversation). After we hang up, I finish writing as much as I can, often leaving big blanks for them to fill in, or questions in parentheses. I

DIVERSIFYING

mail or fax them the first draft. Then they call me with revisions.

Susan Ireland
Dynamite!! Resumes
Kensington, CA

COMPUTER LESSONS

Dear Yana: I have recently added WordPerfect lessons to my list of services. Our adult education programs offer word-processing classes; therefore, I target people who want a one-to-one learning environment. I have found that the lessons often go hand-in-hand with my resume services. Many of my clients are office support people who want to enhance their office skills. WordPerfect software takes some time to learn, but is a versatile and popular program.

Vicki Law-Miller
Scribbles to Script
Montrose, CO

WRITING JOB DESCRIPTIONS

Claude Whitmyer, coauthor of *Running a One-Person Business,* suggests that resume writers expand into other kinds of writing to create additional "income streams"—for example **writing job descriptions for personnel departments**. He adds, "A writer could promote this service by stressing that they could save employers time by composing job descriptions that would effectively screen out inappropriate applicants.

The (Infamous) Federal Form SF-171

For those who have been thus far spared the experience, let's just say that filling out a many-paged, detailed federal job application blank—called the Standard Form-171, or SF-171 for short—can be an intimidating process. On the other hand, for those who are willing to take on the challenge and master the process, there is a niche market of grateful job-hunters who gladly pay handsomely to turn this . . . um . . . odious task over to someone else! Obviously the author is biased, so you should hear from others who DO take on this task:

DEVELOPING TEMPLATES FOR THE SF-171

Dear Yana: A new wrinkle for resume writers is answering questions and filling in blanks for the federal job form SF-171. This clumsy form calls for a mini-resume type answer for every job or relevant experience.

I calculated the form in WordPerfect 5.0 and am now able to complete answers and develop a presentation for laser printing. My charge for writing and completing the form is $300 to $400, depending on additional forms required. The finished result is especially nice. I have developed the form in such a way that I can expand Sections A, B, C, etc., to a full page, OR I can answer in the smaller 1R page section, as necessary.

Mary Ann Finch-Vandivier
Pacific Beach Writing Service
Solana Beach, CA

Now if that piques your interest, read on for some tips on preparing an SF-171 for your client . . .

USING A RESUME TO SUPPLEMENT THE FEDERAL SF-171

by Robert G. Smith

For federal jobs the Standard Form 171 is the required application form. I think the way most employees prepare 171s does them more harm than good.

To get you past the screening panel into the interview, you should write an application for each job you apply for. What you say should show how you are a top candidate for the job, based on the requirements of the vacancy announcement.

A good resume can supplement the SF-171. When the review panel members meet to rate each of the applications submitted for a job, they must score each application on a set of rating factors. **If you make it easy for them to see that you are highly qualified on each of the rating factors, you will get a high score. If you make it difficult you will get a low or average score, regardless of your qualifications.**

There are two ways to make it easy for the review panel to see your qualifications:

The first is to place your experience that is related to the rating factors at the head of the description of each job you have had when you complete the 171.

The second is to prepare a supplement in which your experience, education, training, and even related reading is listed under each of the rating factors. I think you should do both. And that is where the *Damn Good Resume Guide* by Yana Parker comes in.

The typical resume describes the skills of the applicant in a list of "skill areas," each followed by several one-liners that show exactly what you did. Substitute "rating factor" for "skill area" and you have the basis for the supplement. In fact, you might have skill areas under each rating factor, followed by appropriate one-liners. The *Damn Good Resume Guide* contains three aids to resume preparation that can be useful to those preparing Forms 171 and Supplemental Data Sheets. The first is a list of ninety-six skills areas. The second is a page of "action verbs" for describing specific work under such headings as management skills, financial skills, research skills, and so on. These word lists can be useful when you would like to sharpen your descriptions of what you did. The third aid is a list of ten tough questions that might arise, and how to handle them.

SOME SUGGESTED FORMATS

Format A—for when there is only one skill area in a rating factor.

SUPPLEMENTAL DATA SECTION

Rating Factor 1

- Skills and Experience (one liners)
- Education and Training (one liners)
- Related Off-duty experience (one liners)

(Continue as above for rating factors.)

Format B—for more than one skill area per rating factor.

SUPPLEMENTAL DATA SECTION

Rating Factor 1

Skill Area A

- Skills and Experience (one liners)
- Education and Training (one liners)
- Related Off-duty experience (one liners)

Skill Area B

(Continue as above for other skill areas and rating factors.)

Excerpted and reprinted courtesy of Federal Times; Copyright by Times Journal Company, Springfield, Virginia.

DIVERSIFYING

AN INSIDER'S TIPS ON PREPARING THE SF-171

by Jan Hurley

The SF-171, Application for Federal Employment, is a form like no other—long, complex, and confusing at times. Professional preparation of the 171 requires an insider's understanding. Here are some pointers I've developed from the inside as a former employee and supervisor in the federal government.

The Right Stuff

The SF-171 must serve the needs of two audiences. In the federal hiring process, personnel specialists first screen incoming applications using detailed classification guides called the X-118 Standards. These specialists like detail, precision, and completeness, and they will usually read every word no matter how long the application package. The personnel office selects the qualified applications that will be further reviewed by the employer and other officials.

Reviewing and selecting officials want to find out quickly if a candidate has the particular blend of skills and experience needed for the job. These employers are interested in recent work and volunteer experience, accomplishments, and good references. They likely don't care where the candidate went to high school or how many units were taken in economics. They appreciate a clean, readable application package and probably will not read every word of a lengthy or messy presentation.

So, how can the application satisfy both sides of the federal hiring process? First, meet the need for detail by paying meticulous attention to the required blocks on pages 1, 3, and 4, and the headings for the Experience Blocks. Blocks 31 and 32 on page 3 (Supplemental Training and Special Accomplishments) can often be shown on a separate page as an attachment. If any block is left blank, for example, if there are no licenses or certificates in Block 34; type "N/A" or a double dash "– –" to indicate that the block was not ignored.

Experience Block Format

The Experience Block text must show the full range of the client's work in clear, concise language. I have successfully used a style known as the RDA format — Responsibilities, Duties, and Accomplishments. The sample page illustrates this format for the client's current job.

This format uses two parts: One or more paragraphs describes the responsibilities and duties of the job, giving an overview of the scope and significance of the client's work. A cardinal sin in this area is copying from position descriptions.

The next and most important part is Accomplishments. This describes specific things the client has achieved in the position. Awards can be shown here, as well as on Block 32. In describing accomplishments, I find a two-part statement to be useful. The first part describes the nature of the client's participation in the project, and the second part tells the outcome or significance of the achievement. These parts can be combined in one sentence, although two sentences may be used for major accomplishments.

A good way to generate this material is to ask the client to brainstorm a list of statements about the job. Then sort these statements into responsibilities, duties, and accomplishments. If the client is shy about identifying accomplishments, ask that useful interview question, "What are you most proud of?"

The writing style is similar to that of a detailed resume, although it's fine to use "I" sentences for variety. How long is enough? I recommend no more than two pages for recent or current jobs with major experience. Briefer or more distant jobs can be condensed into one or two paragraphs, and placed on the half-page version of the 171A Continuation Sheet. A typical 171 for someone with ten to fifteen years in the workforce would be about eight to twelve pages long.

Production

I produce 171s on an electronic typewriter that also serves as my computer printer. First I type all of the form blocks (except for Announcement Number on page 1 and Signature and Date on page 4) and Experience Blocks using a self-correcting film ribbon. I type on high-quality photocopies, rather than the printed green forms, because the flat paper of the copies rolls through the typewriter more easily. Then I write the Experience Block texts on my word processor and feed the page with the proper block heading through the typewriter/printer for direct printing of the narrative on the completed form. Of course, I do this only after the Experience Block heading is proofread and corrected!

It sounds complex, but this is the only way I can ensure that the 171 is prepared properly. The form

DIVERSIFYING

itself is a challenge for any typewriter or printer—micro-adjustments in alignment often have to be made as you work through the page. Some spaces require switching from twelve-pitch to fifteen-pitch type—for example, when filling in a lengthy name or phone number.

There are computer programs that claim to prepare the 171. I'm skeptical. For one thing, many agencies will not accept computer-generated 171s, although they do accept photocopies if there is an original signature. The only suggestion I have is to try the program before you buy it—then take a sample to one or more federal personnel offices and ask if they will accept it.

FOR MORE HELP: Visit your local Personnel Office. Have them critique samples of your work and ask to see one or more of the X-118 Standards. Preparing the SF-171 takes patience and attention, but it can be a lucrative adjunct to a resume service. And it's one that clients will definitely appreciate!

> **Jan Hurley**
> **J. Wolff Enterprises**
> **JFH Resumes**
> **Silver City, NM**

WHAT'S AN SF-171?

Now would you like to see what an SF-171 form looks like? Just turn the page!

Application for Federal Employment - SF 171

Read the instructions before you complete this application. *Type or print clearly in dark ink.*

Form Approved:
OMB No. 3206-0012

GENERAL INFORMATION

1 What kind of job are you applying for? *Give title and announcement no. (if any)*

2 Social Security Number

3 Sex
☐ Male   ☐ Female

4 Birth date *(Month, Day, Year)*

5 Birthplace *(City and State or Country)*

6 Name *(Last, First, Middle)*

Mailing address *(include apartment number, if any)*

City   State   ZIP Code

7 Other names ever used *(e.g., maiden name, nickname, etc.)*

8 Home Phone
Area Code   Number

9 Work Phone
Area Code   Number   Extension

10 Were you ever employed as a civilian by the Federal Government? If **"NO"**, go to **item 11**. If **"YES"**, mark each type of job you held with an **"X"**.

☐ Temporary   ☐ Career-Conditional   ☐ Career   ☐ Excepted

What is your **highest** grade, classification series and job title?

Dates at **highest** grade: FROM _____ TO _____

DO NOT WRITE IN THIS AREA

FOR USE OF EXAMINING OFFICE ONLY

Date entered register

Form reviewed:
Form approved:

Option	Grade	Earned Rating	Veteran Preference	Augmented Rating
			☐ No Preference Claimed	
			☐ 5-Points (Tentative)	
			☐ 10 Pts. (30% Or More Comp.Dis.)	
			☐ 10 Pts. (Less Than 30% Comp.Dis.)	
			☐ Other 10 Points	

Initials and Date

☐ Disallowed   ☐ Being Investigated

FOR USE OF APPOINTING OFFICE ONLY

Preference has been verified through proof that the separation was under honorable conditions, and other proof as required.

☐ 5-Point   ☐ 10-Point--30% or More Compensable Disability   ☐ 10-Point--Less Than 30% Compensable Disability   ☐ 10-Point--Other

Signature and Title

Agency   Date

AVAILABILITY

11 When can you start work? *(Month and Year)*

12 What is the lowest pay you will accept? *(You will not be considered for jobs which pay less than you indicate.)*
Pay $ _____ per _____ OR Grade _____

13 In what geographic area(s) are you willing to work?

14 Are you willing to work:

	YES	NO
A. 40 hours per week *(full-time)?*		
B. 25-32 hours per week *(part-time)?*		
C. 17-24 hours per week *(part-time)?*		
D. 16 or fewer hours per week *(part-time)?*		
E. An intermittent job *(on call/seasonal)?*		
F. Weekends, shifts, or rotating shifts?		

15 Are you willing to take a temporary job lasting:

	YES	NO
A. 5 to 12 months *(sometimes longer)?*		
B. 1 to 4 months?		
C. Less than 1 month?		

16 Are you willing to travel away from home for:

	YES	NO
A. 1 to 5 nights each month?		
B. 6 to 10 nights each month?		
C. 11 or more nights each month?		

MILITARY SERVICE AND VETERAN PREFERENCE

17 Have you served in the United States Military Service? *If your only active duty was training in the Reserves or National Guard, answer "NO". If "NO", go to item 22*   YES ☐ NO ☐

18 Did you or will you retire at or above the rank of major or lieutenant commander?

MILITARY SERVICE AND VETERAN PREFERENCE *(Cont.)*

19 Were you discharged from the military service under honorable conditions? *(If your discharge was changed to "honorable" or "general", by a Discharge Review Board, answer "YES". If you received a clemency discharge, answer "NO".)* If "NO", provide below the date and type of discharge you received.   YES ☐ NO ☐

Discharge Date *(Month, Day, Year)*	Type of Discharge

20 List the dates *(Month, Day, Year)*, and branch for all **active duty** military service.

From	To	Branch of Service

21 If all your active military duty was after October 14, 1976, list the full names and all campaign badges or expeditionary medals you received or were entitled to

22 **Read the instructions that came with this form before completing this item.** When you have determined your eligibility for veteran preference from the instructions, place an "X" in the box next to your veteran preference claim.

☐ NO PREFERENCE

☐ 5-POINT PREFERENCE--You must show proof when you are hired.

10-POINT PREFERENCE--If you claim 10-point preference, place an "X" in the box below next to the basis for your claim. To receive 10-point preference you must also complete a Standard Form 15, Application for 10-Point Veteran Preference, which is available from any Federal Job Information Center. ATTACH THE COMPLETED SF 15 AND REQUESTED PROOF TO THIS APPLICATION.

☐ Non-compensably disabled or Purple Heart recipient.
☐ Compensably disabled, less than 30 percent.
☐ Spouse, widow(er), or mother of a deceased or disabled veteran.
☐ Compensably disabled, 30 percent or more.

DIVERSIFYING

NSN 7540-00-935-7150   171-109

Standard Form 171 (Rev.6-88)
U.S. Office of Personnel Management
FPM Chapter 295

WORK EXPERIENCE *If you have no work experience, write "NONE" in A below and go to 25 on page 3.*

		YES	NO
23	May we ask your present employer about your character, qualifications, and work record? *A "NO" will not affect our review of your qualifications. If you answer "NO" and we need to contact your present employer before we can offer you a job, we will contact you first . . .*		

24 READ **WORK EXPERIENCE** IN THE INSTRUCTIONS BEFORE YOU BEGIN.

- Describe your current or most recent job in Block **A** and work backwards, describing each job you held **during the past 10 years**. If you were **unemployed** for longer than **3 months** within the past 10 years, list the dates and your address(es) in an experience block.

- You may sum up in one block work that you did **more than 10 years ago**. But if that work **is related** to the type of job you are applying for, describe each related job in a separate block.

- INCLUDE VOLUNTEER WORK *(non-paid work)*--**If the work** *(or part of the work)* **is like the job you are applying for**, complete **all** parts of the experience block just as you would for a paying job. You may receive credit for your experience with religious , community, welfare, service, and other organizations.

- INCLUDE MILITARY SERVICE-- You should complete **all** parts of the experience block just as you would for a non-military job, including all supervisory experience. Describe each major change of duties or responsibilities in a separate experience block

- IF YOU NEED MORE SPACE TO DESCRIBE A JOB-- Use sheets of paper the same size as this page (be sure to include **all** information we ask for in **A** and **B** below). On **each** sheet show your name, Social Security Number, and the announcement number or jo

- IF YOU NEED MORE EXPERIENCE BLOCKS, use the SF 171-A or a sheet of pa**IF YOU** NEED TO UPDATE (ADD MORE RECENT JOBS), use the SF 172 or a sheet of paper as described above.

A

Name and address of employer's organization *(include ZIP Code, if known)*	Dates employed *(give month, day and year)* From: To:	Average number of hours per week	Number of employees you supervise
	Salary or earnings Starting $ Per Ending $ Per	Your reason for wanting to leave	

Your immediate supervisor Name	Area Code	Telephone No.	Exact title of your job	If Federal employment *(civilian or military)* list series, grade or rank, and, if promoted in this job, the date of your last promotion

Description of work: Describe your specific duties, responsibilities and accomplishments in this job, **including** the job title(s) of any employees you supervise. *If you describe more than one type of work (for example, carpentry and painting, or personnel and budget), write the approximate percentage of time you spent doing each.*

_____

For Agency Use (skill codes, etc.)

B

Name and address of employer's organization *(include ZIP Code, if known)*	Dates employed *(give month, day and year)* From: To:	Average number of hours per week	Number of employees you supervise
	Salary or earnings Starting $ Per Ending $ Per	Your reason for wanting to leave	

Your immediate supervisor Name	Area Code	Telephone No.	Exact title of your job	If Federal employment *(civilian or military)* list series, grade or rank, and, if promoted in this job, the date of your last promotion

Description of work: Describe your specific duties, responsibilities and accomplishments in this job, **including** the job title(s) of any employees you supervise. *If you describe more than one type of work (for example, carpentry and painting, or personnel and budget), write the approximate percentage of time you spent doing each.*

_____

For Agency Use (skill codes, etc.)

DIVERSIFYING

EDUCATION

25 Did you graduate from high school? *If you have a GED high school equivalency or will graduate within the next nine months, answer "YES".*

26 Write the name and location *(city and state)* of the last high school you attended or where you obtained your GED high school equivalency.

YES ▶ If "YES", give month and year graduated or received GED equivalency:

NO ▶ If "NO", give the highest grade you completed:

27 Have you ever attended college or graduate school? YES ▶ If "YES", continue with 28. NO ▶ If "NO", go to 31.

28 NAME AND LOCATION *(city, state and ZIP Code)* OF COLLEGE OR UNIVERSITY. *If you expect to graduate within nine months, give the **month** and **year** you expect to receive your degree:*

Name	City	State	ZIP Code	MONTH AND YEAR ATTENDED From	To	NUMBER OF CREDIT HOURS COMPLETED Semester	Quarter	TYPE OF DEGREE *(e.g. B.A., M.A.)*	MONTH AND YEAR OF DEGREE
1)									
2)									
3)									

29 CHIEF UNDERGRADUATE SUBJECTS *Show major on the first line*

	NUMBER OF CREDIT HOURS COMPLETED Semester	Quarter
1)		
2)		
3)		

30 CHIEF GRADUATE SUBJECTS *Show major on the first line*

	NUMBER OF CREDIT HOURS COMPLETED Semester	Quarter
1)		
2)		
3)		

31 If you have completed any other courses or training related to the kind of jobs you are applying for *(trade, vocational, Armed Forces, business)* give information below.

NAME AND LOCATION *(city, state and ZIP Code)* OF SCHOOL	MONTH AND YEAR ATTENDED From	To	CLASS-ROOM HOURS	SUBJECT(S)	TRAINING COMPLETED YES	NO
1) School Name City						
	State ZIP Code					
2) School Name City						
	State ZIP Code					

SPECIAL SKILLS, ACCOMPLISHMENTS AND AWARDS

32 Give the title and year of any honors, awards or fellowships you have received. List your special qualifications, skills or accomplishments that may help you get a job. *examples are: skills with computers or other machines; most important publications (do not submit copies); public speaking and writing experience; membership in scientific societies; patents or inventions; etc.*

33 How many words per minute can you: TYPE? TAKE DICTATION?

Agencies may test your skills before hiring you.

34 List **job-related** licenses or certificates that you have, such as: *registered nurse; lawyer; radio operator; driver's; pilot's; etc.*

LICENSE OR CERTIFICATE	DATE OF LATEST LICENSE OR CERTIFICATE	STATE OR OTHER LICENSING AGENCY
1)		
2)		

35 Do you speak or read a language other than English *(include sign language)? Applicants for jobs that require a language other than English may be given an interview conducted solely in that language.*

YES ▶ If "YES", list each language and place an "X" in each column that applies to you.

NO ▶ If "NO", go to 36

LANGUAGE(S)	CAN PREPARE AND GIVE LECTURES Fluently	With Difficulty	CAN SPEAK AND UNDERSTAND Fluently	Passably	CAN TRANSLATE ARTICLES Into English	From English	CAN READ ARTICLES FOR OWN USE Easily	With Difficulty
1)								
2)								

REFERENCES

36 List three people who are not related to you and are not supervisors you listed under **24** who know your qualifications and fitness for the kind of job for which you are applying. At least **one** should know you well on a personal basis.

FULL NAME OF REFERENCE	TELEPHONE NUMBER(S) *(include Area Code)*	PRESENT BUSINESS OR HOME ADDRESS *(Number, street and city)*	STATE	ZIP CODE
1)				
2)				
3)				

DIVERSIFYING

		YES	NO
37	Are you a citizen of the United States? *(In most cases you must be a U.S. citizen to be hired. You will be required to submit proof of identity and citizenship at the time you are hired.)* If **"NO"**, give the country or countries you are a citizen of: _____		

NOTE: It is important that you give complete and truthful answers to questions 38 through 44. If you answer **"YES"** to any of them, provide your explanation(s) in **Item 45. Include** convictions resulting from a plea of nolo contendere *(no contest)*. **Omit:** 1) traffic fines of $100.00 or less; 2) any violation of law committed before your 16th birthday; 3) any violation of law committed before your 18th birthday, if finally decided in juvenile court or under a Youth Offender law; 4) any conviction set aside under the Federal Youth Corrections Act or similar State law; 5) any conviction whose record was expunged under Federal or State law. We will consider the date, facts, and circumstances of each event you list. In most cases you can still be considered for Federal jobs. However, **if you fail to tell the truth or fail to list all relevant** events or circumstances, this may be grounds for not hiring you, for firing you after you begin work, or for criminal prosecution (18 USC 1001).

		YES	NO
38	During the last **10 years**, were you **fired from any job** for any reason, did you **quit after being told that you would be fired,** or did you leave by mutual agreement because of specific problems?		
39	Have you **ever** been convicted of, or forfeited collateral for **any felony violation?** *(Generally, a felony is defined as any violation of law punishable by imprisonment of longer than one year, except for violations called misdemeanors under State law which are punishable by imprisonment of two years or less.).*		
40	Have you **ever** been convicted of, or forfeited collateral for **any firearms or explosives violation?**		
41	Are you **now** under charges for **any** violation of law?		
42	During the **last 10 years** have you forfeited collateral, been convicted, been imprisoned, been on probation, or been on parole? Do **not** include violations reported in 39, 40, or 41, above		
43	Have you **ever** been convicted by a military **court-martial?** If no military service, answer **"NO"**.		
44	Are you **delinquent** on any Federal debt? *(Include delinquencies arising from Federal taxes, loans, overpayment of benefits, and other debts to the U.S. Government* **plus** *defaults on Federally guaranteed or insured loans such as student and home mortgage loans.)*		

45 If "YES" in: 38 Explain for each job the problem(s) and your reason(s) for leaving. Give the employer's name and address.
           39 through 43 - Explain each violation. Give place of occurrence and name/address of police or court involved.
           44 - Explain the type, length and amount of the delinquency or default, and steps you are taking to correct errors or repay the debt. Give any identification number associated with the debt and the address of the Federal agency involved.
      NOTE: If you need more space, use a sheet of paper, and include the item number.

Item No.	Date (Mo./Yr.)	Explanation	Mailing Address
			Name of Employer, Police, Court, or Federal Agency
			City State ZIP Code
			Name of Employer, Police, Court, or Federal Agency
			City State ZIP Code

		YES	NO
46	Do you receive, or have you ever applied for retirement pay, pension, or other pay based on military, Federal civilian, or District of Columbia Government service?		
47	Do any of your relatives work for the United States Government or the United States Armed Forces? Include: *father; mother; husband; wife; son; daughter; brother; sister; uncle; aunt; first cousin; nephew; niece; father-in-law; mother-in-law; son-in-law; daughter-in-law; brother-in-law; sister-in-law; stepfather; stepmother; stepson; stepdaughter; stepbrother; stepsister; half brother; and half sister*.		

if **"YES"**, provide details below. If you need more space, use a sheet of paper.

Name	Relationship	Department, Agency or Branch of Armed Forces

SIGNATURE, CERTIFICATION, AND RELEASE OF INFORMATION

YOU MUST SIGN THIS APPLICATION.   Read the following carefully before you sign.

- A false statement on any part of your application may be grounds for not hiring you, firing you, or for firing you after you begin work. Also, you may be punished by fine or imprisonment (U.S. Code, title 18, section 1001).
- If you are a male born after December 31, 1959 you must be registered with the Selective Service System or have a valid exemption in order to be eligible for Federal employment. You will be required to certify as to your status at the time of appointment.
- I **understand** that any information I give may be investigated as allowed by law or Presidential order.
- I **consent** to the release of information about my ability and fitness for Federal employment by *employers, schools, law enforcement agencies and other individuals and organizations,* **to** *investigators, personnel staffing specialists, and other authorized employees of the Federal Government.*
- I **certify** that, to the best of my knowledge an belief, **all** of my statements are true, correct, complete, and made in good faith.

48	SIGNATURE *(Sign each application in dark ink)*	49	DATE SIGNED *(Month, day, year)*

DIVERSIFYING

Resume Workshops: Another Way to Diversify

Resume-writing **workshops** will almost certainly appear on your agenda sooner or later. **You might seek out opportunities** to do some teaching as one way to market your services and increase your income. OR **you may be invited to do a presentation** because the need exists and your talent has come to someone's attention.

To stimulate your thinking along these lines, I'll list **some of the circumstances under which I have presented resume workshops:**

- Two- or three-hour events **for the public**, at nonprofit community career centers—for example, those housed at the local YWCA.
- One-hour presentations **for the public** at job fairs.
- Brief seminars on resume writing **for professionals** in different fields, at their monthly or annual association meetings.
- One-hour presentations **for unemployed executives** at their weekly self-help job club meetings.
- Three-hour workshops **for reentry women** at special community college job programs.
- Classroom presentations **for at-risk high-school students** in the public schools.
- As-needed training and support **for volunteer resume writers** who work with homeless job-hunters.

- All-day entrepreneurial workshops that I present quarterly **for professional resume writers and career counselors**.
- Three-hour in-service training in resume writing, **for community agency staff** working with special populations.
- Half-day workshops **for corporate career center managers,** who in turn taught their staffs throughout the state.

As you can see, there are virtually endless possibilities, because **excellent resume writing is a skill in great demand and short supply**. If you can effectively help others sharpen THEIR skills in this critical area, you will find yourself in demand as a workshop leader.

Tips for Leading an Effective Resume Workshop

KNOW THE AUDIENCE

Each audience has its unique character and needs, even though I am virtually always talking to them about resumes from one angle or another. So, to best address their needs, I request that they send me in advance a packet of typical examples of their work (the resumes they produce or evaluate). Viewing that advance packet gives me a sense of their skill level and the nature of the problems they are facing, so I can arrive with the right kind of help—ideas targeted to their population plus good resume examples they can relate to.

BRING ATTRACTIVE GOODIES!

I make it a point to ALWAYS bring some high-quality, graphically appealing giveaways when I do any presentation or workshop. People like to have something to take home. Handouts help them remember the key points and minimize the need to take notes.

The three handouts I use most are:

1) A 3-by-8-inch **"Bookmark Mini-Guide"** that is packed with information— including the essential steps to writing a powerful resume, plus some provocative concepts to get people thinking. (*Of course*, it has my name and phone number at the bottom, so it can double as a soft-sell marketing piece. The Bookmark is shown on page 325.)

This Mini-Guide can act as an OUTLINE for a brief presentation, as well as a generator of comments and questions from the audience. It covers all the **basic concepts for creating a good resume**, and these concepts, I find, **need to be repeated endlessly**, for ALL audiences.

2) A **Self-Teaching Template**. (See Chapter 3.) I choose the one that seems the most appropriate for the particular audience—a simple version for students, a sophisticated version for unemployed professionals, a functional style for re-entry women and others making big career changes.

3) A **good sample resume** that illustrates effective resume writing—again, choosing one that's appropriate for my audience.

I always print my **handouts on good-quality COLORFUL paper**, choosing the warm, intense colors that provide sharp, readable **contrast** to the black text. (Lime green, golden yellow, and light hot pink are excellent.) In a noisy, crowded room, it is easy and efficient to call out, "Let's all look at the GREEN sheet next," and it minimizes paper shuffling and confusion.

Finally—and this is a personal preference—it's my trademark to include humorous cartoon-like graphics in all my handouts. I definitely find that people warm up to these handouts.

I've included a few **typical examples of handouts I use in workshops**:

On pages 327 to 329 "Accomplishments," "Job Titles," and "Looking for a New Job" were used in a two-hour pre-resume-writing workshop for a group of employees about to be laid off. The purpose was to get them all thinking about their imminent job search and get them ready for resume writing—in a supportive environment where they were able to work *together* on this anxiety-producing task. The little cartoons were intended to lighten the atmosphere.

On page 331, "Some Essential Characteristics of an Effective Resume" was designed as a handout for a job club of unemployed white-collar workers, to help the members evaluate their own resumes.

PARTICIPATION IS THE KEY

The one feature of my workshops that I consider most important is **active participation** of everybody. I get people involved from the very beginning; if it's a workshop for the job hunters, for example, I get them involved by having them introduce themselves and tell their job objective (or their current position) as well as their agenda for being at the workshop. If it's a workshop for professionals, I make it clear at the start that this won't be a lecture—that I will share what I know, but I expect THEM to jump in and share what THEY know too, so there is a rich stew of knowledge dished up and shared.

Then—whether the workshop is for job hunters or for career-development people—I pull them into the action repeatedly with provocative questions that keep them on their toes. I include questions that **provide a chance for participants to help each other** by sharing their information and support. Invariably, people get more out of a workshop where they are actively involved. And I consider it MY responsibility to create a stimulating atmosphere where involvement is *irresistible*!

WHAT'S ON THE AGENDA?

On the following pages are the descriptions or agendas for three very different kinds of resume workshops I present.

1. For job hunters (a two- to three-hour workshop)

2. For resume writers (a two-hour workshop)

3. For resume writers (a one-day workshop)

WRAP-UP EVALUATION

Finally, you'll find on page 332 the evaluation form I use at the end of the one-day workshop. One question, #5 on the form, turned out to be extremely fruitful. It simply asked for "Surprises—unexpected outcomes," but it brought out feedback that was invaluable.

DIVERSIFYING

A Two-Hour Workshop for Job Hunters

The main thing I try to accomplish in a brief workshop for job hunters is to jar people loose from their old assumptions about resumes—to get them to see their old resume as an obsolete albatross that can be replaced by a really lively document that does them justice and that's really interesting and helpful to the reader. They need to DARE to be themselves on the resume, to be a trifle outrageous in their honest appreciation of their talents. (In fact, they are delighted to be encouraged in this direction. Most people are pretty depressed at what their old resume looks like, and are very relieved and excited to find out that it doesn't HAVE to look like that.)

I start a two-hour resume workshop by briefly outlining the the five basic concepts for superior resume writing that appear in Chapter 2 on pages 18-19 (using my "Bookmark Mini-Guide" as a handout and outline.) I point out how the resulting resume differs from the traditional (job obituary) type of resume.

Next, I ask each person in the room to introduce themselves by their first name and to state their current job objective—in ten words or less. I urge everyone else to listen carefully to the job objective so they can later contribute leads and ideas to each other.

(If there is time, I also ask each person to briefly state the one thing they want to get out of the workshop before they leave—and then toward the end I'll check in to make sure they all got what they needed.)

As each person expresses their job objective, I comment on whether it is clear and concise, i.e., whether it reflects an actual job title and some explicit level of responsibility. It should be as focused as possible.

After we've gone all around the group, I have each person write down three skill areas related to the job objective they chose. Then everybody briefly shares what they wrote and I comment again on each one, emphasizing the need to zero in on skills that are directly relevant to the job objective they earlier named.

Next, I ask them to come up with one solid accomplishment that illustrates one of the relevant skills they mentioned (more, if they have time). Again, they share this with the group and I comment on the effectiveness of each accomplishment in illustrating the skill and supporting their job objective.

By now, the participants have got some hands-on experience in dealing with the heart of their resume: the objective, the relevant skills, and the supporting accomplishments. In the process of struggling with these, they bring up a great many problems and dilemmas to ask me about, and I answer these as they come up. I find this strategy —addressing problems as they emerge in the exercise—is an effective way of introducing the resume-writing process. In this short period of time, we do not attempt to write the whole resume—just to get off on the right foot.

We wrap up with a question-and-answer period on the issues that will come up in their Work History and Education . . . such as, "Can I leave off dates?" (*No!*) and "Do I say 3/87 to 11/87?" (*No, just say 1987.*) "How far back shall I go?" (*Ten to fifteen years, usually.*)

I urge the job hunters not to ever consider their new resume as a finished product, but rather to see it as a dynamic one that constantly changes as they get new information and new inspiration. (It's best if it's word-processed, for that reason). I also remind them to get feedback over and over again about what works on their resume and what doesn't work—to find out how various parts of it "feel" to the people who read it.

Aside from the actual content, as I said before, I find that a workshop goes well to the extent that the participants are actively involved. I avoid lecturing at them and get *them* talking very early in the game. Lecturing puts people to sleep; participating energizes them. The more I can lure them into helping each other—with feedback, networking, brainstorming, and sharing their own stories —the more everybody enjoys the workshop and reports that they learned a lot.

DIVERSIFYING

A Two-Hour Workshop
for Resume Writers

An entirely different approach was used for a two-hour in-house staff workshop held to upgrade the resume writing skills of counselors in a city agency, who worked with difficult-to-place job hunters. We reviewed six resumes, one at a time. The resumes were actual examples taken from the agency's current files, and were written by the participating staff members.

First, I asked the staff members to try to set aside their normal, decent human values and to role play. "Pretend—just for now—that you are a cynical, sexist, racist, elitist employer. Really try to get into it." (They were a little shocked and wary, but they did get into it!)

Then I asked them to examine the first resume very critically, from the perspective of this "pretend employer," and to **find all the reasons NOT to employ this person**. "Find every shred of evidence you can, to support a decision NOT to interview her."

Next, I asked them to reexamine the same resume from a positive viewpoint, and to **dig for every shred of evidence that this job hunter MIGHT be a GOOD candidate.**

Finally, we took a quick straw vote: "What's the overall impression we get of this candidate? What's **working** on this resume—what's working

that we should keep? What should we discard? What should we play up, or play down? Is there anything we need to add?"

The staff discovered, for each of the six examples, **the overall impact or image created by the resume**. This image is the sum total of many subtle messages that can be "read between the lines" when you carefully scrutinize a resume.

The trick here is for the staff to learn to routinely stand in the shoes of the would-be employer whenever they help design a resume. Before the job hunter goes out the door with their resume, the counselor can help them be sure the right kind of messages, both subtle and obvious, are being conveyed to the employer by the choice of words on the resume.

In one of the resumes we reviewed, for example, the staff noticed that a "**mommy**" image was being created *inadvertently* by detailed descriptions of the job hunter's work at a Montessori school and by the "cute" name of one of her employers, Mother Dear's Bakery. Further, the staff noticed that a **passive** image was being created by the way the job hunter's employment was described ("**worked at** the courthouse," "**took care of** the children").

In two short hours, the staff realized the great value of even this brief period of *teamwork*, reviewing their own work together and jointly sharpening their writing, critiquing, and counseling skills.

Great Workshop Warm-up

Speaker Pat Katz used this warm-up exercise at a lecture event I attended. It got the whole room humming loudly in no time, and was an excellent ice-breaker and energizer. (She says she uses it at ALL her parties.)

At the very beginning, she provided paper and pen for everybody, and gave us an assignment. We had to connect briefly with every other person in the room and ask one question, jot down the answer, give the other person a chance to ask US a question, and then move on quickly to another person. We had to work quickly and try to get to every person in the room in the allotted time—only ten to fifteen minutes, and there were more than fifty in the gathering.

Each person asked each OTHER person:

"What's one thing you do best?" We were not to get into a conversation about it—just record it. And if we found somebody's answer particularly interesting, we could follow up on it later.

She reminded us, "You do not have to give everybody the same answer. You can name something else you do well—or even make something up."

In a recent resume writing workshop, I used this warm-up and proposed this question for the participants to ask each other: "What's your favorite skill? . . . something you know so well that you could teach it to somebody else?" This exercise brought out some memorable answers and got the workshop off to a high-energy start.

DIVERSIFYING

Front of bookmark

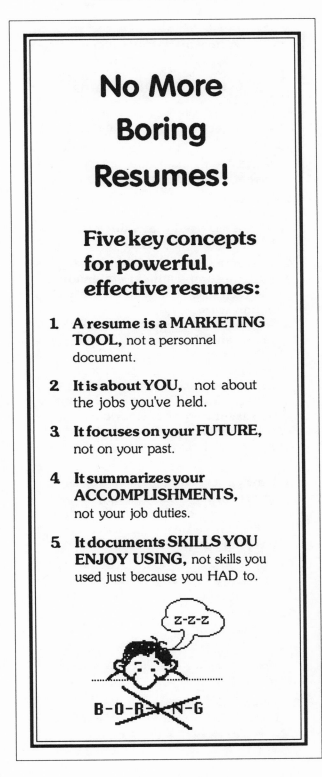

No More Boring Resumes!

Five key concepts for powerful, effective resumes:

1. **A resume is a MARKETING TOOL,** not a personnel document.

2. **It is about YOU,** not about the jobs you've held.

3. **It focuses on your FUTURE,** not on your past.

4. **It summarizes your ACCOMPLISHMENTS,** not your job duties.

5. **It documents SKILLS YOU ENJOY USING,** not skills you used just because you HAD to.

Back of bookmark

- A Bookmark Mini-Guide -

SEVEN TIPS On Writing A "Damn Good Resume"

1 Always start with a clear, concise **Job Objective**—a job title if possible.

2 Identify about 3 to 6 **essential skill**s required to do that job, or the most **essential functions** of that job.

3 For each essential skill or function, **recall several situations** where you successfully **used that skill** or did something similar (for pay or not).

4 **Describe what you did in brief, lively accomplishment statements.**
   – In each statement, **lead off with an action word.**
   – Spell out the resulting **accomplishment, and the benefit** to others.
   – Do not use job descriptions ("duties included…"). Instead, present your **uniquely effective way of doing things—how YOU got good results.**
   – **Present only the experiences you found satisfying.** Omit, or at least play down, tasks and roles you don't want to repeat in future jobs.

5 Arrange your accomplishment statements **either chronologially** (under each job title) **or functionally** (under skill groups related to the objective), **keeping the resume lean**.

6 Top it off with a 4 to 5 line Summary outlining your strengths and qualifications, plus one prime accomplishment.

7 **Get feedback** before you use it.

Taken from Yana Parker's books:
• *Damn Good Resume Guide*
• *Resume Catalog: 200 Damn Good Examples*
• *Resume Pro: The Professional's Guide*

Ten Speed Press, Berkeley (510) 845-8414
Damn Good Resume Service (510) 540-5876
© 1992, Yana Parker

DIVERSIFYING

ACCOMPLISHMENTS

Things you did that gave you a real sense of satisfaction or accomplishment—they could have happened on your job, or in your volunteer work, or in your personal life. They can derive from projects you worked on, something you built, a great idea you developed, a hobby, a problem you solved.

You don't need the details here—just a few words to remind you of the accomplishment.

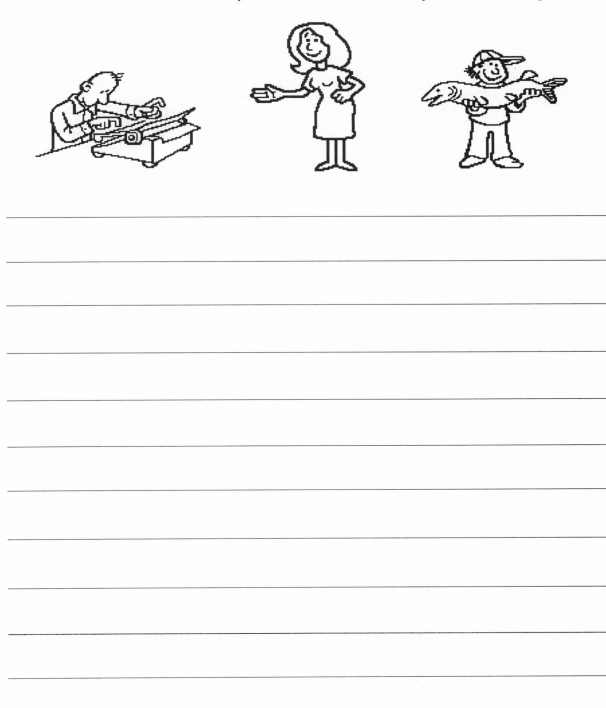

_____

_____

_____

_____

_____

_____

_____

_____

_____

DIVERSIFYING

327

JOB TITLES

that would be appealing and appropriate for my very next job
(which might be my ideal job OR a BRIDGE to a better job).

These should be *actual job titles*, like "full charge bookkeeper," "executive secretary," "vice president of marketing," "human resources trainer," "paralegal." Jot down every job you can think of that you'd be willing to do and are probably able to do (even if you're not absolutely sure you're qualified). It's okay to *guess* at what the job might be called.

_____

_____

_____

_____

_____

_____

_____

_____

A handout used with laid-off workers at a brief resume-writing workshop warm-up

BRAINSTORM
on ideas for getting started

LOOKING FOR A NEW JOB

The obvious places to start looking:

1. Classified ads
2. Job placement agencies
3. Leads from friends and relatives

_____

_____

_____

_____

The not-so-obvious places to look:

1. College career center listings
2. Community career center listings (YWCA, etc)
3. Civil service listings (County or City Business Library)
4. Referrals from "information interviews"

_____

_____

_____

_____

_____

DIVERSIFYING

329

This is an example of an agenda for a resume workshop for professional resume writers. I find that participants appreciate having an outline so they know what to expect.

AGENDA CREATING POWERFUL RESUMES USING SELF-TEACHING RESUME TEMPLATE
MORNING THEME: Anatomy of powerful resumes
AFTERNOON THEME: Strategies to deal with unique problems

9:45-10:00 Get your snapshot taken (please). Get fee receipt.

No breaks. One hour lunch at 12:15. Feel free to get up and stretch or leave the room whenever you want to. There are beverage machines in the hallways.

10:00 OPENING Ice-breaker 10-15 minutes

10:20 Quick review of Agenda
10:25 INTRODUCTIONS (2 minutes each) - Total 35 minutes
Someone will ring a little bell to remind you when 2 minutes is up. Tell us all
1. Your name, job title, where you work. (Hand out your business card if you have one.)
2. What you want to gain from this workshop. (What do you want to leave with?)
    (Write that down for yourself, and at 2:00 pm, TELL US if you still haven't got it)
3. Look on the Participant Name List and tell us all if your name, telephone, or address IS NOT correct.

11:00-11:55 Yana talks on CONCEPTS. Refer to the Templates Manual and Bookmarks as referenc
See Functional format, page xx
See Features and Advantages, page xx
See Information Interviewing, page xx and xx

12:00-12:15 RESUME-WRITING EXERCISE (15 minutes) *[We ALL "applied" for the job of Mayor*
(We will look at the results AFTER lunch)

12:15 - 1:10 LUNCH in the cafeteria. Follow anybody who looks like they know the way.

1:15-1:35 QUADS (20 minutes — 5 minutes per person)
Each person take 5 minutes to quickly present their resume results while the other 3 practice their interviewing skills to draw the person out and make sure they didn't miss any relevant skills or achievements.

1:40-1:45 Back in the larger group (5 minutes) to share anything unusual about this exercise.

PROBLEMS: In three segments below, we'll be building a sort of TOOL BOX of creativ
IDEAS for solving tough problems such as how to draw out the client.

1:50-2:10 (20 minutes) PROBLEM EXAMPLE - Susan Ireland's client, "Nancy Paralegal"
(Older worker; first entry into workforce; "conscious communication")

2:10-2:30 (20 minutes) PROBLEM EXAMPLE - Yana Parker's client, "Roger Arrowhead"
(Minimal credible work history; older worker; no experience in new profession)

2:30-2:50 (20 minutes) GROUP CRITIQUE of inmate resume
(What's wrong with it? What could he do?)

3:10-3:20 10 minutes (evaluation form)
3:20-3:40 Share about "any surprises?"
Thank any other participants from whom you learned something, if you wish.

A handout designed for use at a job club of unemployed white-collar workers to help the members evaluate their own resumes.

Some Essential Characteristics
Of An Effective Resume

1. A good resume has a FOCUS, and the focus is on your FUTURE JOB OBJECTIVE — not on your past work history EXCEPT as it relates to your future job.

    A resume that merely outlines your past experience puts the *reader* in the position of *interpreter* of your experience. But:
    a) The reader DOESN'T WANT that responsibility.
    b) The reader SHOULDN'T HAVE that much authority over your career.

2. It repeatedly ANSWERS the question "SO WHAT?"
    For every accomplishment or statement you list, ask yourself *"So What?"* Check to see if you have answered it by emphasizing the BENEFIT of that action — saved money, increased productivity, cut expenses, improved the company's public image.

3. It's "LEAN & MEAN" — lots of white space; a crisp, clear layout. In contrast, telling EVERYTHING on your resume — the "more is better" approach — has a negative impact. Far from impressing people, it does the opposite: it makes you look insecure. (*"If I don't tell it ALL they'll never know I'm great."*)

4. It's straightforward, HONEST, and gutsy.
    You don't need to exaggerate, lie, or mislead.
    You also don't need to confess, apologize, or be modest.

5. It's CLEAR, easy to read, powerfully simple, and user-friendly.
    Important information, such as dates and job titles, almost jumps out.

6. It reflects the REAL YOU at your best.
    It's consistent with your personality and your values.
    Your special qualities and your uniqueness show up.
    It pleases you to look at it. You feel a bit proud of it AND it's all true.

DIVERSIFYING

331

I use this form at the close of my one-day workshops for professionals. Question #5 generates the most enlightening responses.

Participant Evaluation of the Workshop

1. Overall **value of the workshop** to you on a scale of 1 to 100 — 100 meaning "I'm fully satisfied."

   10   20   30   40   50   60   70   80   90   100

2. What you **liked** about the workshop:

   _____

   _____

   _____

   _____

3. What you **didn't like** about the workshop:

   _____

   _____

   _____

   _____

4. Recommendations for **additions or changes** in workshop **content or method**:

   _____

   _____

   _____

   _____

5. **Surprises** — unexpected outcomes:

   _____

   _____

   _____

6. **Anything else you want to say:**

   _____

   _____

   _____

   _____

This can be anonymous, OR you can sign it.

CLOSING

Go for It!

GO FOR IT!

CLOSING
Go for It!

GO FOR IT!

Well—did all that turn you on? Are you inspired to give it a try? Or to give it a brand NEW try if you're already doing resume writing?

Then GO FOR IT! You have nothing to lose but some boring job you're eager to leave—or some way of working that you've outgrown.

There is SO MUCH job satisfaction available to those who dare to break out of their rut and risk making change—risk doing something that reflects THEIR priorities, interests, and personal style. This is true even if change initially happens by accident, or—as in my case—something fell through and you were forced to try a new tack. It isn't what happens to you that determines your career fate: it's what YOU DO about what happens to you. So now is a great time to take charge of your own career future and at the same time enjoy the satisfaction of making your unique contribution to the whole realm of work, job search, and career satisfaction.

Reread the chapters that caught your imagination or tapped into your particular passions, and **take one step now** toward the exciting goal of a career that YOU design.

Reporting In: Job Satisfaction and Opportunities Do Make a Difference

I've told you my story, in bits and pieces throughout this book. Now I'll share a few of the letters I've received from other resume writers. They tell of the job satisfaction they enjoy from their daily work, as well as their excitement about the many new directions available to their creative minds.

LETTERS

Dear Yana: It's so rewarding when a client is truly appreciative of my efforts to provide them with a perfect resume, and many of them truly are. It's often more special when they send a note or call with good news, such as the two phone calls I got from my client, Deborah.

She called me just a week after I did her resume to let me know that the first place she sent it—a hospital where she was wanting to work—asked her to come in for an interview. Her second call was about three weeks later to tell me that they made an offer and she accepted! She kept on repeating "I owe it all to you! How can I ever thank you for all you've done for me?" She was so pleased that she referred her sister in Cincinnati to me.

Incidentally, Deborah and I never actually met face-to-face until I delivered her resume package. We did the whole thing via phone and fax! I'm doing her sister's resume the same way.

Judi Robinovitz
Resumes That Work!!
Vero Beach, FL

SUPPORT IS WHAT CLIENTS VALUE MOST

I think that what my clients value most is the support they get while putting the resume together. Either they are not very objective about themselves, or they find it difficult to say nice things about themselves. Most of them have grown up learning to be modest, so when their resume writer identifies certain strengths during the interview, it becomes easier for them to acknowledge those assets.

My own satisfaction comes from empowering others, and in the process I empower myself, so this work has been a boon to my self-esteem as well as theirs.

Charlene Rashkow
Redondo Beach, CA

Dear Yana: Here's an interesting story about one of my clients. Readers familiar with the Los Angeles area know a one-hour commute one-way to a job is not an uncommon circumstance. Such would have been the case for this applicant. Her company was laying off due to government cutbacks. We wrote a very concise and targeted resume (using the *Damn Good Resume Guide*, of course) highlighting her capabilities. She sent her resume and cover letter to a potential employer and easily won an interview.

But, the morning of the interview, there were two major accidents on the freeway. Her one-hour commute turned into a two-hour trip, making her an hour late for her interview. She decided that if she couldn't make it to something as important as her initial interview, there was no way she could make it on time daily.

She got off the freeway, called the interviewer, and explained that the commute would be too much for her. To her surprise, the interviewer offered her the job over the phone—BASED ON HER RESUME ALONE!

He stated that no other applicant had presented herself in a way that addressed what he was looking for. Her resume led him to believe that she had an understanding of his needs and that she was the obvious best choice for the job! She was tremendously flattered, but turned the job down anyway.

A week later, a supervisory position opened up at the company she was working for. Armed with the same resume (and a bushel full of confidence from the job offer she turned down) she applied for the advancement and got it!

Stories like these make me happy I'm in the resume-writing business. It is tremendously satisfying to know that I can help other people help themselves.

L. Denise Cross
Cross Executive Services
Rolling Hills Estates, CA

Opportunity to Make a Difference

As you can see, there is much opportunity here to make a difference in other people's lives by doing superior resume work.

And beyond that, even, the doors are wide open for expanding the ways you apply your expertise to a myriad of related issues. Remember, **since you're self-employed, there's nobody to clip your wings** and say "No, sorry, you can't go off in that direction." You CAN go off in any direction that commands your interest, responding to invigorating opportunities to develop your skills and perhaps even collaborate with others on the solutions to problems related to the world of work.

Here is an example of such an opportunity that is currently opening new and challenging doors for me:

 Dear Yana: I am the Counseling Coordinator for the Oakland Unified School District and I'm concerned about the marketability of our culturally very diverse population of students. Statistics are not in their favor! We need to develop tools that will better highlight these students' talents, interests, and attitudes that could make them more marketable.

At the same time we need to address the issues of self-esteem and limited experience. Research shows there are several factors that predict success for minorities in college and on the job. **I'd like to apply this information somehow. Can you help?** Would you be interested, for example, in working on a resume-related tool or product that could address these issues?

Marilyn Harryman
Counselor at Large,
Div. of Instruction
Oakland Unified School District
Oakland, California

Dear Marilyn: Yes, certainly I'd like to work on that. It seems to be a wide open area where some great ideas and superior "tools" could make a very positive impact on students' lives. Let's get together and see what we can come up with. —yp

P.S. to other readers—If you have any input on this, write to Marilyn and/or Yana. We will report in the Resume Pro Newsletter *(see below) on our pro-*

gress in designing innovative resume writing tools and software for high school students—particularly those with minimal experience.

Commencement!

Now I'd like to come full circle back to these two paragraphs from the introduction:

"I wrote this book to show you how to create superior resumes, but I had another goal in mind beyond that. I want this book to **get you excited and inspired about how YOU could use YOUR talents in this field**. I want you to see that there IS a place for your VISION here, that this isn't a cut-and-dried business! **You can make a difference.** Your job can actually influence the world of work and contribute to the quality of a lot of other people's lives. THAT's something to get excited about!

"Finally, I want to say that this book is not a finished product. *Resume Pro: The Professional's Guide* is meant to be the **beginning of an ongoing dialogue** and sharing among resume writers across the land. A quarterly newsletter will keep that dialogue going between editions, and I am **eagerly awaiting your contribution** to it."

Resume Pro Newsletter

The newsletter referred to above will be called the *Resume Pro Newsletter* and will provide an open forum for sharing all kinds of information and inspiration related to resume writing. The tone will be informal and fun-loving, as we support and encourage the growing community of dedicated, creative, "*damn good*" professional resume writers in their quest to *make a living that makes a difference.*

You are invited to write for subscription information and to submit letters-to-the-editor, articles, and samples of your resume work.

Now, go for it!

APPENDIX

Pow!-litzer Prizes

APPENDIX
Pow!-Litzer Prizes

Some Damn Good Resumes

Here are more than 40 resumes to inspire you toward great resume writing. These are examples written by both professional resume writers and by job hunters, applying the "damn good resume writing" principles.

I think they are exceptionally good examples of effective resume writing. "Exceptionally good" does not necessarily mean "perfect," so if you find a minor blemish please try to be forgiving. The resume writer nevertheless did good work. (On YOUR resumes, however, make every effort to be *perfect*. Always, always check your spelling and then have two people proofread it.)

Here is the criteria I used for selecting these "damn good" examples:

- Scanable in seconds, so the reader can get a quick overview of structure and content.

- Meets the employer's needs for adequate and easy-to-find information.

  —a clear, concise objective (stated or implied)

  —a clear, concise, chronological work history (or equivalent)

- Somehow distinguishes the job hunter from the masses of other applicants. Some distinctive, engaging touch to set it apart.

- Graphically appealing at first glance.

- Free of tired old resume jargon.

- Free of information that could trigger discrimination.

- The resume WORKS, even if it misses on some of the criteria above.

Now, below you'll find a little note relating to each of the resumes in this chapter. These notes tell what I found particularly appealing about each resume, and in some cases include comments from the resume writer about the problem they were attempting to resolve.

FIRST: RESUMES DONE BY *JOB HUNTERS* THEMSELVES

- Yvonne Lee, page 345. A clear, concise job objective and a great layout that is super-easy to scan. Nice balance of text and white space. Explicit, colorful, engaging accomplishments. Clarity about where things happened even though it's a functional format.

- Tom Harper, page 346. Clean, crisp graphics that demonstrate the skills he wants to use in his new position. Concise; immediately conveys the critical information.

- John Holland, page 347. One of my favorites— an immediately engaging resume that you want to read, word for word, all the way to the end. My associate read it and commented: "I feel like I know this guy—he's fun, he's funny, he's creative, he's smart, he likes a challenge, and he likes Asian food. Using this resume he'll never get a job he doesn't like."

- Karen Hanks, pages 348 and 349. Two resumes creating an interesting contrast of functional and chronological formats.

  —Karen Sue Hanks, Account Manager. Gorgeous first impression, distinctive logo, very easy to scan, extremely clear, well organized, explicit accomplishments, objective says a lot about her attitude.

  —Karen Sue Hanks, Technical Director. Gorgeous; easy to scan; job titles jump right out; clear objective; strong accomplishment statements.

- Steven Dinkowitz, pages 350 and 351. Cover letter and resume.

  —The cover letter: Here Steve is using yours truly, the author, as a typical (if unlikely!) prospective employer to whom he might address this excellent "broadcast letter" (a term used when you are fishing for a position that hasn't yet been advertised.) This letter sounds self-confident and engaging; it shows initiative—he's not waiting for an opening; it talks about *their* goals rather than his; and it closes with a direct suggestion for follow-through ("Let's get together.")

  —The resume: Dynamic overall impression. Attractive graphic design that is scanable in seconds. Clear, simple job objective; job titles stand out clearly; explicit accomplishments; free of irrelevant material; language appropriate to the industry.

NEXT: RESUMES DONE BY *RESUME WRITERS* OR OTHER PROFESSIONALS IN THE CAREER FIELD.

(Their full business names and addresses are found on page 399.)

By resume writer Jeff Lewis:

- Frances Dayan, page 352. Unique objective (wordy but it works); powerful summary; one-liners that show her unique strengths and explicit benefits to the employer.

- Donna Malone, page 353. Strong accomplishments in a brief and powerful layout; emphasizes benefits to the employer. She could use as-is for "Information Interviewing" and then make the Objective more explicit when she applies for a specific job.

- Alison Arons, page 354. A new graduate; got the job despite widespread downsizing in her field; a unique presentation of job hunter's motivations; powerfully simple and brief yet succeeds in conveying this student's uniqueness.

- Mark Alexander, page 355. Resolves problem of very frequent career moves by presenting the TOTAL years of experience at the top (instead of chronological work history) and putting a strong emphasis on his impressive achievements. Omitting dates like this is risky and won't always work, but it worked in this case; he came in #2 out of 900 applicants for the job.

- Harry Hall, page 356. In rare cases such as this, it can work to omit dates (which otherwise would have made this job hunter's history look fragmented) and focus entirely on impressive accomplishments and well-known clients to capture the reader's attention. Clear objective, powerfully simple and brief; strong presentation of results and benefits.

- Thomas Chaney, page 357. The objective presents his military experience as an asset; strong summary; accomplishments transformed into cost-saving, business-oriented benefits; bold, brief, powerful, scanable in seconds. He got the job he wanted with a major airline.

- Debra Rabin-Posner, page 358. Refreshing approach: first draws attention to the problem, then proposes the solution, her services. At first glance it doesn't look like a resume, but it is marketing Debra's services, just as a good resume does, emphasizing benefits to the employer.

- Ms. Lupe Matz, page 360. Resolves potential age discrimination problem for an older worker by presenting the total number of years worked rather than the specific dates. It takes a strong resume like this one to get away with breaking the rules and omitting dates.

By resume writer Claudia Jordan:

- Debra Nauman, page 361. Effectively resolves a few problems. The resume writer notes that she had to deemphasize the client's age (very young to have such senior responsibility), and downplay her current job (her best experience was in her previous position). This conservative chronological format, with lots of pizazz in the highlights, got her foot in the door and landed a senior management position within two months.

- C. Ryan Howard, page 362. Succeeds in the tricky business of translating an ex-clergyman's experience into business language. The next step in his career change is "Information Interviewing" to explore positions in counseling, training, and public speaking.

- Gordon Kent, page 364. "Juicy" accomplishments with measurable results help to generalize his business experience. The resume writer says, "Gordon's business for the past eight years was mostly marketing Arabian horses and some restaurant management/investing. We had to communicate what he had done in general business language, showing his business savvy without labeling him a horse person."

  (Note: The resume writer also could have *dropped the bottom 3 items in the Employment History*, starting that section with 1980.)

- Julie Pavlich, page 366. Claudia explains what the problem was: only two years' experience to support the management level objective, but highly successful achievements in a short period of time. Solution:

Emphasize impressive results and abilities on page one, and put dates on page two.

- Beverly Dail, page 368. Good example of combination chronological/functional format. The most difficult obstacle, says Claudia, was showing her chutzpah and business savvy without it sounding like puffery and bragging. They created the "Event Planning" section on page two to show her amazing organizational/social skills.

By resume writer Yana Parker:

- Matt Parker, page 370. Here we've designed a unique format to fit the situation, ignoring paid work history (he earns his living as a professional plumber) and focusing on what matters most to band members: attitude, commitment, style, reliability, skill, experience, and equipment.

By resume writer Susan Ireland:

- Susan Tall, page 371. Clean, crisp, unique layout, very easy to read and scan. Functional headings (marketing, events coordination) are documented, showing where the accomplishments occurred. All the bases are covered, including relevant and measurable accomplishments.

- Thomas Colman, page 372. Concise, extremely easy to scan; makes the most of minimal experience. Resume writer's comments: "Since it's difficult to measure the effectiveness of teaching, Thomas chose to demonstrate his understanding behind what makes a good teacher, giving the reader a feeling for what he's like in the classroom. His resume led to an immediate interview and a job offer."

- Bill Furner, page 373. Simple, clear format that fits the information being presented.

- Allison Page & John Lawrence, page 374. Succeeds in blending the work experience of two people who work together as property managers. Clear and easy to scan despite a unique format covering a lot of information.

- Maureen Wells, page 376. Work history shows how to indicate promotions within a company efficiently. The Professional Experience section shows one way to organize one-liners by both function and by

company, all at once. (Not always practical, but sometimes it works.)

- Jeannette Parr, page 378. Here is one good way to present the unpaid volunteer work experience of a woman returning to the commercial workforce after full-time parenting. Notice that the experience is listed as "work," not as "volunteerism." Good strategy.

By resume writer Judi Robinovitz:

- Ruthanne Rosen, page 379. Makes the most of a new grad's summer work experience, beefing it up with a list of relevant courses.

- Karen Brett, page 380. Outstanding graphic design; just about everything has been done to make it easy for the reader to scan the contents quickly. Accomplished by repetition of bold text, caps, and bulleted substatements, consistently throughout the document.

- Rebecca Shidel, page 382. Clear objective; strong, relevant accomplishments and it's clear where they happened. One recommendation: Switch back to regular type instead of italics, because it's easier to read in large blocks of text.

By resume writer Cynthia Mackey:

- Lawrence Gere, page 384. This resume says a lot in just a few words, illustrating how a chronological format (often ideal when staying in the same industry) can be very powerful when you talk about *results* rather than duties and job descriptions.

- Carlton Mackey, page 385. Cynthia comments: "My brother asked me to update his resume. The original resume (chronological) made him look like a regular job hunter rather than a consultant. Also, some of his contracts were short and this made him look like a job hopper. I chose a functional format, grouping similar skills under the heading Representative Accomplishments, and listed job titles first (rather than years first) under Experience. The result: He mailed 27 copies and within two days received a job interview and a job offer, plus five other responses."

By resume writer Kim Coats:

- Kelly McCombs, page 386. Beautifully designed format; powerful accomplishments; packs maximum punch for minimum words.

- Donald Smeltzer, Jr., page 387. Very strong design that's easy to scan. The use of bold plus a large type size for headings results in a crisp, clean, high-contrast look.

By career professional Rogene Baxter:

- Jane Foster, page 388. There are times when you can get away with throwing out the guidelines and going with your guts. Here is an example of a successful resume for a talented writer. It went out just as it appears here, to the top companies in her area, and she had her pick of job offers. Resume reprinted, with permission, from *Do-It-Yourself CareerKit* by Rogene Baxter and Marcelle Brashear (Bridgewater Press, 1990).

By resume writer Calvin Baird:

- Dale Wickett, page 389. Clearly and concisely presents the information the employer needs, uniquely organized to fit the objective.

By resume writer Vicki Law-Miller:

- Ronlyn Henegar, page 390. Here Vicki accommodates the client with a conservative resume appropriate to the field. She writes, "Ronlyn felt that any employer would be put off by a cover letter (perhaps even by a resume) since the industry standard was application forms. She already had to deal with sex discrimination, so we tried to keep it simple yet include everything (see Summary) that Ronlyn felt was important for the interviewer to know."

By resume writer Jan Hurley:

- Brian Briarsson, page 392. A good "blue collar" example by resume writer Jan Hurley, who says: "The features I like best about this resume are the way the client's accomplishments are highlighted in the first two job fields, and the way I managed to use some of the client's own phrasing, for example 'job is done on time' and 'ran crews.' This gives a true flavor of the skilled construction worker, in the context of a polished format."

By resume writer Hinda Bodinger:

- Zachary Curtiss, page 393. Clean, crisp, easy-to-scan, compact one-pager. In the skilled trades where excellent resumes are rare, a document as user-friendly as this is sure to be well received.

- Lee Craig, page 394. Clear objective and very relevant summary statements under the Highlights. Lots of measurable accomplishments in a compactly designed resume that is very easy to scan.

By resume writer Sallie Young:

- Gerard Villaseñor, page 395. Thoroughly covers the technical details that are important to a potential employer in this field, and then adds the personal touches (in the Highlights section) that could tip the scales in the job hunter's favor and generate an interview.

By resume writer Karen Staggs:

- Jenny Lin, page 396. All the relevant information is here and easy to scan for this student's internship application.

- Craig Ash, page 397. Another easy-to-scan example packed with the right data. On most resumes you would NOT include this personal information but it's appropriate for this job objective.

YVONNE L. LEE

725 Mariposa Avenue •Mountain View, Calif. 94041 • Work: (415) 329-3571

OBJECTIVE

A position as reporter in the general press

HIGHLIGHTS

- Write clearly on topics from technology to legal issues to sports
- Can analyze news for long term social and legal implications
- Unusually strong vocabulary; in top 3 percent of Americans who entered graduate school
- Familiar with electronic research methods, as well as traditional reporting techniques

EDUCATION

Stanford University, Master of Arts, Journalism, 1987
Rutgers University, Bachelor of Arts, Political Science, 1982
conversant in French, Spanish; studied elementary Japanese

PROFESSIONAL SKILLS & ACCOMPLISHMENTS

News Analysis

- Reported on lawsuits and explained the possible impact of precedents they set.
- Examined policies and practices surrounding new communication technologies and explained their social and legal implications.
- Presented updates on current technology and how it relates to business managers' needs.

News Gathering

- By monitoring electronic data networks, discovered the Xerox-Apple lawsuit in time to prevent my paper from missing the story.
- Covered activities of technological companies such as Word Perfect, 3Com, Novell, Banyan, Lotus, Oracle, Sybase, and ccMail for *InfoWorld*.
- At *InfoWorld*, related computer use to real world events, such as the October 17, 1979 Northern California earthquake and Persian Gulf War.
- Wrote ...product announcements, ...technology explanations, ...lawsuit analyses, ...features, ...sports accounts, ...personality profiles.
- Was the first reporter to uncover that Carl Lewis' 1984 100-meter gold medal had been buried with the athlete's father in 1986.

Writing

- Presented technological announcements clearly to a business audience at *InfoWorld*.
- Wrote lively features for freelance articles and on the city desk of the *Press Democrat*.
- Met daily deadlines at *InfoWorld* and *The Press Democrat*.
- Wrote profiles of famous athletes including Edwin Moses, Carl Lewis, Calvin Smith, Jackie Joyner-Kersee for *Track and Field News*.
- While stringing for the Bryan-College Station, TX *Eagle*, I got a routine sports event on the front page of the Pepsi Games supplement by targeting to the paper's audience.

Editing

- Substituted for senior networking editor while a senior writer at *InfoWorld*.
- Copy-edited, proofread, and verified facts in multi-volume *Petersons Guide to Graduate and Professional Study*.

WORK HISTORY

1990-present	**Senior Writer**	InfoWorld, Menlo Park, Calif.
1989-1990	**Reporter**	InfoWorld, Menlo Park, Calif.
1987-1988	**Staff Writer**	Track & Field News, Mountain View, Calif.
Summer 1987	**Intern**	Press Democrat, Santa Rosa, Calif.
Summer 1986	**Data Editor**	Petersons Guides, Princeton, N.J.
1985-present	**Freelance Writer**	

- Resume written by Yvonne Lee -

THOMAS F. HARPER 11-36 31ST AVENUE LONG ISLAND CITY, NY 11106 718.267.1515

Resume & Qualifications

Computer Skills

✣ Specialized in Quark XPress 2.1, PageMaker 3.0, and Microsoft Word for typesetting and page layout.

✣ Full knowledge of popular graphic programs with emphasis on Adobe Illustrator 88 and Aldus FreeHand 2.0 for high resolution PostScript output.

✣ Experienced in a corporate environment producing charts and graphs of financial data with programs such as Microsoft Excel, Informix Wingz and Cricket Graph.

✣ Extensive knowledge of the Macintosh based graphic production environment. Assisted in set up and supervision of an Ethernet Network consisting of 6 Mac II work stations with a 1.2 gigabyte file server.

✣ Familiarity with networking software includes AppleShare, EtherTalk, and TOPS.

✣ Expert with all production and printing processes utilizing the Linotronic L-300. This expertise includes different methods of color separation as well as basic knowledge of the PostScript language.

✣ General software experience includes familiarity with data base, financial, spread sheet, and telecommunications packages.

Management & Organization

✣ Over ten years supervising and training personnel in the entertainment industry.

✣ Three years training and consulting in the field of Macintosh graphics.

Work History

'89   Computer Typographer/Artist
      PDR Computer Impressions
      New York, NY

'88   Corporate Graphic Designer
      United Illuminating
      New Haven, CT

'87   Macintosh Graphics Consultant
      Freelance
      New Haven, CT

'78-86 Tour/Equipment Manager
      Champion Entertainment
      New York, NY

Related Education & Affiliations

Pratt Institute,   New York, NY
School of Visual Arts,   New York, NY
Graphic Artists Guild,   New York, NY

346

- Resume writer: Thomas Harper -

John Holland
2419 Haste St. #11
Berkeley.CA.94704
415.843.5685

**In 1984 I used my first Macintosh.
In less than five minutes, I knew my life would never be the same.**

Since then, I've used just about every design package for Macintosh, ranging
from the early stuff, like MacPaint and MacDraw, to the amazing stuff, like
Illustrator, FreeHand, PageMaker, Quark XPress, PhotoShop, and Studio 8.

It's 1990 now, and I believe it's just the beginning. If there's one thing I want
out of a job, it's the same thing I want out of life: To create images that work.
In short, put a mouse in my hand, a tough project on my desk, and I'm happy.

A Private CD ROM Project
In early 1990, I was asked to work for Lewis Browand & Associates in Oakland on a CD ROM catalog
containing more than 50 10" x 15" element sheets for one of their advertising projects. The first question
the Art Director, Tyler Vogel, asked me was, "Do you like Chinese food?" I thought the job was going to be
easy. I was wrong. I spent the whole month on a Macintosh IIci, occasionally twiddling my thumbs waiting
for Lino, and worked more overtime than I'd like to remember. I finished ahead of schedule, and it was no
surprise to me they decided to put my work on CD.

A Corporate Identity
The people at Master Your Mac in Berkeley needed an identity that looked clean and professional. Even
though I know my stuff, I was a little worried about doing work for a company that specialized in Macintosh
training. Nevertheless, I called up one of my graphic artist pals, and we got right to work designing a logo
and then slapping it all over their stationery and brochures, which we also designed on my faithful little
Macintosh SE. We even helped them find a good printer. It all worked so well that it led to some work
training Pac Bell employees on the Mac. I've never eaten so much Thai food and had so much fun in my life.

Technical Illustration (and Head of Macintosh Information Services)
I never thought I'd find myself hanging out with a bunch of engineers and construction workers, but when
I was contracted by Bechtel to provide Macintosh support on a $130 million construction project, that's
exactly what I did. I accepted the job, mistakenly believing everything would be pretty basic, but these
folks were always thinking up new things for me to do! I set up networks, scanned big (and I mean BIG)
drawings, authored HyperCard stacks, and drew almost anything you can imagine. The best part: I got to
keep my hard hat.

P.S. I created everything on this resumé in under an hour and laser printed it at home. I'm saving up for a Linotronic. Just kidding.

- Resume writer: John Holland -

347

KAREN SUE HANKS

9923 Lenel Place • Dallas, Texas 75220 • (214) 956-9652

Objective
Account Manager with an aggressive company that believes in providing business solutions, not just products, to their clients

Qualification Highlights
- Experience in selling to small/medium businesses and Fortune accounts
- Clear and professional presentation skills
- Solid familiarity with DOS and Windows, advanced understanding of the Macintosh platform
- Successfully developed loyal vendor and client alliances; reputation for ethical relationships
- Tenacious, resolute, systematic, resourceful, adaptable and profit motivated

Relevant Skills & Experience

DIRECT SALES/MARKET DEVELOPMENT
- Developed system configurations and solved various pre/post installation problems for clients
- Successfully turned a $3k/month account into a +$100k/month account
- Maintain high profile within niche market by participating in clubs and user groups
- Maintained customer database used for informational mailings, seminar invitations, etc.

ACCOUNT MANAGEMENT
- Demonstrated interest in clients by remembering personal details, advising them of appropriate new products and upcoming special events of their particular interest
- Personally administered software/hardware support
- Resolved service issues, billing concerns and misunderstandings
- Followed through promptly to resolve customer complaints with patience and sensitivity
- Located hard-to-find parts for clients by whatever means necessary
- Responds effectively in high pressure emergencies such as needing equipment overnight and getting a downed network up again
- Special ability to transform serious problem accounts into amicable clients by re-establishing parameters of vendor/client relationship

PRESENTATION/COMMUNICATION
- Prepared professional, detailed formal proposals including: equipment descriptions, timeline of implementation, appropriate justifications, executive summary, financial options, etc.
- Addressed individuals, small or large groups in private demonstrations and user groups
- Demonstrated features and benefits of computer products to decision makers and various size meetings in private demonstrations or user groups and successfully negotiated closings

Employment Experience

Corporate Sales Representative	JWP Businessland	1990
Designer/Technical Consultant	Direct Marketing Direct Advertising	1989
Director of Lasertype/DTP	Kinko's of Winter Park	1988
Typesetter/Graphic Designer	Florida Choice Food & Drug Stores	1988
Production Artist	Typo-Graphics	1987
Narrator	Sea World of Florida	1986
Freelance contracts during and post-college		1983-88

Education
BACHELOR OF SCIENCE, Ad Design • Northwestern State U • Natchitoches, LA • 1985
Attended U of Innsbruck, Austria, Summer 1984; Who's Who Among American Colleges & U's; Sigma Sigma Sigma Sorority; Art Club Pres 1984; Phi Delta Theta & Sigma Tau Gamma Lil' Sis

Other Information
Willing to travel or relocate (current passport) • Other interests: sketching, reading, swimming, traveling, watercoloring, community involvement, home improvement, marine life, genealogy

References and further information happily provided upon request

- Resume writer: Karen Hanks -

K A R E N   S U E   H A N K S

9923 Lenel Place • Dallas, Texas 75220 • (214) 956-9652

Objective

Technical Director position where I can utilize my extensive background in electronic publishing to maintain network and participate in occasional design projects.

Employment Experience

GRAPHIC SPECIALIST • JWP Businessland (formerly MR.MICRO) • Dallas, TX • August 1990
Recommended and implemented high-end graphic system configurations. Provided hardware and software support. Spearheaded and participated in seminars targeted to the publishing industry. Demonstrated scanning, digitizing, photo manipulation, and a myriad of software packages.

GRAPHIC DESIGNER • DMDA • Carrollton, TX • September 1989
Personally researched, purchased and implemented a state-of-the-art color electronic publishing system. Responsible for maintenance of system, training art director and freelancers and answering technical questions. Used system to execute my designs as comprehensives and mechanicals. The system cost justified itself within the first 6 months and consistently enabled 3 and 4 day projects to be rendered in 3 or 4 hours.

DIRECTOR OF LASERTYPE/DTP • Kinko's • Winter Park, FL • December 1988
Single-handedly initiated department for this location of a growing nationwide network of electronic printshops which had recently entered the DTP market. Among other challenges, this included: establishing a solid clientele; developing customer awareness of department capabilities; determining price structure; hiring/training support staff; producing customer projects; and interfacing this department with pre-existing departments and services offered. After 3 months, department posted a 7% profit which continued to grow under my supervision.

TYPESETTER/DESIGNER • Florida Choice Food & Drug Store • Maitland, FL • March 1988
Hands on production of all printed materials such as store signs and banners, newspaper inserts and ROP advertisements, special promotional pieces and mailed circulars. Executed layouts, camera work and all departmental typesetting for camera ready mechanicals. Voluntarily participated in production of videos, store grand openings and community awareness programs.

GRAPHIC DESIGNER (Freelance) • Harcourt Brace Jovanovich • Orlando, FL • December 1987
Retained to assist in the production of a textbook series for elementary schools: assembled pages, rendered 'quickie' illustrations, and proofed pages.

PRODUCTION ARTIST • Typo-Graphics • Orlando, FL • June 1987
Assembled mechanicals, worked extensively with rapidiograph pens and shot camera work for major advertising agencies and public relation firms in Central Florida.

GRAPHIC DESIGNER (Freelance) • EPOCH Properties • Winter Park, FL • August 1986
Scheme designer for Polo's, a apartment complex targeted to the 'yuppie' market. This included developing logo, color choices and interior/exterior murals. Monitored the aesthetic development of complex from ground breaking until completion of property. Of the 4 complexes in the area which opened at the same time, Polo's was the first to fill to capacity.

September 1983 to December 1985 • Contracted a variety of freelance jobs while attending college in which my original designs were produced on stationery, clothing, store signs and menus.

Education

BACHELOR OF SCIENCE, Ad Design • Northwestern State U • Natchitoches, LA • 1985
Attended University of Innsbruck, Austria, Summer 1984; Who's Who Among American Colleges & Universities; Art Club President; LASCO Club Sponsor; Sigma Sigma Sigma Social Sorority; Phi Delta Theta & Sigma Tau Gamma Lil' Sis.

Other Information

Willing to travel or relocate (current passport) • Other interests: sketching, reading, swimming, traveling, watercoloring, community involvement, home improvement, marine life, genealogy.

References and further information happily provided upon request.

- Resume writer: Karen Hanks -

STEVEN DINKOWITZ

9778 LOWER RIVER ROAD   GRANTS PASS, OREGON 97526   (503) 479-01

November 19, 1990

Ms Yana Parker
ATTN: <u>Damn Good Resume</u>
PO BOX 3044
Berkely, CA 94703

Dear Ms Parker:

Although your firm has no published openings at this time, I have enclosed a copy of my resume for your review.

I think you will find evidence of a versatile, flexible engineer, with a broad background in electronics technology, including significant programming experience.

Additional skills and qualifications, left out of the resume because of size considerations, include marketing, advertising, technical writing/publication, and personal computer fluency (PC/AT), as well as drafting (CAD and mechanical), front panel design, and machine tool experience (vertical mill, lathe, precision grinder).

If you like what you see, let's get together: we could talk about Resumes' current projects and direction, and determine where I would fit on the team to help achieve your goals.

Thank you for the time you spend considering this matter.

Sincerely,

Steve Dinkowitz

STEVEN DINKOWITZ

9778 LOWER RIVER ROAD   GRANTS PASS, OREGON 97526   (503) 479-0134

OBJECTIVE: TEST ENGINEER / TECH SUPPORT

To design equipment and procedures which will economically test electronic assemblies.
To develop software on PC/AT for data acquisition/analysis, and process/test control.

SUMMARY OF QUALIFICATIONS

Twenty years involvement with electronics manufacturing and test
Innovative thinker, able to quickly resolve problems
Excellent communication skills
Exceptionally flexible, with broad experience
Adept at kludging a quick fixture or developing automated test equipment from scratch
★ Able to discern the goal and to work with a team ★

RELEVANT SKILLS & ACCOMPLISHMENTS

Qualified to Design and DeBug Test Equipment, Develop Software and Write Test Procedures for RF, Analog and Digital Electronic Products. Scale of projects has been from quick jigs for screening components, to fully automatic test sets for CCAs and sub-assemblies, including Digital, HVDC, Pulse, RF and Microwave.

Decoded and improved customer-supplied HP Basic software designed for automated RF testing on the GPIB. Wrote original programs for an automated RF test station utilizing HP Basic and C.

Designed and built fully automated GO-NOGO CCA test sets for JIT manufacturing line. The test set verifies risetime, amplitude, and width of various pulses in 1/2 second.

Designed and built all Special Test Equipment for Navy Active Electronics Buoy, a micro-processor controlled device combining a powerful microwave transmitter and high sensitivity receiver in one compact, air-dropped package:

   • Received special recognition for writing software to automate required calculations and graphs •

   • Traveled to a remote site to train technicians and organize a test shop to conclude contract •

   $ Collected cash bonus for a successful effort $

Produced all special test equipment, documentation and procedures for Army airborne Azimuth Display Unit. Designed and fabricated special incoming test set to measure all CRT and Deflection Coil parameters. Received special recognition for developing proprietary GO-NOGO CRT brightness tester.

Developed fiber optic instrument links for monitoring high power DC transmission line test equipment. Gained valuable experience in RFI and EMI protection.

EMPLOYMENT HISTORY

1977 - 1990 **Test Engineer:** Dalmo Victor Company, Grants Pass, Oregon
1976 - 1977 **Assistant Trainer:** Stepping Stone House, Grants Pass, Oregon
1974 - 1976 **Associate Engineer:** Hughes Aircraft Co., Research Labs, Malibu, California
1972 - 1974 **Associate Engineer:** Omnicron Instruments, Pasadena, California
1969 - 1972 **Engineering Technician:** Systron Donner Corporation, Van Nuys, California
1966 - 1969 **US Army Electronics:** Electronics Training, Electronics Instructor, PIO

EDUCATION

Cal State, Northridge, Northridge, CA: **BA, English Literature**. Minor Subject: Art.
Ft Monmouth Electronic Training Center, Monmouth, NJ: Radar Repair, Military Instructor

351

- Resume writer: Steven Dinkowitz -

FRANCES DAYAN
14895 Moorpark Avenue
Sherman Oaks, California 91403
(818) 980-3723

The Ultimate Executive Secretary/Assistant to Upper Management; a valuable "Right Arm", fulfilling all Clerical needs, plus the Implementation of Projects requiring Judicious Planning, Good Judgement, Intuition, & Creativity

SUMMARY OF QUALIFICATIONS

- ☐ Excellent typing skills; computer literate in MacIntosh & IBM; familiar with Word Perfect 5.1, Microsoft Word, & Lotus 123 (taught to staff); special expertise in Speedwriting, Dictaphone, & Dictation

- ☐ Responsible decision maker; achieves Management's diverse goals through intelligent research, development, & personal implementation of all projects from inception to completion with minimum of supervision

- ☐ Dedicated, detail-oriented, creative; a fast study; quickly fulfills present needs by transferring clerical, administrative, & executive skills honed in other industries; brings order out of chaos utilizing understanding & diplomacy

- ☐ Adept at spotting clerical and administrative procedural problems; institutes corrective measures, resulting in greater effectiveness and productivity

SPECIAL ACHIEVEMENTS

Piccadilly Designs, Los Angeles, an Interior Design Company (1985 - present),
- In charge of diverse clerical and paperwork for four designers
- Following dictation of business correspondence & PR texts, was depended upon to rewrite for greater effectiveness prior to typing
- Researched, composed, structured, & typed complex contracts, especially designed to cover specific projects and clients
- Supervised other clerical staff; restructured accounting ledger; evaluated work done by clerical staff and on-site project workers
- Responsible for judicious financial selection of purchases; assured that all products arriving, and all work being done was on schedule

Dimex Corporation, Los Angeles, an Import/Export Company (1983 - 1985)
- Executive Secretary to President of Company
- Saved Company $19,200 annually by accomplishing same functions as predecessor, in half the time
- Achieved 50% increase in productivity & 50% decrease in costs by teaching Lotus 123 to staff, replacing longer manual method

Zip Temporary Personnel Agency, Beverly Hills (1980 - 1983)
- Promoted to Personnel Manager in six months
- Conceived & implemented new interviewing procedure & filing system for a savings to ZIP of $4800 annually, plus assurance of obtaining best qualified "Temps" for such clients as: Bank of America, Security Pacific, Allstate Insurance, and California Federal
- Saved California Federal as an account for the company

Education:
Los Angeles City College, AA, Business (1984)
UCLA Extension (Present) Accounting/Finance Program

References Available Upon Request
- Resume writer: Jeff Lewis -

DONNA P. MALONE
21058 Rolling Hills Drive
Northridge, California 91326
(818) 705-6509

An astute Executive, highly skilled in Sales, Marketing, Business Management, Customer & Public Relations, Image-Building, Advertising & Promotion

SUMMARY OF QUALIFICATIONS

☐ Familiar with most facets of Apparel & Restaurant operations, planning, coordinating, supervising, & implementing all aspects of complex projects

☐ Successful at maintaining customer satisfaction/patronage and expanding client base due to intuitive understanding of, and satisfying their needs

☐ Plans, coordinates, supervises & implements all facets of multi-faceted projects

☐ Detail-oriented & dedicated; committed to goal achievement; a decision maker; diplomatic approach to supervision resulting in greater productivity

PROFESSIONAL ACHIEVEMENTS

- Conceived, developed & promoted own apparel import company (Beau Gio); generated $1MM+ gross sales within three seasons in up-scale shops nationally; totally knowledgeable in sales, promotion, sales staff hiring, administration, quality control, shipping, & successful Trade Show planning & exhibiting
  (Beau Gio, Owner/Manager, 1988 - Present)

- Successfully transformed restaurant concept into operational reality; as integral member of select staff (3), designed, planned all details, hired & trained staff, and wrote training/operational manual for prototype of Captain Pepper's Shrimp Boat Cafe; developed customer base, and achieved goal of maintaining & expanding repeat business
  (Seafood Consortium, Project Manager, 1984 - 1987)

- Promoted within six months at each of two restaurants, first to assistant manager, then to manager; thoroughly trained in all phases of restaurant management, hiring & training of staff, customer and public relations, plus image-building and enhancement
  (Pelican's Retreat & Bob Burns, Asst. Manager/Manager, 1978 - 1983)

Education:
California State University, Northridge
Special courses in Business Administration, Economics, Marketing, Accounting

Special Accomplishments:
Operated a Real Estate Investment Company; successfully purchased, renovated, and sold residential properties, bringing net profits to the investors

References Available Upon Request

353

- Resume writer: Jeff Lewis -

ALISON ARONS
12065 Addison Street
Studio City, California 91604
(818) 783-7218

Objective: To be a highly effective Elementary School Teacher, always aware that today's lessons become integral components of tomorrow's leaders; to be remembered by each student as the teacher who transformed learning into an exciting experience

Teaching Credentials:
Point Loma College, Pasadena, CA (1991)
Clear Multiple Subject Teaching Credential

Education:
University of Colorado
B.A. English (1990)
University of Pittsburgh (1/89 - 5/89)
Semester at Sea
(Concentrated studies in multi-cultural backgrounds)

Special Studies:
Method courses in Music & Art
(to be integrated into daily schedules)
Additional Method Courses in:
Social Studies, Science, Math, Reading, & Language Arts
Multi-Cultural Analysis & Understanding

STUDENT TEACHING EXPERIENCES & ACHIEVEMENTS

☐ **Carpenter Elementary School, Studio City, CA (1991)**
Taught 2nd & 4th grades; used "hands-on" experiences; involved in team teaching; conceived learning centers for groups of varying ability levels; created "spelling lists" to achieve greater story vocabulary understanding; initiated concept of "popcorn" reading, improving reading ability & maintaining concentration; took over class when regular teacher left for week

☐ **University of Colorado (Junior Year, 1988/1989):**
Simulated teaching 4th grade class to her classmates for discussion & evaluation of peers and professors; rated in top 5% of total class

☐ **University Hill Elementary School, Boulder, CO (Sophomore Year, 1988):**
Special Education Tutor for 5th & 6th grade students 3 - 4 days every week

MOTIVATIONS & COMMITMENTS

- "Fire in Stomach" to make a constructive difference by being an effective teacher

- Committed to emulating teacher who first motivated her to feel a "Yearn to Learn"

- Complete flexibility in approach methods; if one doesn't work, will try another

- Total involvement; sincere & equal caring about each and every student

- Feels students should know direction teacher is taking, goal to be reached, that teacher is organized but flexible, and consistent in implementation of decisions

INVOLVEMENTS & ACHIEVEMENTS

- ◆ **LA Children's Hospital (Summer, 1987):**
Volunteered three nights weekly in Pre-Operating Playroom, minimizing traumatic fear of children from 3 - 9 years old, during both Pre and Post-Operation periods

- ◆ **Meadow Oaks Camp (Summer, 1989):**
Volunteer counselor for three groups of 20 girls each; became personal mentor, constantly available to discuss and try to solve problems of various natures

Honorary Affiliations:
Pi Beta Phi - Colorado Alpha

354   **References Available Upon Request**   *- Resume writer: Jeff Lewis -*

MARK ALEXANDER
16741 Vanowen Street
Encino, California 91406
(818) 376-0613

**A top echelon Marketing Executive, whose Accomplishments reflect 16 years of
Creative Development Concepts, Profitable Media Placements, and Successful
Market Penetrations for some of the world's top Consumer Products & Services**

PROFESSIONAL QUALIFICATIONS

☐ Unique ability to research, analyze, & advise re: product success potential;
intuitive expertise...how and where to institute improvements

☐ Conceives, develops, and implements total marketing campaigns to commence
and/or increase market penetration; hands-on supervision from conception to
successful completion

☐ Excellent and creative negotiator in all types of media placement; enviable
reputation for special skills in utilizing barter concepts to achieve mutual benefits

OUTSTANDING ACHIEVEMENTS

◆ Expanded Mid-West Market for **Pleasant Hawaiian Holidays**; increased net profit
by 9% within one year, while maintaining costs at same level

◆ Successfully supervised "Gain" program for **State of California**; resulted in
retraining & employing 32 thousand Hispanics & Blacks within three years

◆ Restored $27.3MM of consumer sales to **Weingarten Supermarkets** (Houston)
by developing recipe campaign, demonstrating how cooking differently results
in feeding family nutritionally and inexpensively

◆ Started **Halston's** meteoric rise by disassociating the original Halston
Men's Fragrance from the Max Factor image, resulting in Halston's introduction
as an up-scale stores product, with first year gross sales of $5.5MM

◆ Successfully conceived, developed, and implemented the original **Mazda** launch;
instituted national radio campaign (including the famous "....Mazda motors go
Hmmmm"; campaign sold a year's production of Mazdas in the US within 4 months

◆ Conceived "Trade-In" program for **Mattel's Barbie** dolls; tackled a Barbie saturated
market & sold 360,000 new Barbies over the next two years; also initiated first
nationwide TV network commercial advertising of toys directed at children, increasing
over-all sales more than 400% in two years

◆ Additional clients have included: **P&G "Cheer", Breck's Shampoo,
American Express, Chrysler Corporation, Manufacturers Hanover Trust,
Johnson & Johnson, General Foods' Minute Rice & JELL-O**

Education:
City University of New York, (MBA)
University of Miami, (BA, Economics)

References Available Upon Request

- Resume writer: Jeff Lewis -

HARRY HALL
Post Office Box #5823
Sherman Oaks, California 91403
(818) 789-7865

Objective: **Senior Executive, in charge of National Sales, Marketing & Promotion, for a major Manufacturer of Consumer Products**

SUMMARY OF QUALIFICATIONS

- More than twenty years top level management experience in Sales, Marketing, and Promotion
- Special expertise with diverse classes of trade
- Total familiarity with production techniques, bottom line cost/profit factors, and sales training procedures
- Conceived, developed and implemented "Management To Management" presentations, resulting in closer understanding, and more mutually profitable relationships between vendors and retailers

SPECIAL ACHIEVEMENTS

☐ Increased sales at EVAN-PICONE by convincing major department stores' top management to adopt a policy of uninterrupted replacement of basics

☐ Reduced HANES KNITWEAR CORPORATION's cost-of-sales more than 50%, replacing a network of national wholesalers with a salaried national sales staff, working directly with retailers

☐ Increased BALI COMPANY's annual volume from $34MM to $77MM, and profits from $34K to $5.1MM by restructuring field sales and absorption of SG&A

Successfully moved the BALI line from 12th place to 2nd place at MERVYN'S; from $110K to $2MM (1st place) at MAY COMPANY, Los Angeles; from $67K to $6.5MM at J. C. Penney; increased Belk volume from $80K to $3.5MM within a three year period

Succeeded in opening and developing C. R. Anthony

Education
Auburn University
Degree: B.S. Business Administration
Whorton School of Business
Graduate: "Effective Executive"

Honors
Past President: City of Florence School Board
Past President: Florence Exchange Club
Past President: Delta Sigma Phi Fraternity (Auburn University)
Past President: Tri-Cities Quarterback Club
Vice President: AAMA Consumers Affairs Committee

Fraternal Memberships
Masons
Shriners
Elks

References available upon request

356

- Resume writer: Jeff Lewis -

THOMAS M. CHANEY
11306 Chimineas Avenue
Northridge, California 91326
(818) 360-0442

An Operations Leader Whose Expertise (eleven years of Marine Corps training) includes Administration, Logistics, Cost & Quality Control, plus Cargo/Personnel Transportation

SUMMARY OF QUALIFICATIONS

- Problem Solver, (identifies problems, creates successful solutions), Decision Maker, & Planner; Goal-Oriented, Organized; determined to succeed at any project

- Cost-Conscious; simultaneously manages several multi-faceted, detail-oriented projects/programs with minimum supervision, from concept to completion on schedule, and within or below allocated budget

- Unique ability to work well under pressure; intense Marine Training & creativity has forged an Operations Leader; creates, plans, organizes, initiates, coordinates, supervises, & implements procedures for all operational functions; "team" approach to staff supervision increases productivity, and improves efficiency

Employment History:
U.S. Marine Corps. (1980 - 1992)
(Last Rank: Captain, [Major select], Squadron Flight Leader)

OUTSTANDING ACHIEVEMENTS

Operations (& Asst. Operations) Officer

- ☐ Successfully managed **all operational activities** of 250 man flight squadron; supervised 10 officers, 11 enlisted men, plus maintenance & other crews

- ☐ **Increased squadron's efficiency** 20% while reducing training time 20%, allowing more judicious use of allocated funds; initiated successful tracking readiness program, adopted by other squadrons in Group

- ☐ **Conceived, wrote & implemented training plans & programs,** achieving new pilots' proficiency in aircraft tactics, while saving $450,000; created "reconciliation reports", attaining 10% increased proficiency, plus keeping Group Commander constantly aware of squadron's progress; This procedure now used by all 5 squadrons in Group (100 aircraft)

Embarkation & Logistics Officer

- ☐ Deployed squadron/equipment (1,950 tons) 15 times from embarkation to destination, on schedule, 10 times within budget, 5 times under budget

- ☐ Initiated new deployment guidelines, saving $90,000+ over three years; high probability that this one procedure is now utilized by other embarkation bases, with savings of additional millions of dollars

- ☐ Increased flight training proficiency & maintenance productivity by 8% by restructuring & rescheduling activities during deployment preparation days

- ☐ Saved $100,000+ by judicious purchasing & negotiating for operations' needs

Special Honor:
Newest Captain, most Junior Officer to be selected to train for & fly the new AV8B jet aircraft

Education:
BS in Business Administration (Emphasis on Management) (1980)
California State University, Northridge

References Available Upon Request

357

- Resume writer: Jeff Lewis -

PROPOSAL FOR SERVICES

Presented to: HUGHES AIRCRAFT COMPANY
Presented by: Debra S. Rabin-Posner, Licensed Speech Pathologist, (818) 907-6311
                         15427 Camarillo Street, Sherman Oaks, California 91403
Subject: Elimination of language problems shared by many Hughes' employees

---

THE PROBLEM

A substantial percentage of Hughes' employees have difficulties in speaking English clearly, resulting in several adverse ramifications. Some of the most important are:

Communicating incomplete, inadequate, or incorrect data
    Results: Misinterpretation; productivity reduction

Limitation of otherwise qualified employees from promotion

    Results: Upper management deprived of added brain power contributions.
                    False impression that Hughes' promotion policies are discriminatory.

Attitude and confidence suffer due to difficulty in exchanging thoughts and
                    ideas with co-workers and superiors

PROPOSED SOLUTION

Hughes' Learning Center to offer a series of weekly workshops, given over a four-to-six month duration, taught by Ms. Debra Rabin-Posner, an experienced and licensed Speech Pathologist.
GOAL: TO ELIMINATE LANGUAGE PROBLEM AREAS SUCH AS:

```
* Sound Errors              * Vocabulary              *
Auditory Discrimination     * Speaking w/Mouth Closed  *
 Pronounciation           * Speaking Too Quickly
* Intonation                  * Non-Verbal Communication
             *   and more....
```

After identifying, evaluating and diagnosing the various problem areas, Ms. Rabin-Posner's remedial techniques and approaches include: Auditory Models; Tapes; Articulator usage demonstrations; Team Pair-ups; Phonetic and Orthographic Representations of each problem sound; and other Scientifically-Approved remedial procedures.

An abbreviated list of Ms. Rabin-Posner's past clients include:

> Los Angeles Unified School District
> Los Angeles Municipal Court
> Santa Monica Community College
> University of Judaism

(Please turn to page 2)

From: Debra S. Rabin-Posner, Speech Pathologist
To: Hughes Aircraft Learning Center
Re: Language Problem Elimination Proposal

(Page 2)

Professional Affiliations
American Speech, Language & Hearing Association
California Speech, Language & Hearing Association
National Association of Teachers of Singing

Education & Cerification
California Board of Medical Quality Assurance
State Licensure...Speech Pathology #SP5734 (1985)

American Speech & Hearing Association
Certificate of Clinical Competence (1985)

Stanford University
Clinical Fellowship/Speech Clinician Certification/Audiometry (1975)
Masters Degree...Speech Pathology (1978)

California State University, Northridge
Clinical Rehabilitative Services Life Credential (1978)

Cedars-Sinai Medical Center
Clinical Fellowship...Speech Pathology (1977)

University of California, Los Angeles
Bachelors Degree...English Literature/Linguistics (1973)

References available upon request

Debra S. Rabin-Posner, Licensed Speech Pathologist
15427 Camarillo Street
Sherman Oaks, California 91403
(818) 907-6311

- Resume writer: Jeff Lewis -

MS. LUPE MATZ

16116 Royal Mount Drive
Encino, California 91436
(818) 783-9536

A creative, people-oriented Executive, whose unique Bi-Lingual and Bi-Cultural background is reflected in 20+ years of Public Relations & Business Successes on behalf of companies associated with both Hispanic & American clients

SUMMARY OF QUALIFICATIONS

◆ Mexican born; schooled in U.S. through Junior High, and in Mexico through College; innate ability to speak & think fluently in either language, relate instinctively to either culture, and adapt instantaneously from one to the other

◆ Establishes immediate & total trust, through intuitive understanding of, compassion for, and ease in relating to people and their needs

◆ Detail-oriented, with sound business sense and logic; a perfectionist, challenged by the opportunity to conceive & structure new procedures to attain desired results

◆ An unusually fast learner, quickly capable of planning, coordinating & implementing any multi-faceted project from conception to completion with minimal supervision

SPECIAL ACHIEVEMENTS

☐ **Matz, Bryman, Zinman & Brenner, Los Angeles**

(13 years functioning as combination **office manager, efficiency expert, and translator** [when needed] for husband's Law Firm)

✓ Improved productivity & company image by structuring creative solutions to administrative and other problems; "peacemaker" for 25 member staff, by intuitive use of total and equal diplomacy

✓ Responsible for the signing of every Hispanic client due to translation skills and ability to relate to them as a Hispanic

✓ Planned & Hosted two major theme-oriented special events annually, each resulting in expanding the company business

✓ Saved Company approximately $25,000 annually by initiating more cost-effective purchasing of office products

☐ **Magana, Cathgart, Marin & Pierry, San Diego**

(3 years **Public Relations and legal-oriented activities** in charge of one-person office for a Century City based Law Firm, which represented Personal Injury clients within the commercial fishing industry)

✓ Responsible for over $6MM in contingency fees due to bi-lingual expertise plus the innate ability to achieve & maintain client rapport

☐ **Radiology Medical Group, San Diego**

✓ (4 years as **Patient's Advocate**, calming Hispanic & Non-Hispanic patients' anxieties re: X-rays and/or cobalt treatments; completely categorized, translated, and typed in Spanish all applicable pre-visit instructions, allowing non-Spanish speaking staff to properly instruct Hispanic patients, eliminating Company losses due to unused appointments

Education:

Instituto Cuauhtlatohuac (Degree: AA)

References Furnished Upon Request

- Resume writer: Jeff Lewis -

Debra Nauman

5039 E. Paradise Drive ♦ Scottsdale, AZ 85254 ♦ (602) 996-5334

OBJECTIVE: Mortgage Banking Management

HIGHLIGHTS of QUALIFICATIONS

♦ Outstanding leadership skills, an effective manager able to energize a crew and willing to roll up sleeves and pitch in when needed.
♦ Well versed and knowledgeable in all phases of mortgage banking.
♦ Excel in developing harmonious customer relations in both retail and wholesale lending.
♦ Committed to producing results above and beyond what's expected.

PROFESSIONAL EXPERIENCE

BRANCH MANAGER
Franklin Mortgage Company, Phoenix, AZ 1990-1991
♦ Direct development of residential mortgages, processing and closing procedures, accounting department, and staff of fifteen.
♦ Involved in start-up of company, which evolved from Ben Franklin Mortgage Company.

SENIOR VICE PRESIDENT
Benjamin Franklin Mortgage Company, Scottsdale, AZ 1985-1990
♦ Instrumental in start-up and on-going operation of company, achieving status of #1 lender in Maricopa County in 1988 and 1989.
♦ Directed and co-directed all aspects of mortgage lending and company operations from loan production to loan closing/shipping.
♦ Loan production of company in excess of $200 million annually.
♦ Ensured all loans met turnaround time and clients served in an efficient, professional manner.
♦ Effectively managed growth of staff from three to sixty employees.
♦ Established and oversaw company policies, procedures, and systems.
♦ Personal loan approval up to $300,000.
♦ Supervised accounting department; proficient in accounting procedures.
♦ Opened and relocated ten offices in four years, all on schedule.

LOAN SALES SUPERVISOR
Merabank, Phoenix, AZ 1983-1985
♦ Supervised the shipping of $35 million per month, underwrote and approved loans purchased by the association, and coordinated all accounting procedures for department.

PREVIOUS EXPERIENCE

Corporate Collector - American Express; retail credit and finance positions.

EDUCATION

B.S. Business Administration, Major: Finance - Mankato State University, MN

- Resume writer: Claudia Jordan -

C. RYAN HOWARD
8384 Linwood Avenue, Cincinnati, OH 45226
(513) 321-1330

Career Objective: To motivate and train people to excel
in total life management.

QUALIFICATION HIGHLIGHTS

* Planned, conducted, and participated in numerous seminars, retreats, and orientations attended by 20 to 4,000 people.
* Highly skilled in motivating both small and large groups.
* Extensive counseling of individuals and family units in total life management.
* Very experienced in negotiation, conflict resolution, communication, and crisis management.
* Enjoys a zest for life and the daily challenge of motivating people to excel in all aspects of life.

PROFESSIONAL EXPERIENCE

PUBLIC SPEAKING
* Lectured at various world-wide motivational seminars with attendance from 2,000 to 5,000 people on subjects such as conflict resolution and personal motivation.
* Planned and conducted six workshops on marriage and parenting for groups up to 600 people.

LEADERSHIP and TRAINING
* Directed and co-directed internship training program for nine years. Instrumental in designing the program and its start-up.
* Trained groups and leaders in start-up and establishment of new organizations. Established four new organizations nation-wide, still operating successfully.
* Senior level leadership in organization which grew from 250 to 800 members in 3 years.
* Recruited and trained 120 leaders of on-going groups dealing with total life management issues such as interpersonal relationships and productive careers.
  - oversaw training groups of 100-200 people per year for five years.
  - offered continuous classes in conflict resolution, learning and applying counseling skills, developing communication skills, small group interaction, and time management.
  - strengthened and saved many marriages throughout program. Says one married man two years later, "We have seen how to make it, we're happy and have hope."

COUNSELING - Group and Individual
* Counseled single and married professionals in finance, sexuality, communication, parenting, and conflict resolution.
* Designed and conducted "Life Talk" program for juvenile detention center.

EMPLOYMENT HISTORY

1989-present	Senior Leader and Program Coordinator	Cincinnati Church of Christ Cincinnati, OH
1985-89	Senior Leader and Program Coordinator	Chicago Church of Christ Chicago, IL
1976-85	Director, Co-Director Internship Training	Mid County Church of Christ St. Louis, MO
1973-75	Student	Harding Graduate School

MILITARY EXPERIENCE

1971-72	Aircraft Maintenance Officer	4th Tactical Fighter Wing, USAF

Selected from 180 cadets to be Personnel Services Officer.
Received Vice-Commandant Award for outstanding performance.

EDUCATION

Masters of Theology, Harding Graduate School, TN, 1984   3.5 GPA
BA and BS (Geology), Clemson University, S.C., 1970   3.0 GPA

PERSONAL

Happily married with two children; enjoy sports. I am deeply committed to excellent performance, productivity, and the highest of ethics.

- Resume writer: Claudia Jordan -

Gordon Kent

5039 E. Paradise Drive ∎ Scottsdale, AZ 85254 ∎ (602) 996-5334

INTENT: BUSINESS MANAGEMENT

QUALIFICATION PROFILE

∎ Special talent for promoting ideas, projects, and goals into successful, profitable, business ventures.
∎ Excel in planning and directing complex events and projects.
∎ Highly organized, detail oriented, committed professional with unquestioned integrity.
∎ Adept at achieving superior performance from employees.
∎ Lifelong experience and enthusiasm in business management.

PROFESSIONAL EXPERIENCE AND ACCOMPLISHMENTS

BUSINESS MANAGEMENT
∎ Successfully managed operation of nationwide company expansion from one to four locations and employee increase from 40 to 250.
∎ Ensured smooth and profitable growth transition by recruiting capable talent, restructuring management systems for growth, encouraging open line of communication and feedback from new managers, and promoting customer service.
∎ Resulting gross annual company sales were upwards of $20 million.
∎ (Executive Manager, Lasma Corporation)

CONSULTING, SALES and MARKETING
∎ Planned, promoted, and orchestrated high caliber auctions throughout the United States grossing several million dollars. Auctions were attended by international audiences.
∎ During start-up of company, planned nationwide trip to establish customers, select, and market product. Grossed over $1 million in sales in two month tour of fourteen states.
∎ Counseled clients, marketed and promoted their investments; resulting sales were substantially greater than the original offering.
∎ Increased $35,000 sector investment to $225,000 through specific promotion and marketing, within one year.
∎ In five months, turned a $100,000 niche market investment into a $170,000 sale through promotion and marketing.
∎ (President and Owner, Kent Ltd.)

INVESTMENTS and MANAGEMENT
∎ Bought restaurant for investment purposes. Analyzed business, remodeled facility, implemented new management systems, revised menu, reduced number of employees, and restructured business hours.
∎ Increased profit margin by 25% and sold business 17 months later at a profit.
∎ (Owner and Manager, English Bear Delicatessen)

Gordon Kent

INVESTMENTS and MANAGEMENT

- Obtained control of national franchise for potential investment. Promoted customer service as top priority. Negotiated with corporate executives and won approval to introduce new products.
- Increased annual gross sales by 35%, during 14 month tenure.
- (Manager/option to buy, Swensen's Restaurant)

EMPLOYMENT HISTORY

1983-present	President and Owner	KENT LTD.
1989-90	Manager, with option to buy	SWENSEN'S RESTAURANT
1988-90	Owner and Manager	ENGLISH BEAR DELICATESSEN
1981-83	Executive Manager	LASMA CORPORATION
1980-81	General Manager	ZICHY-THYSSEN ARABIANS
1979-80	Supervisor	ROHR INDUSTRIES, INC.
1978-79	Director/Safety & Security	SHERATON-UNIVERSAL HOTEL
1964-78	Sergeant of Police	LOS ANGELES POLICE DEPT.

EDUCATION and TRAINING

Business Administration Major - Texas A & M
Degree in Police Administration - Los Angeles City College

OTHER FACTS

Reared in Central America, speak fluent Spanish, have current business contacts in Central and South America.

- Resume writer: Claudia Jordan -

Julie K. Pavlich

5039 E. Paradise Drive, Scottsdale, AZ 85254   (602) 996-3951

PROFESSION: Dental Financial Management, specializing in Collections

HIGHLIGHTS of QUALIFICATIONS

* Highly skilled in reduction of Accounts Receivable and bad debt collection.
* Completed one year Dental Practice Management Program with The Center For Professional Development; successfully implemented program.
* Expertise in evaluating, improving, and setting up financial management policies and systems.
* Ability to develop rapport, inform, and instruct others.
* Organized, thorough, and dedicated - willing to "go the extra mile."

PROFESSIONAL EXPERIENCE

DENTAL FINANCIAL MANAGEMENT
♦ Directed financial aspects of two-office dental practice, with $745,000 in annual revenue.
♦ Instrumental in profit margin increase of 24% through financial management efforts.
♦ Collected 57% of existing bad debts within 10 months, including bad debts up to five years old. Researched and selected capable collection agency to handle remainder of debts.
♦ Reduced overhead by 46% in one year.
♦ Trained front desk personnel in effectively collecting fees from patients in a timely and professional manner.
♦ Managed accounts payable/receivable, account reconciliation, general ledger, payroll, purchasing, and inventory control.
♦ Adapted accounting procedures to computer program. Proficient and knowledgeable with financial management software.
♦ Initiated tag system for inventory and purchasing control: requested bids and negotiated with dental suppliers.

LEASING and PROPERTY MANAGEMENT
♦ Set up IBM property management computer program for new apartment complex; computer literate and usage competent.
♦ Updated financial property status reports weekly and monthly.
♦ Performed accounts payable/receivable and collection duties, monitored overhead and rent roll.
♦ Hired, trained, and supervised leasing agents.
♦ Developed rapport and worked with prospective residents. Consistently top leasing producer.

EDUCATION and TRAINING

The Center For Professional Development, Practice Management Program,
Scottsdale, AZ - 1990-91

Loma Linda University, Infection Control, San Bernadino, CA - 1991

International Computer Systems, Five Minute Manager, San Diego, AZ - 1990

Implant Seminar, Elko, NV - 1990

Arizona Real Estate License, Phoenix, AZ - 1988

EMPLOYMENT HISTORY

1989-91	FINANCIAL MANAGER	Jeffrey Bartley, D.D.S. Ely, Nevada
1988-89	ASSISTANT PROPERTY MANAGER	Robertson Properties Scottsdale, Arizona
1987-88	LEASING MANAGER	Granada Management Corp. Phoenix, Arizona
1984-87	MANAGER of LEASING and RESIDENT RELATIONS	Hast & Company Denver, Colorado
1981-83	ACCOUNTING CLERK and RECEPTIONIST	Glicksman, Woodrow, Shaner, Babich & Savage Denver, Colorado

- Resume writer: Claudia Jordan -

BEVERLY DAIL

5039 E. Paradise Drive, Scottsdale, AZ 85254   (602) 996-5334

OBJECTIVE: Public relations and business management.

HIGHLIGHTS of QUALIFICATIONS

-- Enthusiastic, energetic, and polished professional with strong
   interpersonal skills and a willingness to "go the extra mile."
-- Accomplished in promoting public relations, especially in liaison roles.
-- Expert in business, property, and financial management.
-- Masters talent for planning and directing major events.
-- Easily establishes and maintains an important cadre of business and
   social contacts.

PROFESSIONAL EXPERIENCE

CORPORATE IMAGING / PUBLIC RELATIONS / MARKETING_____

* Identified desired image for an upscale, specialty shopping center and
  developed a marketing concept to attract an affluent clientele. Made
  presentations to key community members, meeting planners, hotels, and tour
  bus groups. Restructured weekend entertainment and organized charity
  benefits. Merchants reported very positive results from efforts.
--(MARKETING CONSULTANT, Westcor Partners - el Pedregal, 1990-present)

* Highly effective public relations representative and liaison between
  sophisticated member/owners and the corporate office for a master-planned
  community development. Set-up initial sales office and expertly assisted
  in real estate procedures and the administration of contracts. Served on
  Public Relations - Design Review Board for overall project.
--(MANAGER-COORDINATOR, Desert Mountain Development, 1985-90)

BUSINESS, PROPERTY, and FINANCIAL MANAGEMENT_____

* Managed three development complexes, supervised construction projects, and
  located new development property. Activated collection and eviction
  proceedings without the use of attorneys. Negotiated three lawsuits and
  settlements within one month. Developed landlord/tenant handbook for
  property management.
--(VICE PRESIDENT of ARIZONA OPERATIONS - Land Development & Mgmt,
  Affiliated American Corporation, 1984-85)

* Executed all business aspects of oil and real estate holdings, investments,
  and partnerships, as a Personal Business Manager. Performed as power of
  attorney for financial matters with authority to make decisions involving
  significant sums of money. Coordinated proper administration of assets
  with CPA, stockbroker, financial advisor, attorney, and bank officer.
  Served in a public relations capacity and as liaison between employer,
  business associates, and the general public.
--(PERSONAL BUSINESS MANAGER, A.J. Field Petroleum Consultant, 1976-83)

BEVERLY DAIL

Page Two

* Managed three office buildings, hotel, restaurant, apartment building, and
  condominium complex. Interfaced directly with tenants, resolved problems,
  and maintained high level of tenant satisfaction. Handled Accounts
  Receivable, Accounts Payable, Payroll, and Financial Statements. Prepared
  and maintained four complete sets of books.
    -Reduced monthly water bills in apartment complex by 25%.
    -Found $10,000 in uncollected rents, produced evidence, collected.
  --(PROPERTY MANAGER and BOOKKEEPER, William E. Ward & Assoc., 1975-79)

EVENT PLANNING_____

* Planned and orchestrated the Grand Opening of Desert Mountain Development
  with 1500 people attending. Managed and coordinated promotions/marketing,
  caterers, staff, entertainment, flowers, photograghers, etc. Project was
  within budget and effectively contributed to positive image of company.
  Organized numerous special events and social functions for company.
  --(MANAGER-COORDINATOR, Desert Mountain Development, 1985-90)

* Directed major annual fund-raiser. Planned and coordinated menus,
  caterers, and entertainment for 1200 people; conducted a raffle. Event
  raised $70,000 after costs.
  --(FUND-RAISING CHAIRMAN, Assistance League, 1982)

EARLIER EXPERIENCE

Office Manager/Secretary on the Board of Directors for an oil firm.
Office Manager for a Medical-Dental Center.
Other: Loan Officer, Escrow Officer, Executive Secretary.

EDUCATION

Washington State University, 3 years - Lower Columbia College, 1 year.

Real Estate License - current Arizona, prior California.
Notary Public - Arizona and California.

Wheaton School of Business - Financial; American Management Continuing Education
courses; Savings & Loan Continuing Education courses; Escrow courses; and
various management seminars.

ACTIVITIES

Arizona: Carefree/Cave Creek Chamber of Commerce - Secretary on the Board of
            Directors; Make a Wish Foundation - Member
California: Assistance League - Fund-raising Chairman, Secretary, Treasurer,
            and Newsletter Editor
            South Hills Country Club - Vice-Chairman of Ladies Golf
            Association, Social Director
            Soroptomist Club - Secretary, Treasurer

369

- Resume writer: Claudia Jordan -

Matt Parker
Guitarist – electric and acoustic
3056 Hillegass Avenue
Berkeley CA 94705
(510) 540-7750

Looking to play lead and rhythm guitar in an established, versatile dance band with
...pro attitude ...good equipment ...playing a good mixture of cover and original music

- ★ Serious, committed musician (singer, song writer, performer)
  who knows how to have a good time. No drug problems.
- ★ Over 15 years experience playing guitar in bands.
- ★ Contribute actively to making a band an exciting entity; good at
  working with a group to establish its unique sound.
- ★ Own quality equipment; willing to help pay for rehearsal space.
- ★ Available to practice weekly, or more if needed.
- ★ Stage show oriented – into lighting, mood, sweat, romance;
  dynamic and charismatic on stage; enjoy stimulating the crowd.

BAND EXPERIENCE

STORM (1974-75) Cooperstown NY - early metal hard rock (high schools)
  Lead Singer, Lead Guitar - founder

IRON HORSE (1975-76) Cooperstown NY - early metal hardrock (very theatrical/showy)
  Rhythm Guitar, Backup Vocals - cofounder

FIREHOUSE (1976) Oneonta NY - blues and hard rock (clubs)
  Rhythm Guitar, Backup Vocals

SOUTHERN ADIRONDACK HARD TIME BAND (1978-79) Oneonta NY - rock country, bluegrass (clubs)
  Lead Guitar, Backup Vocals

WHISKEY RIVER BAND (1979-80) Oneonta NY - southern blues, country rock, bluegrass (clubs)
  Lead Guitar, Backup Vocals

BUZZARD MOUNTAIN (1980-81) Oneonta NY - southern rock, blues rock, kickass dance band (clubs)
  Second Lead Guitar, Backup Vocals - cofounder

ROADHOUSE (1986-87) Berkeley CA - country and rock club dance band (clubs, parties)
  Lead Guitar, Backup Vocals - cofounder

THE MERCURIES (1987-89) Oakland - original and cover rock & roll, '60s-'80s dance music (clubs)
  Lead Guitar, Backup & Lead Vocals

LOOSE DIAMONDS (1990-Present) Bay Area/Contra Costa - Bluegrass-oriented rock, cover and originals
  Guitars, Mandolin, Vocals - cofounder   (parties, clubs, weddings, special events)

TECHNICAL SUPPORT

- Provided **lighting equipment** for all the bands I've worked with since 1979.
- Extensive **roadie work** with other bands (driving, lighting, set-up/tear-down, repairs).
- Own and provide **sound reinforcement** and **home recording equipment**.

EQUIPMENT OWNED

Amplification & Sound Reinforcement
- Yamaha MR-1642 mixing console
- Mesa Boogie Mark III combo amp
- GK bass amp
- Nomad guitar amp
- Fender Deluxe Reverb Amp
- Tascam 238 Syncaset 8-Track
- Yamaha RX-21 drum machine
- A.R.T. Multiverb III Effects Processor
- Shure microphones (one 58, one 57)
- Boss foot pedals, personal selection

Guitars
- Jackson Soloist solid body electric
- Gibson Firebird
- Yamaha APX-7 Electric Acoustic
- Guild D-40

Other instruments
- R.L. Givens Mandolin, A-style
- Spector Bass - Jazz/Precision

- Resume writer: Yana Parker -

SUSAN C. TALL • 800 Duboce Ave. #101 • San Francisco CA 94117 • (415) 552-5264

OBJECTIVE

A position as Public Information/Marketing Coordinator at U.C. Santa Cruz

SUMMARY OF QUALIFICATIONS

- Effective marketer with a record of achieving results through team leadership.
- Three years as manager for a performing artist.
- Proficient in database management, word processing, graphics, desktop publishing.
- Strong written, verbal, and interpersonal skills.
- Over eight years work experience in the CSU system.

EDUCATION

MBA, Marketing, Santa Clara State University, 1990
BA, Psychology, Sonoma State University, 1984

RELEVANT ACCOMPLISHMENTS

MARKETING

As Associate Director of the Center for Professional Development:
- Developed and directed marketing plans, resulting in revenue growth of $1.2 M.
- Expanded sales 15% by repositioning the Center in the seminar market.
- Increased revenue 8% by soliciting training contracts with Bay Area companies.
- Designed and implemented an intensive marketing plan for a new SFSU Center program that exceeded enrollment objectives.
    - Identified target market using database analysis.
    - Created low-cost, professional posters using a Macintosh graphics program.

As Manager for Allen Plane, a performing vocalist in the San Francisco Bay Area:
- Created a public image that attracted a loyal following from diverse audiences.
- Designed all promotional materials including press kits, logo, and fliers.
- Oversaw the production and distribution of a promotional video.

EVENTS COORDINATION

As Events Coordinator for Periwinkle & Hammer Public Relations:
- Assisted in media relations for New Langton Arts' Annual Christmas Store & Auction, and the Women in Architecture exhibition at the Western Merchandise Mart.
- Solicited vendor donations and managed databases to promote the Annual Gala Ball held at the California Academy of Sciences.

As Manager for Allen Plane:
- Arranged and managed numerous club performances; oversaw sound, lighting, staging, musicians, and scheduling.
- Coordinated Allen's participation in large fundraising events.

RELEVANT WORK HISTORY

ALLEN PLANE, VOCALIST/SONG STYLIST
    1988-present   **Manager**
SANTA CLARA STATE UNIVERSITY
    1990-present   **Office Manager**   Department of Public Affairs
    1988-90   **Research Administrator**   Physics Department
    1985-87   **Associate Director**   Center for Professional Development
PERIWINKLE & HAMMER PUBLIC RELATIONS
    1988   **Event Coordinator**
SONOMA STATE UNIVERSITY
    1983-84   **Student Programs Assist.**   International Student Programs

- Resume writer: Susan Ireland -

Thomas A. Colman

1370 Byron Dr., #5
Salinas, CA 93901
(408) 422-1650

OBJECTIVE

A position as a Multi-Subject Teacher

HIGHLIGHTS

- Achieve personal satisfaction through facilitating a child's social and intellectual growth.
- Talent for establishing rapport with students that encourages relaxed instructional interaction and mutual respect.
- Strength in lesson planning and delivery.
- Committed to contributing to society through the teaching profession.

EDUCATION AND CREDENTIAL

California State Teachers Multi-Subject Credential
Dominican College, Ukiah, CA, 1991

B.A., Liberal Arts
St. Johns College, Annapolis, MD

TEACHING EXPERIENCE

LESSON PLANNING
- Planned lessons appropriate to different learning modalities and ability levels for: Mathematics Social Studies Science English
- Generated material such as charts, maps, and tests to accompany established curriculum.
- Developed science lesson for Yosemite field trip.

CLASSROOM TEACHING
- Strive to deliver lessons in a meaningful and appropriate manner, encouraging interest, participation, and questioning.
- Recognize the need for proper pacing and wait time to ensure all students understand.
- Establish a relaxed, open, and two-way communication that empowers students to "buy into" the learning process.

CLASSROOM MANAGEMENT
- Develop and maintain proper educational environment by
  - clearly stating the school and classroom rules;
  - holding students accountable for their actions; and
  - being consistent and fair in administering positive and negative consequences.

PARENT-TEACHER RELATIONS
- Involve parents as fully as possible, recognizing the importance of family support.
- Participate in parent-teacher and I.E.P. conferences.

WORK HISTORY

1991-present	*Student Teacher*	**Laytonville Elementary School, Laytonville, CA**
1990-91	*Substitute Teacher*	**Laytonville Elementary, Middle, & High School, Laytonville, CA**
1989-90	*Carpenter*	**King Construction Company, Ukiah, CA**
1988	*Salesman*	**Pacific Sierra Insurance Company, Santa Rosa, CA**
1986-87	*Sales Support*	**Xerox Corporation, Santa Rosa, CA**
1980-85	*Route Manager*	**Silla Music Company, Oakland, CA**

- Resume writer: Susan Ireland -

Bill Furner, Classical Guitarist
Available for long- and short-term engagements

CLASSICAL & POPULAR
performed with recorded backgrounds produced especially for the artist
Repertoire includes:
Concierto De Aranjuez by Joaquin Rodrigo
Sleepers, Awake! by J.S. Bach
Arioso by J.S. Bach
Classical Gas by Mason Williams

RAGTIME, FLAMENCO, FINGER STYLE BLUES , & NOVELTY SONGS
repertoire includes original compositions as well as:
Maple Leaf Rag
Winnin' Boy Blues
Original Flamenco Solo

PERFORMANCES
Over 20 years experience performing in formal and informal settings, for large and small groups, for profit and nonprofit. Occasionally perform with Donna Salarpi, second violinist of the Marin Symphony.

Colleges/universities including:
Bringham Young University, The Marriott Center, audience - 13,000
Sonoma State University
College of Marin

Community Groups including:
Vietnam Veterans' Association, San Francisco Civic Auditorium & Old Waldorf
Marin County Mariners Cove Association
Waikiki Resort Area

Churches:
Numerous Mormon Churches throughout Marin County

Cafes including:
Dominic's Restaurant, San Rafael
Sleeping Lady Cafe, Fairfax
Crossroads Cafe, San Anselmo

PROFESSIONAL RECORDINGS
Composed and performed guitar pieces for professional recording entitled "Who is This Man Called Joseph?" Recording featured Scott Beach, John Brebner, and Steve O'Hara, and was distributed throughout the United States.

PERSONAL STATEMENT
Committed to educating the public about the beauty of classical music while incorporating original novelty songs into the performance.

TRAINING
Student of George Sakellariou, Head of Guitar Dept., San Francisco Conservatory of Music
Synthesis (Big Band), Brigham Young University
Influenced by John Williams' recordings

Bill Furner • *(415) 924-7417* • *7 Harbor Drive* • *Corte Madera, CA 94925*

- Resume writer: Susan Ireland -

ALLISON PAGE & JOHN LAWRENCE

Business: (415) 000-0000	1970 Pale Street #10
Residence: (415) 000-0000	San Francisco, CA 90000

JOB OBJECTIVE: Property Managers

SUMMARY OF QUALIFICATIONS

- Experienced in residential property management.
- Ability to perform building repairs including electrical, mechanical, plumbing, carpentry, and painting.
- Skilled at facilitating tenant cooperation; adept at settling disputes.
- Demonstrated effectiveness in upholding building policy and enforcing tenant compliance.
- Excellent references upon request.

EXPERIENCE

PROPERTY MANAGEMENT

- Managed a 60 year old apartment building in San Francisco for over three years, requiring consistent maintenance.
- Immediately after the 1989 Earth Quake:
  - Checked gas and water mains, and inspected building thoroughly for damage.
  - Provided emergency lighting during the 24-hour blackout.
  - Met with tenants regarding fire prevention, security, and safety procedures.
- Managed indoor and outdoor property maintenance:
  - Performed repairs, resulting in significant savings to the owner.
  - Hired and oversaw contractors for extensive jobs.
  - Personally conducted ongoing maintenance including plumbing, electrical, mechanical, carpentry, painting, swimming pool service, and gardening.
- Protected the owner against possible liability by establishing a rotating schedule for contracted maintenance of facilities and equipment.
- Represented the owner in tenant interactions by:
  - Showing apartments.
  - Reviewing building policies with new residents to promote cooperative atmosphere.
  - Encouraging tenant discussion to resolve disputes, intervening when necessary.
- Accurately documented problems with tenants; provided verification to owner for legal recourse.

TECHNICAL SKILLS - Allison Page

- As a Communications Contractor, performed prewiring for residential and commercial construction projects; read blueprints to determine specifications.
- Assisted carpenters building commercial and residential structures.
- Gained working knowledge of electrical wiring and plumbing as a helper to professional contractors during residential construction.
- As pool owner, maintained pumping and filtering systems, analyzed water to determine chemical use, and vacuumed and cleaned pool regularly.
- Planted and maintained various types of gardens, utilizing manual and power tools.

(Continued)

TECHNICAL SKILLS - John Lawrence

- As swimming instructor and life guard at the Parks and Recreation Departments of the Appleton and Milwaukee, WI:
    - Maintained pumping and filtering systems for public pools.
    - Monitored water quality and regulated chemical content.
- Assisted a licensed contractor in the remodeling and maintenance construction of residential and commercial properties.
- Landscaped and maintained grounds for the Parks and Recreation Departments of the Appleton and Milwaukee, WI.
- Managed the upkeep of buildings and grounds at Brush Ranch School, involving:
    - Structural carpentry and plumbing
    - Fence building and repair
    - Interior renovation
    - Installation of household appliances

EMPLOYMENT HISTORY and EDUCATION
Allison Page

1988-present	**Property Manager**	San Francisco, CA
1985-present	**Technical Consultant**	U.S. SPRINT: San Francisco, CA
1981-85	**Telecom Contractor**	G.E. BENDICKSON, S.F. Bay Area
1980-83	**Communications Tech**	EXECUTONE, Sacramento, CA
1976-80	**Technician**	PACIFIC TELEPHONE, Stockton, CA

• • • • • •

1973-75	**Business Administration**	San Joaquin Delta College, Stockton, CA
1976-80	**Industry Training**	Pole Climbing Electronics Key Systems, PBX, EPABX Voice/Data Communications & Networks

EMPLOYMENT HISTORY and EDUCATION
John Lawrence

1990-present	**Therapist**	CASTLE MEDICAL CENTER, Wailuku, HI
1988-1990	**Property Manager**	San Francisco, CA
1989-90	**Research Associate**	UNIVERSITY OF CALIFORNIA, San Francisco, CA
1987-88	**Therapist/Case Mgr.**	ST. MARY'S MEDICAL CENTER, Reno, NV
1984-86	**Therapist**	WASHOE MEDICAL CENTER, Reno, NV
1983	**Student**	UNIVERSITY OF WISCONSIN, Milwaukee, WI
1981-82	**Residential Counselor**	BRUSH RANCH SCHOOL, Santa Fe, NM
1980-81	**Health Educator**	YMCA OF METRO MILWAUKEE, Wauwatosa, WI

• • • • • •

1984	**Master of Science**	Rehabilitation Counseling University of Wisconsin, Milwaukee
1981	**Bachelor of Science**	Health Education and Recreation University of Wisconsin, La Crosse & Stout

- Resume writer: Susan Ireland -

Maureen Wells

Home: (540) 786-2248

150 Arrowhead Way
Patterson, CA 91738

OBJECTIVE: A position in Training or Management Development

SUMMARY OF QUALIFICATIONS

- Strength in strategic planning, group facilitation, presentation, and program development.
- 12 years experience in training/counseling/educating.
- 4 years experience in developing effective training materials.
- Skilled at understanding and relating to people from a wide variety of cultures and socioeconomic backgrounds.

WORK HISTORY

1991-present	**Health Educator**	WEST PATTERSON HEALTH CENTER
1987-1990	**Trainer** **Interview Board Member** **Team Leader** **Customer Account Coor.**	ANDERSON CORPORATION, Oakland
1985-87	**Anchor/Reporter** **Writer/Producer**	KCPO NEWS DEPARTMENT, San Jose
1984-85	**Assignment Editor**	KRUK NEWS DEPARTMENT, Redding

PROFESSIONAL EXPERIENCE

NEEDS ASSESSMENT

Anderson Corporation:
- Determined a need for extensive team building to successfully convert the work style from American individualism to Japanese teamwork.
- Initiated the concept of a pilot team, which proved effective in setting the tone for team development throughout the company.
- Established the need for cross-functional training without interruption of daily operations.
- Set priorities with regard to each worker's training requirements.

Paterson Health Center:
- Determined target groups involved with tobacco use in order to provide relevant health education.
- Analyzed problems of addressing this population and determined appropriate means of communication.
- Tested clients to evaluate their knowledge of tobacco use and its effect on the body.
- Worked individually with clients to determine what triggers their addictive behavior and how to treat it.

(Continued)

MATERIALS DEVELOPMENT

Anderson Corporation:
- Created all training material for each job in the Oakland Division (approximately 25 people). Identified functions, wrote modules, and developed visual aides.

West Patterson Health Center:
- Authored workbooks designed to teach clients of varying levels of ability, taking into consideration a wide range of cultural backgrounds.

KCPO and KRUK:
- Developed stories that captured the attention of viewers and evoked positive responses.

PRESENTATIONS

Anderson Corporation:
- Professionally trained at an intensive "Train the Trainer" seminar; recognized for my natural ability to communicate effectively.
- Conducted instructional and hands-on job training. Tested participants, most of whom passed with scores of at least 95%.

KCPO and KRUK:
- Consistently maintained high rating for my segments of the news broadcasts, often getting complimentary calls from the public.

West Patterson Health Center:
- Conducted twice-daily workshops in tobacco education to groups of up to 30 participants.

EDUCATION

Bachelor of Arts, Liberal Arts, San Jose State University, 1976
Master of Arts, Applied Linguistics, San Jose State University, 1978
Master of Arts (in progress), Clinical Psychology, Fairmount University

- Resume writer: Susan Ireland -

JEANETTE PARR
392 Happy Mountain Road • Biddeford, CA 91548
(307) 741-1832

OBJECTIVE

Assistant to the Events Coordinator

HIGHLIGHTS

- Experienced at assisting in special events production.
- Excellent at performing administrative duties including office support, telephone work, and bookkeeping.
- Resourceful; ability to quickly find what is needed within budget.
- Skilled at implementing on-site logistics.

RELEVANT EXPERIENCE

SPECIAL EVENTS
- Currently assisting the producer of an annual fashion show for 550 people, a fundraiser projected to raise $30,000 for the Biddeford Volunteer Center.
  - Coordinate rehearsals, fittings, schedules, and logistics for approximately 63 models, ages 5 to 18.
  - Solicit See's Candy and Macy's for product donations.
  - Regularly collaborate with executive committee to plan event and monitor progress.
- Co-managed an auction for Happy Mountain School which raised $20,000.
  - Determined budget, solicited donations, and designed system for collecting cash during event.
  - Arranged logistics including event location, catering, and personnel.
- Served as hospitality chairman on numerous committees, being fully responsible for meeting arrangements.

ADMINISTRATION
- Managed a dental office for over 5 years (prior to work history below), including scheduling, bookkeeping, and personnel management.
- Coordinated 12 committees, as P.T.A. President, which collaborated with school administration on major fundraising projects.

RECENT WORK HISTORY (while full-time parent)

1990-present	**Assistant Event Producer**	Biddeford Volunteer Center, Biddeford
1990-1991	**Philanthropy Co-chairman**	National Charity League, Biddeford
1989-1990	**Parliamentarian**	Powell Junior High P.T.A., Biddeford
1987-1988	**P.T.A. President**	Happy Mountain School, Biddeford
1985-1986	**Fundraiser/Chairperson**	Happy Mountain School P.T.A, Biddeford
1984-1985	**Vice President**	San Ramon Dental Auxiliary, San Ramon

EDUCATION

Liberal Arts, San Anselmo State University, San Anselmo, CA

Additional coursework:
Dale Carnegie: Basic Communication and Management Skills
Empowerment Training
Communication and Motivational Skills

- Resume writer: Susan Ireland -

RUTHANNE ROSEN
8 Dorchester Drive
East Brunswick, New Jersey 08816
(908) 254-1839

OBJECTIVE

Entry Level Position in Sales/Marketing.

SUMMARY OF QUALIFICATIONS

- *Readily inspire the confidence of clients; special talent for relating well to all types of people.*
- *Ambitious, goal- and profit-oriented; well organized and resourceful.*
- *Capable of performing industry analysis, including profitability, growth, and market share.*
- *Familiar with international marketing techniques.*

RELEVANT EXPERIENCE

1990 (Summer)   **Marketing Intern**   *LEHMAN BROTHERS, New York, NY*

- *Assisted stock brokers in expanding client base:*
  - *contacted potential clients through extensive cold calling.*
  - *consistently ranked in top 10% among interns for creating new client relationships.*
  - *developed record keeping system for tracking calls.*
- *Developed good working knowledge of the stock market through observation and intern training.*

1989 (Summer)   **Sales Associate**   *JERSEY CAMERA, East Brunswick, NJ*

- *Successfully sold video and audio equipment on a commission basis:*
  - *provided customers with technical specifications about merchandise.*
- *Developed excellent rapport with clients:*
  - *enhanced client loyalty to store and resolved customer service problems.*

1986 (Summer)   **Sales Associate**   *BENNETON, Beach Haven, NJ*

- *Assisted customers in selection and purchase of clothing.*

EDUCATION

B.S. *(cum laude), Business Administration (concentration in Marketing), 1991 - UNIVERSITY OF HARTFORD*
Dean's List
GPA in major: 3.7

Relevant Courses

- *Strategic Marketing Management* • *Multinational Marketing* • *Management Policy and Strategy*
- *Market Research* • *Principles of Retailing* • *Consumer Behavior* • *Finance* • *Advertising*
- *Quantitative Analysis* • *Managerial and Financial Accounting* • *Human Behavior in Organizations*

AWARDS AND ACTIVITIES

American Marketing Association
Founder of SIGMA DELTA TAU Sorority at University of Hartford

- Resume writer: Judi Robinovitz -

KAREN LYNNE BRETT

402 April Drive • Atlanta, Georgia 30322 • (404) 712-0444

OBJECTIVE **Senior management position in consumer financial services.**

HIGHLIGHTS
- ★ More than 10 years' senior executive experience in customer service and banking.
- ★ Recognized expert in consumer financial services policy and delivery.
- ★ Special sensitivity to re-engineering workflows to enhance service and improve staff productivity.
- ★ Proven record of success with managing large organizations.
- ★ Strong analytic and problem solving skills.
- ★ Member of the Bar in Virginia and District of Columbia.

PROFESSIONAL EXPERIENCE

1989-present

Vice President, Customer Service
MASTER CARD, TRAVEL RELATED SERVICES, Atlanta, GA

Responsible for round-the-clock inbound telephone operation, annually handling 13 million customer service calls and 1 million disputes:

- Manage a staff of 1,000 employees in several departments:
  - Dispute Resolution   - Customer Service
  - Telemarketing Administration   - Credit Administration
- Administer an annual budget in excess of $30 million.
- Designed and implemented innovative programs to re-engineer workflow, enhancing productivity and quality.
- Success reflected in consistently exceeding exacting quality, timeliness, and unit cost goals.

1986-1989

Vice President/Chief of Staff
METRO INVESTMENT BANK, New York, NY

Organized and administered syndicated loan department:

- Directed the competitive deal-making activities of transactors and sales associates.
- Achieved pre-tax earnings almost 50% higher than projected.
- Managed departmental budgets and financial reporting requirements, including MIS requirements, expense management and control, and computer applications.
- Identified and resolved legal and accounting issues inherent in product innovation.

1984-1986

Vice President
METROCORP (USA), INC., Los Angeles, CA

Initiated or directed all Metrocorp government, public relations, and marketing initiatives in 16 western states:

- Designed and implemented programs to effectuate legislative goals at the federal, state, and local levels:
  - instrumental in achieving passage of interstate banking legislation in California.
- Favorably positioned Metrocorp and its subsidiaries in 16 western states through:
  - media and advertising   - contributions programs   - community activities
- Pioneered Metrocorp's emergence as a major player in the retail and corporate markets in California.

380

- continued -

KAREN LYNNE BRETT

PROFESSIONAL EXPERIENCE (continued)

1983-1984

Vice President
METROCORP SAVINGS, San Francisco, CA

Appointed as a member of the initial senior management acquisition team:

- Managed the merger of 2 subsidiaries involving over 100 branches.
- Supervised branch financial reporting and analyzed branch productivity.
- Developed a marketing strategy for entrance into and positioning in the Northern California savings and loan marketplace.

1978-1982

Director, Office of Consumer Affairs
FEDERAL CREDIT UNION ADMINISTRATION, Arlington, VA

Directed the regulation and examination of 13,000 federally chartered credit unions for compliance with federal and state consumer credit laws:

- Hired and managed a staff of 90 policy-makers and examiners.
- Designed and oversaw the national complaint program covering 23,000 members of credit unions.

1973-1978

Attorney Advisor/Hearing Officer
NATIONAL SERVICES ADMINISTRATION, Bethesda, MD

Ensured the quality, legal sufficiency, and consistency of Board hearings and decisions on disputes, frequently involving multi-million dollar claims.

EDUCATION

1977

L.L.M., EMORY UNIVERSITY LAW SCHOOL
Major: Government Contracts

1973

J.D., HARVARD COLLEGE OF LAW

1971

B.A. (summa cum laude), NORTHWESTERN UNIVERSITY
Majors: Philosophy and Anthropology

Continuing Education:

1981-1982

OFFICE OF PERSONNEL MANAGEMENT, Senior Executive Service
Management Training Program

PROFESSIONAL AFFILIATIONS

1974-Present   Member, Virginia, Maryland, Georgia, and Illinois Bars

1978-Present   Member, Committee on Consumer Financial Services, American Bar Association

1976-1978   Member, Consumer Advisory Council to the Federal Reserve Board

1987   Registered Securities Representative, National and New York (passed Series 7 and 63)

Rebecca Kaminsky Shidel

10667-1 Montgomery Road • Cincinnati, Ohio 45242 • (513) 489-7019

OBJECTIVE

Management position in marketing, promotions, or public relations, with responsibility for planning corporate events.

HIGHLIGHTS

★ *20+ years of management experience in sales, marketing, and public relations.*
★ *Successful with planning and implementing events.*
★ *Demonstrated talent for educational training and implementation.*
★ *Proven record of generating new business and increasing sales volume.*
★ *Charismatic and persuasive; able to build instant rapport.*
★ *Proficient using IBM PC and Macintosh computers; skilled in DOS, PageMaker, WordPerfect, and BASIC.*

EXPERIENCE

Sales/Marketing
- *Designed and produced all promotional materials for major programs at GEORGIA TECH RESEARCH INSTITUTE and STEWART'S:*
  - *organized advertising campaigns, press releases, media contacts.*
  - *wrote original copy, designed layouts, created clip art.*
  - *selected appropriate advertising agencies, printers, and mail houses.*
- *Created a major new market for STEWART'S, inaugurating a teen board.*
- *Actively participated on a team to create the new corporate image and logo, "Where Else But Stewart's," winning an award for creative advertising.*
- *Most productive ENVIRONMENTAL PERSONNEL recruiter, locating candidates on a national basis to fill positions in the environmental industry.*
- *Made cold calls to find new clients to sell BERNINA merchandise, increasing their base by 75%.*

Event Planning and Promotions
- *Coordinated GEORGIA TECH RESEARCH INSTITUTE's conferences and training programs, both on- and off-site:*
  - *developed all promotional materials and coordinated their production.*
  - *determined target markets.*
  - *arranged conference facilities, travel, accommodations, and catering for 50-2,500 attendees and presenters.*
- *First employee to create events designed to increase STEWART'S customer base; organized all aspects of major store events for 8 department stores:*
  - *coordinated all press releases, TV appearances, and other publicity.*
  - *arranged physical logistics.*
  - *enlisted national personalities as guest speakers.*
  - *hosted events and resolved on-site problems.*

- continued -

Rebecca Kaminsky Shidel

EXPERIENCE
(continued)

Communications/Media Engagements

- *Made personal appearances on TV and radio to promote upcoming events at STEWART'S, BERNINA, and LYNTEX.*
- *Keynote speaker at colleges and department stores across America, discussing diverse topics, from women's issues to fashion merchandising.*
- *Featured in LYNTEX and BERNINA press releases and as a lead speaker at their national conferences, introducing their newest products.*
- *Conducted week-long formal BERNINA product training programs for store owners and staff.*
- *Taught college level courses to prospective retailers:*
  - *advertising*   - *event planning*   - *marketing*
  - *merchandising*   - *salesmanship*   - *public relations*

Management

- *Managed public relations and marketing departments for all employers, supervising teams of up to 12 people:*
  - *trained new staff members in effective marketing/media techniques, monitored and reviewed staff performance.*
  - *coordinated staffing and delegated responsibilities for major events and conferences.*
  - *monitored operational budgets, especially for advertising.*
- *Supervised all promotions and advertising for 48 stores in 4 states selling BERNINA sewing machines.*
- *Second in command at ENVIRONMENTAL PERSONNEL: made ultimate decisions about interviews, billing, advertising, client/candidate contacts.*

WORK HISTORY

1989-present	**Account Executive/ Technical Recruiter**	*ENVIRONMENTAL PERSONNEL SERVICES, Cincinnati, Ohio*
1988-89	**Marketing Director of Continuing Education**	*GEORGIA TECH RESEARCH INSTITUTE, Atlanta, Ga.*
1986-88	**Detail Account Executive**	*SANDOZ CORPORATION, Atlanta, Ga.*
1983-86	**Retail Merchandising Instructor**	*SPENCERIAN and BAUDER COLLEGES Louisville, Ky. and Atlanta, Ga.*
1978-83	**Public Relations Director/ Special Events Coordinator**	*STEWART'S DEPARTMENT STORES, Louisville, Ky.*
1976-77	**Merchandising Department Head**	*BRADFORD COLLEGE, Pittsburgh, Pa.*
1972-76	**SE Regional Sales Manager**	*SWISS-BERNINA, INC., Atlanta, Ga.*
1969-72	**Sales Coordinator**	*LYNTEX CORP, New York, N.Y.*

EDUCATION

M.S., *Education, UNIVERSITY OF LOUISVILLE, Ky. (in progress)*
B.S. *(cum laude), Education/Home Economics, HUNTER COLLEGE, N.Y. (Major GPA: 3.8)*

- Resume writer: Judi Robinovitz -

LAWRENCE GERE

505 H Canyon Oaks Drive
Orinda, CA 94605
(415) 766-7616

OBJECTIVE:

To utilize sales expertise in an account management capacity.

SUMMARY OF QUALIFICATIONS:

- Twelve years sales, technical manufacturing, and management experience
- Specializing in mainframe, mini-computer, and personal computer sales, and their applications in workstations and network topologies
- Stimulated account development with Microsoft Inc., Georgia Pacific, Weyerhauser, National Semiconductor, and Sunstrand Data Control
- Excellent oral and written communication skills
- Surpassed all sales goal expectations consistently
- Innovative strategies for new account penetration

EMPLOYMENT HISTORY:

12/83 - 12/89   **Digital Equipment Corporation**, Bellevue, WA
Account Manager
- Created and managed new account opportunities in the high technology manufacturing arena
- Achieved recognition awards for consistent budget attainment
- Exceeded averaged sales quota of $1.8 million by 60%
- More than doubled fiscal year 1989 sales quota by 265%
- Actively participated in community organizations to develop and broaden customer base

11/82 - 12/83   **Swan Computers**, Bellevue, WA
Account Manager
- Managed major corporate account in Washington and Oregon
- Nationally ranked as the leading dealer sales representative for Apple Computers for 1983
- Exceeded sales quota by 150%

10/81 - 11/82   **Sears Business Systems Center**, Bellevue, WA
Sales Representative
- Designed optimal personal computer solutions for various retail customer requirements
- Ranked top sales representative in the retail facility in 1982

EDUCATION:

California State University, Dominguez Hills, Carson, CA
Bachelor of Science in Management, 1974

University of Southern California, Los Angeles, CA
Graduate Administration Studies, 1976

Miscellaneous experience includes six years in Procurement in the Semi-Conductor Industry.

REFERENCES AVAILABLE UPON REQUEST

- Resume writer: Cynthia Mackey -

CARLTON MACKEY
Information Systems Specialist

1121 Magnolia Street
Oakland, CA 94607
510-451-5279

PROFILE

- Over 8 years of experience in the field of information systems hardware and software.
- Built and troubleshot networks within a majority of the popular architectures.
- Integrated and diagnosed Novell and OS/2 microcomputer LANs, and LANs utilizing Windows 3.0.
- Knowledgeable on 10baseT and thin-net Ethernet, coaxial and twisted pair ArcNet and IBM Token Ring.

REPRESENTATIVE ACCOMPLISHMENTS

System Design and Implementation

- Installed and configured OS/2 applications.
- Configured Windows 3.0 on OS/2 LAN.
- Designed, sold, and installed microcomputer LANs.
- Worked with clients on problem definition and solutions.
- Integrated PS/2 systems into SNA environments.
- Interfaced PCs to DECnet LAN.

Maintenance and Diagnostics

- Troubleshot crashed file servers and stabilized environments.
- Analyzed application software conflicts on LAN.
- Supported customers for PS/2 and PC Token Ring LAN.
- Diagnosed faults in the network to wiring closet level.
- Tested and troubleshot microprocessor based circuit boards by programming 68000 emulators.
- Troubleshot prototype circuits and ran computer circuit simulations using CAD.

Training

- Trainer to MIS staff on multi-server IBM OS/2 LANserver LAN (100 + users).
- Created user and administrator manuals.
- Developed and taught OS/2 training sessions.
- Taught basic electronics, digital electronics, PC systems troubleshoot and repair, and MS DOS.
- Instructed "How To Use The Novell Operating System" and "Manage The Novell Operating System"

Applications

OS/2, Knowledgeware, Microfocus, XDB, Novell Netware on 10baseT, PC 5250 terminal emulation for IBM AS400 communications, Assembly language, Basic, Circuit board design using CAD, Lotus 123, WordPerfect 5.1, Microsoft Word, Dbase, PARADOX, Q&A, and similar popular software packages.

EXPERIENCE

Information Systems Consultant	Mervyn's, Hayward, CA	1991 - present
Systems Designer/Analyst	Pyramid Business Systems, Berkeley, CA	1990 - 1991
Systems Engineer	Western Computer Group, Burlingame, CA	1990
Systems Integrator	Vitalink Corporation, Fremont, CA	1989 - 1990
Instructor, Electronics	Inter-City Services, Berkeley, CA	1987 - 1990
Systems Engineer	DataNet, Oakland, CA	1989
Engineering Technician B	Siemens Ultrasound, Pleasanton, CA	1985 - 1987
Engineering Technician C	Gould/AMI Semiconductor, Santa Clara, CA	1983 - 1985

EDUCATION

Cogswell College, San Francisco, CA
<u>A.S.</u>, Electronics Technology, December 1982
Four years towards Bachelors Degree in Engineering

385

- Resume writer: Cynthia Mackey -

KELLY D. McCOMBS

27664 Blackhawk Court • LeClaire, IA • 52753
(309) 764-2477

PROFILE

A highly motivated individual oriented to a fast-paced retail sales and marketing environment through 13 years experience. Excellent interpersonal and speaking ability with a talent for training and motivating others. Proven skills in market trend analysis, budgeting, product selection, merchandising and management; emphasis on client services, needs assessment and negotiations.

RELEVANT EXPERIENCE

BUYING
- Bargain assertively and effectively with vendor representatives locally, in New York and Dallas.
- Increased *Men's* department sales by 35%, with a volume of $1,186,300 in a four year period.
- Increased *Misses* department sales by 179%, raising volume from $1,273,000 to $3,547,800 in eight year period.

MERCHANDISING/MANAGEMENT
- Analyze stock levels, product turnover, markup and markdown procedures; project budgets based on sales/market trends for monthly and annual goals.
- As Buyer for eleven outlets of private department store, travel to each store to supervise and merchandise the product assortment.
- Present semi-annual corporate seminars on product knowledge and merchandise assortments.
- Participated in preparations for openings of eight new stores.
- Implemented a major vendor fashion presentation by organizing the efforts of the manufacturer representative and four buyers.

EDUCATION

Western Illinois University
Major - Textiles and Clothing • Minor - Business

EMPLOYMENT HISTORY

1978 - present
VON MAUR • DAVENPORT, IOWA
Buyer - Misses Update Better Sportswear *(6/83-present)*
Buyer - Men's Clothing *(1/79-6/83)*
Clerical - Men's Division *(8/78-1/79)*
Intern *(6/78-8/78)*

- Resume writer: Kim Coats -

DONALD H. SMELTZER, JR.

260 27th Street SW · Naples, Florida 33964 · (813) 455-9305

Objective: Warehouse/Inventory Control

PROFILE

Over 19 years stable employment history, utilizing many talents in variety of fields. Obtained broad scope of shop experience for a major manufacturer of construction and farm equipment parts, demonstrating loyalty until terminating due to plant closing.

STRENGTHS

★ Fast learner with a wide range of practical skills.
★ Adept at performing routine inventory control warehouse functions - experienced at handling shipping and receiving.
★ Knowledgeable with industrial equipment and manufacturing processes.
★ Skilled machine operator - wide background of experience on numerous machines.
★ Proven track record of performing with little or no supervision.

EMPLOYMENT HISTORY

CASE IH, East Moline, ILLINOIS, September 1990 to April 1991
Machine Operator
- Maintain quality control in various areas of production.
- Operate numerous machines, i.e., drills, mills, hones, lathes and grinders, to ensure economic and timely production of company products.

WEIGOLD & SONS AIR CONDITIONING, INC., Naples, Florida, 1989 to 1990
Warehouse Inventory Control
- Managed and preserved organization of company products and equipment stored in warehouse.
- Monitored incoming and outgoing shipments, facilitating efficiency in delivering sold goods and acquiring new inventory.

AQUALETIC SWIM CLUB, Rock Island, Illinois, 1979 to 1989
Seasonal Maintenance Worker
- Responsible for all aspects of maintenance on 3 outdoor swim pools including plumbing, electrical, carpentry and cement upkeep/repairs.
- Assisted Manager in club operations - conducted facility tours, completed membership paperwork, responded to telephone inquiries.

CASE IH, Rock Island, Illinois, 1972 to 1988
Production Worker
- Performed multiple jobs during term of employment, obtaining numerous skills:
  - Operated various machines
  - Used holding devices
  - Assembled component parts
  - Performed set-ups
  - Worked with hydraulic cylinders
  - Operated forklift

MILITARY

VIETNAM VETERAN - HONORABLE DISCHARGE
Ft. Riley, Kansas

EDUCATION/TRAINING

BLACK HAWK COLLEGE, Moline, Illinois
Introduction to Numerical Control Machining

- Resume writer: Kim Coats -

JANE FOSTER
592 SURREY CIRCLE
SINCLAIR, WA 98305
TELEPHONE: HOME 739-8226
           OFFICE 742-9140

I WRITE . . .

. . . FACT: Straightforward explanations of technical obfuscation, precise analysis of
                 complex laws, deciphered engineering jargon, accurate accounts of news
                 events and probing interviews with newsmakers . . .

. . . FLACK: The honing of a candidate's rhetoric, boosting of a brainstorm, promo for a
                 product, ballyhoo for a rally, packaging of a product . . .

. . . FLUFF: Breezy pieces on coping, hoping, getting along in a mad world; features,
                 columns, reviews, anecdotes, sense and nonsense . . .

. . . FINAL DRAFTS: Impeccable punctuation, verbs and nouns in complete harmony,
                 graceful syntax, accurate spelling, precise wording, proper references,
                 readable prose and fluid text . . .

I AM LOOKING FOR A JOB THAT DEMANDS A GOOD COMMUNICATOR

Staff Writer	Public Energy Company	1987 - present
Tax Editor	Commonweal Clearing House	1982 - 1986
Editor	American Bay Press	1979 - 1982
Woman's Page Editor	Sinclair Constitution	1964 - 1967
General Reporter	Grand City Independent	1963 - 1964

Dale J. Wickett
11670 N.E. 18th. St.
Miami, FL 33166
(305) 887-1801

Objective: Position as Assistant Golf Professional I or II under a class "A" Golf Professional.

SUMMARY OF QUALIFICATIONS

- ▸ Strong desire to establish a career in pro- golf field.
- ▸ Sociable, enjoy the challenge of working with people to bring out their best.
- ▸ Exceptional success in establishing rapport with members of all cultures and economic levels.
- ▸ Aggressive, enthusiastic and energetic self-starter.
- ▸ Thoroughly enjoy coordinating and managing projects.

RELEVANT SKILLS AND BACKGROUND

P.G.A. affiliation
- Began P.G.A. apprenticeship in 1989.
- Have accumulated twenty-six points towards membership.
- Successfully completed Business School #1.
- Play in as many section and chapter events as schedule permits.

Pro-Shop
- As Assistant II controlled day to day operations including:
    -opening and closing shop - sales -pricing -ordering -receiving
    -collecting cart and green fees -posting handicaps.
    -keeping payroll and other records relating to retail operation.
    -stocking of all golf merchandise, equipment and clothing.
- Daily, using three computers, entered data on inventory, handicaps, cart and green fees.
- Solely responsible for all clubs in the shop.
- Acted as liaison between our club and other country clubs and guests, in properly billing accounts.
- Assisted in organizing multiple tournaments with different formats, verifying guests handicaps.
- Conducted Junior Clinics, and instructed five to seven hours per week.

Caddie Master
- Worked as Assistant to Starter ensuring proper starting time procedures.
    -handled all Bagroom operations, including billing of club and cart rentals.
    -made sure carts available and in good order.

EMPLOYMENT HISTORY

1989-91	Asst. golf pro. II	HIALEAH COUNTRY CLUB, Hialeah, FL
1987-89	Asst. golf pro. II	DAVIE SHORES COUNTRY CLUB, DAVIE Shores, FL
1985-87	Owner/Operator	QUALITY PATIO, Miami, FL
1984-85	Accountant	TAMARIC HOTELS AND RESORTS, Miami, FL
1979-84	Aircraft mechanic	U.S. NAVY

EDUCATION AND TRAINING

AA-BROWARD COMMUNITY COLLEGE, Davie, FL
P.G.A. Business School #1, Kansas City, MO
A.M.S.-U.S. Navy, Virginia Beach, VA

389

- Resume writer: Calvin Baird -

RONLYN R. HENEGAR
7 Brown Road
Montrose, Colorado 81401
303/249-6501

_____

OBJECTIVE: A position as a heavy equipment operator for a company located on
the Western Slope of Colorado.

HIGHLIGHTS OF QUALIFICATIONS

* Over 9 years experience as an operator on heavy equipment.
* Operated a D9 dozer on the McPhee Dam Project.
* Consider the over-all project as important as my direct responsibilities;
creative and proud of work.
* Learn quickly and willing to work hard; known for physical and mental strength.
* Work as a Dozer Instructor at Rancho Murieta Training Center, which has the
reputation of being the best in the world.

RELEVANT EXPERIENCE

Dozer Operator
•Operated D9; D8H; D7; D6D; D6C; D5; and Kamatsus.
•Pioneering, building roads, logging, and finishing in very steep, rocky, dangerous
terrain. Successful as a finish hand with clay fill on D9 - McPhee Dam Project.
•Off-shore work; mixing mud from a dredger. Able to keep up with larger dozers
while operating a D7.
•Successful at finish work with large dozers, saving blade time and money.

Blade Operator
•12 and 14 Cats; rough blade haul roads, ditching.
•16 Cat; haul road maintenance.

Backhoe Operator
•Trenches; remove silt from ponds; lay pipe.

Excavator Operator
•Bantam and Cat 245; steep pioneer road pulling up huge granite rock from slope;
finishing fill slopes.

Loader Operator
•988; 980; 950; loaded trucks with shot rock.
•966; grade check

Linkbelt Operator
•18 ton crane; tearing down mining operation.

Oiler
•140 and 60 ton cranes; moving, rigging, putting together 140 ton trucks.

Scraper
•Cut and fill.

Grade Checker
•8 mile project

- CONTINUED -

RELEVANT EXPERIENCE - continued

Compactor
- Roller
- 825 compactor

Dozer Instructor
- D9; D8H; D6D; D6C; D5;
- Write and follow curriculum. After being on the job only one month, was trusted to write my own curriculum.
- Directed safety meetings.
- Trained over 150 people, majority being men; 148 students passed course.
- Taught apprentices and journeymen: leach ditching, sloping, pioneering, finishing, pushing scrapers, following grade stakes.
- Oversaw C-Testing for non-union members to become union journeymen.
- Developed hand-out on techniques of moving dirt.
- Served as member of review board, determining disciplinary action.
- Successfully solved everyday personnel and logistical problems by making good decisions and using sound judgement.

WORK HISTORY

1989-Present **Dozer Instructor** RANCHO MURIETA TRAINING CENTER Rancho Murieta, CA
1987-1989 Pregnancy Leave - Household Management
1985-1987 **Heavy Equipment Operator** SIERRA CONSTRUCTORS San Francisco, CA
1985 **Dozer Operator** GUY F. ATKINSON (NKA SIERRA CONSTRUCTORS) Terminal Island, CA
1980-1984 **Dozer and Blade Operator, Oiler** GUY F. ATKINSON McPhee Dam Project Dolores, CO
1979 **Grade Checker** SCHMIDT & TIAGO Grand Lake-West Vail Denver, CO

EDUCATION

1979 - Operating Engineers (Local 9) Apprenticeship Program

SUMMARY

I am a 34 year old single mother of one with the desire to live on the Western Slope of Colorado. I am willing to take a cut in pay in order to make this move. Over the past 11 years, I have made a place for myself in what is typically known as a man's world by working hard and being accountable for my own responsibilities. I have earned the reputation of being a fast and accurate operator. In the past, I have handled any personnel problems, created by being a woman in this occupation, without costing management time, headaches, or money. I strongly feel that my experience and enthusiasm would be a good addition to any company. I am available for interviews at your convenience.

- REFERENCES AVAILABLE UPON REQUEST -

- Resume writer: Vicki Law-Miller -

BRIAN BRIARSSON
9999 West Highway 999
Silver City, NM 99999
(999) 999-9999

SUMMARY: Experienced in pipeline and oilfield construction work.
Since 1986, specialist in asbestos abatement, including
job management and crew supervision.

Work History:

1989-present   GENERAL SUPERINTENDENT, SPRAY SYSTEMS
                  ENVIRONMENTAL, PHOENIX, AZ. Superintendent for
                  asbestos abatement contractor at Chino Mines of
                  Hurley, NM. Supervise 30-person crew, set up
                  jobs, oversee safety, order materials, assure
                  that job is done on time.

                  * Current job involves setting up freestanding
                  asbestos containments around 70-foot-high boilers
                  in a working copper smelter. This has been
                  accomplished with no disruption to plant
                  operations or personnel.

1986-89   SUPERINTENDENT, BCP CONSTRUCTION, PHOENIX, AZ.
                  Asbestos abatement for schools, hospitals, office
                  buildings from Kentucky to California. Ran crews
                  of one to 45 workers.

                  * Supervised complete asbestos abatement
                  project for three floors of a high-rise building
                  (Mera Bank) in Phoenix, Az.

1980-86   APPRENTICE WELDER, WAYNE HOUSTON WELDING,
                  MEDICINE HAT, ALBERTA, CAN. General welding
                  duties, pipe cutting, and job set-up.

1975-80   ASSISTANT DRILLER, ROUGHNECK; VARIOUS OIL
                  COMPANIES, ALBERTA, CAN. Worked on large oil
                  rigs.

Education / Training:

1989   Advanced Supervision of Abatement, Georgia Inst. of
               Technology.
1988   Certificate, abatement work in schools under Asbestos
               Hazard Emergency Response Act, Hager Labs.
1987   Abatement Supervisor Training, Georgia Inst. of
               Technology.
1985   Certificate, Welder First Class, Southern Alberta Inst.
               of Technology.

- Resume writer: Jan Hurley -

ZACHARY CURTISS
35 WEST HARBOR ROAD
MASSAPEQUA, NEW YORK 11758
(516) 789-8765

OBJECTIVE: SERVICE TECHNICIAN IN AN AUTOMOBILE DEALERSHIP

HIGHLIGHTS OF QUALIFICATIONS:

* Relate easily with all levels of Co-workers and Customers
* 7 Years Hands-on Experience with Automotive Electronics,
   Electronic Fuel Delivery Systems and Computers
* Adapt readily to both Domestic and Foreign Car Repair
* Responsible, Capable and Hardworking

EDUCATION: **A.A.S. Degree - AUTOMOTIVE ENGINEERING TECHNOLOGY**
SUNY College of Technology   Farmingdale, NY

May 1991   Graduated Cum Laude,   College and National Dean's List

AUTOMOTIVE SERVICE SPECIALIST CERTIFICATIONS:
   - Automotive Electricity
   - Combustion Engines
   - Automotive Transmissions
   - Automotive Electronics & Computerized Control

ADDITIONAL RELEVANT COURSE WORK:
   Automotive Merchandising and Inspection
Computer Science   Business Management

**WORK
EXPERIENCE:**   AUTOMOTIVE REPAIR BUSINESS   1986 - Present
-Repair, rebuild and maintain over 100 foreign & domestic
 automobile engines annually
- Manage all aspects of my own business

AUTOMOBILE MECHANIC   1985 - 1988
Rosco Service Station   Northport, NY

- Provided general & preventive maintenance on foreign and
 domestic automobiles
- Interacted with customers

ASSISTANT MANAGER/NEW CAR DEPARTMENT   1984
Anchor Toyota   Oakdale, NY

- Oversaw Department personnel and operations
- Executed repairs and installation of vehicle options
- Prepared new automobiles for delivery to customers

REFERENCES: Available Upon Your Request

393

- Resume writer: Hinda Bodinger -

LEE CRAIG
254-39 Peachtree Lane
Bayside, New York 11364
(718) 997-8594

OBJECTIVE: **Executive Chef** in charge of Corporate Dining Facilities & Events

HIGHLIGHTS OF QUALIFICATIONS
Graduated with honors from the Culinary Institute of America
Over 10 years successful experience in restaurants and catering
Effective manager with proven ability to train, motivate and direct staff
Consistent performance of highest quality and creativity levels within budget
Full range of experience in developing & presenting menus of diverse ethnic & cultural styles

RELEVANT SKILLS & EXPERIENCE
MANAGEMENT:
- Managed kitchen and support staff of 10 - 20, preparing menus for off-premise events
- Supervised & coordinated presentation of events ranging from elegant seated dinners, to
    corporate cocktail and large theme parties - Clients included:
    Tiffany, Philip Morris, Citibank, The NYC Ballet, Boys Harbor, Ann Taylor, Julliard
- Maintained and often surpassed a targeted 25% food cost
- Developed and implemented policies and standards of quality for private catering business
- Directed a cafeteria-style lunch operation serving 50 - 90 members daily
- Supervised and produced menu preparations for lunch, dinner, brunch, catered events and daily
    specials at a 125-seat "healthy foods" restaurant
- Purchased all food for 300-seat restaurant and banquet facilities
- Trained staff in basic skills; taught seasoned employees enhanced preparation & presentation skills
- Directed layout and design of two full-service kitchens

TECHNICAL & CREATIVE EXPERTISE:
- Instituted a plan for menu and recipe development for own catering company, significantly
    increasing menu repertoire
- Created standardized recipe and accurate costing systems
- Conceived and priced menu for 160-seat restaurant serving lunch, dinner and brunch
- On-site chef for events ranging from seated dinners for over 100 to cocktail parties for over 1000
- Designed, developed and executed menus including the following:
    Regional American, French, & Italian; Middle Eastern, English Teas and Spa Cuisines

EMPLOYMENT HISTORY

1987-1991	**PARTNER/EXECUTIVE CHEF**	Lee Craig Catering	NYC / The Hamptons
1984-1987	**HEAD CHEF**	S.K. Williams Catering	NYC / The Hamptons
1983-1984	**CONSULTANT**	The West End Cafe	New York City
1982-1983	**DAY PRODUCTION CHEF**	Natalie's	New York City
1980-1982	**RECEIVING STEWARD/LINE COOK**	Windows on the World	New York City

EDUCATION
THE CULINARY INSTITUTE OF AMERICA   Hyde Park, NY
Associates in Occupational Science - 1980   Graduated with Honors, Perfect Attendance

- Resume writer: Hinda Bodinger -

Gerard Villaseñor

2020 Thomas Drive • Sunnyvale, CA • 94086

(408) 734-9365

Objective: Position as Roofing Superintendent.

Highlights of Qualifications

- Energetic, enthusiastic, dedicated professional.
- Self-motivated; knows what it takes to get the job done.
- Inspires and supports others to work at their highest level.

- Good decision-maker; resourceful and responsible.
- Talent for picking the right people for the job.
- Ability to prioritize, delegate, and motivate.

Roofing and Construction Experience

New Construction

- Worked extensively in new construction for commercial and industrial projects, including $750,000 Hydro-tech waterproofing project for Codorniu Winery in Napa; Bentonite waterproofing and single-ply PVC membrane for New Children's Hospital at Stanford; and single-ply EPDM and two-piece tile for Monterey Sports Center.
- Incorporated variety of roofing and waterproofing techniques, most notably for Syntex Evergreen in San Jose, which used BUR, Polyken, Mameco Vulkem, Xypex, and a complete paver system on pedestals.
- Reviewed plans and developed schedules with architects, contractors and subcontractors, assuring proper coordination, efficiency and profitability.
- Supervised crews for all types of roofing and waterproofing:
  – BUR: hot, cold and modified;
  – single-plies: EPDM, PVC, PIB, Hypalon;
  – fluid applied: roof membranes, traffic topping;
  – steep roofing: composition shingles, tile, shakes;
  – waterproofing: sheet membranes, blacklines, Bentonite.
- Dispatched tractor-trailers, 3X dump trucks, debris bins, asphalt tankers and truck-mounted crane.

Reroofing

- Achieved consistent high quality control in compliance with building codes and inspection standards.
- Assured strict adherence to projected scheduling and costs.
- Interacted with variety of roof consultants, building inspectors, and owners or their representatives for effective scheduling and maximum quality control.
- Completed wide range of projects involving Tremco materials, working closely with their sales and technical reps.
- Coordinated sheet metal, mechanical, electrical, plumbing and core drilling subcontractors as the prime contractor for various reroofing projects.
- Handled wide range of public works, including NASA, Cupertino School District schools and City of San Jose.

Repairs and Maintenance

- Dispatched personnel promptly for leak calls and other needed repairs.
- Scheduled and satisfactorily completed minor roof maintenance work in a timely manner.

Work History

1987-91	**Field Production Superintendent** (1990-91)	Blue's Roofing Co., San Jose
	Dispatcher/Assistant Superintendent (1988-90)	"
	Journeyman Roofer (1987-88)	"
1984-87	**Freelance Roofer**	Clients in Santa Clara, San Mateo counties
1971-84	**Foreman** (1976-84)	Andy's Roofing Company, Mountain View
	Journeyman Roofer (1973-76)	"
	Apprentice (1971-73)	"

Education

Roofing Apprenticeship Program, Local Union 95 • San Jose City College, 1971-73

Ethnic Studies, Foothill College, 1972-73

- Resume writer: Sallie Young -

JENNY H. LIN
4005 Cowell Boulevard, #210
Davis, California, 95616—(916) 756-9515

Objective: Work experience internship position with an organization in the hospitality industry (hotel-restaurant).

Education
B.A. Linguistics/Japanese, University of California-Davis, June 1990
Summer School, Sophia University, Japan, 1989

Summary

With my travel and practical/academic experiences, I have demonstrated skills in customer services-relations, general office support, oral/written communications, and public/international relations. Related course work (listed below), has increased my desire to choose a career that is very people-oriented and offers unlimited opportunities for seeking a challenging, stimulating, rewarding occupation.

Basic Accounting   Management of Firms (business methodology of Japanese firms)
English (4)   Psychology (2)   Geography (2)
Linguistics (10)   Japanese (5)   Cantonese

Highlights of Skills—Qualifications
✳ Lifelong exposure to cultural & language differences.
✳ Very sociable and comfortable working with the public.
✳ Sincere, enthusiastic, and committed to doing a job right.
✳ Willing to learn, work hard, and expand current level of skills.
✳ Bilingual: fluent Chinese & English; speak/write/read Japanese.
✳ Familiar with MacWrite, MacDraw, Microsoft Word–Macintosh WP

Relevant Work Experience

RECEPTIONIST **American General Insurance Company, Los Angeles-CA** **Summer F/T, 1987**
Screened phone calls and routed to appropriate staff.
Handled client inquiries effectively.
Courteously directed clients to appointment meetings with staff.
Made appointments for agents to provide intercultural service to non-English speaking Asians.
Typed routine correspondence and business forms.
Organized and maintained insurance application profiles and general office files.
Experienced with handling multi-line communications switchboard.

NURSES AIDE **Lin's Hospital, Taipei, Taiwan** **Volunteer/Fall F/T, 1986**
Assisted patients in day-to-day routine functions.
Provided caring communication assistance between professional staff and recovering patients.

SALESPERSON **Contempo Casuals, Los Angeles, CA** **P/T, 1985 - 1986**
Obtained information from customers on services desired.
Determined type and quality of merchandise wanted and showed various items.
Effectively handled customer service complaints and resolved purchasing problems.
Planned and displayed merchandise to promote customer interest in buying.
Counted and recorded weekly product inventory sheets for supply/demand purchasing.
Tallied sales receipts and balanced cash register on a daily basis.

ACADEMIC & SOCIAL EXPERIENCES

Asian Student Union, UCD 1989-present
Alpha Phi Omega (Co-Ed International Service Fraternity), UCD 1990
Traveled throughout Asia: Japan, Singapore, Hong Kong, China, lived in Taiwan 12 years.
Thoroughly enjoy travel, cross-country skiing, biking, and camping.

–References Available On Request–

- Resume writer: Karen Staggs -

Craig K. Ash

Address

Current: 1340 Hazelwood Court, Dixon, CA 956201
Permanent: 118 Kings Court, North Mankato, MN 56001

Telephone
(916) 678-6383
(507) 387-6940

JOB OBJECTIVE   *Career Flight Officer*

CERTIFICATES   Airline Transport Written (completion date, 15 April 1989)
Flight Engineer Turbojet
Flight Engineer Written (FEB 96%/FEJ 96%)
Military First Pilot
Medical Certificate: FAA Class I – No Limitations

FLIGHT TIME
- 1371 Total Time
- 752 Pilot in Command
- 1070 Heavy Multiengine Jet
- 1314 Multiengine Jet
- 147 Simulator Category II

EXPERIENCE   *Nov 1987 - Present: C5A/B First Pilot.*
Certified in air refueling.

Performed as First Pilot and Co-Pilot on worldwide airlift for a crew of 13 - 22 members and up to 72 passengers.

Provided domestic and international all-weather airlift carrying highly sensitive cargo and passengers.

Functioned as Pilot in Command in the following areas:
- Continental U.S.
- Europe
- Japan
- Alaska
- Korea
- Philippines
- Guam

Operated into some of the world's busiest airports such as Frankfurt and Honolulu.

EDUCATION   *Bachelor of Science in Business Administration, 1986*
University of Texas, Austin, Texas

TRAINING   Feb 1989 — C5B First Pilot, Travis AFB, CA
May 1988 — C5A Air Refueling Training, Travis AFB, CA
Feb 1988 — C5B Co-Pilot Qualification, Altus AFB, OK
Aug 1987 — T-37/ T-38 Undergraduate Pilot Training, Williams AFB, AZ

PERSONAL   Date of Birth: 9 Feb 1963
Marital Status: Single
Height/Weight: 69"; 165 lbs.
Health: Excellent * Non-smoker * 20/20 Uncorrected Vision
Sports: Jogging * Tennis * Golf * Racquetball

Available April 1989 ● Willing to Relocate
References Included

- Resume writer: Karen Staggs -

ADDRESSES

Resume writers and allied professionals whose correspondence and articles appear in this book:

Donald Asher
Resume Righters
2444 Polk St.
San Francisco CA 94109
(415) 543-2020

Calvin Baird
DATACO Resume Service
1101 East Sixth Court
Hialeah FL 33010
(305) 887-1637

Rogene Baxter
100 Whitethorne Dr., Ste. #400
Moraga, CA 94556
(510) 376-3872

Julie Benesh
Career Consultant
1303 Lancaster Drive
Champaign IL 61821-7027
(217) 355-8188

Hinda Bodinger
Career Planning Techniques
69-16 229th St.
Bayside NY 11364-3119
(718) 631-3635

M. Lea Cabeen
A•Leaco/A•Script Group
8 Dalton St.
Newburyport MA 01950
(508) 463-4356

Clara Carter
Scholarship Resources Services
510 Union Ave.
Patterson NJ 07522
(201) 904-0210

Kim Coats
A Better Resume Service
2127 Fifth Ave.
Moline IL 61265
(309) 764-2470

Joe Costa
331 Duperu Drive
Crockett CA 94525

Joan Cousins
Career Counselor
1480 West St.
Pittsfield MA 01201
(413) 443-1154

Denise Cross
Cross Executive Services
715 Silver Spur Road, Suite 204
Rolling Hills Estates CA 90274-3632
(213) 544-7171

Robert Davidson
Executive & Professional Resume Svc.
11 Vanderbilt Ave, # 220
Norwood MA 02062

Lynn Desker
99 Lorong N.
Republic of Singapore 1542

John Ellis
Assistant Director, Career Services
College of Saint Rose
432 Western Ave.
Albany NY 12203
(518) 454-5141

Mike Farr
JIST Works, Inc.
720 North Park Ave.
Indianapolis IN 46202-3431
(317) 264-3720 or 1-800-648-JIST

Mary Ann Finch-Vandivier
Pacific Beach Writing Service
125 N. Acacia Ave., #113
Solana Beach CA 92075
(619) 488-0625

Rhonda Findling
Rubicon Programs, Inc.
2500 Bissell Ave.
Richmond CA 94804
(510) 235-1516

Lisa Gessner
14 Margaret Street
Glen Cove NY 11542
(516) 759-2388

Oliva G. Gorey
Ideal Resume Service
19 Bayview Terrace
Portland ME 04103
(207) 774-5231

Marilyn Harryman
Counselor at Large, Div. of Instruction
Oakland Unified School District
1025 Second Ave., Harper Bldg.
Oakland CA 94606
(510) 836-8257

Bryan Howard
10 LaButte
St. Albert, Ontario
Canada K0A 3C0
(613) 987-5342

Drema Howard
University of Kentucky
University Career Center
201 Mathews Building
Lexington KY 40506
(606) 257-2746

Marty Hughes
Accu-Pro Data Management
PO Box 4932
Hayward CA 94544
(510) 582-8211

Jan Hurley
J. Wolff Enterprises
JFH Resumes
P.O. Box 5158
Silver City NM 88062
(505) 388-5834

Susan Ireland
Dynamite!! Resumes
237 Colgate Avenue
Kensington CA 94708
(510) 524-5238

Claudia Jordan
2513 E. Yucca Street
Phoenix AZ 85028
(602) 992-0144

Michelle Jurika
Career & Personal Development
1425 Leimert Boulevard
Oakland CA 94602
(510) 530-5477

Nancy Malvin and Carla Culp
Keyboard Connection
P.O. Box 338
Glen Carbon IL 62034
(618) 692-9673

Vicki Law-Miller
Scribbles to Script
820 South Tenth
Montrose CO 81401
(303) 249-7451

Jeff Lewis
A Better Resume
15010 Ventura Blvd., Suite 223
Sherman Oaks CA 91403
(818) 788-8232

Josephine Loo
1681 - 20th Ave.
San Francisco CA 94122

Cynthia Mackey
Winning Strategies
PO Box 6746
Oakland CA 94614
(510) 533-0589

Linda Marks
Work Options Consultant
1177 Green Street
San Francisco CA 94109
(415) 441-4520

Joe Meissner
155 Sansome, 7th Floor
San Francisco CA 94104
(415) 392-7097

May Nolan
Paper Chase Secretarial & Temporary Services
5291 Highway 20
Oak Harbor WA 98277
(206) 679-2918

Dianne E. Paroli
Dept. of Education
Bureau of Corrections
State Correctional Institution, Muncy
P.O. Box 180
Muncy PA 17756

Phyllis Pechman
Pechman Professional Services
508 South Clinton St.
Iowa City IA 52240
(319) 351-8523

Judi Robinovitz
Resumes That Work!
999 U.S. 1
Vero Beach FL 32960
(407) 778-8001

Nancy Rosenberg
The Right Resume
149 Whaler's Cove
Babylon NY 11702
(516) 661-7395

Chris Schneider
Schneider Word Processing
651 Lancewood Court
Mobile AL 36609
(205) 666-6651

N. Victoria Sisson
804 Woodland Way
Richardson TX 75080
(214) 231-6031

Karen Staggs
AccuWord Processing & Resumes
26837 Contignac Drive
Murrieta CA 92562
(714) 698-8455

Justine Stelling
Resumes Plus
1291 E. Hillsdale Blvd, Suite 209
Foster City CA 94404
(415) 573-1657

Rene Stelzer
A Scribe to Greatness
1809 Redwood Place
Denton TX 76201
(817) 383-8390
(214) 804-9277

Bernard Stopfer
Resumes Plus
2855 West Cactus Rd.
Phoenix AZ 85029
(602) 789-1200

Sallie Young
Impressions by Sallie
2773 Custer Dr.
San Jose CA 95124
(408) 978-7278

Doug Zeiger
100-1/2 Market Street
Mt. Clemons MI 48043
(313) 468-5170

Louis Zirin
7 Carlton Rd.
Marblehead MA 01945

INDEX

A national newsletter for professionals, exploring and promoting excellence in resume writing

The Damn Good Resume Pro Newsletter

• Published quarterly by Yana Parker, Damn Good Resume Service   • Editor, Susan Ireland

This Book Is Not Done Yet ... if ever.

RESUME PRO: The Professional's Guide is not a finished guidebook — it is an *ongoing* journal on the state-of-the-art in resume writing. It will be updated and revised periodically.
Meanwhile . . .

. . . **Resume Pro <u>Newsletter</u> is an extension of the book**, and is published every three months to keep readers informed of developments in the field. (This material, plus some of *your* letters and articles, will appear in the NEXT edition of this book.)

But more important, **the Newsletter provides a public forum** for sharing all kinds of information and inspiration related to resume writing. **We're waiting to hear from you!**

Write To Us

We welcome articles, letters, resume problems to be solved, ideas for new columns and features. Our address is below.

Subjects We Want To Discuss

Anything of interest to resume writers (and allied fields) can appear in the Newsletter. In upcoming issues, we'd especially welcome letters, articles, and resumes related to:

- Military downsizing
- Youth and joblessness
- Small business and the economy.

Feature Columns in the Newsletter

Regular columns that appear in the Newsletter include:

- Entrepreneurship (money, marketing, client services)
- Spin-offs, income streams
- Profiles of resume writers
- Employers' needs/wants
- Special populations
- New technologies
- Writing techniques
- Resume Clinic (problems and solutions)
- Graphic design for resumes
- "Pow-Litzer" prize-winning resumes.

Subscription to Resume Pro Newsletter

☐ $20 for **one year** (four issues) — US $25 Canada & foreign

☐ $5 **sample issue** (if you like this book, you'll like the newsletter)

☐ Free detailed subjects-list of **back issues.**

Please make check payable to "Yana Parker" and send to:
P.O. Box 3289, Berkeley CA 94703.

Name _____

Company/Title _____

Street _____

City/State/Zip _____

Phone: _____   _____
             Work   Home

The disk contains:

- Templates in a variety of sharp looking design layouts for each of the four most useful resume configurations:
    - Chronological   - Functional   - Combined Chronological/Functional   - Accomplishment

    Each template has built-in step-by-step directions for what to say in every section of the resume, and the formatting and placement are already done for you. (Just type over the existing text with your own words.)

- Templates and models for special purpose resumes and letters, including:
    - Information Interviews
    - Job Promotions and Change of Status
    - Recommendation Letters
    - Cover Letters
    - Thank You Letters

- All of the above provided in one or more of the most popular word processing programs.

The 48-page manual provides:

- "Hard-copy" illustrations of all the resume templates.

- Very simple and complete instructions **for job hunters** on using ReadyToGo Resumes templates — including the features and advantages of each format, and how to choose the best layout for your situation.

- Guidelines **for professional resume writers, career counselors, educators, word processors**, and other professionals on how to use the Templates with your customers or clients.

- "Problem Patches" to handle problems such as:
    - Complex work history
    - No experience
    - Major career change
    - Erratic work experience
    - Time out for parenthood and family issues
    - Period of unemployment

- Eight sample resumes designed in the ReadyToGo Resumes formats.

NOTE: WordPerfect and Microsoft Word are registered trademarks of (respectively) WordPerfect Corp. and Microsoft Corp.)

- -

Order Form

Please send "ReadyToGo Resumes" @ $39.95

Quantity		Cost
☐	IBM PC Compatible 3.5" disk (in WordPerfect <u>and </u>Microsoft Word) *Yes, it works with "Windows"*	_____
☐	IBM PC Compatible 5.25" disk (in WordPerfect <u>and </u>Microsoft Word)	_____
☐	Macintosh 3.5" disk (Microsoft Word) (write for availability of other formats)	_____
	Add **$3.50* per item for shipping** (* $4.00 to Canada)	_____

☐ Check here if you want info about a Newsletter for Resume Writers

Total: $ _____

Mail your order and payment to:
Yana Parker
(software department #10)
P.O. Box 3289
Berkeley CA 94703

Ship to:

Name _____

Title/Company _____

_____

Street _____

City _____

State _____ Zip _____

Phone (_____) _____

Method of Payment (US currency only):
☐ Corporate Purchase Order. PO# _____
☐ Check or Money Order **payable to Yana Parker**

P.S. At your local bookstore there's more help from Yana:
- *Damn Good Resume Guide*
- *The Resume Catalog: 200 Damn Good Examples*
- *Resume Pro: The Professional's Guide*